Understanding Badiou, Understanding Modernism

Understanding Philosophy, Understanding Modernism

The aim of each volume in **Understanding Philosophy, Understanding Modernism** is to understand a philosophical thinker more fully through literary and cultural modernism and consequently to understand literary modernism better through a key philosophical figure. In this way, the series also rethinks the limits of modernism, calling attention to lacunae in modernist studies and sometimes in the philosophical work under examination.

Series Editors:
Paul Ardoin, S. E. Gontarski, and Laci Mattison

Volumes in the Series:

Understanding Bergson, Understanding Modernism
Edited by Paul Ardoin, S. E. Gontarski and Laci Mattison

Understanding Deleuze, Understanding Modernism
Edited by S. E. Gontarski, Paul Ardoin and Laci Mattison

Understanding Wittgenstein, Understanding Modernism
Edited by Anat Matar

Understanding Foucault, Understanding Modernism
Edited by David Scott

Understanding James, Understanding Modernism
Edited by David H. Evans

Understanding Rancière, Understanding Modernism
Edited by Patrick M. Bray

Understanding Blanchot, Understanding Modernism
Edited by Christopher Langlois

Understanding Merleau-Ponty, Understanding Modernism
Edited by Ariane Mildenberg

Understanding Nietzsche, Understanding Modernism
Edited by Douglas Burnham and Brian Pines

Understanding Derrida, Understanding Modernism
Edited by Jean-Michel Rabaté

Understanding Adorno, Understanding Modernism
Edited by Robin Truth Goodman

Understanding Flusser, Understanding Modernism
Edited by Aaron Jaffe, Rodrigo Martini and Michael F. Miller

Understanding Marx, Understanding Modernism
Edited by Mark Steven

Understanding Barthes, Understanding Modernism
Edited by Jeffrey R. Di Leo and Zahi Zalloua

Understanding Kristeva, Understanding Modernism
Edited by Maria Margaroni

Understanding Žižek, Understanding Modernism
Edited by Jeffrey R. Di Leo and Zahi Zalloua

Understanding Nancy, Understanding Modernism
Edited by Cosmin Toma

Understanding Bakhtin, Understanding Modernism
Edited by Philippe Birgy

Understanding Badiou, Understanding Modernism
Edited by Arka Chattopadhyay and Arthur Rose

Understanding Cavell, Understanding Modernism (forthcoming)
Edited by Paola Marrati

Understanding Badiou, Understanding Modernism

Edited by
Arka Chattopadhyay and Arthur Rose

BLOOMSBURY ACADEMIC
NEW YORK • LONDON • OXFORD • NEW DELHI • SYDNEY

BLOOMSBURY ACADEMIC
Bloomsbury Publishing Inc, 1359 Broadway, New York, NY 10018, USA
Bloomsbury Publishing Plc, 50 Bedford Square, London, WC1B 3DP, UK
Bloomsbury Publishing Ireland, 29 Earlsfort Terrace, Dublin 2, D02 AY28, Ireland

BLOOMSBURY, BLOOMSBURY ACADEMIC and the Diana logo are trademarks of
Bloomsbury Publishing Plc

First published 2024
Paperback edition published 2026

Copyright © Arka Chattopadhyay and Arthur Rose, 2024

Each chapter copyright © by the contributor, 2024

Cover design: Eleanor Rose
Cover image © Candida Slater / Alamy

All rights reserved. No part of this publication may be: i) reproduced or transmitted in any form, electronic or mechanical, including photocopying, recording or by means of any information storage or retrieval system without prior permission in writing from the publishers; or ii) used or reproduced in any way for the training, development or operation of artificial intelligence (AI) technologies, including generative AI technologies. The rights holders expressly reserve this publication from the text and data mining exception as per Article 4(3) of the Digital Single Market Directive (EU) 2019/790.

Bloomsbury Publishing Inc does not have any control over, or responsibility for, any third-party websites referred to or in this book. All internet addresses given in this book were correct at the time of going to press. The author and publisher regret any inconvenience caused if addresses have changed or sites have ceased to exist, but can accept no responsibility for any such changes.

A catalogue record for this book is available from the British Library.

A catalog record for this book is available from the Library of Congress.

ISBN: HB: 978-1-5013-8440-0
PB: 978-1-5013-8444-8
ePDF: 978-1-5013-8442-4
eBook: 978-1-5013-8441-7

Series: Understanding Philosophy, Understanding Modernism

Typeset by Deanta Global Publishing Services, Chennai, India

For product safety related questions contact productsafety@bloomsbury.com.

To find out more about our authors and books visit www.bloomsbury.com and sign up for our newsletters.

Contents

Series Preface ix

Introduction: Badiou, the Modernist *Arka Chattopadhyay and Arthur Rose* 1

Part I Badiou's Modernisms: Debts and Contestations 11

1 Mal/Bad, Beck/Worse: How to Think Poetically through Mallarmé, Plato and Beckett with Badiou *Jean-Michel Rabaté* 13
2 Alain Badiou's Dialectical (Non) Gesture of Modernity: Poetry, Mastery, Undecidability *Soumyabrata Choudhury* 26
3 Badiou, Hegel and the Thinking of Modernist Thought-Action *Justin Clemens* 37
4 The Eternal Return of the Modern: Poetry, History, Philosophy *Bruno Bosteels* 50
5 Badiou, Lacan and Mathematical Modernisms *Arka Chattopadhyay* 66
6 Badiou and Mad Love *Arthur Rose* 81

Part II Modernisms' Multiple Badious: Conditions and Manifestations 95

7 Twisting Modernism around Mallarmé's White Hair: Badiou versus Rancière *Joseph Shafer* 97
8 Reflections on Cinema and Philosophy *Alex Ling* 113
9 Modern Love Theory: James, Badiou and "The Story in It" *Sigi Jöttkandt* 127
10 Derrida's and Badiou's Absolute Modern(ist) Surfaces *James Martell* 138
11 Approaching a Non-Modern Historical Theory: Catholic Theology, Alain Badiou and Antihistory *Michael J. Kelly* 153
12 Badiou, Music, Novelty *Adity Singh* 168
13 The Thinking of Representation: Badiou and Modernist Theater *Eloïse Mignon* 186

Part III Glossary 201

14 "The Age of Poets" *Christian R. Gelder* 203
15 Maoism *Robert Boncardo* 212

| 16 | Grace *Baylee Brits* | 218 |
| 17 | Ontology and Greater Logic *John Cleary* | 227 |

Notes on Contributors 237
Index 240

Series Preface

Sometime in the late twentieth century, modernism, like philosophy itself, underwent something of an unmooring from (at least) linear literary history in favor of the multi-perspective history implicit in "new historicism" or, say, varieties of "presentism." Amid current reassessments of modernism and modernity, critics have posited various "new" or alternative modernisms—postcolonial, cosmopolitan, transatlantic, transnational, geomodernism or even "bad" modernisms. In doing so, they have not only reassessed modernism as a category, but also, more broadly, rethought epistemology and ontology, aesthetics, metaphysics, materialism, history and being itself, opening possibilities of rethinking not only which texts we read as modernist, but also how we read those texts. Much of this new conversation constitutes something of a critique of the periodization of modernism or modernist studies in favor of modernism as mode (or mode of production) or concept. Understanding Philosophy, Understanding Modernism situates itself amid the plurality of discourses, offering collections focused on key philosophical thinkers influential both to the moment of modernism and to our current understanding of that moment's genealogy, archaeology and becomings. Such critiques of modernism(s) and modernity afford opportunities to rethink and reassess the overlaps, folds, interrelationships, interleavings or cross-pollinations of modernism and philosophy. Our goal in each volume of the series is to understand literary modernism better through philosophy as we also better understand a philosopher through literary modernism. The first two volumes of the series, those on Henri Bergson and Gilles Deleuze, have established a tripartite structure that serves to offer accessibility both to the philosopher's principle texts and to current new research. Each volume opens with a section focused on "conceptualizing" the philosopher through close readings of seminal texts in the thinker's oeuvre. A second section, on aesthetics, maps connections between modernist works and the philosophical figure, often surveying key modernist trends and shedding new light on authors and texts. The final section of each volume serves as an extended glossary of principal terms in the philosopher's work, each treated at length, allowing a fuller engagement with and examination of the many, sometimes contradictory ways terms are deployed. The series is thus designed both to introduce philosophers and to rethink their relationship to modernist studies, revising our understandings of both modernism and philosophy, and offering resources that will be of use across disciplines, from philosophy, theory and literature, to religion, the visual and performing arts, and often to the sciences as well.

Introduction

Badiou, the Modernist

Arka Chattopadhyay and Arthur Rose

What does it mean to think of Alain Badiou—philosopher, novelist, playwright—as a modernist?

From his philosophical project, which seeks to explain how newness enters the world, through his political commitment to the revolutions of 1789, 1871, 1917 and 1968, his stylistic debts to Samuel Beckett, Stephane Mallarmé and Arthur Rimbaud, his profound engagement with modern mathematics, to his mourning the contemporary crisis of love, Badiou encapsulates what Harry Levin called "this paradoxical state of feeling belated and up-to-date simultaneously" (Levin 1960: 622). Far from being difficult to apply the label "modernist" to Badiou and his writing, their concerns and sources positively invite it.

Understanding Badiou, Understanding Modernism explores Badiou's engagement with, and formation by, diverse aspects of modernism. In his philosophical project, aesthetic orientation and political leanings, Badiou is a product of, and a leading advocate for, European modernism. From the milieu of the May 1968 student protests in Paris to the contemporary "postmodern" ethos, Badiou returns, time and again, to avant-garde modernist texts—aesthetic, political, philosophical and scientific—as inspiration for his response to present situations. This book locates Badiou in this complex intersection of critical and conceptual paradigms. Drawing upon disciplines as varied as cinema, theater, music, history, mathematics, poetry and philosophy, the book shows how Badiou's contribution to philosophy must be understood within the context of his decades-long conversation with modernist thinking.

Still, our efforts to contextualize Badiou in a modernist matrix should not be taken as a straightforward identification of Badiou as a modernist. Several of our contributors raise the problems such an identification poses. If so much of Badiou's work challenges the neatness of academic categories like modernism, Justin Clemens wonders, how then one might construct "a relation between 'Badiou' and/or 'modernism' that doesn't presume or falsify what's in question." Soumyabrata Choudhury argues that Badiou's affirmation of universals raises problems for integrating his philosophy "in any consistent program or ideology of 'modernism.'" Reciprocally, the assumption that a philosophy of political, scientific, artistic and amorous innovation can automatically be labelled modernist appears wedded to a notion of modernism that the (not-so) new modernist studies has sought to challenge for the last twenty years. Instead of simply avowing Badiou a modernist, or modernism "Badiouian," in round terms, the chapters collected here try to address the consequences of specific coincidences between Badiou's thought and the ideas, texts and figures associated, for better or worse, with modernism.

To navigate these concerns, this volume develops two analytic programs, examining the situation of Badiou as a modernist in aesthetics, politics and philosophy and the transformations modernism undergoes in the wake of Badiou's philosophical interventions. Using Badiou's own critique of postmodernism to argue for a return to modernism, we identify the avant-grade concern, explicit in Badiou's emphasis on newness as the goal of eventual truth in *Being and Event* (1988). Badiou's criticism of postmodernism and its nexus with globalization in *The Century* (2005) paves the way for his return to the rigors of the modern (Badiou 2007: 199). Badiou credits Mallarmé as an eventual inventor of "modern writing" in this book (6). For him, the modernist rigor puts the "universe of representation to ruin" (36) and this destruction produces the new. *The Century* identifies the modernizing temporality as a time of de-subjectivation (106). Badiou's philosophical project seeks to bring back the subject by posing a modernism against this modernity. If the contemporary lacks the present, as we noted at the beginning of this introduction, Badiou champions the modernist avant-garde in *The Century* for focusing on the creative act that can "only be thought in the present" (136). He reflects: "[f]or the avant-gardes, art is much more than the solitary production of works of genius. Collective existence and life itself are at stake. Art can no longer be conceived without an element of violent aesthetic militancy" (134). This political rigor of modernism would look beyond the bodies and languages to generate an exceptionality in the "materialist dialectic" Badiou develops in *Logics of Worlds* (2006): truth. In his system, all four fundamental conditions of philosophy (art, love, politics and science) have a modernist streak written into them. Badiou's own readings of scientific, political and aesthetic (which includes the thematics of love as a condition) modernisms are utilized to form the ground for the chapters in Part I.

The volume then goes on to consider the ways in which Badiou's work impacts and extends modernist studies at large, such as, how Badiou's thinking on the event resonates with the idea of socio-political change in modernist aesthetic debates. The chapters in the second part widen the encounter between Badiou and modernism by using his philosophy as a critical and heuristic lens to read modernism. Badiou's work enables new ways of encountering modernism through ideas like the relation between the subject-body and the event, the logics of appearing in the world and so on. The readings that comprise Part II testify to the extensional capacity of Badiou's work in engaging with modernism, beyond the trappings of his own investigations. Finally, we gloss over the chapters in Part III through entries on important terminological concerns vis-à-vis Badiou and modernism. Here we cover an intense diversity, ranging from the mathematical frameworks used in approaching modern ontology and phenomenology to the crucial phrase, "the age of poets," Badiou's thoughts on politics as a condition for philosophy, and his work on St. Paul and grace in relation to modernity and modernism.

At the same time, it seems necessary for this introduction to ask why modernism remains such a conflicted issue for Badiou's readers. Bryan Cooke argues as much when, in response to the question "what do people hate when they hate (the philosophy of) Alain Badiou," he offers as a possible scapegoat "the philosopher's modernism," which he glosses as

> Badiou's penchant for the apodeictic mode and the rhythms of the manifesto; his avant-garde (but also Pauline) preoccupation with rupture and with novelty [...]; his penchant for numbered theses; for definitions, axioms, scholia and schemata designed to *cut through* [...] the phenomena under discussion. (Cooke 2018: 159)

Even when Cooke moves beyond objections to Badiou's style, the tension he identifies between "the formal, indeed *formalist* underpinnings of Badiou's philosophy and the intransigent political commitment which both animates and impels his corpus" (Cooke 2018: 159) appears to mimic the preoccupations with form and its limits in studies of modernism from the 1960s and 1970s (Levin 1960; Beebe 1974: 1072). In the wake of the historicist reappraisal of modernism—from Andreas Huyssen's *After the Great Divide* (1986), through the founding of *Modernism/Modernity* in the mid-1990s, to the birth of the new modernist studies in 1999 (Mao and Walkowitz 2008: 737) and its necessary and overdue expansion of the modernist canon to include people marginalized for reasons of gender, race, sexuality, class and nation—Badiou's identity as a modernist seems as best reactionary, harking back to earlier definitions of modernism, and, at worse, based on a caricature of what modernism was. When identifying the "modernism" of a philosopher as self-evidently modernist in ambition, predilection, project and style as Alain Badiou, we must necessarily ask whether the juxtaposition brings much profit to either.

Understanding Badiou, Understanding Modernism demonstrates that much can be learned by putting the two into direct conversation. The chapters achieve this by leading the reader through Badiou's rich and varied engagement with modernism in all its cultural, sociological and philosophical guises. But it also raises more complex questions about the temporality of modernism that remain intractable in contemporary modernist studies. Badiou opens his 2013 essay, "The Pornographic Age" with a notion of contemporaneity that "is lacking." To articulate this point, he rests on the referential shoulders of two eminent modernist poets, Stephane Mallarmé and Arthur Rimbaud: "'A present is lacking' is Mallarmé's formula. And Rimbaud: 'we are not in this world'" (Badiou 2020: 1). A contemporaneity that lacks the present is symptomatic of the involuted temporality of modernism. This, one could argue, is the line that divides the modern from the modernist. The modernist is not reducible to the contemporary; if at all, it is a contemporaneity without the present. This complex temporality is then furnished by a reading of Jean Genet's avant-garde play *The Balcony* (1956) that would reinvoke the literary-dramatic history of Francophone modernisms after the echoes of Mallarmé and Rimbaud. William Watkin in his commentary on Badiou's aforementioned essay maintains that for Badiou, modernity is a set that doesn't have a concept which extends across objects to characterize them as modern (Watkin

2020: 85). This is another kind of lack. What does this lack mean for modernism in contradistinction with modernity? How does the previous discussion present Badiou in relation to modernism? This is our moot question.

We begin by outlining the major modernist aspects of, and inclinations in, Badiou's works. The first section of the book consists of chapters that explore Badiou's readings of aesthetic, political and scientific modernities, both introducing his system and pointing to how Badiou offers manifold readings of Modernism. The middle portion of the book connects Badiou's thought with the various strands of aesthetic, philosophical, amorous and political modernisms in relation to which it can be extended. Here we open up a conversation between Badiou and his philosophical contemporaries to see how we can use his philosophy as a heuristic framework to engage with modernism. The final section of *Understanding Badiou, Understanding Modernism* is a glossary of key concepts and categories that Badiou uses in his interface with modernism.

The chapters in this first part examine Badiou's multipronged readings of aesthetic, scientific and political modernisms. They introduce his encounter with manifold modernisms and offer critical and analytical contexts for as well as responses to this encounter. Jean-Michel Rabaté addresses two of Badiou's most sustained engagements with the European canon of literary modernism in the form of Stephane Mallarmé and Samuel Beckett. Rabaté investigates Badiou's conjunction of Mallarmé's "*Un Coup de Dés*" and Beckett's *Worstward Ho* to critique his logic of converging the two texts in their terminal moments. He offers a detailed reading of Badiou's latest piece on Beckett's poetry from *The Immanence of Truths* to show how Beckett's uncovering and recovery of the infinite from the modern coverings of finitude initiates a fresh ethical dialog with modernism. In this ethics of the infinite, the political task of modernist art becomes both immanent and absolute as it has effects on history from a distance. Soumyabrata Choudhury's chapter studies Badiou's philosophical gesture of dialectics vis-à-vis the theatrical gesture in his evental philosophy. He connects Mallarmé with Badiou's co-invocation of Labid, a sixth–seventh-century Arabian poet, thus complicating the modernist timeline and its critical geography. Choudhury deals with Badiou's development of the dialectic around the notion of deciding upon the undecidable. He reflects on the relation between undecidability and modernity, on a political plane, revolving around the idea of impasse in mastery. The chapter ends with a counter-positioning of Badiou's Beckett against Badiou's Mallarmé. If Mallarmé's master hesitates facing the undecidable, Beckett's courageous saying attempts to go deeper into undecidability by worsening it.

Continuing with the dialectic, Justin Clemens approaches Badiou's reading of Hegelian infinity to draw out a critique of philosophical modernism. Clemens begins by complicating any unambiguous categorization of Badiou as a modernist and goes on to find his relation to Hegel's thought on qualitative and quantitative determinations of infinity. Clemens situates this reading within the Francophone reception of Hegel and Marx via Badiou's master Althusser. He then goes on to interpret the various stages of Badiou's reworking of the political logic of Hegelian dialectics to comment on his re-imagining of modernist politics in terms of the infinite. Bruno Bosteels in his chapter delves into Badiou's reworking of the Platonic tension between poetry and philosophy via the missing third term of history. He engages with Badiou's readings of modernist poets from Stephane Mallarmé to Paul Celan, connecting modernity with the finite and the infinite. Forming an interesting contrast to Michael's evocation of history in relation to Badiou's system of philosophy, Bosteels draws attention to Badiou's insistence on reading the poem away from its historical contextuality. The chapter makes a pivotal distinction between the two meanings of the finite, the good and the bad "modern" in Badiou and contributes to a new thinking of the affirmative finitude in *The Immanence of Truths* that culminates in an eternal return of the modern in his system.

Arka Chattopadhyay's chapter focuses on mathematical modernisms and the gap between the modernity of finitude and the modernism of the infinite. It examines the modernist gesture toward mathematical formalization in Badiou's system, tracing it back to the Platonic dialectic between the "matheme" and the poem and Lacan's mathematization of psychoanalytic discourse. Chattopadhyay addresses Badiou's evocation of Cantorian set theory as a post-Lacanian move and shows how it can be problematized by a late-Lacanian idea of infinity. He also reads Badiou's seminar on Lacan, attempting to understand the complex relation between mathematics and politics in Badiou through Lacan. Arthur Rose turns to the sporadic references to surrealism through Badiou's work to consider that movement's influence on his notion of love. Although many of Badiou's love examples are taken from a canon of nineteenth-century musical and poetic works, he shares with surrealism the desire to realize Rimbaud's ambition, articulated in *Une Saison en Enfer*, that love must be reinvented. To consider how modernist Badiou's understanding of love actually is, this chapter follows its intersections with surrealism.

Apart from extending Badiou's system as an analytical tool for reading modernisms beyond his own readings, the chapters in Part II aim to create links between Badiou and his contemporaries in a philosophical tradition and field. This approach is consistent with Badiou's idea about the "intra-philosophical" effects of art, literature, politics and science where all these domains are considered autonomous methods of thinking about their own conditions. Joseph Shafer's chapter begins the section on a critical note by discussing the differences between Badiou and his contemporary, Jacques Rancière, in the context of Modernism. While Rancière posits aesthetics as politics, Badiou takes a counter-position toward "inaesthetics." What does this inaesthetic mean for modernism? Shafer unpacks what Rancière calls Badiou's "modernism with a twist" and places Badiou's and Rancière's differing interpretations of Mallarmé as a dialectical stage for the dice throw. The whiteness of the page as surface, the whiteness of the foam and the siren's white hair as all that remains of the eventical are traces that divide modernism between the mimetic and the anti-mimetic. The chapter explores the paradoxes in Badiou and Rancière's differential readings of Plato and modernism's negotiation with a language that transcends communication. From poetry and art, we move on to the ontology of cinema and its relation to Badiou's vision of philosophy in Alex Ling's chapter. Approaching how cinema thinks by converting time into perception and its inherently impure character as image that goes back to its paradoxical relation with art and non-art, the chapter addresses the status of subtraction in Badiou's cinematic modernism. As Ling shows, cinema artistically purifies its immanent impurity as non-art and yet becomes democratic by making this impurity a thing in itself. This is a crucial exercise to determine Badiou's relation with modernism that rests on the dialectical, democratizing movement ceaselessly transforming non-art into art.

Sigi Jöttkandt in her chapter complicates Badiou's thesis on love through a reading of Henry James's short story, "The Story in It." Beginning with a contextualization of love among the three friends in James's story in a literary-historical debate about the notion of love and adventure in French culture, Jöttkandt goes further to bring in Badiou's "modern" and rupturous thesis on the two of love. For her, James introduces a torsion into Badiou's theorization of love's capacity to disrupt the "count-as-One." As the chapter shows, James's story questions whether the secret amorous relation in which romance rests on the beloved's not knowing it, can sustain love's division in the two. James Martell's chapter examines the notion of surface in modernisms as he brings Jacques Derrida into dialog with Badiou. Martell sees the figure of the "inexistent" as a deconstructivist point when Badiou spells it "inexistance" *a la* Derrida's "différance." Weaving in Beckett's idea of punching holes on the surface of language, the chapter connects Badiou's concept of the absolute in *The Immanence of Truths* with the idea of the surface. It constructs a topological map for Badiou's V as absolute surface in *The Immanence of Truths* and Derrida's figure of the checkboard and its spatial matrix.

Michael J. Kelly approaches Badiou's relation with modernism from the vantage of history. He takes up the question of truth's eternity in Badiou's philosophy and thinks through its implications for history by comparing these with those of Catholic theology. The chapter shows how Badiou's project develops resonances with works of Visigothic thinkers like the seventh-century bishop of Toledo, Ildefonso, and, in so doing, moves beyond modernist historiography. The disruptive novelty of truth in relation to history in an accidental trinitarian fashion (shared by Badiou and the theologians) generates what Kelly postulates as a speculative objectivity. Adity Singh focuses on music and modernism in Badiou's philosophical investigations of this artform. She begins by pointing to the absence of music in Badiou's essays on "inaesthetics" and goes on to ask how music paves the way for novelty in Badiou's thought. She engages with the scholium in *Logics of Worlds* on the "Schoenberg-event" for a discussion of "metaphysics of the subject" and the analysis of Messiaen's "Le merle noir" to illustrate the "form" of an artistic work in *L'Immanence des vérités*. Her essay argues for the musical event of the new, emerging through a dialectical and insurrectionary relation with the old.

Eloïse Mignon's chapter sees theater as an essential artistic component of Badiou's thinking of the relation between philosophy and modernism. She traces Badiou's dialectic of Theater/theater in which the former is statist and the latter produces evental truths away from the state. Mignon addresses the problematic of theatrical representation and argues how philosophy takes upon itself the task to index the ontological split of theater into two (Theater/theater). The chapter considers Badiou's references to modernist theater (Brecht, Artaud, Beckett, etc.) as well as his own plays (the *Ahmed* tetralogy) and highlights the need to preserve the interruptive agency of the theatrical event.

The third and final section of the book offers a glossary of concepts, categories and expressions that are pertinent to the critical confluence of Badiou and modernism.

Christian R. Gelder begins the section by glossing one of Badiou's key aesthetic concepts, "The Age of Poets", which has a complex history in Badiou's work immediately after the publication of *Being and Event*. Unlike traditional forms of modernist periodization, Badiou's category does not designate a defined historical period. Instead, "the age of poets" diagnoses several shared philosophical concerns that preoccupy a number of poets from the late nineteenth and early twentieth century: Mallarmé, Hölderlin, Celan, Trakl, Stevens, Beckett, and Rimbaud. Gelder's entry goes on to rehearse how Badiou locates the thinking of these concerns in the singular verse practice of these poets, as well as how his own reconceptualization of the relationship between mathematics and poetry serves to decisively bring this poetic age to a close.

Robert Boncardo's entry speculates on whether there is a specifically "modernist" political dispensation and whether Badiou's politics fits within this framework. He explores the modernist features in Badiou's style of thought—from his declarative style, the penchant for polemic and for writing manifestos, like a member of an early twentieth-century aesthetic avant-garde, to his defense of notions of truth and history. Boncardo shows how he both reinscribes and decisively displaces the sense of these "modernist" motifs. In particular, he explores in what sense Badiou's account of political action takes up the modernist taste for manifesto-like declarations, while at once ontologically grounding the force of these declarations and showing how they might unfold in an absolutely inconsistent political situation, more akin to a postmodern understanding of the political.

Baylee Brits's entry picks up on Badiou's "subjective" work on religion in *St Paul: The Foundation of Universalism* to pose "grace" as a significant concept. She discusses Paul as a militant figure, brought into being by an event that gives rise to a universal truth procedure. Brits concentrates on the fabulous element of the Christ-event that underpins Paul's "militancy" for Badiou and goes on to highlight the term "grace" in relation to modernity and truth. Brits asks why Badiou leaves religion out of his "conditions" for philosophy, in spite of his very convincing and sympathetic approach to Paul's own particular truth procedure. John Cleary's entry on ontology and "greater logic" focuses on the philosophy of mathematics in Badiou. Badiou's ontology (being-*qua*-being) in *Being and Event* is based on Zermelo-Fraenkel set theory, while *Logics of Worlds* presents his phenomenology (being-*qua*-appearing) in terms of topoi and category theory. *The Immanence of Truths* revisits these ontological conditions of truths via a branch of set theory, the theory of large cardinals, which constructs models of set theory in which exist infinite sets that surpass those in ZFC. The entry delves into Badiou's mathematical choices in establishing his philosophical system, elaborating on relativity, multiplicity, truths and the absolute.

Perhaps the one text, most notable in absence of a chapter-length treatment, is the book that remains Badiou's masterpiece and the cornerstone of his system: *Being and Event*. Though there are references to the book throughout this volume (most sustained in Justin Clemens and Bruno Bosteels) unfortunately, circumstances beyond our control meant that the essay we commissioned on *Being and Event* could not be completed. In lieu of this fuller discussion, which must be deferred to a future publication, it has to be noted that *Being and Event*, originally published in 1988, draws on mathematical ontology to reflect on the status of the event. In its patient exploration of the irruption of the new in the same, it models the workings of modernism, as a project to "Makes It New." The very idea of the event as rupture imports a counter-emphasis into the modernist commonplace of literary works where nothing happens by way of plot-events. Badiou's idea of the event allows us to see how eventality is and must be considered an axiom of the modern, if not the modernist.

In terms of reference too, poets like Mallarmé and Hölderlin, both proto-modernists in their own ways, appear at crucial junctures of the book. Meditation 19 on Mallarmé highlights the importance of the poem in fixing eventual sites: a place for the aleatory event. On a broad level, this reading helps shifting the accent from temporality to spatiality in modernism and allows us to rethink the eventual in its ambit. Mallarmé's thematization of number in "*Un Coup de Dés*" brings the event in connection with the mathematical. Badiou's reading privileges the urge for action over modern nihilism, recasting modernism in affirmationist terms. This is a modernism that shows the courage to take up the undecidability of the event and decide on it by saying yes to it.

In "Meditation Twenty-Five" of *Being and Event*, Badiou reads Hölderlin as an exemplar of the fidelity to the event with an ability to inhabit the eventual site. This reading activates the idea of the transnational, discussing how Hölderlin thematizes Germany, Greece and Asia as sites. It also touches on questions of law and divinity among others. Going back to historical and colonial sequences of modernity, Badiou's work makes way for questioning the complex relation between modernity and modernism.

Finally, the form of the book itself inherits something of modernist projects that sought to revitalize the present through the rediscovery of traditional forms. Its conscious evocation of Descartes's meditations seems, on first glance, a strange approach for a work that announces the end of the Cartesian subject. And yet, this form allows Badiou to parallel semi-autonomous sections that (1) reconstitute the history of Western philosophy through the mathematical approach taken to ontology, (2) correspond this history to the logico-mathematical procedures since Cantor and Frege and (3) reflect on the doctrine of the subject. The form of the meditation is not simply an affection; it is a vital structure for the development of three lines of argument that function heteronymously.

No single definition of modernism emerges from this collection of chapters; rather, read together, they challenge the regressive pigeon-holing of Badiou to one definition or another. Modernism, here, runs the historical gamut from Visigothic Spain to the present and across the genres of philosophy, mathematics, music and theater. In turn, its influence on the different parts of Badiou's project proves to be heterodox and surprising: often upsetting its own apparent canonicity in the diverse and divergent treatments of its modernist precursors. In the essay referred to earlier, Cooke observes that the tension between Badiou's formalism and his commitments often manifests as a demand for "a greater degree of *mediation* within Badiou's corpus," or a "mutual implication of the abstract and the concrete" (Cook 2018: 160, 161). For Cooke's

Badiou, "a consistent philosophy is also one which should derive the categories *with which it thinks from the material which is the object of its thought*" (Cook 2018: 165). As the chapters that follow show, this commitment produces its own contradictions, convolutions and impasses, whose infinite multiplicities make for as many modernisms as there are "Alain Badious."

Works Cited

Badiou, A. (2007), *The Century*, trans. Alberto Toscano, Cambridge: Polity.
Badiou, A. (2020), *The Pornographic Age*, trans. A. J. Bartlett and J. Clemens, London and New York: Bloomsbury.
Beebe, M. (1974), "What Modernism Was," *Journal of Modern Literature* 3:5, 1065–1084.
Cooke, B. (2018), "Everything Must Become Nothing (and Vice Versa): Love and Abstraction in Badiou and Lacan," in A. J. Bartlett and J. Clemens (eds.), *Badiou and His Interlocutors: Lectures, Interviews and Responses*, 159–176, London: Bloomsbury.
Levin, H. (1960), "What Was Modernism?," *The Massachusetts Review* 1:4, 609–630.
Mao, D. and R. L. Walkowitz (2008), "The New Modernist Studies," *PMLA* 123:3, 737–748.
Watkin, W. (2020), "Brothel as Category," in A. J. Bartlett and J. Clemens (trans.), *The Pornographic Age*, 65–112, London and New York: Bloomsbury.

Part I

Badiou's Modernisms

Debts and Contestations

1

Mal/Bad, Beck/Worse

How to Think Poetically through Mallarmé, Plato and Beckett with Badiou

Jean-Michel Rabaté

My starting point is a question that has dogged me for some time: Why did Badiou begin to read Beckett via Mallarmé, as he did in his sustained discussion of *Worstward Ho*? (See Rabaté 2005, 2010 and 2016: 135–57). In order to answer, I survey Badiou's early engagement with Mallarmé in *Theory of the Subject*, then return to his main readings of Beckett, before tackling more recent engagements in *The Immanence of Truths*. I will argue that he finds a new point of departure and an original critical vocabulary when he approaches Beckett as a poet and not as a prose writer in *The Immanence of Truths*. Moreover, this approach, while introducing different concepts, also corrects recurrent distortions due to "strong readings" that took little notice of the texts' literary nature. Badiou shifts the focus of his engagement with Beckett when the 2018 book foregrounds the role played by infinity in finite artistic forms by introducing the conceptual couple of "uncovering" and "covering-over," in which I see a productive turn.

One of the first discussions of poetry in Badiou's work is the dialog staged between Mallarmé, Hegel, Marx, Lenin and Mao Zedong in the fifty pages that he devotes to the former's poetry in *Theory of the Subject*. *Un Coup de Dés*, the famous experiment in free verse set like a musical score and whose main statement is: "A Throw of the Dice Will Never Abolish Chance," which is presented from the start as a "revolutionary" poem in the most literal way. Mallarmé is seen as politically progressive, he allies himself with the struggle of the Parisian *Communards* or anarchists throwing bombs and dreaming of the *Grand Soir*, hoping for a spontaneous rebellion of the people against the bourgeois status quo. What distinguishes Badiou's reading from historicizing critics like Julia Kristeva and many others is that Badiou adds to this political dimension a systematic theory of the subject. One key point is the perception that if Mallarmé is a materialist poet, for him there is a "rock" that serves as a foundation for the Real. We see this in his poem: "some rock [. . .] which laid / a limit on the infinite" (Mallarmé quoted in Badiou 2009: 19).

Such a materialist foundation entails a "limit," which poses a problem for Badiou. Hence the affirmation that Mallarmé is not only a "materialist" thinker but also a "prodigious dialectician" (Badiou 2009: 65) produces in his work a poetic logic capable of favoring revolutionary politics, a tool as powerful as Hegel's *Logic* or Marx's *Capital*. Mallarmé formulates a dialectical theory of the subject, and appears as the progenitor of the historical avant-gardes that follow him, from futurism to Dadaism and surrealism. This derives from the fact that his poetics is founded on radical destruction, as stated in a letter from 1867: "Destruction was my Beatrice" (Badiou 2009: 87). Here is how Mallarmé can empower the masses or "the crowd," and not be out of place in Tiananmen Square during the Cultural Revolution (Badiou 2009: 66–7). He also understands the lack of the masses, because he anticipates Lacan's concept of the lack of a lack (Badiou 2009: 73). This original interpretation is exemplified by a close of reading of one sonnet, "A la nue accablante tu," here translated by Bruno Bosteels:

> Stilled beneath the oppressive cloud
> that basalt and lava base
> likewise the echoes that have bowed
> before a trumpet lacking grace
>
> O what sepulchral wreck (the spray
> knows, but it simply drivels there)
> ultimate jetsam cast away
> abolishes the mast stripped bare
>
> or else concealed that, furious
> failing some great catastrophe
> all the vain chasm gaping wide
>
> in the so white and trailing tress
> would have drowned avariciously
> a siren's childlike side. (Badiou 2009: 75)

This 1895 poem sketches the plot of *Un Coup de Dés* published two years later. Similar elements feature: we have a shipwreck, a raging storm, a siren appears only to vanish while the sea, clouds and rocks exchange their properties. An apocalyptic end of the world is sublimated by a poetic writing which takes place in times of social and political upheavals. Badiou considers the paradoxical trope of a drowning siren: "furious for not having had any ship to disappear, the abyss (sea and sky) has swallowed a siren, of which the white foam would no longer be anything other than the hair" (Badiou 2009: 75). He untangles the dialectical images at work in a poem that offers contradictory metaphors; the notions of a blank space is contradicted by an image of the sea-sky-foam; from this continuum two metonymic chains issue; one stresses disaster, the ship wrecked, the mast stripped, the horn ineffectual; the second foregrounds resilience with the siren who may have drowned but whose hair figures a "dolphin's leap" (Badiou

2009: 79). Shifting gradually from foam to hair, we go through the motions of the negation of the negation, a dialectic echoed by Maoist theory: "we also must produce the destruction of the bourgeoisie twice. First, the old bourgeoisie, the classical one, for which Leninism provides the means to destroy its apparatus. And then of the new one, the state bureaucratic bourgeoisie, which as Maoism teaches us sprouts up even among the instruments of the first destruction, the Leninist party and the socialist state" (Badiou 2009: 80). How can revolutionary masses perform such a double negation without abolishing their nature? This is a crucial issue, which can be compared with Lenin's hesitation about the withering away of the state after the revolution (Badiou 2009: 83).

Badiou fleshes out his dialectics of the subject by adding that politics, like literature, finds its being "in a structure of fiction" (Badiou 2009: 85). He then returns to "A la nue . . ." creatively, adding one extra stanza to the poem. In a gesture that is less a forceful appropriation or a show of one-upmanship than as a suggestion about how commentaries can politicize literary texts, Badiou's additional tercet offers both a convincing conclusion to his own meditations and a new poetic paradigm. Here is his tercet:

> Left dead by the song's excess
> Except that hatred the mast annuls
> From foam the plunging ride
> ["*Morte à l'excès qui fut son chant*
> *Sinon qu'annule de sa haine*
> *Le mât d'écume naufrageant*"]. (Badiou 2009: 345)

"Haine" rhymes back with "Sirène" of the previous tercet, while the rhyme of "chant"/"naufrageant" develops echoes from the last tercet of the original ("*dans le blanc cheveu . . . avarement . . . le flanc enfant . . .*"). In this brilliant pastiche of Mallarmé, Badiou not only shows his poetic virtuosity but also creates a loop that triggers another de-centering. His gloss on the added lines already sketches the issues of *The Immanence of Truths*:

> The poem, which is supposed to be finite, does not end in a loop, nor does it suggest the principle of an iterative descending into infinity. // I leave it to you to judge whether my looping—defounding—addition which annuls the siren and re-establishes the ship produces a paradox for the operations accepted by the Mallarmean theory of poetic sets: metaphor, metonymy, vanishing, annulment. The latter, I repeat, articulate all the concepts of the structural dialectic: chain effect, vanishing term, causality of lack./ Mallarmé stops. //Mao does not stop. To Stalin's loop he prefers the other slope of the unfounded, of the real as impossible: the infinite descent. (Badiou 2009: 91)

Here, Badiou has managed to re-unite Lacan, Hegel, Marx and Mao by splicing two themes, the theory of the subject as exception, and the dialectical twist of the lack of the lack. Mallarmé's "nothing" negates the object which allows language to enact a double negativity, introducing a dynamic lack in which one can perceive a dialectical movement. The poetic logic of the double negation offers a dialectical tool whose proper application is revolutionary politics.

This rather free treatment of Mallarmé can be compared with another discussion of poetry when Badiou translated Plato in his notorious "hypertranslation" of the *Republic*. In this freewheeling version, Badiou modernized Plato's dialog inserting numerous anachronisms; thus his *Republic* includes the French Revolution, the Soviet uprising of 1917, along with Stalin, Hitler and Mao. Rewriting Plato's text in French, Badiou deletes, adds, combines characters and even invents a feminine philosopher he calls Amantha. Whenever Plato's dialog mentions the "gods," they become a Lacanian "big Other." Socrates's discussion of irrational numbers turns into a disquisition on Cantor's transfinite numbers.

Hellenists and classical philosophers have screamed in horror but the overall result is truly exciting, highly controlled and thought-provoking. Whereas Plato's *Republic* is rarely read in its entirety, Badiou forces one to engage fully with a text that asks us to define the ideal political system. Plato repeatedly poses the questions of the nature of truth; he is eager to avoid the mistakes of Sophists and Cynics who reduce truth to subjective opinion. Accepting such a program, Badiou asks why communism has remained a possible option, and also how mathematics can still give access to a scientific and materialist ontology. However, he cannot avoid dealing with Plato's notorious exclusion of poets from his ideal city, and indeed his version does not bypass this tricky passage. Plato had concluded that despite all their creativity poets must be exiled from the *polis* because the new order that the philosophers are building only needs music, prose and mathematics. *Amantha* interjects that given its internationalist scope, the political utopia planned cannot have borders:

> The proletariat has no country. A communist border agent would be a pathetic oxymoron!
> —Which only proves, *Socrates shot back*, that what I was suggesting was an *image*, that I was speaking metaphorically. Trust me, this vision of the poet, banned from the city, will become famous!
> —Oh, then *you*'re the poet with the deceptive language and the enticing images!
> —Well, *concluded Socrates*, I entrust you with the task of personally seeing to my deportation.
> They all burst out laughing. (Badiou 2012: 88–9)

The passage that has consternated generations of poetry-lovers aghast at Plato's strictures turns into another game of dialogical one-upmanship thanks to a paradox: How can poets be excluded from an internationalist and cosmopolitan republic whose borders remain open? The paradox is redoubled as soon as we remember that Plato was also a poet, a frustrated playwright and a mimetic artist himself. He should have excluded himself from his own utopia! His exclusion of poets is replayed in a series of dialectical reversals that entail a similar double negativity. If poets are dangerous, their double negations in which one glimpses a certain infinity are revolutionary. Here is where Beckett comes into play.

Badiou's attitude has been confrontational facing the previous reception of Beckett. Badiou repeatedly attacks a doxa that was prevalent in the 1950s when Beckett was portrayed as "a writer of the absurd, of despair, of empty skies, of incommunicability and of eternal solitude" (Badiou 1995: 38). The refutation is inscribed on the cover of the book: "No, Beckett's oeuvre is not what was always said about it—that it was despair, absurdity of the world, anxiety, solitude, decrepitude" (Badiou 1995: cover). *Beckett: l'increvable désir*, this short guide to Beckett's entire work restates in less technical language the analyses of the Irish writer Badiou has provided in 1989 with "The writing of the generic." After that, a chapter of his *Handbook of Inaesthetics* was devoted to *Worstward Ho* in 1998. Commenting these, Andrew Gibson's book on Badiou and Beckett assumes that one cannot follow Badiou's reading of Beckett without having understood his entire system. Gibson is honest, never hushing his doubts facing Badiou's offhand treatment of some texts. He sums up Badiou's position as an attempt to find in Beckett concepts such as "subtraction, restricted action, actual infinity, the event, subjectification, the logic of appearance, naming, fidelity, apagogic reason, the waiting subject, investigation, inexistents, patience, vigilance, objectivity; undecidables, indiscernibles, and unnameables, *événementialité* or the event of the event" (Gibson 2006: 285). Are these concepts that come from Beckett or from Badiou? Indeed, the slim book on Beckett might be taken as a condensed version of Badiou's system of thought. Badiou's philosophical program had been launched with the hope of reconciling Sartre's negative ontology and Blanchot's conception of an autonomous literary language. He wished to "complete the Sartrean theory of freedom through a careful investigation into the opacities of the signifier" (Badiou 2003: 39). If the second part of the program was never fully implemented, Badiou has come more and more close to it recently.

The second half of the programme started being sketched when Badiou began seeing Beckett not only as a political and ethical writer but also as a poet whose works were founded on a certain conception of beauty. Affirming the courage to keep on desiring in spite of endless obstacles, Beckett not only teaches a truth about desire, language and being but also aims at creating a beautiful form. Beckett knows that it is essential never to yield on one's desire when facing collapse, fiasco, moral perversion, intellectual bankruptcy and impotence; however, his main model remained Joyce, the consummated artist, even when he stated that his method would be the exact opposite of Joyce's belief in artistic power. Beckett opposes to this a model of impotence, poverty and lack, but such a model feeds the ethical affirmation giving courage and helping to keep on living. The more Beckett multiplies the arguments showing how impossible his position is, the more his writing is seductive.

Beckett did not reach such a position all at once, and Badiou sees a divide in Beckett's career, more precisely finds that there would have been a break between 1950, when the progression toward silence loomed larger and larger in *Texts for Nothing*, and ten years later, with the new departure of the dark novel *How It Is*. At the same time, a new minimalism generates daring experiments in the theater and other media like film, radio and television. This movement culminates with the second trilogy, *Nohow On*, which for Badiou embodies the highest point of Beckett's language and thought. Beckett's operations follow logically a "methodical askesis" going back to Descartes and Husserl, his main wish being to "suspend" everything deemed inessential. The clownish humor and the nihilistic elements of existential despair are merely ironical instruments for that end. When Beckett reduces human subjects to paralyzed cripples or ectoplasms in a jar, when he fits Winnie up to her neck in an earth mound in *Happy Days*, when he imagines the Unnamable as an egg-like sphere with minimal apertures, he enacts a Cartesian and Husserlian *epoché* (Badiou 2003: 44) so as to expose what is "generic" in humanity. The investigation of thinking humanity proceeds by way of destruction: one has to discover what resists, what remains indestructible. Only then can there be a stable foundation for ethics.

In *Handbook of Inaesthetics*, Badiou calls *Worstward Ho* a "short philosophical treatise, as a treatment in shorthand of the question of being" (Badiou 2003: 80). He offers a reading that is philosophically rigorous while staying so close to the letter of Beckett's text that it uses only words already in the text, but broken down into a series of propositions. First, the injunction "on" marks the imperative of saying, which is the first and only law of the text; then pure being is equated with the "void" thanks to a systematic exercise in disappearance. All subjects are inscribed in being, like the characters of this fiction, the one of woman and, the two of an old man and a child. The universe is a void infested by shades because "dimness" is the condition of being. Whatever or whoever is inscribed in being is defined as that which can "worsen." Existence is a constant "worsening" caused by language, since it is always possible to say "worse" or "iller" what has already been said only badly. However the worst that language is capable of can never let itself be captured by absolutely nothing. Thought is produced by a head or a skull in whose confines the drama of the Cartesian cogito is replayed endlessly. Three types of exercises in worsening that bear on the one, on the two or on the skull. These exercises in worsening testify to the sovereignty of language: in Beckett's language addition is equal to subtraction. Worsening is a labor that demands the courage of truth.

Since there will be no termination of saying, this courage is founded upon a strong rapport between words, truth and beauty. If the void is posited as "unworsenable," an absolute limit, nevertheless worsening aims at getting always closer to the void. The void can only be crossed in an event that remains unspeakable. What has been gained by exercises in worsening is a more rigorous definition of the two of love as the root of migration and change, and a sense of joy and beauty that come from the link posited between words and truth. Beauty surges when we understand that the path of words goes counter to the demand of thought. Finally, at the end of the text, on the last page, we go beyond the pattern linking being, existence and thought; there we witness the irruption of an event. This irruption is similar to the way a "constellation" appears in the sky at the end of Mallarmé's *Un Coup de Dés*. The event is signaled by "enough," a word that appears in the penultimate paragraph and introduces a rupture with what precedes. The word is spoken when the old woman turns into a grave. However, the imperative of language remains: all will begin again.

In the looping of the circle, Mallarmé and Beckett overlap or are combined fully (Badiou 2003: 81–96).

Badiou's strategy is to quote only terms provided by Beckett, and these terms are then harnessed in a philosophical syntax that provides a meta-narrative. The commentary, which doubles in length Beckett's prose poem yields a coherent set of philosophical statements thanks to a rare feat of close reading that is also a radical re-translation. While I admire the consistency of the commentary, I do not follow its conclusion when Badiou has to introduce an "event" emerging at the end. The "event" would appear in a last page of *Worstward Ho,* read as marked by a final explosion:

> But once the recapitulation is complete there brusquely occurs—in a moment introduced by "sudden"—a sort of distancing of this state to a limit position . . . there emerges, in a suddenness that amounts to a grace without concept, an overall configuration in which one will be able to say "nohow on." Not an "on" ordained or prescribed to the shades, but simply "nohow on"—the "on" of saying reduced, or leastened, to the purity of its possible cessation. (Badiou 2003: 109–10)

If the penultimate paragraph indeed may call up a certain limit ("Enough. Sudden enough. Sudden all far. [. . .] At bounds of boundless void. Whence no farther" [Beckett 1992: 128]), this is not the first time that "sudden" appears: one finds it on page 107. Badiou's intertextual detour via Mallarmé justifies this reading, because he can assert that the "event" is the appearance of a constellation shining at the moment of death. Gibson took seriously the idea of an extra-textual event included into the text or leaving a hole for the emergence of truth. Gibson's commentary also identified modernity with the event: "The event defines modernity" (Gibson 2006: 257) accepting Badiou's reading of the last page of *Wostward Ho.* He qualified this by adding that what is at stake is only the "evenementiality of the event." And the analysis has trouble identifying the event, which is both an absence and a presence: "Beckett's commitments to aporetics is precisely a commitment to a writing that, in the absence of events, produces and sustains a consciousness of *événementialité*" (Gibson 2006: 287). Of what event are we talking? Badiou links the event with fidelity to what happens, like a political revolution, falling in love or the irruption of scientific inventions. Even if we can agree that Beckett's text ends with a suggestion of the death of the old woman, there is no reason to link it with an "event" in Badiou's sense.

Happily, the chapter on Beckett in *The Immanence of Truths* modifies the previous approaches. Above all, Badiou refrains from mentioning any event when reading Beckett's poetry. The term only crops up briefly at the end in a discussion of Love (Badiou 2018: 613, 635). *The Immanence of Truths* is a huge book of some 700 pages presented as the third volume of a philosophical trilogy, completing *Being and Event* (1988) and *Logics of Worlds* (2006). Shorter chapters are devoted to literary texts, sections of a few pages each on René Char (89–92), Victor Hugo (107–10), Emily Dickinson (131–3), Paul Celan (151–5), Osip Mandelstam (169–72), Fernando Pessoa (191–6) and Bertolt Brecht (211–13). Finally, Beckett (231–6) marks a climax. After Beckett, there are only artistic examples: an analysis of Breughel's painting of the

"Fall of Icarus" (548–51) and a discussion of Olivier Messiaen's musical piece "The Black Robin" (551–60). These pithy and vibrant pages are written with a degree of condensation and poetic flair that contrasts with the extensive sections plunging us at length in mathematics and logical theory.

The first examples, all of which concern poems, exemplify modern forms of finitude. Then Beckett's poems are adduced to introduce the binary of "covering-over" (*recouvrement*) and "uncovering" (*découvrement*). The first sections also include numerous passages from Badiou's play, *Ahmed Philosophe*, disseminated throughout the text. However, if the number of pages devoted to Beckett is limited, and is followed only by two passing allusions, it seems that the literary analyses are more than "interludes," as they are called. Indeed, they pave the way to the exposition of a comprehensive thesis on art and infinity that is presented in the later chapters (section VII, Chapter C22 "General theory of works-in-truth" and section VIII, Chapter C23, "Works according to the object: Art, science").

Badiou defines "covering-over" as the modern, as opposed to classical, form of finitude. The discourse of "covering-over" does not deny that a potentially revolutionary situation has happened, but it translates any emergence of the infinite into the language of the finite. The infinity deployed has been masked or distorted in order to maintain the status quo (Badiou 2018: 75). "Covering-over" conceals and hides infinite multiplicities by reducing them to constructible multiples. "Covering-over" is a mechanism by which a system's chains of infinities are inverted into finite segments perpetuating a closure that maintains the status quo. "Covering-over" refuses anything that might be in excess and makes the new look old, banal or simply impossible. It will "asphyxiate" the teeming possibilities contained in the infinities; it attempts to prevent any new infinity from emerging in a situation (Badiou 2018: 222).

"Covering-over" rejects in advance any risk and blocks new departures. For instance, the potential for the infinite can be seen as the communist idea against the capitalist state, or as the possibility of love, since love creates a new life between two individuals, which can be resisted by jealousy, as one sees with Proust. To give another example, the revolutionary protests of May 1968 will be reduced to a movement of "sexual liberation" (Badiou 2018: 227). The infinite potentiality of the movement will be neutralized and rationalized reductively. At bottom, the subject interested in such covering-over is defined by Lacan's concept of the "non-dupes" who err (*les non-dupes errent*) (Badiou 2018: 228). The "*non-dupe*" is a "renegade of infinite potential" (Badiou 2018: 229). This corresponds with people who resent having been taken in romantically, decide not to be deceived again and find a determined footing with which they reduce all infinities. Given their enlightened false consciousness, they deceive themselves all the more, for in the end, those "non-duped" repeat the homophonic phrase of "the nom-du-Père," the name of the Father that keeps the symbolic order of culture and religion tightly under control.

It is in this context that Beckett is called upon to bring about his breakthrough. There was a "covering-over" for him: it corresponded to how mystified first readers saw in him existential despair, nihilism or the death of God. Paralleling his objections from the 1995 book, Badiou again rejects those readings that reduce Beckett to a "decorative anxiety" (Badiou 2018: 231). Even if these opinions hark back to the 1960s and do not quite correspond to the current critical consensus, Badiou does not care. He is not interested in the evolution of Beckett scholarship because he thinks through the Beckett who marked his generation, who defined his own sense of history and whose philosophical questions are tackled through poetic texts.

Against any "covering-up" passed or to come, Beckett's Heraclitan poem from 1977 asserts pure flux: "flux cause / that all things / while being / all things / thus that thing here / even that one there / while being / is not / let's talk about it" (Beckett 2012: 213; my translation). Badiou agrees with the ending and praises the idea of talking along with the universal flux: "Talk about the weakness of usual 'saying' that misses the infinity of the real flux because it covers it over with identities that only freeze it outside its real. Indeed, the task is nothing less than the invention of a new saying, which will be a saying-the infinite-of-the-finite-as-discovered" (Badiou 2018: 232). The hyphenated compound combines two main concepts to show the clash between the finite and the infinite. This points to the work of "uncovering" or "discovering" that Beckett's poetry accomplishes. Beckett shows how the infinite can emerge from the finite, instead of reducing the infinite to its biographical circumstances, to identity politics or to some historicist framing in a mystifying contextualization.

In those impassioned pages, Badiou avoids the recurrent problems betrayed earlier with the translations he would quote, mostly because the two main poems he glosses were written in French. For this one, Beckett provided a translation under the title of "what is the word." I'll quote the beginning of the English version:

folly—
folly for to –
for to –
what is the word –
folly from this –
all this –
folly from all this –
given –
folly given all this—
seeing –
folly seeing all this — (Beckett 2012: 228)

This last exercise in poetic panting sends us back to *How It Is*, with its jerky breathless rhythms, but here punctuation intervenes by multiplying dashes that can appear as so many minus signs. They interrupt the lyrical breath, but also send it back on itself for renewed utterances. As Badiou explains, the "folly" or "madness" expresses the risk taken by Beckett as a poet. The madness alludes to the poet's "desire to reach beyond the ordinary state of language, which is doomed to covering-over" (Badiou 2018: 233). In *The Unnamable*, Beckett had called the language that he needed to express himself a *charabia* (gibberish). This gibberish imposed from the outside is a code that he wants if not to destroy wholly at least to subvert from within. Here lies the "folly," the idea that a new language can be created, and that it can exceed the issue of the given as visible: "the perception of the visible is here torn away from language to go and see, one might say to see-beyond (*outrevoir*) what flux allows to be in non-being" (Badiou 2018: 233). Badiou's critical idiom coins words like "outrevoir" (it does not exist in French) and keeps flirting with paradoxes and oxymorons. Like Rimbaud, who had called "folly" his entire poetic endeavor, Beckett invents a vibrant saying that pierces through any "covering-over" because it reaches the heart of the "infinite nudity of what is true" (Badiou 2018: 232).

Badiou turns to a French poem evoking Kant and the Lisbon disaster, a poem written after Beckett had read through the collected works of Kant in German. The poem connects the catastrophic Lisbon earthquake of 1755, an event that shocked the whole of Europe, and Beckett's own losses. Lisbon, one of the main European capitals, was almost destroyed. Kant wrote no less than three essays about the catastrophe in one year, as Beckett learned from Ernst Cassirer's biography. From a population of 200,000 people, one-quarter died, and 80 percent of the buildings in Lisbon were destroyed. It looked as if religion had been attacked by the earthquake which was unleashed on All Saints' Day: most people were in churches that collapsed on them. Kant, who was twenty-four then, argued wrongly that the catastrophe was caused by exploding gases arising from the underground caverns. Beckett contextualizes this by including previous catastrophes, like the unknown cause leading to the extinction of mammoths (Beckett 2012: 98). The text is quoted in full by Badiou. Here is my translation:

> thus will one in vain
> by good weather or by bad weather
> imprisoned at one's place imprisoned abroad
> as if it was yesterday remember the mammoth
> the dinotherium the first kisses
> ice periods bringing nothing new
> the great warming up of the thirteenth century of their era
> on Lisbon still smoking Kant coolly bending
> dream in generations of oak trees and forget one's father
> his eyes whether he wore a moustache
> whether he was a good man what he died of
> one is none the less eaten up without appetite
> by bad weather or by worse weather
> imprisoned at one's place imprisoned abroad. (Badiou 2018: 236)

Beckett's poem unfolds as a single sentence with interpolations. This is a poem of mourning expressing Beckett's loss after his father died in 1933 from a sudden heart-attack. The aftermath of the traumatic loss led Beckett to begin a psychoanalytic cure with Bion. He states that if one measures personal pain by comparing it with huge periods of time defined by glacial ages, there is little difference between one's first kisses and the thawing of glaciers, between remembering or forgetting the loved one. One might say that a certain terrestrial infinity is used as solace in moments of intense pain. But this is not the way Badiou reads the text.

Beckett had found in Fritz Mauthner's *Beiträge zu einer Kritik der Sprache* (Mauthner 1982: 644–8) an analysis of the disappearance of the mammoths, the fact that oak trees live for one thousand years, the time it takes for linguistic changes, and quotes from Joseph Alphonse Adhémar who in *Révolutions de la mer: Déluges périodiques* (Adhémar 1860) calculates that the earth experienced periodic catastrophes in cycles of 15,000 years, each time the earth tilts on its orbital axis. A similar scientific approach was shared by Kant, hence his "coldness," his indifference to the suffering of the inhabitants of Lisbon. His cold wisdom offers a good example of "covering-over" personal or collective pathos in times of horrible disaster. Such scientific calculations might offer a consolation, but they stop and block in the name of a spurious infinity. As Badiou shows, the only solution is movement, a refusal to stay in the same place, as Kant did since he was rumored never to have left his city of Königsberg. Rejecting the facile consolation of great numbers, Beckett instead opted to choose exile, moving to Paris and taking Joyce as a model. Badiou gives us this original interpretation:

> The evil that is invisible but caught up in the "what is the word" corresponds to being "imprisoned at home imprisoned abroad," which means: imprisoned quite simply, imprisoned in the finite of *chez*, whether it is "at their place" (*chez eux*) or "at one's place" (*chez soi*). Whoever takes shelter in an unequivocal *chez* is lost. All infinity requires errancy. Otherwise, there is no point in invoking the common places of past grandeur to fight against the law of the Father: the imprisoned one will be, just because he is imprisoned, in-finitized (*en-finitudisé*), eaten up by the worse. (Badiou 2018: 236)

Again, a coining, the invented verb "en-finitudiser," parallels wandering as errancy and the acceptance of risk and error, in opposition to the "non-duped" subject who would remain in his father's house and never questions the ideology of patriarchy. If one can reach outside, face existential pain and risk, then the "covering-over" of pseudo-science will vanish. The risk is worth the effort: for once it is confronted, what looked like the worst appears small and derisive. Badiou concludes this chapter by quoting the first "mirlitonnade":

> en face
> le pire
> jusqu'à ce
> qu'il fasse rire. (Badiou 2018: 236)

It might be translated as:

> Face
> the worst

until it makes
you laugh.

Badiou analyzes this poem in a sentence that recapitulates previous readings:

> Instead the errant, faithful to "what is the word," he who sees in the small daffodil the infinite genesis of spring, he who can say "we have our being in justice I have never heard anything to the contrary," he who sees the night as he sees himself seeing the night, he who experiments further than the here and there of the named thing, he who is not in-finitized, he faces the worst. And then he sees its entire derision. (Badiou 2018: 236)

One may be intrigued by the insertion of a sentence from *How It Is*. I have discussed Badiou's reading of *How It Is* elsewhere (Rabaté 2020: 43–7) and will just call up one objection. My criticism was that Beckett used the term "justice" ironically or critically, for he hinted that Dante's idea of justice could be reduced to calculations of equivalences. In *How It Is*, we are far from the universal law one expects from true justice. Justice is reduced to a "contract," the Dantean *contrapasso*, which moreover is grafted onto a parody of Nietzsche's law of eternal return. Everyday life is allegorized as a perpetual crawling through mud, muck and shit. Aimless and desperate progression, from which death cannot free us, is caught at the end in endless calculations. Here, "justice" cannot be taken as an opening to the incalculable or to infinity, for it remains bound to the law of mortality, to a system of counterparts that can be calculated when meted out. The ethical experience proposed by the voice, if we imagine it expecting something "to the contrary," that is the ethical voice has been silenced.

In fact, this notion fits the thesis launched in *Immanence of Truths*. If Badiou had been more consistent about this small detail, he would have revisited his previous reading of *How It Is* in light of the theory of the "covering-over," since it seems clear that in Beckett's strange hell, even justice reintroduces a "bad infinity," which appears by the fact that the last twenty pages of the novel multiply sequences of numbers, before concluding that all these calculations were idle:

> when the panting stops an ear above somewhere above and unto the murmur ascending and if we are innumerable then murmurs innumerable all alike our justice one life everywhere ill-told ill-heard quaqua on all sides then within when the panting stops ten seconds fifteen seconds in the little chamber all bone-white if there were a light oakum of old words ill-heard ill-murmured that murmur those murmurs. (Beckett 1964: 146)

Thus the concept of infinity is stronger than the belief in "honour and justice" (Beckett 1964: 147), even when the speaker admits in the very end that all the panting-speaking-murmuring was his, that he was alone and alone fabricated a parody of Dante to avoid thinking about his impending death.

To conclude, I suggest that the main obstacles to a convincing practice of literary commentary of Beckett, the fact that Badiou did not pay enough attention to the letter of the texts analyzed, or did not distinguish between poetic texts and their translations, or imposed a grid borrowed from another poet (as Mallarmé for Beckett), have been overcome in *The Immanence of Truths*. What stands out is a remarkable attempt at reading literary texts poetically, philosophically and politically, showing how a finite work—a poem or a "work"—avoids turning into a "waste" or *déchet* because it impacts history even at a distance, keeping alive its revolutionary charge and chances, allowing the infinity it contains to remain alive. Art can thus accomplish its work of beauty and emancipation by generating a truth that is both immanent and absolute.

Works Cited

Adhémar, J. A. (1842, 1860), *Révolutions de la mer: Déluges périodiques*, 2nd ed., Paris: Dunod.
Badiou, A. (1995), *Beckett: L'increvable désir*, Paris: Hachette.
Badiou, A. (2003), *On Beckett*, trans. N. Power and A. Toscano, Manchester: Clinamen.
Badiou, A. (2009), *Theory of the Subject*, trans. B. Bosteels, New York: Bloomsbury.
Badiou, A. (2012), *Plato's Republic: A Dialogue in 16 Chapters*, trans. S. Spitzer, New York: Columbia University Press.
Badiou, A. (2018), *L'immanence des vérités. L'être et l'événement, 3*, Paris: Fayard.
Beckett, S. (1964), *How It Is*, London: John Calder.
Beckett, S. (1992), *Nohow On: Company, Il See Ill Said, Worstward Ho*, London: Calder.
Beckett, S. (2012), *The Collected Poems*, eds. S. Lawlor and J. Pilling, London: Faber.
Gibson, A. (2006), *Beckett and Badiou: The Pathos of Intermittency*, Oxford: Oxford University Press.
Mauthner, F. (1982), *Beiträge zu einer Kritik der Sprache, Zweiter Band: Zur Sprachwissenschaft*, Stuttgart: Ullstein.
Rabaté, J.-M. (2005), "Unbreakable B's: From Beckett and Badiou to the Bitter End of Affirmative Ethics," in G. Riera (ed.), *Alain Badiou: Philosophy and Its Conditions*, 87–108, Albany: State University of New York Press.
Rabaté, J.-M. (2010), "Philosophizing with Beckett: Adorno and Badiou," in S. E. Gontarski (ed.), *A Companion to Samuel Beckett*, 97–117, Oxford: Wiley-Blackwell.
Rabaté, J.-M. (2016), *Think, Pig! Beckett at the Limit of the Human*, New York: Fordham University Press.
Rabaté, J.-M. (2020), *Beckett and Sade*, Cambridge: Cambridge University Press.

2

Alain Badiou's Dialectical (Non) Gesture of Modernity

Poetry, Mastery, Undecidability

Soumyabrata Choudhury

Introduction: Is the Philosopher's Gesture a Subtraction from the History of Gestures?

If one were to ask a mime artist to show the audience what it is to walk, the artist wouldn't actually walk from one spot to another. She, standing at the same spot, would mobilize all her limbs from the toenail upwards to express and embody the *gesture* of walking. In this sense, she wouldn't confuse the essence of walking with merely taking a walk but, instead, attempt to show "walking" as such.

If one were to ask an actor brought up on, let's say, the exercises of Jerzy Grotowski's "poor theatre" to show us "seeing," this actor wouldn't actually turn to an object in her surroundings to intently focus on it; she would in all likelihood, use her two hands to widen her eyes such that from the pupils to the iris, every visible part (of the eyes) would themselves come into a kind of rarefied field of vision.[1] The eyes wouldn't merely see; the very act of seeing would become a pure gesture without any necessary object or focus outside its performance.

Now if one were to ask an actor, a mime, a dancer to show us "thinking," it is difficult to imagine where the gesture of this thinking would be localized. That is to say, for the specialized art of expressing and codifying a gesture of thinking, it would be difficult to unequivocally home in on an *organ* of thinking in the same way that one seizes the limbs or the eyes as organs, radiating the gesture of walking and seeing. Of course it is very likely that when called upon to show "thinking," the artiste would resort to the conventional gesture of stabbing her forehead with an insistent finger as if to think with great force and animation. But in no way would this purely conventional action, common to our gestural habits, including those of the most refined virtuosos, signify that the head or the brain inside the head is the real organ of thinking. It's as if the real of thinking eludes both localization within an organ and the gestural radiation which can extend an organ into an artistic form. One is reminded of Jacques

Lacan's quip in a rather sardonic allusion to Noam Chomsky's popular thesis on the human brain as a source of the anthropological capacity for all structures of developed thought, beginning with language that he had seen many a brain-scan but never a single thought in them (Roudinesco 1997: 379).

If the philosopher's gesture has something essentially to do with the genesis and act of thinking, then the question arises: What is the archetypal philosophical gesture of thinking? One will notice that even with the examples of walking and seeing, while the gestural forms of these actions in their artistic expression do not result in any empirical evidence of a walk taken or a thing seen, the very localization of these actions in specific organs as their source of gestural radiation, point to a certain logic of *knowledge* that is implicated in these non-instrumental performances: the mime, the actor or the dancer, even without any explicit stakes in empirical knowledge take their specific materiality from the same source and element from which the constitution of knowledge proceeds. That is to say, the performance of a pure gesture of walking or seeing must still originate in a kind of "real" of an organ that in the first place must be perturbed by the compulsion to walk, to see and so on. Whether art or knowledge, both must find their initial forms of constitution into their respective "gestures" within this real of an encounter between material bodies, their organismic organization and the contingent triggers of the world.

When comparing the philosophical gesture with the artistic or the epistemic one, the impasse of finding a properly philosophical organ, that is to say, an organ of thinking raises the question of whether the philosopher's labor can be included within the historical repertoires that one can extract from the archive of artistic and epistemic gestures, constituting a history of knowledges as it were, which corresponds to the contingencies of sensory and perceptual perturbations that keep arising in the real world. At the same time, if one is not to fall into an idealistic temptation for philosophy, the latter must have something real to do with these sensory upsurges in the world and their historical constitution into particular knowledges, including the scientific and the artistic ones.

In his own philosophical repertoire, Alain Badiou has in various articles and books placed the term "event" at this delicate cusp between the "history of gestures" and the real of a thinking which is not spontaneously generated by this history. This feature of thinking without a proper organ of its generation / gesture leads to significant consequences for the history of knowledges. What Badiou calls "event" takes place in history even while the world, which is subject to the historicity of this event, has not prepared a "place" for it. That is to say, in Badiou's proposal, event has a singular historicity but does not *belong* to any historical place—which exactly marks a certain crisis of historical knowledges and the real of thinking and its lack of a proper "organ." But he also examines the logic of the event in relation to the form of thinking one calls "dialectics" as a preoccupation with the philosophical method particularly in a kind of virtual conversation with Hegel and Marx. Before proceeding any further it is important to note that Badiou does not offer the notion of event upto any kind of mystical epiphany beyond the rationality of knowledge(s). So the philosophical search for a *concept* of the event is central to Badiou's reason as much as to his passion. This is the specific articulation between a certain subjective "leap" (or in more ludic terms a wager or gamble) that any affirmation indicates and a search for method that does not cease to give up on a passion for formalization, with the unfolding of its conceptual gestures yet never quite folding back into a form of "knowledge." This chapter is situated along the amplitude of this movement between a subjective affirmation and an objective conceptual horizon, an amplitude evidently contained in the very phrase "affirmative dialectics."

It is only recently that Alain Badiou has suggested the possibility of an affirmative dialectics as a form of thinking about the event—a form to be differentiated from a historical or a methodological dialectic. In either case the dialectic operation would seem to effectuate a new state of affairs whether in the world or in thought which arises from a certain moment of the negative. Hegel's *Phenomenology of Spirit* could be seen as the unfolding of a world historical repertoire of gestures corresponding to the different moments of the negative that result in the great epochal changes structuring world history.[2] In Hegel, the success of this gestural project is truly encyclopedic because each unit of historical change and epistemic transformation corresponds to, as if, a gestural unit so minute yet so saturating that it leaves no space for what Alain Badiou calls the affirmation of a true creation (2013: 1). In his lecture/essay, "Affirmative dialectics: From Logic to Anthropology," Badiou points out that Marx could be said to initiate a new direction of thinking, not so much in relation to the constitution of new knowledges (for instance, the knowledge of capitalism) as in relation to something outside the ongoing dialectic of history and knowledge. This Badiou calls the outside of revolutionary thought or the thinking of revolution that does not fall under any historical knowledge. What is challenging in Badiou's thesis is that the outside of Marx's historical situation is *immanent* to that situation—which demands to be thought. Alain Badiou's own vocation seems to remain within this demand of thinking and his "philosophical gesture," in its own reconstitution, must be subtracted from any discernible historical "result" corresponding to gestures of history, including the empirically verifiable revolutionary ones. In a conversation with Jean-Luc Nancy, Badiou expresses some doubt whether Marx can be called a "philosopher" in so far as the German thinker did not ever entirely subtract his gesture of thinking from his epic analytical, scientific and epistemological preoccupations (2018: 25–8). At the same time, we cannot neglect the fact that Marx in the eleventh thesis of *Thesis on Feuerbach* when pronouncing the verdict that philosophers have hitherto only interpreted the world, did not explicitly declare that the "gesture" of *changing* the world was obligatorily a philosophical one (1969: 13–15). The thought of change remains an open one in the *Thesis on Feuerbach*; Marx does not actually prescribe a form or a gesture—whether artistic or political—for the provenance of change that the world needs. The question of change is an invitation to affirm the same without the support of a historical gesture. And yet this very event of change demands to be thought and invites the capacity for such a thinking to find its form and gesture. It is this edge of the dialectic and history of forms/gestures seen as a dialectical process that can also be termed the non-dialectical edge of any dialectic. But one has to be careful to note that this edge is neither a structural property of nor a simple exclusion from the dialectic but, in Alain Badiou's thinking, its affirmative condition even before the logic and productivity of the negative has set in.

In Marx's own time, the revolutionary conditions which were not a simple matter of historical knowledge but the very creation of a new *subject* whose subjective process consisted in affirming such a revolutionary capacity, opened up the condition for both the accumulated gesture (s) of history to lose its encoded efficacy (whether understood instrumentally or artistically) and this new capacity itself to be affirmed as a gesture of that very "outside" which history had eventually secreted. The historicity of the outside remains a passionately dialectical affair and yet it has the peculiar topology of an "outside dialectic," which does not mean being outside the dialectical process. It is this method of the so-called immanent exception or the affirmative labor of finding a name for this exception which makes the philosophical gesture after Badiou a truly intriguing one: following Marx, the affirmation of change, while casting grave doubts on the philosopher's historical disposition and ideology hitherto seen, itself doesn't have to issue from philosophical knowledge as such. The subject of this affirmation is now *anyone*, not simply as an empirical possibility but as a revolutionary or eventual capacity (Choudhury 2013: 157–98). But seeing from the vantage point of Badiou's labors, the very name "event" is the effect of a philosophical gesture. His point is precisely that the condition for this effect is not a philosophical one but something which arises out of the real of historical change whose initial dialectical (non) gesture was performed by Marx (2013: 1–2). Badiou, as a philosopher affirms the initial affirmation and does not cease to do so while traversing the several and often contestatory consequences of that initial affirmative (non) gesture. To this extent, philosophy itself does not have an internal historical consistency but in being subtracted from the stories, gestures and effects of history, this very subtractive (non) gesture introduces, with each eventual historicity a new affirmative dialectics or, what has been called earlier, an "outside dialectic" (Badiou 2013: 13).

The Dialectic of Gesture and Non-Gesture: Poetry, Mastery, Undecidability

It is not difficult to see that the idiom of gesture is borrowed from the art of theater. In the modern period we can see at least two attitudes in the history of theater to the question of gesture that hold particular interest. The first is the Brechtian attitude which treats gesture as a unit of social rationality at a particular historical moment. In this sense, for Brecht, gesture is not simply the localization and expression of a sensory upsurge through particular bodily organs but it is the further complication of bodily actions and dispositions which produce certain *significant* historical contradictions and crises. For example, in the play *The Life of Galileo*, the central contradiction of the history of science is expressed by the question whether the venerable scholars and philosophers of the Italian court would accept Galileo's nearly unctuous invitation for them to turn the telescope toward the Heavens—which till the very end they refused to do (Brecht: 2006). It is this refusal of a sensory action that produces the true significance of the historico-social gesture divided between the traditionalist disavowal and the Galilean act of looking at the sky through a new instrument, mediating sensory perception. Clearly, the Brechtian attitude to gesture in its very negative presentation of a historical crisis remains didactic. Brecht, through the gestic contradiction of the play, would like to teach the audience/reader the real gesture *required*—the gesture of "change."

The second attitude to gesture in the modern period with a theatrical logic as its stake, is Mallarméan. In Alain Badiou's extraordinarily subtle essay from *Handbook of Inaesthetics* "A Poetic Dialectic: Labid ben Rabi'a and Mallarmé," the author speaks of the French poet from the nineteenth-century imperial period surrounded by high bourgeois culture as a singular instance of a kind of gestural undecidability (2005: 46–56). It is true that in this essay Badiou refers to Mallarmé's poem "Coup de des" instead of his theatrical works to present the problem of gesture but what is interesting is that the very nature of the poetic object, the poem as a fixed form, is internally destabilized by the image of a master's gesture, which in its very performance "hesitates," so as to make this performance equally a non-gesture. So hesitation is not a simple psychological action, emerging from the poem's narrative, but instead is a kind of mobile standstill, whose form can only be captured by the dynamic yet disoriented stillness of the Mime, an archetypal Mallarméan figure.[3]

Though he doesn't say this explicitly, Badiou's reading of Mallarmé's poem in the context of a crisis of mastery can be thought of in terms of the master, who hesitates at the crucial moment of mastery and making a decisive choice (to throw the dice from his place of mastery), survives this undecidability at the heart of his hesitation only as a Mime.[4] In this sense even though Badiou reads Mallarmé as a poet, the very intensity of this reading which can only be called philosophical, finds its own movement of thought, oscillating between the figures of the master and the mime. Alternatively put, the intensity of thought makes both the question of mastery and gestural mimeticism not anymore the insistent exercise of organic vitality but the effects of a kind of problematic intellectuality. This intellectuality can now only be poetically said rather than corporeally performed. This is Alain Badiou's philosophical forcing of the problem which both pushes the form of poetic expression to a saying of thought and immobilizes that thought to a constitutive absence of any corporeal presence or bodily possibility.

So the Mallarméan attitude to gesture in Alain Badiou's philosophical figuration is one of presenting mastery as a problem without the support of the master's vital intervention. This, in Badiou's terminology, is an attitude to and of the "void." The master's place is a void-place and yet the void, as if shimmers with the problem of an absent mastery which only the poem/ mime can say/perform. This is the limit point of a modern crisis of gesture where the dialectic of gesture and non-gesture is presented through the master's self-negating hesitation (Badiou 2005: 50). But one can also not go beyond this self-negation and so at the Mallarméan level of modernity there is no "teaching" to be gained, no didactic requirement to follow.

For such didactic requirement to be arrived at, even the negative dialectic of modernity has to be more sufficiently traversed and this is what Badiou does in this essay. Instead of choosing to write about a so-called consistent modern figure like Mallarmé and show the inconsistency of the logic of modernity through a consistent example Badiou compares, in a robustly anachronistic move, the nineteenth-century poem with a pre-Islamic Arabic ode by Labid ben Rabi'a. Both poems raise the question of mastery in situations of intense negativity, pictured in one case through the master's hesitation and in the other by a kind of desertification of a nomad people, who have to abandon their encampment in the face of Nature's "revenge" against all cultural and institutional authority or settlement (Badiou 2005: 48). Yet in the Arabic ode, the master returns from within this very crisis forced upon a people by the storm, the rain, the desertification of the desert as it were. And this return is again made possible by the forcing of language into a poetic "reawakening" (48). Despite the anachronism between the two instances, both the poetic sayings say the crisis though in two different modes and with two different attitudes. With Mallarmé the master has to entirely disappear in his own gesture of hesitation—so what takes place in the gesture of this disappearance is the place itself—while with the Arabic saying of the crisis, the negative is recuperated by the Master's return as one among the people who now can be blessed by the poem itself with the grace of the phrase that he is the "master of choices" (47). In Mallarmé's poetic instance, the master is entirely sacrificed but, yes, the moment of grace does arrive with the event of the Constellation up in the sky of transcendence (46). In Badiou's vocabulary this contrast between an immanent return of master from among a people in crisis and the transcendental substitution of the master by an event of impersonal grace, is the essential problem of *truth* as it unfolds in modernity. Modernity is characterized by the dialectic of the figure of the master who survives in his disappearance through the persistence of the void place of mastery and the filling up of a voided place of mastery with the figure of the master returned from the people itself to a position of choice and decision. In Badiou's estimation at this level of anachronistic yet contemporaneous dialectic between a master whose gesture and non-gesture cannot be distinguished anymore (to the point that the mime and the master becomes undecidable) and the immanent though arbitrary choice of a master who *can* decide, there is no resolution. No didactic lesson can follow from this poetic saying of the problem of modernity so as to emancipate the problem into a new *truth*. For the requirement of the thought of any truth, Badiou needs to change his register even within his infinite exploration of a poetic dialectic, which remains a kind of negative dialectic, into a saying of *affirmation*.[5] In other words, Badiou from being the philosopher who reads gestures of thought in poetic sayings, must now affirm something philosophically.

Conclusion: The Effect of Modernity Subtracted from Any Modernism

I believe the principal challenge faced by contemporary thought is the following: To discover a thinking of choice and of the decision that would go from the void to truth without passing through the figure of the master, that is, without either invoking or sacrificing the master. (Badiou 2005: 54)

It is interesting to note that Badiou's use of "contemporary" in the above is predicated upon an analysis of the historical epoch one calls "modern" or even "modernist," and an effect of an anachronistic comparison of two singular poetic works from entirely different historical periods. And, further, the diagnosis of a "contemporary challenge" is made to precisely take up that challenge and *didactically* supply what is required to go beyond the impasse diagnosed. That is why, Badiou having illustrated the impasse between a crypto-christic sacrificial master and a nostalgically restituted tribalist one, as the very undecidability of the modern decision on mastery prescribes that we philosophically affirm the need for a thought of truth without mastery.

But the didactic orientation of this prescription is that it cannot merely belong to a particular historical period, whether pre-modern or modernist. The very meaning of Badiou's philosophical desire which cannot be separated from a methodological didacticism is that the prescription and affirmation must be *universalized*. That is why Badiou's philosophy cannot be included in any consistent program or ideology of "modernism." At the same time in his essay on the poetic dialectic between Mallarmé and Labid ben Rabi'a, he diagnoses the impasse of mastery in extremely precise and subtle terms—of the structure of a transcendental impersonal master supported by the grace of the Constellation (Mallarmé) and the immanent individualized master, supported by the grace of a popular or clannish love and obedience (Labid ben Rabi'a) (2005: 52). One could add a third form of mastery, pertaining to the impasse of any modernism, which is the substitution of a kind of "self-mastery" for the undecidability of the true master (or master of truth). In a way this is the very paradigm of modernism, which on the one hand absolutely hollows out the foundation of any consistent modernist principle, that is to say any principle or ground of a *sovereign* master (whether that ground be immaterial Capital or the despotic State) and on the other hand, populates this hollow itself with the subjective figures of self-fashioned individuals who tirelessly stylize their modern existence into "forms of life."[6] This third cultural perspective on the possibility of self-mastery can be traced back to that very nineteenth century of which Mallarmé was a part, when Charles Baudelaire transmitted his poetic-prosaic sayings *as* effects of a style of life. If the undecidable impasse between Mallarmé and Labid ben Rabi'a can be schematized as the persistence of a "negative dialectic," the historical indexes populating modern life from nineteenth century onwards to at least the first half of the nineteenth century could be encapsulated by Walter Benjamin's imagery of "a dialectic at a standstill."[7] Alain Badiou's affirmative dialectics must be strictly differentiated from these other dialectical perspectives. And the real force of this distinction comes from the affirmative prescription that Alain Badiou wants to transmit through his universalized teaching-philosophy.

Having created this schematization, we must also note that there is a central ambiguity in Badiou's philosophical desire to affirm a universal process of "truth," which would avoid the impasse of mastery at the most general level and yet take its specific constituent elements from the very modern poetic combinatory that he eventually wants to subtract his universal affirmation from. Thus Badiou says that the contemporary challenge is to be able to think of a truth process without the need of the figure of the master while retaining the elements of anonymity and impersonality from

Mallarmé and the immanence of a kind of popular capacity for decision and choice in Labid ben Rabi'a. Of course as already noted, Badiou's methodological terms are anachronistic not because both poets don't belong to the same historical period; but the main project of constituting a *subject* of truth, which is anonymous and immanent, cannot but respond to extremely empirical and punctual historical questions of modern democracy and capitalism. The entire communist desire is to be able to traverse the impasse constituted by the conjunction of democracy and capitalism so as to open up a thought of egalitarian truth without sovereign mastery. At the same time this opening up cannot be a purely dialectical operation of the negation of the negative dialectic of modernity.

It must emerge from what Alain Badiou repeatedly calls an *axiomatic* freedom to enunciate or affirm something supplementary[8] and to that extent non-dialectical, which is nevertheless immanent to the situation of history—in this case the axiom of an egalitarian truth without mastery. So even in his more recent essay on affirmative dialectics we see a repetition of the same ambiguity: on the one hand Badiou clearly says that philosophy and its affirmation do not constitute a consistent history; they belong to a kind of reversible eternity of truths (in the gestural dramaturgy of this eternity Plato and Badiou or Lacan and Marx could be rendered reversible and indiscernible). On the other hand, the new contemporary challenge is precisely to make this affirmation in a punctual historical crisis of the modern *state*. That is why Badiou feels compelled in the first twenty years of the twenty-first century to speak of an affirmative dialectics at a distance from the state as different from the classical revolutionary dialectics which involves the occupation of the state and its new proletariat synthesis into socialist society (2013: 9). Everything depends on the understanding of this constitutive distance. So at the end let us make a few remarks on the relationship between the notions of distance and void with the philosophical terms of being and existence, as situated within sites of thought that must at least partly subtract themselves from any consistent historical program of modernity or modernism—but cannot entirely free themselves from a certain historical ambiguity.

In *Handbook of Inaesthetics*, Alain Badiou writes a philosophically indefatigable essay on Samuel Beckett called "Being, Existence, Thought: Prose and Concept." There is indeed in this essay an axiomatic insistence on "saying"—saying not anymore as the poetic idiom of a constitutive modern impasse of the being of mastery but a minimally affirmative saying which is existential and subjective. This is what recurs in Samuel Beckett's novella *Worstward Ho!* as the saying of an "on," that is to say, the recurrence of the axiom that one must say exactly when it is impossible to speak propositionally. Against Wittgenstein's famous aphorism that one must be silent thereof whereof one cannot speak, Badiou reads Beckett as saying "on" exactly at the point of the persistent impasse (2005: 99–100). Mallarmé's poetry of the imperial nineteenth century is still at a minimal discursive distance from its constitutive ontological problem: the undecidable gesture of the master's hesitation. Language was still a kind of stable anchor to present this crisis of gesture and the crisis of gesture was epochally ontological since, at the most general level, the being of the master had dissolved into the very void which had propped him up in the first place. This could be called modernity's shattering exposure to ontology. With Samuel Beckett something else happens when the very utterance of language becomes an axiomatic gesture; language is not anymore both the residue and illustration of a crisis. In Badiou's reading, Beckett's novella is the *turn* within the crisis itself toward a minimal opening of the very courage of speaking; to speak "on" is equally to walk on, to see on, to think on . . . to gesture on insofar as the very inscription of the "on" is the gesture.

In Badiou's essay on Beckett the philosopher again extracts a kind of teaching from *Worstward Ho*: according to Badiou Beckett teaches us not to fall into what could be called "the temptation" of the void received as ontologically pure and exhausted (2005: 101–2). Exactly when Mallarmé's master is seen to hesitate, the temptation is to absorb the scene of this hesitation into a state of total disappearance, such that the landscape of the "dark" that is modernity becomes the dark ideology of modernism—a pure desert or a pure foundationless void. Instead of this ontological temptation, Badiou sees in Beckett the possibility of an existential commitment to "worsen" which is to say to never cease taking one more step within the very crisis of undecidability and disappearance. Strangely the gesture of "worsening" is not simply the empirical phenomenon of a worsening crisis going toward a catastrophe. Beckett's worsening is paradoxically affirmative and an act of delocalization within the denuded or voided space that one is tempted to absolutize. In this sense Beckett's "worsening" is not different from the gesture of "love" which is always a kind of delocalization within the locality of an organ, a body, a space (113–14). So we could actually observe in Alain Badiou's method of reading Beckett, a remarkable and singular articulation between dialectics and topology but both these operations serve only to produce an *effect* or "event" whose truth requires an universalizing infinite subjective process. Clearly, this process cannot be a function of mere historical circumstances but it cannot also not be situated within the amplitude of a real historicity. It is to Alain Badiou's singular credit that he makes this ambiguity immeasurably productive without ever abandoning the search for new philosophical organs to localize this infinity in and existential gestures to measure it by.

Notes

1 See Grotowski's exercises featuring Ryszard Cieslak in Grotowski (2002: 219).
2 In this context, see Lyotard (1981). For the logic of a result-oriented *effectuation* through linguistic operations of the dialectic.
3 See Gilles Deleuze's concept of counter-actualization by the actor/mime. Deleuze (1993: 148–54).
4 We'll come back to this in some detail during the conclusion but already it is evident that Badiou's implication of the master's residual capacity to survive the crisis of mastery only as a Mime in the mode of a simulacrum of the master, is essentially a part of a modern dialectic of mastery and undecidability. Though it does not comprise the methodological references of this article it must be pointed out that the reason for Badiou's psychoanalytic construction of mastery lies precisely within this modernist dialectic.

5   It is not feasible for an article with a concentrated focus of attention—the dialectic of mastery and undecidability expressed by a singularly modern poetic logic subtracted from multiple imaginaries of modernism (or, alternatively from "possible modernisms")—to extend its field of references to every bit of relevant literature that carries the resonance of a developing thought in a philosophers oeuvre during a particular period. But as a parallel though not unfolded layer of texts, Badiou's second "big book" within his great trilogy *Logics of Worlds* (after *Being & Event* and before *Immanence of Truths*) must be mentioned in which the extremely fertile contrast between the corrosive constitution of a "democratic materialism" and the generic creativity of a "materialist dialectic" is presented. This presentation governs ours too though without recourse to the vocabulary of *Logics of Worlds*. Indeed, Badiou's short text on affirmative dialectics is a lucid summarization of the generic creativity that such a philosophical notion enjoys. But this philosophical enjoyment, which also corresponds to a certain political enthusiasm Badiou has noted in our otherwise claustrophobic neoliberal times emerging out of such events as those of the Arab Spring and the Greek "exception" within the market society of the EU, is only made possible by the tireless labors that have gone into the construction of a theory of "worlds," with its law of places and distribution of functions setting the conditions for a kind of *objective phenomenology*. So the subjective excess of an affirmative dialectic with its lack of "place" in the world achieves its true liveliness and creativity only in contrast to the oppressive closure of a "world" (whether one calls this world neoliberal or democratic or modern is a matter of vocabulary). The question of a genre of poetry, literature or art with its particular aesthetic effects embody and localize this general liveliness but the conditions of a "new life" irreducible to the extent laws of the world are equally conditions for a generic or universal creativity opening up spaces for artistic singularities whose lawful name can no more be read within the legible sign of any "modernism" (Badiou 2008).

6   For Badiou's projection of the Labid ben Rabi'a example of an immanent arbitrary master onto the experience of the twentieth-century despotism of the socialist state(s), see Badiou (2005: 53); "forms of life" is part of a popular cultural phraseology whose more sophisticated philosophical articulation in our times comes from Giorgio Agamben's works. Agamben has never shied away from revealing his subjective alliance with Michel Foucault's Last Style, so to speak, which consisted in both writing about and practicing "styles of life" which never ceased to desubjectify the dominant regime of the subject in the modern epoch. It's interesting that Agamben reconfigures Foucault's experiments with alter-modern styles of life—which could also be understood as a continuous desubjectification of the modern tyranny of what Foucault called "the truth of the subject," a strikingly different usage of the word from Badiou's—as alter-cultural or even alter-religious "forms of life" where the form of the subject and the force of subjectification cannot be distinguished anymore. This program of an alter-modernism of "forms of life" *is* a modernism, from which the effect of modernity can only be subtracted by a universalizing operation of the subject that cannot be in any way defined by either a cultural or historical logic. See Agamben (1998).

7   The singular project (whose unchosen almost non-oriented facticity is the opposite of the instrumental orientation of the word "project" in present-day neoliberal capitalism) must be Walter Benjamin's *The Arcades Project*—which was literally a collection of historical indexes of a particular urban milieu shimmering with subcultural fragments,

whose aesthetic grip on the sensorium couldn't be separated from a *perpetuum mobile* of capitalist crises in this period. "For the historical index of the images not only says that they belong to a particular time; it says, above all, that they attain to legibility only at a particular time . . . each 'now' is the now of a particular recognizability. In it, truth is charged to the bursting point with time . . . image is that wherein what has been comes together in a flash with the now to form a constellation. In other words: image is dialectics at a standstill . . . Only dialectical images are genuinely historical" (Benjamin 2002: 462).

8   "Every process of truth begins with an event. An event is unpredictable and incalculable—it is a supplement of the situation" (Badiou 2005: 54).

Works Cited

Agamben, G. (1998), *Homo Sacer: Sovereign Power and Bare Life*, trans. D. Heller-Roazen, Stanford: Stanford University Press.

Badiou, A. (2005), *Handbook of Inaesthetics*, trans. A. Toscano, Stanford: Stanford University Press.

Badiou, A. (2008), *Logics of Worlds*, trans. A. Toscano, London and New York: Continuum.

Badiou, A. (2013), "Affirmative Dialectics: from Logic to Anthropology," *The International Journal of Badiou Studies* 1:1, 1–13. Available online: https://badioustudies.files.wordpress.com/2016/11/alain-badiou-affirmative-dialectics-from-logic-to-anthropology-pp-1-13.pdf.

Badiou, A. and J.-L. Nancy (2018), *German Philosophy: A Dialogue*, ed. J. Völker, trans. R. Lambert, London: MIT Press.

Benjamin, W. (2002), *The Arcades Project*, trans. H. Eiland and K. McLaughlin, Harvard: Harvard University Press.

Brecht, B. (2006), *Life of Galileo*, trans. J. Willet, London and New York: Bloomsbury.

Choudhury, S. (2013), *Theatre Number Event: Three Studies on the Relationship between Sovereignty, Power and Truth*, Delhi: IIAS.

Deleuze, G. (1993), *Logic of Sense*, trans. M. Lester, New York: Columbia University Press.

Grotowski, J. (2002), *Towards a Poor Theatre*, ed. E. Barba, London and New York: Routledge.

Lyotard, J.-F. and G. Bennington (1981), "Analysing Speculative Discourse as Language-Game," *Oxford Literary Review* 4:3, 59–67, Edinburgh: Edinburgh University Press, http://www.jstor.org/stable/43973631.

Marx, K. and F. Engels (1969), *Marx/Engels Selected Works, Volume One*, Moscow: Progress Publishers.

Roudinesco, E. (1997), *Jacques Lacan*, trans. B. Bray, New York: Columbia University Press.

3

Badiou, Hegel and the Thinking of Modernist Thought-Action

Justin Clemens

Is Badiou Modernist?

Modernism is generally considered to constitute a radical cultural phenomenon at a planetary scale, involving a self-conscious revolution across all received artforms, which emerged in the early twentieth century and rapidly has become a kind of "dominant" across all the arts, introducing an astonishing and irreversible series of innovations whose consequences we are still working on—and out (Friedman 2015). As Alain Badiou puts it in *The Century*:

> The twentieth century kicks off in an exceptional fashion. Let us take the two great decades between 1890 and 1914 as the century's prologue. In every field of thought these years represent a period of exceptional invention, marked by a polymorphous creativity that can only be compared to the Florentine Renaissance or the century of Pericles. It is a prodigious period of excitement and rupture. (Badiou 2007: 6)

Badiou's is self-professedly a study that focuses on (what university discourse would agree to call) *modernist* writings of all kinds. It simultaneously identifies, periodizes and canonizes, even as it revisions and radicalizes; it traces affiliations as much as differences. In doing so, it constructs a concept of "the Century" as being marked by "a passion for the real," a formula that ultimately characterizes something like a *Zeitgeist* or event-character of the epoch, in which otherwise very different works in very different genres participate, equally and together.

Yet "modernism" is itself an academic, taxonomizing and periodizing term, linked to the problematic of inheritances and educational institutions. It is, in other words, a *representational* label—the very thing that Badiou opens this book by criticizing. For Badiou, it is not the current *representations* of the century—whether as "the Soviet Century" of wars and revolutions, the "Criminal Century" of genocides and mass suffering, or the short "Liberal Century" of the triumph of parliamentary capitalism in the 1970s—that should guide the inquiry, but, à la famous phenomenological catchcry, *a return to the things themselves*. This method is expressly revisionist: it seeks to break with received traditions of interpretation, their orientations and terminologies, by returning to what the texts say about their own location and ambitions. It is not reception but production, not transmission but event, that is at stake; this very approach in itself suggests that the dominant representations are themselves limited, partial, symptomatic reductions or misrepresentations of the real issues. Badiou thereby becomes an important critic of "modernism" in a number of senses—not least of the viability of the label itself. In fact, Badiou's own theory expressly treats "representation" as the signature operation of the state form: one which essays to evade at all costs the threat of the void in the name of "inclusion" and "inclusiveness."

However, if Badiou is an important critic of the very idea of "modernism," he is himself often considered an exemplary modernist thinker by much of the authoritative secondary literature on his work. Peter Hallward, for example, does so in what still remains the most extended and detailed commentary on Badiou's work, and for reasons that are to some extent incontrovertible (see Hallward 2003). First of all, "Make It New!," the great modernist slogan promulgated earlier by Ezra Pound is certainly a non-negotiable aspect of Badiou's thought, integrally linked, moreover, to his doctrine of the truth (along the lines of "only the new can be true"). Second, many of Badiou's determining references are themselves usually considered among the high points of modernism: Stéphane Mallarmé's poem "*Un coup de dés*"; Georg Cantor's development of the mathematics of the infinite; Sigmund Freud and Jacques Lacan's prosecution of psychoanalysis; post-Marxian political movements; Schoenberg's development of the twelve-tone system; and much more besides. Third, Badiou regularly deploys such genres—in the commonplace literary understanding of this term—as the manifesto and the intervention, which bring with them certain well-established expectations about the status of audience and address. In a phrase, the typical ideals, authors and genres of modernism dominate in Badiou's work; Badiou should therefore be considered a modernist. We might even say, Badiou's philosophy is the continuation of modernism by other means.

There are however a number of serious problems with such an enumeration of these putative affiliations, let alone with such a conclusion. First of all, what would be the point—whatever the stated motivations or details—of declaring somebody "modernist" today? Is it to circumscribe their achievements historically or conceptually? To mark limits that then enable a difference to be forged or even a dismissal to be prosecuted? Indeed, to call somebody a "modernist" in the present conjuncture is perhaps also to imply something like the following: modernism made novelty a value; novelty is also your value; you are therefore a modernist; but modernism is now out of date; so your being a modernist shows you both to be self-contradictory *and* out-of-date; therefore what you say is not up to the challenges of the present. QED.

This is not even to broach the contemporary critiques of modernism that—with absolute probity—assail the canonical texts of European modernism as synecdoches of capitalism, colonialism, patriarchy, racism and ecological disaster, among other complicities (see Kanth 2005). Although Badiou, as would be abundantly clear from even the most glancing acquaintance with his work, is himself explicitly, constitutionally anti-capitalist, anti-colonialist, anti-patriarchal and anti-racist, the inherent and essential limitations of the canon with which he is working would nonetheless, in and by themselves, necessarily simultaneously limit the sense and reference, the extensions and implications, of his demonstrations.

Even if we attempted to avoid the accusatory sense of such acts of nomination, it remains the case that the troika I just invoked—of innovation, canon and genre—is, without further specification and despite appearances, an external, received determination, not an immanent one. For instance, if modernism exhibited a widespread enthusiasm for novelties of all kinds, it was not the first "movement" to make novelty a value. Novelty and modernism are not coeval, and certainly not reducible. Perhaps we should rather say that modernism was a movement that made novelty an *absolute* value? But if this were the case, in rendering innovation an absolute *obligation* or *injunction* according to one or another modality, such a becoming-obligatory of the production of novelty simultaneously threatens the freedom of invention (or a certain idea of it at least). Novelty is forced to break with a certain repetition in the name of a more profound repetition—a necessarily unrecognizable one, given it thereby wouldn't repeat positivities or predicates (e.g., according to received forms or themes), but indeterminable ruptures. And if we still insisted on characterizing this operation as typically modernist, then "modernism" would no longer simply be a name for a period or movement, since it would simultaneously indicate, even incarnate, an atemporal power of disruption, as well as undermining "the genetic principle that necessarily underlies all historical narrative" (de Man 1979: 101–2).[1]

Alternatively, we might maintain that modernism *pluralized* the sense and import of "novelty," a term which therefore covers a multitude of sins. Indeed, it might even be suggested that modernism pluralizes novelty in such a way that the latter's conditions, justifications, aims and ends become obscure—to the extent that "modernism" itself becomes a misleading misnomer. There would only, at best, be "modernism*s*," which would not be justifiably unifiable according to a time, a place or a concept. Yet another, related concern would be that the processes of correlation and causation, affiliation and influence, should perhaps be more carefully considered when thinking about the application of such a term in any case. Whichever way you turn it, then—making "novelty" contingency, injunction or pluralization in modernism—there is something imprecise and *a fortiori* suspicious about denominating Badiou a "modernist" without further examination.

So "modernism"—in this context, but obviously not only in this context—marks an enigma. And yet we can also see how all the key terms so briefly raised earlier—novelty, negation, repetition, history, genre and so on—also certainly remain inflected as "modernist" in some way (if possibly only for scholars of modernism!). And we can also see that Badiou undoubtedly has something to do with all these phenomena. But, given the reservations listed, it seems that there is not any immediate or straightforward way of constructing a relation between "Badiou" and/or "modernism" that doesn't presume or falsify what's in question. Given such complexities, what would be a way, if any, to reopen the question of "Badiou and modernism"?

The thesis of this chapter is that this is a relationship that can be given several crucial delimitations by reexamining the peculiar developmental relation that Badiou has to the thought of G. W. F. Hegel. This, moreover, is to follow Badiou's own indication in *Logics of Worlds* that, in regards to Hegel's *Science of Logic*, "I have never ceased measuring myself up to this book" (Badiou 2009a: 529). Throughout his philosophical work, from the 1960s to the present, Hegel is a constant interlocutor. Even when the relation is explicitly one of polemic and critique, Hegel and the stakes of the Hegelian dialectic are never not at stake. Pertinently in the current context, Badiou also notes that the "period" we are discussing here—"modernism"?!—is one for which Hegel's dialectic is integrally at play (Bosteels 2014: 137).

An Introduction to the Reading of Hegel: One/a (French) Context

Yet Hegel is himself not exactly or evidently a "modernist philosopher," whatever that would be. Historically, he comes too soon: he is the contemporary of romanticism, the literary "frenemy" of philosophical German idealism. Yet he is also a key founder of and interlocutor for almost all the key thinkers of modernism, not least for a very dialectical reason: without him, the work of Karl Marx is impossible; and, given then the work of Marx, a relation of some kind to Hegel becomes uncircumventable. Whether one considers Hegel as pre-Marx, proto-Marx, non-Marx or anti-Marx, or whether one is indeed pro- or contra- Hegel, he cannot not function as a consequence as a permanent licensor and disruptor of the relation between thought and the political. This, at least, is how Hegel regularly came to function in the particular French intellectual context of which Badiou is today the last living representative. As all the histories testify, moreover, the Hegel problematic in France becomes crucial between approximately 1930 and 1980, as precisely this crucial licensor-disruptor of the thinking of the relation between thought and the political (see Baugh 2003; Butler 1987; Roth 2019; Keenan 2004).

Let me give three key moments in this ambivalent French uptake of Hegel. These are not the only, nor necessarily even the "most important" ones, but they establish the limits of the field in which Badiou's work emerges and into which it intervenes:

(1) Alexandre Kojève's lectures on Hegel as the thinker of the end of history as the end of thinking as historical (Kojève 1969);
(2) Jean Hyppolite's constructions of Hegel as the absolute thinker of sense as the absolute (Hyppolite 1997);
(3) Louis Althusser's rejection of Hegel as a pre-Marxist thinker; or, rather, Marx as effecting a scientific rupture with Hegel and Hegelianism (Althusser 1997).

To rephrase these nominal markers as the establishment of the orientations, aims and limits of a field in terms of themes and operations, we can posit them as sketching: a problematic of history as both determining and inoperative at once; a problematic of sense as both counter-truth and absorbing of truth; a problematic of action as divided between unknowing contradiction and knowing intervention. Moreover, Hegel functions in this way due in large part to his very encyclopedism: he deals with an almost-incomprehensible range of materials as part of the becoming of philosophy itself, including the religious, artistic, scientific, political, historical and so forth.

Let's note, moreover, that these three very different, perhaps indeed incompatible readings of Hegel nonetheless share several conditions and assumptions. First, they mark the assimilation of Hegel into France *via the academy itself*. As the commentators agree: in nineteenth century Germany Hegel's inheritors found themselves split between orthodox academic Hegelians and (significantly!) often extra-academic left-Hegelians; Italy had a major Hegelian school; in England Hegel found such eminent adherents as F. H. Bradley and Bernard Bosanquet in the wake of Edward Caird and T. H. Green. Yet it seems the French almost entirely successfully resisted the importation of Hegel into the official academic and associated intellectual institutions of the time. It is not until the 1920s that Hegel starts to become a figure of some importance: Alain gives lectures on Hegel at the Lycée Henri IV, attended by Hyppolite and perhaps Jean-Paul Sartre too; Charles Andler gives a course on Hegel at the Collège de France; several important works, by Jean Wahl for one, start to appear. All of a sudden, the universities of France got themselves Hegelianized, with extraordinary results. We could note, in passing, that this timing coincides—if in fact it is indeed *coincidental!*—with the high tide of modernism as understood in most studies of the phenomenon, the 1920s and 1930s.

In a dialog with Badiou himself, Jean-Claude Milner recently summarized some of the key consequences of this comparatively late absorption of Hegel into early twentieth-century French thought:

> I accord a major importance to the emergence of what I will call dialectical language. If you take a philosopher-writer like Bergson, his language carries no trace of dialectics. Then, from a certain moment, the philosophy of the French language comes to adopt a dialectical language. Next, in its way, literary criticism and literature itself do the same . . . . The important point is that the French language, as language of the concept, changed in the 1930s. (Badiou and Milner 2012: 174)

It is in this context, then, that the multitudinous works of post–Second World War French thought on the question of thinking—and not just Hegel specifically—come to be, marked by this dialectical language that also entails, as we shall see, a certain dalliance with logics that are tolerant of contradiction. Moreover, from Bataille and Sartre through Blanchot, Derrida, Deleuze, Foucault and many others, the dalliance is self-consciously, explicitly, "ambivalent and conflicted," as Bauch puts it in his own study of the phenomenon:

> nowhere is French philosophy more ambivalent and conflicted in its attitudes toward a philosopher, strenuously resisting and "correcting" Hegel at the very moment it finds him most seductive. The Surrealists want negation, but without limits; Sartre wants negation, but without totality; Derrida and Bataille want

negativity, but not its recuperation in a positive result. Even those who are most explicitly anti-Hegelian, such as Deleuze and Foucault, admit their fascination with Hegel's thought, and sometimes inadvertently demonstrate Hegel's influence on them. It's as if French philosophy of the past century had to deny Hegel in order to affirm him, and affirm him in order to deny him. (Bauch 2003: 1)

To some extent, Badiou conforms to this general situation, if in an exceptional manner. His early published work from the late 1960s, including "Mark and Lack," takes place under the aegis of the Althusserian revisionism of Marxist doctrine. This entails, as I have already noted, a commitment to a certain anti-Hegelianism, in accordance with His Master's Voice (Althusser's!), along with a fundamental commitment to examining the complex relationship between "science" and "ideology." Indeed, Badiou pursues this constitutively anti-Hegelian scientific formalism until contemporary political events make it clear to him that such a formalism is no longer compatible with the temper of the times.

With May 1968, Badiou—like many of his fellow young Althusserians—finds himself forced to break with his teacher. His subsequent commitment to new forms of political activism, to what is now usually broadly named "French Maoism," has two immediate consequences at a directly conceptual level (leaving aside the praxis of the political engagement itself): an enthusiastic return to Hegel, and a concomitant suspicion of the very mathematical and logical formalism he has been pursuing to date. As Tzuchien Tho puts it in his introduction to *The Rational Kernel of the Hegelian Dialectic*: "Hegel, Marx, Lenin and Mao replaced his earlier references to Cantor, Frege, Von Neuman [sic] and Robinson" (Tho 2011: xi). The domination of thought by action demands the repudiation of mathematical formalism in the name of a more dynamic process. One of the many paradoxes of this shift is that it certainly does not affirm an unthinking adherence to the Hegelian project. On the contrary:

> We should begin again at zero, and to ultimately see, philosophically, that Marx is neither the same nor the other of Hegel. Marx is the divider of Hegel. He simultaneously assigns its irreversible validity (the rational kernel of the dialectic) and its integral falsity (the idealist system). (Badiou 2011: 15)

The consequences of this complex position are patent in the published work that in essence summarizes the intellectual labor of Badiou's "Red Years," that is, *Theory of the Subject*, in which we find an exceedingly non-standard, indeed a particularly recondite and abstruse, interpretation of the Hegelian dialectic. Badiou begins by differentiating two integral aspects of the dialectic: first, the operations of an alienating division which, in becoming other, thereby also returns to itself; second, the operations of an irrecuperable scission, which only ever produces disjunctions-without-unity. This, moreover, is only the beginning of Badiou's procedure, which debouches almost immediately into an algebraic-topological formalism. Given an A (any something), Hegel then posits or rather *places* the same A again, which precisely redoubles and contorts the initial something, giving A_p. The minimal difference that emerges from this AA_p is itself the identity of the something itself, that is, $A = (AA_p)$. Yet this doubled identity is also submitted to the operations of placement, that is, $A \to A_p(AA_p)$. And, of course, this redoubled switching in turn comes to split further, given the aggregative-disseminative recombinatory possibilities that the intricated operations of alienation and scission produce. To capture the abstraction of these dialectical intricacies, Badiou proffers two neologisms, *splace* [*esplace*] and *outplace* [*horlieu*], of which he remarks: "The dialectic, in the sawdust-filled arena of the categorical combat, is the outplace against the splace" (Badiou 2009b: 11). Note the algorithmic logic—iterative, divisive, processual—that Badiou engages in here. Hegel's dialectic is transcribed into an esoteric language that simultaneously asserts its control as being that of "real" political action.

Despite the staggering inventiveness and singularity of Badiou's reconstruction of Hegel's dialectic in this period, then, we might still propose that it does not really effectively overturn or exceed the limits of the French situation of Hegel I have noted earlier: history, sense and action remain integrated, if paradoxically so, and in such a way that mathematics itself—when it is mentioned at all—is deployed above all as a metaphor (e.g., Badiou 2009b: 209-10). If we wished to offer a cruel judgment on this project, with all the luxuries of hindsight, we might even say: Badiou's published work of this time remains in the ambit of the very *French academic modernism it purports to contest* insofar as its language, conceptuality, thematics and so forth, remain bound up with the Hegelian legacy of Kojève, Hyppolite and Althusser in this *fundamentally non-mathematical way*.

To Break with Hegel through the Singularity of Certain "Modernist" Emergences

It is with the publication of *Being and Event* in 1988 that Badiou breaks definitively with the Hegelian enterprise. If his position in this fundamental text in some ways constitutes a *return* to his own Althusserian period of mathematical exposition in the period prior to May 1968, it is now with a decisive twist: mathematics is no longer a privileged epistemological instrument, nor conceptually derivative, nor an illuminating metaphor, but is one necessary condition of philosophy itself. Indeed, Badiou's slogan for his new project is now infamous (at least for those working in the wake of contemporary European philosophy): *mathematics is ontology*.

Although there is obviously not the space to discuss this claim in any detail here, a few points must be mentioned in this context. First, the new position derives from Badiou's attention to a mathematics that only emerged toward the end of the nineteenth century, and received its decisive developments in the early years of the twentieth century: set theory. In other words, we are dealing, temporally at least, with a kind of "mathematical modernism." Second, set theory's determining impetus is a new formalization of infinity. As Georg Cantor showed, if we accept infinite sets as actual, then we can also prove that there are infinitely many infinities of infinitely different kinds. In doing so, mathematics gives the infinite a rigorous concept for the first time. In other words, we have a topic historically central to philosophy that philosophy now has to take account of as determining for its own conceptuality (I'll return to this later). Third, a crucial aspect of set theory's development was precisely its axiomatization. If this development is historically complex, encompassing several rival axiomatizations and indeed various rejections of such axiomatizations too, the standard versions of set theory entail further clarifications of associated conceptual issues, such as the role of the empty set, the question of the relation between formalization and existence, and so on. In other words, this development constitutes a self-reflexive *metamathematical* moment, whereby mathematics continues precisely by immanently and practically questioning the status of its own conceptuality.

Certainly, set theory constitutes a mathematical advance that was necessarily unknown to Hegel, and therefore goes beyond Hegel's account of mathematics. But the question still remains: despite the historically novel content of set theory, can Hegel still be said to have accounted philosophically for the role of mathematics in its construction of infinity? After all, Hegel is himself famously the great philosophical thinker of the infinite, in regards moreover to the contradictions that the mathematicians of the calculus were themselves unable to resolve with respect to infinitesimals. In doing so, Hegel notoriously asserts that, while mathematicians *have indeed given a correct concept of infinity*, it is only philosophy that is able to *think* it. In fact, this double aspect of Hegel—mathematics is a condition for philosophy, a condition that philosophy can think from a position of immanent transcendence—can look very much like Badiou's own position. Hegel, moreover, is perhaps the first thinker to rigorously delimit *two* infinities, the bad and the good, the quantitative and the qualitative, and to do so from an express confrontation with the mathematics itself.

As Hegel puts it in his magisterial *The Science of Logic*:

> The mathematical infinite is of interest because of the expansion and the significant new results which its introduction into mathematics has produced in it, but also because of the oddity that this science has to date still been unable to justify its use conceptually ("concept" being taken here in a strict sense). (Hegel 2010: 204)

For Hegel, this is simultaneously a "deplorable situation," insofar as the mathematicians cannot justify their results, and yet it remains crucial because it is by means of this (confused) mathematical infinite, which does indeed truly exceed all the metaphysical notions of infinity, that the true infinite can be determined. Certainly, Hegel is certain that "in its concrete sciences, philosophy must take its logical element from logic, not from mathematics" (Hegel 2010: 181), but it is also the case that philosophy must focus upon the peculiar admixture of nebulosity and precision at work in the mathematics itself.

Yet Badiou's response goes further, and is still more precise. In Meditation Fifteen of *Being and Event* Badiou confronts Hegel with the findings of set theory in such a way as to show that Hegel's own thought is symptomatically unable to think the specificities of the infinite that Cantor's discovery proposes. What he does in the same book, in his other confrontations with Plato, Aristotle, Spinoza and Heidegger, is show how set theoretical concepts of infinity and the void necessarily dismantle the consistency of any pre-Cantorian philosophical edifice, if in a singular way with regards to each. In this meditation, Hegel's devaluation of mathematics will prove determining.

For Hegel, the finite is not something that is surpassed by an external phenomenon but in self-undermining determinateness that sublates its own becoming. Hegel's key operation is something like a "still-more-already": something is determinate insofar as it is tied to thinking the other of the other; this means that the "one" is said of being as much as being is also its own non-being (it is the other of the other). Yet, because for Hegel something's limits derive from what it has introjected of its other, then the breach of a thing's limits comes accordingly to be understood as the being of each, the one surpassing its own non-being. "*Mediation*," as Badiou puts it, "*is the interiority of the negative*" (Badiou 2005: 162).

Otherwise put, the breach of limit (*Grenze*) opens something to its border or frontier (*Schranke*). In doing so, something new emerges between being and the "one" of being, and, moreover, this one is therefore overcome by the very being that it thereby marks. For Hegel there is hence a *law* of being—the self-overcoming of its own determinateness through the operations of determination itself—which entails the emergence of the infinite out of finitude as such.

Hegel, moreover, is very conscious that the *to-have-to-be* of infinity from the finite can only take place as a pure alternation of the void and its limit, which he notoriously names a "bad infinity," an endless iteration of the same. Yet, out of this iteration, a new Other comes: the "good" infinite, the very place of the taking-place of the "bad" infinite, which must be the very *power* of repetition itself. In Badiou's summary:

We can thus see a dividing line drawn between:

- The bad infinity: objective process, transcendence (having-to-be), representation;
- The good infinity: subjective virtuality, immanence, unrepresentable. (Badiou 2005: 166)

Yet, at this point of apparent triumph, Hegel's demonstration finds itself splitting again, this time into two different components, of quantitative and qualitative infinity. Why? As Badiou notes, this is because the status of the "one" is different in quantity and quality. The former bespeaks an indifferent set of "ones," external to each other; the latter, is precisely a one which has introjected its other according to the dialectical machinery. The two "ones" differ in their constitution and machinery of production. The dialectic of quantity and quality, the very movement with which Badiou had opened *Theory of the Subject*, is here re-examined according to an utterly different modality.

For *quality* operates according to a logic of *identification*, whereby the one proceeds from an other that has been interiorized; *quantity*, from a process of *proliferation*, whereby the same repeats without any interiority at all. This is the crux of the issue: the quantitative "one" is not properly determined or determinate for Hegel, precisely because determination derives from a dialectic in which a negation establishes a mark of being (something's limit, the "one" of its being-counted) before that mark is then transformed in turn by a negation of the negation insofar as the being thereby marked comes to interiorize the mark itself (incorporating the gap between itself and its mark, and thereby exceeding its own limit). Being discerns itself *qualitatively* by overcoming the mere indifferent exteriority of a marking as "one." The trouble here is that the "one" as external mark, number as quantity, has no "other"; as Badiou puts it, and so *"its determinativeness is indifferent"* (Badiou 2005: 167). According to Hegel's own principles, then, such a "one" has no proper limit, since limit as such derives from the dynamics of interiorization. And since it has no limit, the proliferation of such a one turns out to be inconsistent dissemination, stripped of any inner principle that would halt its abyssal slew.

This means that in order to re-bind the two kinds of infinite process, the qualitative and quantitative, each operating by means of *two different kinds of one*, Hegel has to name the *qualitative essence of quantity* "infinite." Yet, for Badiou, this is a pure homonymy without concept, a "fragile verbal footbridge" thrown over a fundamental disjunction (Badiou 2005: 170). Again, why? Because proliferation without interiority is precisely *not* infinite in any strict sense that Hegel is able to give it. As indefinite proliferation, it isn't infinite in actuality; as indifferent dissemination, it isn't infinite in its essence, qualitative or otherwise. Descartes, for one, had already drawn on a version of this distinction in the context of number vis-à-vis God: the merely indefinite is irreconcilable with the truly infinite. As set theory also maintains, one needs a special axiom to ensure infinity; it must be a *decision* of the program, not a *law* of being. For his own demonstration of mathematical insufficiency to work, Hegel has to ensure that the quantitative and qualitative are bound together in the infinite. However, by his own logic, this cannot be sustained without the symptom of an unjustified nomination *at the very point that he purports to resolve the dilemma of the infinite*. Whatever the qualitative essence of quantity might be, it isn't the infinite—or, at least, it isn't the infinite in the same sense as the quantitative essence of quality might be.

With this interpretation, Badiou finally breaches the limits of French philosophical modernism: the law of the dialectic is rebuked by the decisions of mathematical axiomatization; the latter is fully separated at the same time from generative processes founded on contradiction, as it is from political or aesthetic intervention; the mathematical modernism of set theory becomes for Badiou a strict and literal condition, an orientation and control, for contemporary philosophy's ontological ambitions. Badiou now literally draws his theses on ontological questions from modernist mathematics, and not any specifically philosophical logic.

Badiou will continue to draw out the consequences of this development in a number of unexpected modalities. In *Conditions*, for instance, Badiou suggests further consequences of Hegel's disentanglement of mathematics from philosophical conceptuality:

Now—and Hegel is decisive in this matter—romantic philosophy will proceed to almost entirely dis-entwine philosophy and mathematics. Romantic philosophy made possible the conviction that philosophy can and must deploy a thinking that at no point internalizes mathematics as a condition of that deployment . . . Empiricist and positivist attitudes, which have been highly influential for the last two centuries, merely invert the Romantic speculative gesture. (Badiou 2008: 95)

Hegel, by subordinating mathematics to philosophy, splitting mathematics and logic and introducing a thematic of endings introduces a deleterious phase for philosophy proper. Shorn of its integral conditioning by mathematics, philosophy thereafter falls into a kind of hiatus, whereby the functions that it would usually fulfill—that is, thinking the world by means of its conditions, which take part independently of each other and prior to philosophy—are taken over by its conditions themselves. This is what Badiou calls "the age of the poets" in his first *Manifesto for Philosophy*, an age which runs essentially from Hegel to Heidegger. This is an epoch dominated by the poem, whereby poetry took on the ontological questioning for philosophy that had hitherto been drawn from mathematics itself (Badiou 1999). Although there is not the space here for a discussion of Badiou's claims in this regard, we should nevertheless underline how Badiou's post-*Being and Event* periodizations tend to cut across and reconstruct received academic historical or thematic divisions, say of "romanticism" and "modernism" by offering an account founded on key events of thought (mathematics, poetry, politics, etc.) that are simultaneously historical insofar as they are integrally bound up with these irreversible, novel events *and* peculiarly atemporal insofar as they offer irreducible conceptual determinations that have both retroactive and proleptic effects.

Conclusion

In the trajectory I have been describing here, Badiou has moved from the rejection of Hegel on formal questions through the affirmation of a radical and non-standard Hegelian dialectic and the use of Hegel as a necessary supplement to praxis, along the lines of the great political revolutionaries from Lenin to Mao. This movement proceeds through a rethinking of the splitting internal to philosophy itself as a return that renders Hegel something other than just a thinker external to action. Yet, as I have shown, the movement concludes with a separation of philosophy from its conditions that also separates Badiou from Hegel on the fundamental questions of negation, infinity, existence and being. To put this more telegraphically, Badiou has traversed the positions: anti-Hegel; Hegel-as-supplement; Hegel-as-self-divided; Hegel-as-provocatory-antagonist.

What has to be strenuously emphasized in this development are, again, its driving anxieties, which concern the relations between action and knowledge, praxis and philosophy. Hence the minatory shadow of Hegel, for whom philosophy alone can render action and knowledge compatible over world history through the contradictory operations of determinate negation that culminate in a Parousia of Absolute Spirit. Against this great vision, Badiou comes to identify singular, non-totalizable processes in which thought and action are inseparable, and which issue determining injunctions to a philosophy they constitutively exceed and frustrate: science, love, art and politics. Moreover, as I have also briefly suggested, Badiou treats these "truths" that are science, love, art and politics as positive and productive procedures that independently operate on the basis of irreducible commitments to heterogeneous forms of negation. Science is concerned with rational consistency, with thinking the powers of (foreclosing) contradiction in asserting the existence of the infinite; love concerns itself with a "sexual" difference that can never be reduced or exceeded without self-dissolution; art is concerned with the mysterious and captivating powers of inconsistency as such, as finitude itself; politics with the revolutionary antagonism between void and State. As such, all are non- or pre-representational processes, each undertaking their own singular problematic of universality, in their own time and in their own way. Yet, *at the same time*, these singularities are, for Badiou, demonstrably compossible insofar as a philosophy, confronted by their heterogeneity, is able to construct a place—that is a Truth, itself stripped of any commitment to a domination by oneness, totality or finitude—which takes aspects of all of them into account.

As I have sought to argue here, while Badiou's theses are in some part ancient (Platonic), romantic (acknowledging the unbanishable power of poetry) and immemorial (aiming at an immanent eternity without time), they also integrally derive from a determining relation to what is generally called modernism—or, at the very least, to certain key emergences of modernist thought. These include the mathematization of infinity with Cantor, the purified verse of Mallarmé and the poetic universes of Pessoa, the love narratives of Beckett and the politics of Lenin and Mao. In fact, it is precisely by attending to the truth of these *modernist* emergences as singular universals that Badiou can establish a definitive break with the Hegelian dialectic or, at least, with the Hegels of academic French modernism. To this extent, then, we would have to agree: Badiou is an exemplary *modernist thinker*. Yet this is only on the proviso that we understand *modernism* in the precise and unique sense that Badiou's work itself provides in its break with Hegel.

Note

1 As de Man often observed, though not of modernism, but *romanticism*. See, inter alia, his remarks on Friedrich Nietzsche's *Birth of Tragedy*: "From a historiographical point of view, it is instructive to see a genetic narrative function as a step leading to insights that destroy the claims on which the genetic continuity was founded, but that could not have been formulated if the fallacy had not been allowed to unfold" (de Man 1979: 101–2).

Works Cited

Althusser, L. (1997), *For Marx*, trans. B. Brewster, London: Verso.
Badiou, A. (1999), *Manifesto for Philosophy*, trans. N. Madarasz, Albany: SUNY.
Badiou, A. (2005), *Being and Event*, trans. O. Feltham, London and New York: Continuum.
Badiou, A. (2007), *The Century*, trans. A. Toscano, Cambridge: Polity.
Badiou, A. (2008), *Conditions*, trans. S. Corcoran, London and New York: Continuum.
Badiou, A. (2009a), *Logics of Worlds*, trans. A. Toscano, London: Continuum.
Badiou, A. (2009b), *Theory of the Subject*, trans. B. Bosteels, London: Continuum.
Badiou, A. (2011), *The Rational Kernel of the Hegelian Dialectic*, ed. and trans. T. Ho, Melbourne: re-press.
Badiou, A. and J.-C. Milner (2012), *Controverse*, Paris: Seuil.
Baugh, B. (2003), *French Hegel: From Surrealism to Postmodernism*, New York: Routledge.
Bosteels, B. (2014), "Hegel," in J. Clemens and A. J. Bartlett (eds.), *Alain Badiou: Key Concepts*, 137–45, Oxford: Routledge.
Butler, J. (1987), *Subjects of Desire: Hegelian Reflections in Twentieth-Century France*, New York: Columbia University Press.
de Man, P. (1979), *Allegories of Reading: Figural Language in Rousseau, Nietzsche, Rilke and Proust*, New Haven and London: Yale University Press.
Friedman, S. (2015), *Planetary Modernisms: Provocations on Modernity across Time*, New York: Columbia University Press.
Hallward, P. (2003), *Alain Badiou: A Subject to Truth*, Minneapolis: University of Minnesota Press.
Hegel, G. W. F. (2010), *The Science of Logic*, trans. G. di Giovanni, Cambridge: Cambridge University Press.
Hyppolite, J. (1997), *Logic and Existence*, trans. L. Lawlor and A. Sen, Albany: SUNY.
Kanth, R. (2005), *Against Eurocentrism: A Transcendent Critique of Modernist Science, Society, and Morals*, New York: Palgrave Macmillan.
Keenan, D. K., ed. (2004), *Hegel and Contemporary Continental Philosophy*, Albany: SUNY.
Kojève, A. (1969), *Introduction to the Reading of Hegel*, ed. A. Bloom, trans. J. H. Nichols, New York: Basic Books.
Roth, M. (2019 [1988]), *Knowing and History: Appropriations of Hegel in Twentieth Century France*, Ithaca and London: Cornell University Press.
Tho, T. (2011), "Introduction: One Divides into Two? Dividing the Conditions," in A. Badiou et al., *The Rational Kernel of the Hegelian Dialectic*, ed. and trans. Tzuchien Tho, xi–xxv, Melbourne: re.press.

4

The Eternal Return of the Modern

Poetry, History, Philosophy

Bruno Bosteels

> *Then we'll allow its defenders, who aren't poets themselves but lovers of poetry, to speak in prose on its behalf and to show that it not only gives pleasure but is beneficial both to constitutions and to human life.*
>
> —Plato, *Republic*, 607d

How can we define philosophy's relation to modern poetry? To what extent does the gap separating the philosopher's truth from mere opinions mimic the high modernist break with the commonplace language of tradition? Does this mimicry complicate the Platonist ban on poetic diction? Finally, could there be something quintessentially modern, even modernist, about the philosopher's appeal to the eternal return of the same truth? If already for Socrates, in Book X of the *Republic*, the quarrel between poetry and philosophy was an ancient one, we might add that in the more than two millennia that have elapsed since Plato composed his most famous dialog, not much seems to have changed in the eyes of Alain Badiou. In fact, for this French philosopher, playwright and novelist, the philosophical act in relation to its truth conditions, which include not only poetry (or art) but also mathematics (or science), politics and love, has remained fundamentally the same. As he explains among other places in *Philosophy for Militants*, philosophy has always tried to seize upon the truths produced in these four conditions by drawing a stark line of demarcation that separates such truths from the circulation of mere opinions. And this division, in turn, has always involved a normative dimension, separating truth and opinion, for example, in terms of ethical criteria such as the good and the bad. In both aspects, philosophy endlessly repeats the same invariant gesture. This allows Badiou to conclude: "So, in philosophy, we have something invariant, something of the order of a compulsion to repeat, or like the eternal return of the same. But this invariance is of the order of the act, and not of knowledge. It is a subjectivity, for which knowing in all its forms is only one means among others" (2012a: 13). Now—to begin raising the questions I have been invited to address in this chapter—what is the place of poetry as one truth condition among others in this eternal return of its quarrel with the act of philosophy? Is this quarrel or antagonism still the same as the one that was already ancient for Plato? Or have the terms of this debate become fundamentally changed under the effects of what counts as modern or even modernist poetry? What is the relation between these two quarrels—that between poetry and philosophy and that between the ancient and the modern? Are these in some way analogous? Or, in a strange loop or torsion back upon itself, does the emergence of the modern retroactively transform the terms of the ancient quarrel between poetry and philosophy? Finally, what are the innovations, if any, that Badiou introduces in this regard in *The Immanence of Truths*, the third and final volume of his philosophical system originally presented under the heading of *Being and Event*?[1]

In *Philosophy for Militants* Badiou is quick to add that philosophy's compulsion always to repeat the same invariant act in connection with its conditions obviously does not preclude its having to take stock of the historical novelty and specificity of the actual events that condition philosophy in each of the four truth procedures: "But if the philosophical act is formally the same, and the return of the same, we will have to account for the change in historical context. For the act takes place under certain conditions" (Badiou 2012a: 15). This difficult articulation between formal invariance and contextual variation—the knot between the conditioned sameness of philosophy's subjective act and the changing historical conditions under which this act repeats itself—sits at the heart of the questions to be addressed in the pages that follow. In fact, I will argue that this difficulty is part of the reason why *Being and Event* needed to be supplemented not once but twice: first with *Logics of Worlds* and then a second time with *The Immanence of Truths*.[2] The reasons for this supplementation, insofar as it entails a repetition-expansion of principles supposed to have been present from the start in *Being and Event*, are by no means self-evident. If already the original volume situated the event in a singular context or situation, as marked by its symptomatic site, at first glance nothing would seem to require a whole additional volume to account for the transcendental logic of such a situation, now rebaptized world, in which truths make a hole with transformative consequences for the totality of what is given. And, furthermore, if all events, in addition to producing universal truths in such a situation or world, from the beginning are also defined as localized exceptions to the existing state of affairs, again there would appear to be no need for second-guessing their immanence to this world.

Why, then, this compulsion to repeat the same gesture of inscribing the truth of an event in the immanence of an ordered state of being? Aside from Badiou's explicit desire to correct common misconceptions about his prior work, could this be because in each new iteration some obscure force time and again pulls the philosopher back toward the affirmation of an absolute and invariant truth, which is the empty concept of the truth as such, subtracted from its variable historical conditions, illustrated with examples from modern poetry or politics, and raised to the eternal dignity of the Idea? And could Badiou's repeated treatment of modern poetry as an exemplification rather than as an actual condition of his major philosophical concepts—being, event, truth, subject, body, work and so on—help us understand not only the need but also the nature of this compulsion? In other words, how does this self-declared Platonist's reliance on modern or modernist poetry help us shed light on some of the tensions traversing his key philosophical assumptions?

In the ancient antagonism between philosophy and poetry as staged and restaged in Badiou's Platonism (a Platonism of the multiple, as he calls it, rather than of the One), I would argue that the missing third term is history. On the one hand, it is because philosophy has a built-in tendency to extract a kernel of eternal and invariant truth from the historical variations and events that otherwise condition it, as witnessed in its exemplary treatments of poetry, that the antagonism or quarrel in question continues to haunt us in the same way to this day, independently of the alleged break between the ancient and the modern. On the other hand, modern poetry itself could be said to operate in a similarly self-sublating way, erasing and subsuming the historical conditions of its own becoming in favor of a finite work whose generic being then shines forth with the infinite and absolute power of a truth that holds for eternity. For this reason, in *The Immanence of Truths*, the work or oeuvre that is a poem—instantiated in the different poems selectively chosen by the philosopher for analysis—can be universalized and applied to the other truth procedures as well. All truths, then, appear not just as infinite processes or procedures but also as finite works that serve as indices of their absoluteness, based on the model of the work of art. This is certainly one of the major innovations introduced in *The Immanence of Truths*, that is, the reliance on art and the poem as models for the finite work characteristic of all other truth conditions as well: "A truth always appears, in a determinate world, in the form of a work, that is to say, that which, in the realm of the finite, is opposed, as a figure of exception, to the ubiquitous figure of the waste product" (Badiou 2022b: 447). As a result of this approach, though, it no longer makes sense, at least not within the parameters of the philosopher's own conceptual system, to describe such poems and artworks as specifically modern, let alone as modernist. For in the process of their inclusion as examples of this philosophy's fundamental concepts the historicity of all such markers has been erased and subsumed under the eternal truth for which they serve as an emblem forever.

All this is not to say that there is no connection whatsoever between the two articulations at work in Badiou's treatment of modern or modernist poetry: first, the theoretical articulation or knot between philosophy and poetry as one of its conditions; and second, the historical link or break between the modern and whatever we call that which comes before the modern—whether the ancient, the classical or the traditional as different names for the pre-modern. Once the philosopher is done with his treatment of the select group of modern poets he has invited into his personal pantheon, however, any attempt to situate them in their original context, in the way a literary historian might want to do, for example, will open itself to the criticism of falling into the trap of a historicist emptying out, or a finitist covering over, of their truth's absoluteness.

As a useful point of departure for discussing these matters let us consider how Badiou, looking back upon his own trajectory at the start of *The Immanence of Truths*, lays out the principal ambitions that would have guided his entire philosophical project beginning already with *Being and Event*:

What has my philosophical strategy been for some thirty years now? It has been to establish what I call the immanence of truths. In other words, to rescue the category of truth and to assert that a truth may be:

- absolute while at the same time being a local construction;
- eternal while at the same time resulting from a process that begins in a determinate world, as an event of that world, and therefore belongs to the time of that world;
- ontologically determinate as a generic multiplicity while at the same time being phenomenologically localized as a degree of maximal existence in a given world;
- a-subjective (universal) while at the same time requiring a subjective incorporation in order to be grasped. (Badiou 2022b: 19)

Here, once again, we can observe how the philosopher's speculative strategy is driven by a compulsion to repeat. In this case, what he repeats is the argument of a certain unity or identity of opposites, marked in each case by the same syntactical conjunction "while at the same time," namely, the unity of opposites of the absolute and the local, the eternal and the temporal, being and appearing, and the universal and the subjectively situated. To be sure, some of these articulations become more pronounced in subsequent volumes, after the first formulation of Badiou's overarching speculative strategy in *Being and Event*. This is the case, for example, of the shift from the ontological to the phenomenological register, or from being to appearing, which comes up for the first time in *Logics of Worlds*; or the renewed emphasis on the absolute, which in *The Immanence of Truths* gains prevalence over considerations of the generic, the singular and the infinite in the previous two volumes. Nevertheless, according to Badiou's own summary, not only should we be able to locate each of these articulations already in *Being and Event*, to the point where the project from thirty years earlier is supposed to embody the same speculative strategy that is named only in the title of the third and final volume. He also wants us to understand how all three volumes are supposed recursively to go over the same ground, as though a central hurdle remained to be jumped over from one book to the next, by adopting different angles and placing different accents in each case.

In the case of poetry, it is the identity of opposites between the eternal and the historical that constitutes the main knot to be tied and untied in *The Immanence of Truths*. The other oppositions, such as the dialectic between the absolute and the local, between the infinite and the finite, or—within the latter—between the finite as an active work (*œuvre*) and the finite as a reactive waste product (*déchêt*), can be said to derive their impetus from that fundamental tension between the eternity of the truths of poetry and the concrete circumstances of their emergence in the time of a particular world. Put differently, poetry in this treatment appears to be caught between the pincers of philosophy and history, with each side pulling and pushing the poem between the extremes of the absoluteness of the true and the timeliness of the given. This pulling and pushing, in my eyes, drives the need to supplement the original volume of *Being and Event* and spread out its speculative strategy into a systematic trilogy.

We can also see this debate over philosophy, poetry and history play out in Badiou's "hypertranslation" of *Plato's Republic*, where the addition of the female character Amantha (introduced in lieu of Plato's brother Adeimantus) allows the French philosopher to include a feisty criticism of the Socratic arguments for banning the poets from the ideal city. In what conventionally is part of Book X of the *Republic* (592b–608b) and what in Badiou's restructuring under the title "Poetry and Thought" becomes the sixteenth and final chapter of the dialog, right before the "Epilogue: The Mobile Eternity of Subjects" (608b–621d), Amantha questions the narrowness of Socrates's attack, which would not apply to all poetry but only to a small subset of poets, devoted to the mimetic reproduction of objects and affects for the purpose of mass consumption:

> Your target—an art that's assumed to be the mere reproduction of external objects and primitive emotions—is very narrow, whereas you act as if it represented practically the whole field. Neither Pindar, nor Mallarmé, nor Aeschylus, nor Schiller, nor Sappho, nor Emily Dickinson, nor Sophocles, nor Pirandello, nor Aesop, nor Federico García Lorca fit into your scheme. (Badiou 2012b: 334)

Through the figure of Amantha, who is Socrates's most outspoken interlocutor in this imaginative recreation-transposition of *Plato's Republic*, Badiou manages to expand the canon of nonmimetic poets, mixing the names of poets both ancient and modern in a steady alternation that at the same time breaks with the strict confines of male normativity that is taken for granted in the Platonic model. The philosophical argument over whether to ban the poets from the ideal regime of government, in other words, is independent of the historical differences that would separate the poets of Greek antiquity from those that belong to the modern or post-romantic era in Europe and the United States, just as it transcends the mimetic reproduction of stable sexual identities. (Incidentally, this also means that arguments over the historical inclusion or exclusion of minority voices do not touch upon the fundamental antagonism at stake in the struggle between philosophy and poetry. It would entail attacking Badiou from the point of view of what he himself calls democratic materialism, which is what the trilogy of *Being and Event* is supposed to overcome in the name of infinite truth.)

Prior to the publication of *Plato's Republic* and *The Immanence of Truths*, admittedly, Badiou had been much more restrictive in his selection of the poets who would be representative of what around the time of *Being and Event* and *Manifesto for Philosophy* he had called "the age of the poets," with the list in question, though not as narrow and Germanocentric as the list of names that we can associate with Martin Heidegger, tending to be all-male and European: Friedrich Hölderlin, Stéphane Mallarmé, Arthur Rimbaud, Georg Trakl, Osip Mandelstam, Fernando Pessoa and Paul Celan (Badiou 1999: 69–77). Of these seven names, as in a constellation of stars against the night sky, only Mallarmé and Hölderlin deserve a full meditation in *Being and Event* (Badiou 2006: 191–8 and 255–61). In *Logics of Worlds*, Badiou would go on to give pride of place to Paul Valéry (Badiou 2009a: 455–75). In *The Immanence of Truths*, Emily Dickinson, Victor Hugo and René Char also make the cut, receiving a short chapter or sequel of their own on a par with Mandelstam, Pessoa (in the person of Alberto Caeiro), Bertold Brecht and Samuel Beckett (Badiou 2022b: 84–7, 99–102, 120–2, 137–40, 151–4, 171–5, 188–90 and 205–10). And in *Badiou by Badiou*, he would further expand the list of the poets of the age of the poets with the inclusion of the name of the Peruvian poet César Vallejo (whose complete poetry in French translation I had given to Badiou as a present more than two decades prior, with an open invitation to expand the horizon of his choices beyond Europe), just as elsewhere, for example in a talk on "Poetry and Communism" (which he offered to me for inclusion in the collection *The Age of the Poets and Other Writings on Twentieth-Century Poetry and Prose*), Badiou would study not only Vallejo's poetry on the Spanish Civil War but also that of the Chilean poet Pablo Neruda, the French Paul Éluard and the Turkish-Polish Nâzim Hikmet (Badiou 2022a: 45 and 2014: 93–108).

Amantha's interruption of Socrates's diatribe against the poets in *Plato's Republic*, however, makes clear that this polemic should not be reduced to a discussion over diversity, equity and inclusion. For Badiou, the point cannot be to produce a more representative list of poets that would be acceptable to the world tribunal of identity politics, because this would run counter to the generic universality of all truth—poetic truths included—in the name of which affect-based mimetic poetry is dismissed in the first place. Based on a conception of the true as generic, universal, but also absolute, it is rather a matter of creating something like a new peace between poetry and philosophy. Thus, answering Socrates's own invocation of an "ancient antagonism," or a "quarrel" that is indeed "a very longstanding one," Badiou has his female character interject: "But why should those old idiotic things keep being repeated? *Amantha stubbornly persisted.* Why not lay the foundations for a new peace between philosophy and poetry?" (Badiou 2012b: 335). To which Socrates, in Badiou's version of *Plato's Republic*, replies as if to concede the argument:

> Look, I don't mind saying that if mimetic poetry in the service of pleasure has any valid argument to make regarding the place it deserves to hold in a communist political community we'd be happy to offer it that place, because we are perfectly well aware that poetry of that sort continues to appeal to us. The fact remains that we're not allowed to betray what for us is the self-evidence of the True. (Badiou 2012b: 335)

After which, turning to Glaucon upon Amantha's suggestion to see if her brother, too, might assent to this compromise, Socrates adds the following proposal, which is Badiou's version of the original statement from Plato's *Republic* quoted in the epigraph:

> Let's go even further. Let's give its defenders, who, like us, aren't poets but only poetry lovers, a chance to defend it in prose and try to prove to us that it's not only pleasant but beneficial for a communist system of government and for ordinary people's lives. Let's give them a sympathetic ear: how advantageous it would be for us if they could prove that it's both pleasant and helpful! (Badiou 2012b: 335)

Much of Badiou's writing on poetry indeed has been and continues to be, especially in *The Immanence of Truths*, an attempt to come up with a defense in prose of poetry's ability to sustain the self-evidence of the True. This also means to overcome the captivating seduction of the affects and identities of bodies, languages and communities, united in their mimetic reproduction for easy mass consumption. Now, insofar as a historicist approach to poetry and to art in general, according to this philosopher, tends to reinscribe their meaning into the archive of their respective identities, languages, epochs, cultures and other such worldly settings, the challenge necessarily would appear to include a radical break with history. In Badiou's version of the ideal city-state, that is, the fifth system of government which he relabels communism, it is not just mimeticism but also and above all historicism and academicism that constitute the principal obstacles for the inclusion of the poets as the bearers of absolute truths. By contrast, insofar as literary critics and art historians according to Badiou tend to reduce art and poetry to the variable conditions of their historical emergence, perhaps it is they who should be banned from the new system of government more so than the poets and artists themselves!

In a rather strange aside in *The Immanence of Truths* Badiou thus mocks the labor of art historians and museum curators who, by relativizing great art in terms of the conditions of its sociohistorical context, fail to perceive the absoluteness of artistic invention as the finite work of an affirmative infinity:

> Indeed, the remarkable self-evidence of great artistic works is relativism's bête noire. To defend its own impotence, cultural ideology is forced to bring back into favor a host of second- and third-rate paintings. Such an array then allows it to claim that great Dutch painting can be entirely explained by the Holland of the time, that it is a cultural context, and so forth. Museums force you to look at a bunch of platters of eggplants and views of Amsterdam painted by fourth-rate Dutch artists, from which—much to the chagrin of the relativists and their historicist supporters—two or three magnificent paintings, which everyone can see are not like the others, stand out. (Badiou 2022b: 96)

In the eyes of the philosopher, relativism, historicism, academicism and culturalism as the dominant ideologies of today's capitalist parliamentarism and democratic materialism go hand in hand in denying the self-evidence of artistic and other truths as touches of the absolute. And yet, insofar as the overarching speculative strategy of his philosophical system, according to the different unities of opposites mentioned earlier, at the same time is supposed to respect the local, subjective and site-specific inscription of all truths—including those of art and poetry—Badiou also will have to find ways to elevate such situated, worldly and finite beginnings to the dignity of an absolute, eternal and infinite truth.

In Badiou's extensive writings on literature both ancient and modern—with Aeschylus and Sophocles for instance receiving careful treatment on a par with Hölderlin and Mallarmé already in *Theory of the Subject*—the principal method for restoring poetry to the self-evidence of its truth is by reading the poem as an absolute emblem of how not just poetry but all truth is supposed to function always and everywhere. Let us give three examples of such an emblematic or allegorical approach, one for each of the three volumes that make up the grand synthesis of Badiou's philosophical system.

In *Being and Event*, Badiou reads Mallarmé's poetry exemplified in *A Dice Throw*, not as an event within the history of post-Hugolian French literature, but as an emblem or symbol of the event-like nature of the event as such. "The event in question in *A Dice Throw* is therefore that of the production of an absolute symbol of the event. The stakes of casting dice 'from the bottom of a shipwreck' are those of making an event out of the thought of the event," Badiou states (2005: 191). And, in fact, this interpretation would be true not just for *A Dice Throw* but for all Mallarmé's poetry: "A poem by Mallarmé always fixes the place of an aleatory event; an event to be interpreted on the basis of the traces it leaves behind. Poetry is no longer submitted to action, since the meaning (univocal) of the text depends on what is declared to have happened therein" (2005: 193; see also Badiou 2009b: 51–110). In reading passages like these, we become the unwitting witnesses to philosophy's appropriation of its own condition, whereby the singular logic of the work of one modern poet becomes generalized, via the reference to any poem whatsoever, to redefine what an event—any event, poetic or otherwise—is always already supposed to be at all times.

About that which makes Mallarmé's poetry into an event within modern French literature, either by itself or as part of a broader movement such as symbolism or modernism, the reader learns next to nothing from Badiou's meditation on *A Dice Throw* in *Being and Event*. Instead, we must wait until *Logics of Worlds* to find a quick side comment in which Mallarmé's poetic project is related to the literary milieu in which it marks an event: "Or the way Mallarmé's poetry affirmed in the French language the inaccessible infinity specific to post-Romantic poetry despite the grid of control imposed by the artificial opposition between symbolism and the Parnasse movement, between Vielé-Griffin's swoonings and Leconte de Lisle's elephants" (Badiou 2009a: 307). This is because for Badiou, contrary to what he believes Jacques Rancière does in *Mallarmé: The Politics of the Siren*, the truth of the poem cannot be reduced to the programmatic statements in Mallarmé's prose pieces about the crisis of traditional verse or the mission of the new theatrical act. In fact, while Rancière criticizes his friend for presupposing and disavowing a modernist conception of poetry and art in general, Badiou for his part in a more recent debate with Rancière and Philippe Lacoue-Labarthe distances himself from any attempt to reinsert poetry's absolute truth in the context of its historical setting—whether of the social or the ontological variety, as in Heidegger's interpretations of Hölderlin. On the contrary, as will become even more crucial for Badiou in *The Immanence of Truths*, the absoluteness of the artwork—like the finite but creative work of any other truth procedure—depends on its ability to break with the historicality of the specific world in which it nonetheless must be inscribed at the same time. To ask the question about the historical inscription of an event in that milieu from which it seeks to tear itself free, however, always risks canceling the truth-value of the event as an absolute novelty.

For Badiou, the status of the Mallarméan poem should not be confused with that of the prose pieces in which Mallarmé announces his dream of a new poetics and a new theater, beyond the Catholic mass and the Wagnerian total work of art. These prose pieces certainly allow us to situate his project in the context of the nineteenth-century imagination of a new community, embodied and consecrated in the work of art as the culmination of what Lacoue-Labarthe and Jean-Luc Nancy (1988) call "the literary absolute," inaugurated in German romanticism. But such a reading according to Badiou not only turns out to be overly historicist, it also appears hard if not impossible to perform such a reading purely from within the resources of Mallarmé's poems alone. Badiou thus tells Rancière:

> But what strikes me is that one has the greatest trouble in retrieving all this based on the poems and that therefore we must in fact admit at a given moment that one will call poem a form for the declaration of thinking, about which it is not certain that it can be located in the same terms that Mallarmé uses in order to locate the poet. What is more, it is possible that, for us, what is thought in the poem, thought by the operations of the poem itself, should be partially or largely disjoined from the operations of localization of poetry and of the poem to which Mallarmé devotes himself in a number of his prose texts. And this is all the more important in my eyes because I think that, if one tries to go from the prose pieces to the poems, one also inscribes Mallarmé too much in a figure of historicality, whereas what matters is to see that the poems, at least, effectuate certain operations of thought that do not pertain to this inscription, to this belonging, or in any case they do not pertain to it entirely. In this sense, they are in part *torn free* from the figure of historicity to which you recall them and to which Philippe calls them even more in a certain way, in a historicity that is even more considerably expansive, since it concerns not only the question of Wagner and the total work of art, but more remotely and more profoundly the question of the destiny of art or of the art project in its quasi-originary Platonic fixation. (Badiou, Lacoue-Labarthe and Rancière 2017: 45–6)

This objection has important consequences for the way in which these French thinkers define their respective approaches to Mallarmé's poems and to art and poetry in general.[3] Clearly, we are still debating the same antagonism between poetry and philosophy that was already ancient for Socrates in Plato's *Republic*. For Badiou, though, it is not just a question of choosing between two unique but otherwise compatible paths of inquiry—an immanent approach to the nature of the poetic act and its intrinsic operations as opposed to the interrogation of its historical inscription. Rather, Badiou's actively rejects Rancière's and Lacoue-Labarthe's interpretations because for him the absolute singularity of the Mallarméan poem, like that of any true poem or artwork, refuses to be understood in terms of historicity. Even in the best of all cases, to try to link the poem or artwork to the site or milieu of its secular inscription would condemn the interpreter to be treated as a mere historian of the archive of available knowledge, which coming from a Platonist is always a bit of an insult. For the philosopher in Badiou, by contrast, the event of poetry—or, rather, the eventfulness of the event that is emblematized in the Mallarméan poem—depends on its capacity to tear itself away from its own historicity or historicality, including the Heideggerian sense of the term.

At this point, we can begin to see a crack opening in the "speculative strategy" behind the overarching project of *Being and Event*. This is because Badiou—at least in his systematic philosophical texts—tends to turn his favorite poems into emblems or illustrations of the absolute event of poetry as such, independently of their historical inscription. *A Dice Throw*, for example, is first treated as an instantiation of the Mallarméan poem in general, which then in its turn functions implicitly as an instance of the event that is *the* poem—not just Mallarmé's but any true poem whatsoever. Finally, this capacity of *all* true poetry to touch upon the absolute, as when Badiou talks about "the absolute event" in his meditation on Mallarmé, will be applied not just to poetry and art but to all truth procedures in *The Immanence of Truths*. However, part of the reason for why Badiou decided to supplement *Being and Event* with two more volumes has to do with a desire, as he puts it in the Sequel on René Char in the third and final tome of the trilogy, "to counter a misinterpretation of my concept of the event, namely, that it must be waited for," for example, as something transcendent like the conventional image of Plato's world of ideas, whereas the infinite truth of an event nevertheless must find ways to inscribe itself within the logic of a given world as its immanent exception. Using Char's words to name this articulation of the finite and the infinite in the work of all truth as illustrated in modern poetry, Badiou concludes: "The work of truth that touches infinity—the end *in truth* of finitude—cannot be waited for from outside; it will have to *reach my waiting*" (2022b: 86–7). Thus, when in order to preserve the absoluteness of the event emblematized in the artwork before being projected on all other truth procedures Badiou tears the poem away from its historicality, he is in a sense canceling the possibility of fulfilling his own speculative strategy behind the philosophical system of *Being and Event*. Or, to put it less negatively, instead of inscribing the event of poetry in the immanence of a particular world, he ends up changing his working definition of the concept of immanence, which henceforth, thanks to the generalization of the artwork's self-sublating absoluteness, comes to be understood as an immanent capacity of the human subject, like the undecidable gesture of the master's dice throw, to touch upon the Absolute.

Similar to how Badiou presents Mallarmé's *A Dice Throw* in *Being and Event* as an absolute symbol of the eventfulness of the event, in *Logics of Worlds* he analyzes Paul Valéry's long poem *The Graveyard by the Sea* as an illustration of how an event, in order to break with the eternal return of the same, must inscribe itself in a finite body capable of drawing all the necessary consequences from its infinite truth: "In our terms, this poem is the story of an event" (2009a: 455). In fact, in a note to the section in which he reads Valéry's poem side by side with the French mathematician Évariste Galois's invention of modern algebra, Badiou himself draws an analogy in this regard between Mallarmé's treatment in *Being and Event* and Valéry's function in *Logics of Worlds*: "It is the question of the 'pure event' that connects the Mallarmé of 'A Dice Throw' and the Valéry of 'The Graveyard by the Sea': under what conditions can the poem capture what lies beyond what is, what purely happens? And what then is the status of thought, if it is true that such a happening strikes at thought's corporeal support?" (2009a: 516). Time and again, philosophy extracts from poetry a thought of the pure event. Contrary to the careful attention Badiou lends to the world of algebra from Lagrange to Cauchy prior to the inventions introduced by Galois, in the case of Valéry he treats the poem as its own world in a kind of retroactive sublation of its thought-practice into the maximal thought of the body of a poetic truth and even of the truth as such.

Finally, in *The Immanence of Truths* poetry plays an even more dominant role than in *Being and Event* or *Logics of Worlds*. Of a total of twenty-six sequels, no fewer than eight are reserved for modern poetry (Char, Hugo, Dickinson, Celan, Mandelstam, Pessoa, Brecht, Beckett), compared to eleven for mathematics (Gödel, Cohen, Ramsey, Scott, Jensen, Kunen), three for philosophy (Plato and Hegel on art, Husserl on science) and one for politics (Mao). This time around, Badiou proceeds to read his selection of poems as exemplifying illustrations of the dialectic between the finite and the infinite as well as between the affirmative finitude of a work as opposed to the reactive finitude or fallout of a waste product. While he offers slightly more contextual information about Dickinson or Mandelstam, for the most part these sequels are all exercises in the philosophical appropriation of the poetic condition. Such exercises seem to work especially well with poems that belong to the post-romantic, high modernist or avant-garde canon, insofar as they break with the language of tradition and illuminate the point where humanity is capable of touching upon the anonymous yet universal appearance of an absolute truth or, conversely, the critical point where an absolute capacity for the infinite can be plunged or embedded within the creative confines of a finite work.

At no point do these readings pretend to locate the poetic experiments in question within the literary situation in which they would mark an unprecedented event. Instead, whether the break occurs between the old and the new, repetition and difference, the finite and the infinite, the work and the waste product, identity and anonymity, academicism and experimentation, or the covering-over and the uncovering of an affirmative infinity, the self-same act of drawing such a Platonic line of separation is seen as the philosophical purport of the poems themselves. Badiou thus reads Victor Hugo, for example, as a serial enactment of the capacity to locate a possible infinity within the desert-like world of a national history and language without truth:

> Hugo is a poet of what might be called the pinpointing of the infinite: he intends poetry to locate—in a world tragically lacking any discernible way out, an unbearable, oppressive, and finite, albeit immense and desert-like, world—the point that can serve as support for a possible infinitization of a path through this situation. This can moreover be considered a metaphor of poetry: how can a poetic truth be brought to light in a national language weighted down by its long history? How can the academic trap be avoided? How can the venerable alexandrine be saved? (2022b: 99)

Here, again, we see how one poet's work comes to be read as a metaphor of poetry as such, based on the break from a tradition defined by the circulation of opinions about history, national identity and commerce, in favor of the novelty of a universal truth. Such a reading gives the impression of providing us at long last with a new peace between philosophy and poetry, but only because the philosopher has turned the poem into an exemplifying metaphor of his own concept of poetic truth.

In Badiou's own terms, we might say that instead of treating events in poetry as conditions for his philosophy, in each of the three volumes of *Being and Event* he turns them into illustrations of his philosophical concepts of the genericity, infinity and absoluteness of the truth of any event whatsoever. In an interview I did with him some time ago, he agrees that this is a legitimate charge to make, perhaps even the only one that he is willing to accept. "If one were to make the objection that I submit the condition to the conditioned, it is rather in the way you've just done that one should proceed, instead of in terms of transcendence," Badiou admits.

> Because it is evident that, first of all, the selection of examples is oriented for me by the fact that the conceptual means that are needed strategically in order to allow for philosophical compossibility push me to choose certain writers or authors in whom precisely there is already present something like an internal disposition toward the event and its consequences. (Badiou 2011: 312)

If we must grant Badiou the right to treat poetry in whatever way he sees fit as a philosopher, however, as a literary critic and theorist I also feel a compulsion to ask how exactly this treatment functions and at what cost. Part of the problem is that in Badiou's Platonist systematization of the age-old antagonism between poetry and philosophy, there is no independent room for literary critics or historians: either they are mere auxiliaries to the philosopher, useful as Gardner Davies is for Badiou in his interpretation of Mallarmé, or else they become the sad custodians of the debris of historicism and cultural relativism with which, like the museum curators of Dutch landscape painting, the academy tries in vain to bury art's infinite potential.

In his critical commentary on Badiou's twisted and disavowed modernism, Rancière mentions two tactics that are typical of this philosopher's repeated appropriation of the poetic condition: the tactic of naming or nominalization, in the sense of extracting names and images from the poems under discussion as metaphors of Badiou's own philosophical concepts; and the tactic that we might call maximalization, in the double sense of extracting a maxim from the poems that at the same time radicalizes the maximalist agenda of the philosopher as an eternalizing Platonist. "But what exactly is thereby *discerned*, that is to say, at the end of the day, *named*? As always, it is the status of the poem both as affirmation and as a metaphorization of the Idea's transpiring," Rancière concludes. "The poem thereby becomes an orientation for thought, and we know Badiou's taste for extracting maxims from poems and giving them a general value" (Rancière 2009: 78–9). The result of this double "torsion" of modern poetry by philosophy back upon itself would explain why Badiou in *Handbook of Inaesthetics* can talk about his approach to poetry and art as a "Platonic modernism" (Badiou 2005: 14).

In the case of *The Immanence of Truths*, we can see these tactics at work in each of the eight sequels dedicated to modern poetry. Victor Hugo, for example, names "blue thistle" the point of infinity that marks a truth, to which he also gives "the dramatic form of a lightning flash in the motionless expanse of the night sky"; these names then allow us to define the essence of poetic truth or to poeticize the task of poetry: "Poetry is assigned the task of expressing what lifts human being out of the abysses of finitude"; and, finally, this self-poeticization of the task of poetry through the lens of the philosopher's conceptual apparatus in turn produces a concluding maxim: "You who are afflicted by finitude, look, see, and ask yourself where the blue thistle is" (2022b: 101–2).

Or take the case of Paul Celan. His work and, at least indirectly, his personal life-and-death struggle, too, are recast as one long battle to avoid the trappings of dominant finitude:

> Paul Celan is a tremendous poet of the traps that the world sets for life, as well as of the ways to avoid them. Accordingly, he attempts to place poetry on the exact boundary between affirmative finitude—the kind that accepts the law of the new infinity—and passive finitude, between the work and the waste product. (Badiou 2022b: 137)

Associating new names drawn from Celan's poems with his own concepts of infinity and of the two types of finitude, then, allows the philosopher to redefine the truth of the poetic work, in the slippery sense of both this poet's work and all poetry in general: "One possible definition of the poetic work, fall and flight combined, might then be: 'sore gain / of a world,'" which in turn provides us readers with a poetic maxim to conclude: "We will heal ourselves from the wound when we discover that the new infinity, too, is also a whole 'world'" (Badiou 2022b: 140).

In addition to the extraction from poetry of names and maxims that would exemplify the philosopher's conception of the work of truth in general, there is another aspect in Badiou's approach to poetry that marks this treatment as uniquely modern, if not modernist. He constantly compares the break between finitude and infinity, or between the passive waste product and the affirmative work, to the break between the old and the new, or between tradition and experimentation. In this sense, we could say that Badiou absolutizes a modern concept of truth, lifting its novelty out of history, which because of this absolutization can no longer be recognized as such. The modern in the hands of the philosopher retroactively erases the prehistory of its break with tradition. To be exact, the break between the old and the new, instead of finding its place *in* history, becomes equated with the work of truth *against* history, a work that is true at all times and in all places. Conversely, any attempt such as Rancière's to historicize the disavowed modernity and/or modernism of Badiou's treatment of poetry can be waived off as just another example of democratic materialism and cultural relativism.

In *The Immanence of Truths*, Badiou for the most part adopts a pejorative concept of modernity, seen as the period of the democratic-materialist or capitalist-parliamentarian covering-over of the infinite potential immanent in any situation: "Modernity means using a new operator, which, rather than highlighting the falseness of everything that touches the infinite, instead covers it over with finite debris, with a solid layer of waste materials, so that any potential infinity, wiped out this way, becomes incomprehensible" (2022b: 181). On a few occasions in the same book, though, Badiou also speaks sarcastically about the culturalist and fundamentalist defense of tradition over and against Western modernity. In such instances, he comes closer again to his affirmative use of "modern" in *Logics of Worlds*, as in the "modern algebra" invented by Galois; or to his plea for taking "one more step" in Cartesian modernity, which he defined in *Manifesto for Philosophy* as the articulation of being and truth via the notion of the subject: "A step within the modern configuration, the one that since Descartes has bound the three nodal concepts of being, truth, and the subject to the conditions of philosophy" (Badiou 1999: 32).

If we study the conceptual history behind the word "modern," however, we realize that since its inception the term has always served to mark a transition or break between the old and the new:

> The word "modern" in its Latin form "modernus" was used for the first time in the late 5th century in order to distinguish the present, which had become officially Christian, from the Roman and pagan past. With varying content, the term "modern" again and again expresses the consciousness of an epoch that relates itself to the past of antiquity, in order to view itself as the result of a transition from the old to the new. (Habermas 1983: 3; referring to Jauss)

Now this highly conventional and at bottom deeply Christian view of modernity, which we can find in the philosophies of history from Saint Augustine all the way to Hegel, is one that Badiou is also not shy to use on those rare occasions in *The Immanence of Truths* where he attempts in a few rough strokes, if not to historicize, at least to periodize the truths of poetry, art or politics. Such periodizations are possible because any finite work, even once it loses its index of the absolute and becomes part of a dead archive, a constructible literary canon or a curated museum collection, is susceptible to becoming reactivated and re-indexed in its absoluteness:

> But when it becomes—and every time a subject reactivates it, it becomes, it is re-indexed—it may point beyond its constructible closure and break through its finite shell. When, for example, the 17th-century theater practitioners revived the Greek and Roman tragedies, they triggered an intense re-indexation of those works, freeing them from the constructible straitjacket of philological and grammatical conservation in the finitude of which they had, somehow or other, come through the Middle Ages. Similarly, by adapting the Icelandic sagas to romantic opera, Wagner, in his tetralogy, revitalized their index, which pierced the covering of the weak finitude to which their anthropological conservation had seemed to destine them. And we know that, throughout the French Revolution, the living meaning of the word "republic" brought back its Greco-Roman resonance, proving that the institutions and battles of Antiquity could be re-indexed in the birth of European modernity. All of this defines the index of a work as the ongoing possibility of undermining the ontological finitude of that work. (Badiou 2022b: 457)

What we see in a passage like this is something we might call the eternal return of the modern. It is a philosophical view of the eternal nature of truth, emblematized in certain events in literature, opera or politics, which presupposes as its defining feature a radical break between antiquity and modernity, between the old and the new, or between finitude and infinity. But this break, once it is absolutized on the models of the literary absolute or the modern political revolution in their struggles against tradition or the old regime, retroactively erases its own historicity and raises itself to the Absolute, as if to illuminate the night sky forever with the constellation of the Great Bear.

Contrary to his ancient model's ban on the poets, the modern Platonist in Badiou would rather exclude the historians—including literary and art historians—from his ideal republic. The philosopher's relentless struggle against the encyclopedia of historical knowledge, which runs parallel to the separation of truth from mere opinions, depends upon the defining turning point of a break between tradition and modernity. And while this battle becomes especially visible in the philosopher's relation of mimicry and appropriation to modernist poetry, once this break has been accomplished its historicity can no longer be retrieved except in a manner that runs counter to the claims to absoluteness of philosophical truth. In this sense Badiou's philosophy in its relation to poetry can be defined as the eternal return of the same modern, capable of sublating its own history into an emblem of eternal truth.

Notes

1 For a broader discussion of the quarrel between poetry and philosophy in Badiou's work prior to *The Immanence of Truths*, see Bosteels (2019).
2 I will not go into my overarching interpretation of Badiou's philosophy (Bosteels 2011), which starts from his *Theory of the Subject* to capture the tensions around the dialectic between the structural and the historical in the overarching project of *Being and Event*.
3 See also Rancière (2011), and for a comparison between Rancière's and Badiou's Mallarmé, see Bosteels (2020).

Works Cited

Badiou, A. (1999), *Manifesto for Philosophy*, trans. N. Madarasz, Albany: SUNY Press.
Badiou, A. (2005), *Handbook of Inaesthetics*, trans. A. Toscano, Stanford: Stanford University Press.
Badiou, A. (2006), *Being and Event*, trans. O. Feltham, London: Continuum.
Badiou, A. (2009a), *Logics of Worlds: Being and Event II*, trans. A. Toscano, London: Continuum.
Badiou, A. (2009b), *Theory of the Subject*, trans. B. Bosteels, London: Continuum.
Badiou, A. (2011), "Can Change Be Thought? An Interview with Alain Badiou Conducted by B. Bosteels (Paris, June 10, 1999)," in B. Bosteels, *Badiou and Politics*, 289–317, Durham: Duke University Press.
Badiou, A. (2012a), *Philosophy for Militants*, trans. B. Bosteels, London: Verso.

Badiou, A. (2012b), *Plato's Republic: A Dialogue in 16 Chapters*, trans. S. Spitzer, intro. K. Reinhard, New York: Columbia University Press.

Badiou, A. (2014), *The Age of the Poets and Other Writings on Twentieth-Century Poetry and Prose*, eds. Emily Apter and B. Bosteels, trans. B. Bosteels, London: Verso.

Badiou, A. (2022a), *Badiou by Badiou*, trans. B. Bosteels, Stanford: Stanford University Press.

Badiou, A. (2022b), *The Immanence of Truths: Being and Event III*, trans. S. Spitzer and K. Reinhard, London: Bloomsbury.

Badiou, A., P. Lacoue-Labarthe, and J. Rancière (2017), *Mallarmé, le théâtre, la tribu*, Paris: Christian Bourgois.

Bosteels, B. (2011), *Badiou and Politics*, Durham: Duke University Press.

Bosteels, B. (2019), "What Are Philosophers For in the Age of the Poets: Badiou with and against Heidegger," in R. Ghosh (ed.), *Philosophy and Poetry: Continental Perspectives*, 248–270, New York: Columbia University Press.

Bosteels, B. (2020), "Rancière's Mallarmé," trans. Erik Vogt, in E. Vogt and M. Manfé (eds.), *Jacques Rancière und die Literatur*, 176–200, Vienna-Berlin: Turia + Kant.

Habermas, J. (1983), "Modernity—An Incomplete Project," in Hal Foster (ed.), *The Anti-Aesthetic: Essays on Postmodern Culture*, 3–15, Port Townsend: Bay Press.

Jauss, H.-R. (2005), "Modernity and Literary Tradition," trans. C. Thorne, *Critical Inquiry* 31:2, 329–364.

Lacoue-Labarthe, P. and J. L. Nancy (1988), *The Literary Absolute: The Theory of Literature in German Romanticism*, trans. P. Barnard and C. Lester, Albany: SUNY Press.

Rancière, J. (2009), *Aesthetics and Its Discontents*, trans. S. Corcoran, Cambridge: Polity.

Rancière, J. (2011), *Mallarmé: The Politics of the Siren*, trans. S. Corcoran, London: Continuum.

5

Badiou, Lacan and Mathematical Modernisms

Arka Chattopadhyay

In a cultural definition of modernity that champions rationality, mathematics often headlines the faculty of reasoning. What Descartes calls a universal mathematical science of "order and measure" (*mathesis universalis*), inclusive of music and astronomy, inaugurates the historical sequence of Western modernity (Descartes 1985: 19). For Kant, it's integral to epistemology as mathematical knowledge works like synthetic *a priori* that goes beyond the empirical (Kant 1998: 143–5). Alain Badiou's mobilization of mathematics goes against such instrumentalist-rationalist approaches to modernity. As we shall see, his philosophical utilization of mathematics is critical of instrumentalist rationality and thereby indicative of a different relation between mathematics and modernity in which the impasse of the former is key to the latter. In what follows, I would tease out the implications of Badiou's "mathematical modernism(s)." This mathematical modernism doesn't get identified with a renaissance or enlightenment model of instrumental rationality. Unlike Jeremy Gray who mobilizes the history of the discipline under the category of "modernist mathematics," (Gray 2008) I will talk about a philosophical culture of modernism that partakes of mathematical ideas and ideologies. Hence the expression, "mathematical modernism(s)." I will trace the modernist gesture toward mathematical formalization in Alain Badiou's system, that comes from what Badiou calls the Platonic dialectic between the "matheme" and the "poem" and Lacan's mathematization of psychoanalytic discourse. Placing Badiou's evocation of Cantorian set theory as a post-Lacanian move, still haunted by Lacan, I will chart the transition from Lacan to Badiou, first in terms of their continuities in envisaging a mathematical modernism and then in their collaboration on a political idea of modernism. We will see how Badiou's work exposes a conflict between modernity and modernism and the latter is militarized to displace the former. How mathematics and politics interact with one another is a question scarcely addressed by Badiou himself. This synthetic exploration of the two thinkers will reveal more permeability between them than what Badiou's strategic departures from Lacan would allow. Our final goal is to arrive at an understanding of this complex relation between mathematics and politics in Badiou's system through Lacan.

Mathematical Formalization between Badiou and Lacan

Let me first place the idea of the "matheme" as a bridge between Badiou and Lacan to show how it shuttles between the Symbolic and the Real. If mathematics is a language, it is also haunted by its Real as the inexpressible of language. Mathematics in this counter-rationalist thesis cannot be identified with any unchanging expressive totality, even if mathematical discourse may have a latent desire for such precision and completeness. In "What Is a Poem?," Badiou reads Plato's famous expulsion of poets from his ideal republic as a dialectic between poetry and mathematics. Poetry offers an "unthinkable thought" while mathematics can be a thought only if it is "immediately written as thought" or made "thinkable" (2005c: 19). This idea of the mathematical as a thought based on writing has a Lacanian echo. For Lacan, mathematical discourse provides a paradigm of writing the impossible Real. We will return to the Real as a key dimension of mathematical modernism, but at this point, let us remember what Lacan says, discussing number theory and the topological geometry of knots, in *Seminar XXV*: "Mathematics makes reference to the written, to the written as such; and mathematical thought is the fact that one can represent for oneself a writing" (session of 10.1.1978). Badiou, likewise, contrasts the "transparency of the matheme" with the "metaphorical obscurity of the poem" (2005c: 19). Does this mean that mathematics transcends linguistic opacities? Is it not a language? This remains a vital question for Badiou and Lacan. What Badiou calls the matheme's "transparency" echoes Lacan's notion of "integral transmission" that can only happen through the "matheme" (from the Greek word "máthēma" meaning "what one learns") which is a Platonic idea of the mathematical letter as self-reference. Lacan reflects:

> signs that are called mathematical—"mathemes"—solely because they are integrally transmitted. We haven't the slightest idea what they mean, but they are transmitted. Nevertheless, they are not transmitted without the help of language, and that's what makes the whole thing shaky. (1998: 110)

As we shall see, this passage is influential for Badiou, but let's note that Lacan hesitates about integral transmission when he considers the dependence of "mathemes" on language. Mathematical letters can be transmitted without meaning but they have to depend on linguistic signs. In "What Is a Poem?," Badiou situates the "unnamable" in the form of a Lacanian Real: "[e]very regime of truth is grounded in the Real by its own unnamable" (2005c: 24). He locates the Real of mathematics in the idea of consistency, as maintained by Gödel: "we know, after Gödel, that consistency *is precisely the unnamable point of mathematics*. It is not possible for a mathematical theory to establish the statement of its own consistency as veridical" (2005c: 24; emphasis original). Badiou agrees with Lacan regarding the tricky reliance of matheme on language: "the unnamable proper to the matheme is the consistency of language" (26). What limits the matheme's complete transmissibility is the very consistency of language that cannot be established by mathematical theory.

Lacan declares:

> Mathematical formalization is our goal, our ideal. Why? Because it alone is matheme, in other words, it alone is capable of being integrally transmitted. Mathematical formalization consists of what is written, but it only subsists if I employ, in presenting it, the language (*langue*) I make use of. Therein lies the objection: no formalization of language is transmissible without the use of language itself. (1998: 119)

Mathematical formalization is empowered by the matheme's integral transmissibility but its foundation in language takes away from the promise of total transmission. In *Conditions*, examining Plato, anti-philosophy and Lacan, Badiou refers to this Lacanian passage:

> For Lacan, mathematics is a kind of formalization, that is to say it is the power of the letter. It is from this viewpoint that we can make sense of the particularly radical statement to be found in the same seminar, namely that "only mathematization touches the real, and in this aspect it is compatible with our discourse, analytical discourse." Only mathematization. This is a strong statement. And you will remark that mathematics has here shifted from the ideal position it occupied a moment ago with regard to the symbolic or transmission to a position of compatibility with regard to the real. For analytical discourse, mathematization is at once the ready ideal of integral transmission, and that real qua impasse of formalization. (2008b: 243)

In Badiou's analysis of Lacan, we see how the matheme oscillates between the Symbolic of language and the extra-linguistic Real. If psychoanalysis takes mathematization as its goal, looking for total transmission *a la lettre*, it must also spot the Real as an impasse in mathematization. Badiou differentiates between the "modern formalizing conception of mathematics and a classical hypothetico-deductive conception" (2008b: 244). Though he doesn't oppose one to the other, for Badiou, Lacan and himself are part of a mathematical modernism that doesn't fall prey to instrumental rationality because they check the total transmission of mathemes with the impasse of the Real as the end of mathematical formalization. The aporia of the Real resists instrumentalist totalization of mathematical forms.

Mathematical Modernism and Infinity

In Badiou, ontology *is* mathematics. This formulation helps us situate "mathematical modernism(s)." To think of ontology or the study of *being-qua-being* as a pure mathematical multiple of set theory is to rethink philosophical modernity, not only in relation to mathematics but also to politics, art and love—all of which activate the multiple in its infinitesimal play. Be it the collective subject of politics, the move from one to two and then to the infinite in the event of love or art and literature that depict infinite multiplicity in their form and content, Badiou's mathematical ontology inflects all the truth procedures and impacts his whole philosophical edifice. Though he is against suturing philosophy to science, Badiou sutures ontology (a branch within philosophy) to mathematics (one among many sciences). With this identification of ontology as mathematics, Badiou anchors a mathematical modernism that is critical of romanticism and/or classicism. As we shall see in what follows, mathematics does not *know* the event because the event can only be a supplement to being. In this sense, Badiou's mathematics is open to the aleatory modernism of the event as a figure of the Real.

For Badiou, modern mathematics (and science in a more general articulation) is one of the four fundamental "truth processes" (others are politics, love and art) that function as the four conditions for philosophy. Philosophy doesn't identify or "suture" itself exclusively to any one condition but deals with the truths produced by all the regimes. This means philosophy has no truth of its own and must make do with the truths that emerge from fields like mathematics. In "Philosophy and Mathematics," Badiou observes with conviction that the link between mathematics and philosophy, once re-established, can make our modernity "post-romantic" (2008b: 98). Rejecting the idea of the postmodern, he identifies two modernities in our history: one, classical and the other, romantic. Mathematics for him will help transcend the romantic (95, 98) and redefine the modern in a post-romantic way. When Badiou identifies the globalized capitalist modernity as a discourse of finitude, he critiques a romanticization of death and finitude in this historical sequence.[1] How do we make modernity post-romantic or non-romantic via mathematics? This is the question I will probe. For Badiou, it is the mathematics of infinity that can create a break with classicism and/or romanticism and reopen the question of modernity or as I would say, "mathematical modernism." To use the set-theoretical language, employed in *The Immanence of Truths* (2022), he opposes the modernity that "covers" up the potential infinity of a situation with finitude and doesn't allow the infinite to emerge from the situation. I argue for a resistance to modernity through modernism in Badiou. Though he doesn't call the infinite operation modernist, we will see that he has two conceptions of modernity, one finite and the other infinite. I choose to call the latter, modernism. In my view, he subverts modernity (classical and romantic) with modernism and contests repressive capitalist modernity with a mathematical modernism that attempts to "uncover" what the modernity of finitude covers up.[2]

As Badiou notes in *The Immanence of Truths* (2022), the dominant ideology may not antagonistically repress the infinite on all occasions but it would utilize the finitude of the situation (significations that are already there in it) to hide its potential infinity (see 205–10). This is a place where mathematics and politics unite in an evental modernism that militates against the modernity of finitude. We see him use mathematics as a way of formalizing political event. The language of "covering" comes from mathematics (set theory) but it is used in a political way to situate the hegemonic operation of power. A set is called finite if all its elements (multiples) are definable parts of another pre-existing set. This is a constructible and definable set that "covers" infinity. It doesn't allow for anything non-definable to take place. Pre-existing significations cover up the possibility of infinite irruption.

Going by the choice of making new sets that are simply properties of old sets, we are always going to remain inside the "covering." This is the fundamental ethical task. To transgress the covering is to make an insurrectionist commitment to the axiom of non-constructibility. If the constructible set (a set that can be created from pre-existing sets through simple operations) is the normative, the non-constructible set interrupts the norm in pursuing the new. The generic set breaks the covering with what is non-definable. Badiou goes to Kurt Gödel and Paul Cohen and highlights the non-constructible or generic set that can produce a pure multiple (a multiple without one, that is, a multiple of another multiple and so on in an infinite order). As politically committed subjects, we must construct the non-constructible set that beats the logic of covering. Badiou devises this mathematical modernism to formalize a political modernism that goes back to his own subjective breakthrough in the wake of the 1968 student protests in France. It is a modernism of non-constructible infinity. The cornerstone of both these modernisms is the generic set as the order of the non-definable and infinite event that ruptures the logic of covering. It is here that Cantor and Mao come together in *The Immanence of Truths*. They are co-invoked as risk-takers, warriors and comrades who seek out the infinite by engaging in the *reductio ad absurdum* proof that opens up a floodgate of contradictions (see 35).

Let us delve deeper into Badiou's mathematics of infinity which commits itself to the event and opens up the space for a mathematical modernism. In "Philosophy and Mathematics" Badiou credits the Hegelian infinite as a milestone in mathematical modernity because it secularizes the metaphysical dogma of divine infinity into a true concept of the infinite, "the thought of which only the dialectic (in the Hegelian sense) can establish" (2008b: 108). He argues that after Hegel, romantic philosophy made philosophy and mathematics the same and this identification disentwined the two (109). His own project consists of restoring the link between mathematics and philosophy by locating the infinite, not in the divine One but in the void. If being is infinite multiplicity, its presentation can only stop at the void:

> there is only the infinite multiple, which presents the infinite multiple, and the unique stopping point of this presentation presents nothing. Ultimately at issue is the void, and not the One. God is dead, at the heart of the presentation. (2008b: 111)

A second important site of mathematical thought that secularizes the infinite is Cantor and in "The Subject and Infinity," Badiou goes back to Cantor via Lacan to demonstrate how the Lacanian gesture only uses Cantor as a detour and remains resolutely finite. Badiou argues that what makes Lacan "modern" is this stress on pre-Cantorian finitude. For him, Lacan invokes Cantor only to "renovate finitude, for the modernity of finitude" (2008b: 226). This reading from *Conditions* is consistent with the reading of modern finitude in *The Immanence of Truths*. It is against this modernity of finitude that Badiou launches a political and mathematical modernism of infinity. Unlike what I contended earlier, here we see Badiou, pushing Lacan into the modernity of finitude and against his own mathematical modernism of infinity. He locates Lacan in a romantic avatar of modernity in which the infinite is reduced to what is inaccessible to the finite. This negative dependence of infinity on the logic of the finite makes Badiou's Lacan "pre-Cantorian" (2008b: 219). This is a refusal of Cantor's actual infinity in Badiou's words: "Lacan had no concept of the infinite other than in terms of operational inaccessibility" (2008b: 219). If Lacan is a "modern" thinker of the finite subject (death-drive as a mark of finitude in the divided subject), what is Badiou? If we accept Badiou's interpretation of Lacan, the latter is romantic in his identification of infinity with inaccessibility. Badiou on the other hand initiates a mathematical modernism that is post-romantic, because he is Cantorian in his agreement with the idea of actual infinity.

Let me go deeper into the Lacan–Badiou debate with an aim to show how Badiou reduces Lacanian infinity to inaccessibility while the infinite is more complex notion in Lacan. In "The Subject and Infinity," Badiou takes Lacan to task for his treatment of 2 as the inaccessible to 0 and 1 in *Seminar XIX*. For Lacan, a number is inaccessible if its smaller numbers can't produce it by way of summation or exponentiation (Lacan 2018: 156). His argument is that 0 and 1 can never produce 2 ($0 + 1, 1 + 0, 0^1, 1^0$) either by summation or by exponentiation (Lacan 2018: 156). This is correct but if we bring in two 1s, the scenario changes dramatically! Badiou is right to point out Lacan's erroneous overlooking of the simple equation, $1 + 1 = 2$. Badiou argues, if 1 and 1, both smaller than 2, can produce 2 by addition, 2 cannot be called inaccessible or infinite, following Lacan's logic. There is no denying Badiou. But despite Lacan's mistake, he has a point that $0 + 1$ doesn't allow us to move to the next number, that is, 2, while $1 + 1$ gives us its successor, 2. The same is true for the following natural whole numbers that produce succession: $2 + 1 = 3, 3 + 1 = 4, 4 + 1 = 5$ and so on. We come from 0 to 1, but the addition of the two numbers makes us stay back at 1. It blocks the succession function. Lacan is right that 0 and 1 by summation or exponentiation doesn't produce a 2. 1 and 1 make a 2 but 0 and 1 don't. As the Lacan of *Seminar XIX* holds, 1 is produced from its lack in 0. Zero is "the mark of lack" (Lacan 2018: 156). How does zero produce one? In *Seminar XXIII*, Lacan returns to this "ambiguity between 1 and 0" via Cantor (Lacan 2016: 10): "Cantor's theory has to start afresh from the pair, but then the set stands in the third place" (Lacan 2016: 10). Since every set contains the empty set as its subset, if you put a 1 into a set ([1]), the set already has two elements ([1, Ø]). This is how 0 is always already counted as 1. This simple operation shows how 1 produces 2. But more important is this ambiguity between 1 and 0 where the latter (Ø) is counted as the former (1). This 0 as 1 is infinitely reproduced in the interval between two natural whole numbers as we move from one number to its successor.

Like Badiou, Lacan uses set theory to ground human subjectivity and its relation to lack and void: "The set is nothing other than the subject. This is precisely why it cannot even be handled without the addition of the empty set" (Lacan 2018: 182). The ambiguity between 1 and 0 points to how the subject is founded by the void. In Lacan's later teachings, mathematics becomes an operative mechanism to reach the impasses of the Real in the unconscious. Be it language or formalization, "matheme" as the literal (and the littoral because the letter punches holes in language)[3] word-body, transmits something of the Real unconscious that the Symbolic order of language or the Imaginary register of meaning cannot convey. Mathematical modernism supplements language and meaning but it can only do so in a partial way at the level of structure alone. More than a residue of meaning is there, and language is still involved in mathematical formalization.

For Lacan and Badiou (who has worked on Lacanian formulas of sexuation), set theory can say something about sexuality as a non-relation. The Lacanian thesis that there is no sexual relation is worked out in variations of Aristotelian modal (propositional) logic but that doesn't mean set theory is left behind. As Lacan says in *Seminar XXV*, sexual relation is like an empty set (session of 15.11.1977). Set theory helps him articulate that sexuality cannot and does not make a relation. Sexual difference is a matter of non-relation. Let's take the same example. If there is a set with an empty set and we put a 1 in it, we get this: [(Ø), 1]. This set has two elements and yet they have no relation. Any set has a default empty set inside it. All we have here is the "One all alone" or what Lacan calls "*il y a de l'Un*" (1998: 67). There is no relation between the 1 of the subject and the empty set as the Other. Responding to this debate between Badiou and Lacan, Duane Rousselle speculates about a Lacanian infinity through the topology of the Borromean knot. He goes from Lacan's knot theory to mathematical physics and discusses infinite loops in space-time. Rousselle's argument lies beyond our scope but his point about the implicit presence of actual infinity in Lacan holds true for set-theoretical infinity as well. He doesn't approach this infinity through set theory in his analysis.

Rousselle observes: "later Lacanian thought, which has been under-represented in the English literature, moves closer toward Badiou's notion of infinity by claiming that strings and other things exist outside of the finite system of buckles, points, and suture" (2017: 163). He dwells on *Seminars XXI* and *XXIII* in which Lacan emphasizes the infinite character of the strings that make the Borromean rings. Following up on the topologist Carlo H. Seqin's discovery that each ring (torus) in the Borromean chain can be made into a Borromean chain, Rousselle constructs a speculative infinity (2017: 169–70). In *Seminar XXI*, Lacan mentions Desargues and his theorem regarding the infinite point on the projective plane (session of 11.3.1975). He discusses the idea that two parallel lines meet at an infinite point. The infinite line (whether straight or not) of the string that is cut and looped into a Borromean ring and eventually a chain, returns in *Seminar XXIII* but again in a projective mode (Lacan 2016: 96). Is this an actual infinity or virtual? Though we can only project the infinity of the line, when it is looped into a ring, the ring maintains a recursive infinity. It can be made into another knot. If we plait three by three (three rings constitute the minimal Borromean chain), we can have a chain, going onto infinity. Lacan hints at a Borromean chain that consists of an infinite number of rings in *Seminar XX* (1998: 125). In *Seminar XXIII*, he defines the "true hole" as the one that is traversed by an infinite line (2016: 16). Casting the Real unconscious as a hole could itself be considered infinite in an immanent way.[4] I cannot develop this thread further, but before returning to set theory, let me say that infinity is not as inaccessible in Lacan as Badiou would have it. Let us see how Lacan thinks infinity in a set-theoretical paradigm. His debt to Cantor is more than a simple detour, unlike what Badiou has us believe.

Delving deeper into the Cantor references and the presence of set theory in *Seminar XIX* (Badiou's Lacanian source in "The Subject and Infinity"), what we find is not the 1 of sameness but the 1 that is "grounded on pure and simple difference" (Lacan 2018: 125). An empty set is called a "singleton" which means it is counted as 1 (2018: 124). This 0 counted as 1 grounds the 1 in its own lack. The 1 appears from the void. As set theory would have it, the interval between 0 and 1 is non-denumerable or uncountable. The set of real numbers between 0 and 1 is non-denumerable. So, the open interval of real numbers [0, 1] is an uncountable set. This is the 1 of difference, grounded on the aleph-nought that is the limit cardinal of the numerical infinite (2018: 125). The axiom of extensionality and the exponential function suggest that the 1 here presents its own difference from the ensuing zero. This leads Lacan to comment that "the One begins on the level at which there is one missing" (2018: 126). He has a problem with the use of "induction" in the infinite set. Instead of *inducing* the non-denumerability (no one-on-one correspondence) of the parts of the infinite set [0, 1], Lacan advocates *partitioning* the infinite set [0 /1]. He links this to the exponential function in which any number raised to the power of 0 would yield 1 or 0 as exponent produces 1 (2018: 141). This 1 emerges from the empty set which is "the reiteration of the lack" (2018: 141). Lacan makes a key distinction between "numerating" and "constructing" numbers (155). For instance, 0 and 1 enumerate 2 insofar as they are 2 numbers (0 and 1), but they cannot construct a 2, that is, $0 + 1 = 1$, not 2. There are echoes here between the Lacanian and Badiouian "non-constructibility." The 0 *as* 1 breaks the repetition of the same by invoking infinite difference between 0 and 1. Contra Badiou, this is an infinity Lacan affirms. The subject of the Real unconscious is an infinite subject, notwithstanding death-drive, just as Badiou's eventual subject is an "immortal" of the situation, despite its empirical mortality. The differences between Lacan and him are not as substantial as Badiou contends. In my reading, they are both crusaders of a mathematical modernism of infinity that goes against the modernity of finitude.

As Badiou reminds us in *Conditions* and *Logics of Worlds*, postmodernism is his arch enemy. In *Conditions*, he calls it a "sophistry" of linguistic relativism (2008b: 7–8). In *Logics*, postmodern is seen as a "democratic materialism" that believes, there are only bodies and languages and no truths (2009b: 2). As opposed to this, Badiou terms his project, "materialist dialectic." It wants to re-establish a politics of truths which stands in exception to the "culturalist" proliferation of bodies and languages. His philosophy returns to the question of the modern via a critique of modernity and its championing of finitude. We have seen the role mathematics plays in that. It opens the "materialist dialectic" up against "democratic materialism" by foregrounding the thesis of ontological infinity. As Badiou says in *Being and Event*: "nature, the moderns said, is infinite" (2005a: 143). In this case, he uses the word "modern" as "modernist" or as a "second modernity." We will return to this second modernity soon. For Badiou, being-qua-being is an infinite multiple. It holds up a "second modernity" that I would name modernism. Mathematics is the condition that delivers this ontological infinity.

In *Number and Numbers*, Badiou marks the break between Greek and modern number theory in terms of the infinite, the one and the zero. He argues that the modern concept of number has to revise the ancient Greek thinking on the end point of a number series. Can this limit be a number? Is it a one or a zero or a collection of numerical units? Here we return to what Lacan calls the ambiguity between 1 and 0. Badiou reflects, "how to *number* unity, if the One that supports it is void? This problem is so complex that, as we shall see, it remains today the key to a modern thinking of number" (Badiou 2008a: 8). The problem is the following: if 1 is built on 0, how do we think about its unifying function? It is from here that Badiou arrives at the evental multiplicity of being as infinity: "We find ourselves under the jurisdiction of an epoch that *obliges* us to hold that being is essentially multiple. Consequently, number cannot proceed from the supposition of a transcendent being of the One" (Badiou 2008a: 8). What breaks this transcendental 1 is the evental ontology of infinite multiplicity. This is the task of mathematical modernism or what Badiou calls the "passage to a second modernity" (2008a: 13):

> Modernity is defined by the fact that the One is not [. . .]. So, for we moderns (or "free spirits"), the Multiple-without-One is the last word on being qua being. Now the thought of the pure multiple, of the multiple considered in itself, without consideration of what it is the multiple of (so: without consideration of any *object* whatsoever), is called: "mathematical set theory." Therefore every major concept of this theory can be understood as a concept of modern ontology. (2008a: 65)

Badiou's mathematical modernism, unlike modern finitude, begins with the infinite and sees the finite as the product of infinity. As he puts it in *The Immanence of Truths*: "*the finite is generally the result of the operative intersection between two infinities of different types* (of different sizes)" (2022: 21; emphasis original). Mathematical modernism declares that infinity exists in the form of number, in the existence of a "limit ordinal" (2008a: 82). It is the achievement of set theory that we have this actual infinity. We move from the zero of the empty set to the succession function and finally to a limit ordinal that doesn't succeed any one particular ordinal but "succeed *all* the ordinals of the sequence of which they are the limit" (2008a: 85). We cannot *deduce* this limit. We have to *decide* on it. This decisionism is central to what Badiou considers modern ("second modernity" or modernist) in mathematics:

> The modern instance of this movement attests to the void and the infinite as materials for the thinking of Number. Nevertheless, none of these concepts can be inferred from experience, nor do they propose themselves to any intuition, or submit to any deduction, even a transcendental one. None of them amounts to the form of an object, or of objectivity. These concepts arise from a *decision*, whose written form is the axiom; a decision that reveals the opening of a new epoch for the thought of being qua being. (2008a: 212)

Badiou's mathematics of infinity *decides* upon a limit that opens itself up to the infinity of the Real and remains staunchly anti-rationalist. Other than the materialist politics of this anti-instrumentalist manipulation of mathematics to formalize ontological infinity, how do we think about the relation between mathematics and politics?

The ontologically infinite subject is consistent with the collective political subject of interruptive eventality in Badiou.

Mathematics with Politics?

When we shift from science to politics as conditions for philosophy, how does mathematical modernism rewrite itself in Badiou's reading of Lacan? This will be our question for what follows. In his seminar on Lacan as anti-philosopher, delivered in 1994–5, Badiou critiques Lacan's axiom from "L'Etourdit" that mathematics is the only science to block the philosopher. Philosophy gets blocked by mathematics: "[e]ven if it knows mathematics, it doesn't understand it" (Badiou 2018: 30). Badiou picks up the second axiom which goes, metaphysics "can only continue by plugging the hole of politics" (Lacan qtd in Badiou 2018: 35). The context for Lacan's axiom is Heidegger's critique of metaphysics. Though the axiom of philosophy getting blocked by mathematics and metaphysics plugging the hole of politics are two unrelated statements in Lacan, Badiou brings them into a liaison. He asks: "[i]s it because one plugs the hole of politics that one is blocked by mathematics" or is it the other way round? (36). He departs from Lacan by arguing that philosophy since Plato has always unblocked mathematics. For Badiou, mathematics is blocked by itself as a thought "because it is essential for it to be aware of its own ontological significance" (36–7). This point resonates with his crucial claim in *Being and Event* that ontology (which *is* mathematics) doesn't know the event: "[t]here is no acceptable ontological matrix of the event" (Badiou 2005a: 190) or "ontology does not recognize any event" (Badiou 2005a: 356). As stated above, this exteriority of the event vis-à-vis mathematics makes mathematics into an opening toward the infinity of the Real. This mathematics of infinity is irreducible to instrumental rationality. Its evental orientation moreover creates a political slant of the Real. We will soon return to this point. Mathematics blocking itself is no news for Lacan by the way. As mentioned earlier, for Lacan, mathematics is a passage to the Real that creates an impasse in mathematical formalization. Once again, Badiou's disagreement hides an agreement.

In Badiou's view, the typical move of the anti-philosopher is to cancel mathematics as a thought but unlike Wittgenstein and Nietzsche (two other anti-philosophers he discusses), Lacan doesn't do that. For anti-philosophy, mathematics is only "grammar" or "logic" but not a "thought" (Badiou 2018: 94). For Lacan though (here I agree with Badiou), mathematics is thought or even "the only possible science of the real" (Badiou 2018: 94). This is where Badiou invokes the "matheme" as an "archi-scientific act" in Lacan (95). He mentions Lacan's engagement with the "impasse of the mathematizable" (95) to explain Lacan's acknowledgment of mathematics as thought. And yet Badiou doesn't admit that in Lacan, mathematics blocks itself in this very impasse. He extracts from "L'Etourdit," the next axiom that in mathematics, "the said renews itself by using a saying rather than any reality" (95). This axiom makes mathematics autonomous qua reality. Mathematics is a matter of saying and said; it is "free of meaning" insofar as the said can be integrally transmitted. As Badiou observes, for Lacan, meaning is always religious and mathematics is the opposite of religion as it eats away meaning (98). Mathematical modernism shows its political color here by taking a stand against the religious consecration of meaning.

Badiou answers Lacan by maintaining that the philosopher gets blocked by mathematics because they "try to ground it where it is not, in the consciousness/reality dyad" (100). Mathematics is about the saying–said relation whereas the philosopher makes the false attempt of trying to ground it in reality and its relation to human consciousness. Badiou proceeds to read a consonance between Plato for whom mathematics is a "prescription of saying" and Lacan who grounds mathematics in axiomatic saying (102–104). Badiou doesn't identify this conception of mathematics as said renewed by saying, with structuralism. Instead, he connects it with his own philosophy of the event: "mathematics is identified as that which [. . .] derives from the event of saying, is evental and contingent" (105). How does this evental mathematics relate to evental politics? If mathematics gets blocked by its own hole, apart from blocking philosophy, metaphysics, the classical avatar of philosophy plugs the hole. But what is this hole of politics or politics as a hole? Badiou's approach is Borromean. He goes to the three holes in the Borromean chain to talk about the politics of holes.

Badiou argues that in the imaginary incarnation, politics is a hole as it is linked with the "group imaginary"; it is an "imaginary hole in the real of capital" (110). In the atomized dispersal of capitalism, politics creates an imaginary hole via the group or the community and this hole produces meaning, which is religious. Badiou calls this politics as "Church Effect" (110). It is an imaginary hole in the real, as Badiou says with extended comparisons between Marx and Lacan and how the latter imitated the former. The group (e.g., the proletariat) wins over the discourse in this imaginary politics (116). To move to the second incarnation, Badiou approaches politics as a Symbolic hole in the "imaginary consistency of discourse" (117). As he notes, politics is not a discourse in Lacan, certainly not one of his four fundamental discourses (hysteric's, analyst's, master's and the university). Politics punches holes in any discourse (117). Following Lacan, Badiou calls politics, a practice (evental) that is, the Marxist idea of revolution, that dislodges the "dominant ideology" and its "imaginary coalescences" (122). Politics here becomes a knowledge-function that can work in "indifference to the particularity of those using it" (122). This is why politics is beyond individuals and personalities. The third and final avatar of the hole in politics is the Real hole in the Symbolic or in the law. These evental ideas of politics make it function as an act of subversion, insurrection and rupture. The three holes of politics are Borromean: Imaginary hole in the Real, Symbolic hole in the Imaginary and Real hole in the Symbolic. Badiou's omission of the central Borromean hole at the heart of the triadic chain is crucial. Strangely, the "inviolable hole" (Lacan *Seminar XXII*: session of 11.3.1975) of the knot where the *object-a* is located has no politics for Badiou. This is the hole that partakes of the three orders of the unconscious: R-S-I. Is there no politics attached to this hole that houses the new object-cause of desire, generated by the psychoanalytic act? If this is a new quilting point around which a new subjectivity takes shape, this external object that doesn't pre-exist analysis produces its own politics of subjectivity.

Badiou locates a discourse without holes that plugs the hole of politics. Philosophy in its metaphysical form is this hole-less discourse. What does it mean for anti-philosophy not to plug the hole of politics? Is there an anti-philosophical radical politics? Badiou pursues this line of inquiry by talking about the political history of psychoanalytic groups and institutions and Lacan's Marxian move to dissolve his own school in 1980. He concludes by claiming that "the hole of politics is unpluggable" (132) and anti-philosophical politics opens it up. Though he feels that Lacanian politics isn't much more than a disbanding act, it is nevertheless a politics of dissensus.[5] In Badiou's surprising formulation, there is no politics of the Real in Lacan, except the hole that metaphysical philosophy plugs. However, as we have seen, the Real as anarchic impasse is political in Lacan as much as it is eventual (a formalization *encountering* its own impasse). It is at this level of the event that the mathematics of infinity becomes political. But for Badiou, there is no Lacanian politics and only political philosophy. In his observation, political organizations are actually philosophical organizations (184). Badiou's conclusion contradicts his previous point about politics as a Real hole in the Symbolic, or an eventual encounter with the void of the situation, to use Badiou's language. His interpretation is paradoxical, if not antinomic: anti-philosophy opens up politics and yet there is no politics in Lacan's anti-philosophy but only a political philosophy. Badiou, I suspect, strategically denies a politics of the Real in Lacan as it stands perilously close to his own political philosophy of the event.

It is against this Lacanian political philosophy that Badiou sets out his "metapolitics." In this orientation, philosophy cannot think politics in its own terms but politics has to drive and condition philosophy. In "metapolitics," philosophy becomes an effect of politics (Badiou 2005b: 55). Though he talks more about infinity in his mathematical ontology, the infinite is not absent from his thinking of politics. The situation in politics is ontologically infinite and Badiou calls this a "stake peculiar to all politics" (21). And then there is a second infinity, that of the state of the situation. This is an "errant" infinity insofar as the state thinks it's infinitely superior to the political situation (22). For Badiou, "every politics of emancipation rejects finitude," death and "summons or exhibits the infinity of the situation" (142). The event in politics is an infinite happening that "fixes" the errant infinity of the state of the situation. This fixing, as he carefully notes, is not a finitude, but a liminal infinity. The event that breaks oneness by supplementing being, makes a shift from an indeterminate infinite cardinal number to a determinate infinite cardinal number (147–8). We move from indeterminate to determinate infinity. For Badiou, infinity is key to political modernism, as much as it is pivotal for mathematical modernism. On this infinite point politics and mathematics meet.

The Immanence of Truths is concerned with the absoluteness of the "work of truth" that produces a finite from two infinities. It is in this absoluteness that politics and mathematics join hands. Badiou maintains that "the universality of mathematics is simply its absoluteness because it has no special character other than being itself its own world" (2022: 512). The absoluteness of mathematics surpasses the other absolutes. Mathematics is intrinsically absolute and doesn't need what Badiou calls an "index" to mark its absoluteness. This for him is its difference with politics that has an "index" of absoluteness in the proper names like Mao and Robespierre (565). Unlike mathematics which *is* its own world with possible forms of multiple-beings, other works of truth operate in "determinate worlds" and therefore require an index of absoluteness to break through the covering-up (512). Politics operates in the determinate world and requires an index but mathematics doesn't. Other than this difference, they are infinite as well as absolute. Their shared absoluteness connects them as much as their shared infinity.

I argue that the hole at the center of Lacan's Borromean chain in which Imaginary as consistency, Real as ex-sistence and Symbolic as the hole—come together, is a rupture that designates a Lacanian politics of infinity. As seen earlier, in his discussion of politics as hole in Lacan, Badiou avoids this central Borromean hole. It is in this hole that the new *object-a* comes to sit; it remakes the subject and inaugurates a new subjective infinity. If this offers a politics of infinity, it takes its support from a mathematical formalization in topological geometry. Translated into Badiou's language, this is the evental encounter with the ontological void of the situation that supplements the state and inaugurates a new situation. This evental supplement produces a new figure of the infinite that is political. It is held in the mathematical structure of set theory (being-qua-being) in *Being and Event* and in the mathematical form of category-theory (being-qua-appearing) in *Logics of Worlds*.

As early as *Theory of the Subject*, we can spot this twin point of mathematics and politics, having an encounter in Badiou via Lacan. In these seminars delivered from 1975 to 1979, Badiou executes a political translation of Lacanian theoretical and clinical practice. To give one relevant example, he reads the Borromean chain of three as a triangulation of state, classes and masses where they have no one-on-one relation and yet the three are striated (see Badiou 2009a: 224–33). Masses for him are a historical name of the Real by which we never understand a substance (228). Citing the Lacan of *Seminar XX*, Badiou situates Borromean topology as a materialist thesis of dialectics (230). Politics, once formalized in a mathematical way, is a philosophical condition that deals with impasses in history via the cut of the event. This is where Badiou's half-silent partnership with Lacan takes on a continuity in mathematical and political modernisms.

Let me end with a splicing of the mathematical and the political modernisms in Lacan. In *Seminar XX*, he identifies "modern science" (in the context of set theory) with the insight that the One and the Other cannot be knotted (1998: 128). We have seen how mathematics supports this thesis of non-rapport [0, 1]. In *Seminar V*, he connects this instability of the Other with "modern politics" in which the Other is an "embodied" Other qua law (2017: 438). The signifier cuts into the Other, bars it, but cannot create a rapport between the Subject (1) and the Other (∅). This has ramifications for both political and mathematical modernisms. The politics of social non-relation is the agonism of capitalist modernity that casts its shadow on mathematics.

To conclude, this collaborative invocation of Badiou with Lacan illuminates Badiou's underplayed debt to Lacan. The return to Lacan underlines the way in which political and mathematical modernisms relate to one another in the shared figures of the evental infinity of the Real, the void and the subject as an ambivalence between zero and the infinite. Badiou mobilizes a mathematico-political modernism of infinity to counter the capitalist modernity of finitude. But as *The Immanence of Truths* would have it, there is another finitude. It resides in the post-eventual work of truth that makes for its immanent absoluteness. It is this second finitude in the absolute work of truth that orients us away from the modern and toward the modernist in both politics and mathematics. The two conditions of philosophy in Badiou's system form a spectrum of modernisms. Eventual politics gets mathematically formalized. Mathematics acknowledges its edge in the deadlock of the Real that politicizes mathematical modernism by resisting instrumentalism. Badiou's mathematics of infinity and aleatoric eventality occludes a debt to Lacan's politics of the Real. The infinity of the event as a figure of the Real helps us grasp the politics of mathematical modernisms that is open to the uncertainty of change.

Notes

1. This thesis remains consistent from *Conditions* to *The Immanence of Truths*. We will spot it in *Conditions* as we go on. The phrase "the modern finitude" ["la finitude modern"] (375) recurs in *The Immanence of Truths*. See section 2 of chapter C7 in which Badiou sees modernity as a process of "covering" the infinite with the finite: "Modernity means using a new operator, which, rather than highlighting the falseness of everything that touches the infinite, instead covers it over with finite debris, with a solid layer of waste materials, so that any potential infinity, wiped out this way, becomes incomprehensible" (181).
2. See section II, chapter C9, "The Ontology of Covering-over" in *The Immanence of Truths*.
3. For more on the letter as a littoral, see Lacan's 1971 text "Lituraterre." (Lacan 2013).
4. I have made some developments on the Real Unconscious as infinite in my book, *Beckett, Lacan and the Mathematical Writing of the Real* (Chattopadhyay 2019).
5. See section IX, chapter C26 of *The Immanence of Truths* for a definition of infinite politics as a "non-consensual discussion about politics itself" (2022: 555).

Works Cited

Badiou, A. (2005a), *Being and Event*, trans. O. Feltham, London and New York: Continuum.
Badiou, A. (2005b), *Metapolitics*, trans. J. Barker, London and New York: Verso.
Badiou, A. (2005c), *Handbook of Inaesthetics*, trans. A. Toscano, Stanford: Stanford University Press.
Badiou, A. (2008a), *Number and Numbers*, trans. R. Mackay, Cambridge: Polity.
Badiou, A. (2008b), *Conditions*, trans. S. Corcoran, London and New York: Bloomsbury.
Badiou, A. (2009a), *Theory of the Subject*, trans. B. Bosteels, London and New York: Continuum.
Badiou, A. (2009b), *Logics of Worlds: Being and Event II*, trans. A. Toscano, London and New York: Continuum.

Badiou, A. (2018), *Lacan: Anti-Philosophy 3*, trans. K. Reinhard and S. Spitzer, New York: Columbia University Press.

Badiou, A. (2022), *The Immanence of Truths: Being and Event III*, trans. K. Reinhardt and S. Spitzer, London and New York: Bloomsbury.

Chattopadhyay, A. (2019), *Beckett, Lacan and the Mathematical Writing of the Real*, London and New York: Bloomsbury.

Descartes, R. (1985), *The Philosophical Writings*, trans. J. Cottingham et al., London and New York: Cambridge University Press.

Gray, J (2008), *Plato's Ghost: The Modernist Transformation of Mathematics*, Princeton and Oxford: Princeton University Press.

Kant, I. (1998), *Critique of Pure Reason*, trans. and ed. P. Guyer and A. Wood, Cambridge: Cambridge University Press.

Lacan, J. (1998), *The Seminar of Jacques Lacan: Book XX On Feminine Sexuality: The Limits of Love and Knowledge 1972-73: Encore*, trans. R. Grigg, ed. J.-A. Miller, London and New York: Norton.

Lacan, J. (unpublished), *Seminar XXII 1974–75: RSI*, trans. C. Gallagher. Available online: http://www.lacaninireland.com/web/wp-content/uploads/2010/06/RSI-Complete-With-Diagrams.pdf (accessed January 20, 2022).

Lacan, J. (2013), "Lituraterre," trans. B. Khiara-Foxton and A. R. Price, *Hurly Burly* 9, 29–38.

Lacan, J. (2016), *The Seminar of Jacques Lacan: Book XXIII: The Sinthome*, trans. A. R. Price, ed. J.-A. Miller, Cambridge: Polity.

Lacan, J. (2017), *The Seminar of Jacques Lacan: Book V: Formations of the Unconscious*, trans. R. Grigg, ed. J.-A. Miller, Cambridge: Polity.

Lacan, J. (2018), *The Seminar of Jacques Lacan: Book XIX: Or Worse*, trans. A. R. Price, ed. J.-A. Miller, Cambridge: Polity.

Rousselle, D. (2017), *Lacanian Realism: Political and Clinical Psychoanalysis*, London and New York: Bloomsbury.

6

Badiou and Mad Love

Arthur Rose

"Love," insists Arthur Rimbaud in his 1873 poem *Une Saison en Enfer*, "needs re-inventing" (Badiou 2012: epigraph). Presented as epigraph to the conversation between Alain Badiou and Nicolas Truong published as *Éloge de l'amour*, it serves as a thesis statement for Badiou's efforts to defend love—one of the four conditions upon which philosophy operates to access its truths—against two threats. The first of these is the "safety threat," promised by online dating apps, which offers "love comprehensively insured against all risks": a love with "nothing random, no chance encounters" (Badiou and Truong 2012: 8; 6). The second denies love's importance and, by extension, the challenge it poses through the "experience of otherness from which love is woven" (Badiou and Truong 2012: 8). Such denial dismisses love in favor of a hedonistic satisfaction of desire. Both positions threaten love as the preservation of an "infinite" difference between two subjects (Badiou and Rousselle 2019: 15). Love mobilizes the means "to make this experiment in difference endure and to increase its scope" (2019: 15). It presents "the world seen by two, according to the two, from the radical duality that fits into two subjects" (Badiou and Rousselle 2019: 15). But it is not enough, Badiou argues, to react to these threats by returning to an earlier concept of love. Love needs re-inventing because "the world is full of new developments and love must also be something that innovates. Risk and adventure must be re-invented against safety and comfort" (Badiou and Truong 2012: 11).

The reinvention of love itself is, of course, a matter for lovers, not philosophers: philosophy, for Badiou, works not to generate truths but, in Justin Clemens's summary, to "transliterate the operations of the conditions [like love] into philosophical jargon [and] by means of such a transliteration [. . .] construct its own 'idea'" (2006: 287). To manage this transliteration, philosophy demands the traces of such operations. But such traces cannot simply be treated as examples; they constitute works, or "a finite, but dynamic, fragment of [a truth] procedure" (Badiou 2022: 451). As Clemens notes, "when reduced to examples, truths are no longer *conditions of* but *objects for* philosophy; as objects, however, these truths cannot support philosophy in the way that it requires; without such support, philosophy collapses into a 'theory' of the logic of appearances" (2006: 278). Understood as works, such examples necessarily affect the philosophy they are harnessed to explain.

What does it mean, then, to invoke Rimbaud as a point of departure for a discussion of love, or, further, to develop an analysis of love using *Une Saison* as a trace of the poet's relationship with Verlaine? What role does "Rimbaud" play as a proper noun that discloses, in addition to the philosophical insights Badiou gleans from him, two distinct "works": a poetic oeuvre and the record of an amorous relationship? Andrew Gibson, writing of Badiou's tendency to read Mallarmé in philosophical terms, observes how his commitment to "an unrelentingly affirmative vision of philosophy" obstructs the possibility of seeing "not how art might contradict his thought, but how it might modulate it, temper it, lend it other intonations" (2006: 116). Sigi Jöttkandt has taken up this challenge to address literature that turns around the conceit of "first love" (2010a: 7). To add a further turn of the screw, literary examples, themselves, add a layer of obfuscation to discussions about love, since their descriptions of love are objects not just for philosophy but for art. *Une saison* is first and foremost a poem; to read it as an account of a love encounter without accounting for its aesthetics cannot but fail to appreciate the way that encounter has modified the poet's understanding of the world.

Badiou generally adopts one of two approaches to this problem in his discussions of love: either he reconstitutes the cultural object as a story that can be told as a linear narrative of two lovers (as in his treatment of Berlioz's *Les Troyennes* in *Logics of Worlds*) or he construes the object as presenting a metalanguage for discussing love's functional parts. The latter is evident in his reading of Samuel Beckett's *Comment c'est*, which turns the narrator's encounter with Pim into an allegory for love's functions (Badiou 2008: 251). This, as we will see, allows Badiou to elaborate on the disjunctive functions of the couple. But it comes at the cost of a certain reflexivity. If "love, as an experience of thought, does not think itself [*s'impense*]," then capturing its unreflective thought cannot be followed through its functions (Badiou 2000: 266). To approach a writing that tries to avoid thinking itself (doomed as that effort obviously is), I want to suggest that "Rimbaud," when taken together with other aphorisms in *Éloge* by "Pessoa," "Aragon" and "Breton," highlights a genealogy of surrealist writing in Badiou's thinking about love. To understand love in Badiou, I argue, we might do well to examine his relationship with surrealism.

In what follows, I give a short précis of Badiou's philosophical account of love, developed in earlier essays "The Writing of the Generic," "What Is Love?" and "The Scene of the Two," the seminar translated as *The Century* through *In Praise of Love*, *Logics of Worlds* and *The Immanence of Truths*. As is often pointed out, this account depends on Badiou's relationship with Lacan and psychoanalysis, where the philosophy of love becomes a science through discussions of transference. But these topics have been admirably treated elsewhere.[1] Instead, I take the central, if superficial, use of Rimbaud in *Éloge*, together with passing references to Fernando Pessoa and André Breton, as an excuse to return to Badiou's brief account of surrealism, there and in *The Century*. It is my contention that surrealism offers Badiou a mode of thinking about love that he risks covering over in his comments. Despite acknowledging that surrealism takes "love as a magnificent poem of the encounter" he ultimately dismisses the movement for having "little interest in that which endured" (2012: 79). By returning to the surrealist texts that Badiou references, I hope to show how love is not merely limited to a miraculous encounter; it presents "the onerous development of a truth that is constructed point by point" (2012: 81). Love, for Badiou, is not only modern but modernist and surrealist. Or, as the surrealists themselves would write, "if you love LOVE, you will love SURREALISM" (Ades and Richardson 2016: 172).

Badiou on Surrealism

Badiou's occasional comments on surrealism suggest complex feelings. On the one hand, there is undoubtable admiration for its political importance as a movement and its aesthetic significance as a program, especially in the work of its sometime leader, André Breton. In *The Century*, Badiou singles out surrealism as exemplary modernist avant-gardes, and Breton in particular, for his development of the manifesto as a genre: "Who more than he, within the century, bound the promises of the new art to the political form of the Manifesto?" (Badiou 2007a: 142). Here, too, he develops a close reading of Breton's later text, *Arcanum 17*, which he praises for "posit[ing] the self-sufficiency of rebellion and the indifference to the pragmatic calculus of results" (Badiou 2007a: 142): "Rebellion is its own justification, completely independent of the chance it has to modify the state of affairs that gives rise to it" (Breton 2004: 89). He also devotes a third of the session on Duchamp in his 2007 seminar to dissecting a single phrase from Breton's 1922 essay on the artist (Badiou 2007b). Most telling, Badiou acknowledges in *Éloge* that "[t]he central Surrealist project was the one we mentioned at the very beginning, namely, following Rimbaud's injunction, to re-invent love" (Badiou 2012: 77). There is, then, in surrealism, as Badiou understands it, a recuperation of Rimbaud's phrase that makes it comparable to his own project on love.

On the other hand, he remains notably critical of surrealism as a project. It endorses "an aristocratic idealism" in his preface to *Logics of Worlds*, preserving "the hope that the intellectual and existential splendours of the past will not be abolished," despite the inevitability that such an endeavor must fail "because it has no chance of being effective" (Badiou 2009: 3). In its adherence to "the Manifesto," it remains committed to "a rhetorical device serving to protect something other than what it overtly names or announces," which fails to incorporate its "real artistic activity" (Badiou 2007a: 138). Again, the most important criticisms for our purposes relate to surrealism's efforts to reinvent love. It suffers from its tendency to think of the reinvention of love as "indissolubly an artistic, existential and political move" that makes no "divisions between the three" (Badiou 2012: 78). Perhaps because he needs to insist on the differences between their project and his own, Badiou explains this further in *The Century*:

> Surrealism was a step in this reconstruction of love as an arena for truth, of love as the procedure that produces a truth of difference. Only a step though, for surrealism still remains in thrall to sexual mythologies that revolve around a fatal and mysterious femininity, the one found walking through the streets of the metropolis, naked under her mantle of fur. (Badiou 2007a: 145)

Surrealism takes a step toward the understanding of love that Badiou wants to develop, which thinks love "not as destiny, but as encounter and thought, as an asymmetrical and egalitarian becoming" (Badiou 2007a: 145). "But," he clarifies, this is "only a step" because the movement is stymied by a unilateral male vision, even if it manages to capture something of the transformation of the world by the Two: "a world refracted and transfigured by contrast" (Badiou 2007a: 145).

Badiou's ambivalence begs the question where the fault lines lie between the two attempts to reinvent love. In so doing, it also offers a suggestive convolute for his relationship with both love and modernism. As much Badiou commentary has made clear, psychoanalysis plays a crucial role in Badiou's efforts to apply a scientific frame to the analysis of love (Jöttkandt 2010b; Park 2021). To clarify these concepts, his examples have often been culled from texts where representation may be taken as a form of realism: the nineteenth-century novel (Badiou 2000), for instance, or Hector Berlioz's *Les Troyennes* (Badiou 2009: 28–33). For all that the "great love stories" are admitted to Badiou's philosophical category of love, "like a syntax made from its semantic fields" (Badiou 2000: 265), these examples remain purely illustrative and unable to challenge Badiou's psychoanalytic "syntax." Badiou's ambivalence over surrealism, however, offers an example that does influence this syntax, insofar as it presents Badiou with both examples of the love encounter and an attempt to think these encounters across artistic and scientific discourses. To understand how, I return to Badiou's thinking on love.

Badiou on Love

In Praise of Love stresses that love is a matter of risk that enables an experience of otherness. In Badiou's more analytical texts about love, the definition becomes more complicated:

> A love encounter is what assigns, eventually, to the atomic and unanalyzable intersection of two sexed positions a double function: that of the object, in which a desire finds its cause, and that of a point from which the Two can be counted, thereby launching a shared investigation of the world. (2022: 538)

To arrive at this definition, Badiou begins by recalling the supplemental role played by love in Jacques Lacan's famous observation that "Il n'y a pas de rapport sexuel [there is no such thing as a sexual relationship]" (2022: 530). "At the very point of the vanishing relationship between the sexes if they are focused only on sex," glosses Badiou, "love can create a relationship, a bond, a connection [. . .] inscribing [. . .] [human beings'] natural materiality into what overdetermines it in terms of language, symbolism, signification" (2022: 530). Love, by this reading, is a compensatory mechanism that rehabilitates the sexual non-relationship by attributing to it a symbolic value: the Two. My desire for an other often stems from attributing to them some aspect that I feel lacking in myself (Lacan's *objet a*). Love, then, names the moment my desire for that part of the other is subsumed into a desire for them as a whole person. It is symbolic and compensatory since, as a matter of pure sexuality, it may be explained away as mere misrecognition: to make my sexual attraction socially acceptable, I call it love. Badiou is clear, however, that this misses Lacan's true insight, which is to insist on the point that there is no sexual relationship. Sexual pleasure remains narcissistic, and therefore an emotional separation of two people rather than the joining together implied by their physical intimacy. There is no relationship as such in sex. For Lacan, love replaces this non-relation, by presenting an attempt to "approach 'the being of the other'" (2012: 19). In the amorous encounter, "you go to take on the other, to make him or her exist with you, as he or she is" (2012: 19). Love, thus, does not properly exist in the situation of sexuality, which is why it is, in Badiou's parlance, an event, that inconsistent multiplicity whose inconsistency is what refuses to make sense within the situation as it is represented. When this event can be named by the subject produced by it—the lovers, who name it by saying "I love you"—it becomes the means of embarking upon a truth procedure: the tracing of the love-events effects on the situation, point by point. In this sense, then, love demands "the object, in which a desire finds its cause" by starting from a narcissistic desire for something that completes me, but also exceeds that object by turning it into a shared investigation of the world.

Of course, there exist many justifications for love that might reconcile it with the situation of sexuality, either by asserting sexuality's dominance (the dominance of the object) or of its mystical transcendental effects (the irrelevance of the object). Badiou explicitly rejects three justifications in his earlier essay, "What Is Love?," as potentially harmful for our understanding of love as the "production of truth" (2000: 266). As has already been suggested, the first highlights love as an illusion, the effect of a "superstructural" bid to render sex more acceptable (2000: 265). This is a position that Lacan "skirts," but ultimately, and paradoxically, contradicts when he also "accords to love an ontological vocation" (2000: 265–6). A second focuses on the "fusion" of two bodies into one through the sexual encounter, a maneuver that suppresses "the multiple" constituted by the love-event by insisting on the primacy of the One that is realized in the moment of ecstasy. The third assumes love to be the "prostration of the Same on the altar of the Other" (2000: 265). In this conception, love is explained by an experience of the Other, rather than, as Badiou would have it, "an experience of the world, or of the situation, under the post-eventual condition that there were Two" (2000: 265). Less a product of sex than the experience of difference, this "ablative" understanding of love shares the mysticism of the "fusional" encounter but turns it outwards to make of love an origin point for ethics. In the *Éloge*, Badiou adds a fourth understanding of love, in which sex is not explicitly mentioned, but which might be understood to be the confirmation of love treated as a contract "between two free individuals [who] never forget the necessary equality of the relationship, the system of mutual benefits etc." (2012: 22) Against these four positions, Badiou will assert that love's equation with relation misses its role as the producer of truth, in which it creates the Two within itself rather than fusing a prior two into one, as an experience of the world, not the Other, in a way that destabilizes the individualities of the parties supposedly "contracted" to it.

In Sigi Jöttkandt's useful summary, "Badiou's concept of an uncounted Two is his stunning contribution to the philosophical dilemma of unity and difference" because it proposes "a space that has been purified of the object relation" (Jöttkandt 2010b: 78). He arrives at this solution by presenting four theses:

1. There are two positions of experience.
2. The two positions are absolutely disjunct.
3. There is no third position.
4. There is only one humanity. (Badiou 2000: 266–7).

Since love is a universal truth, it is indifferent to the particularity of the experience: it is supported by a common humanity. Nevertheless, this humanity is simply the ground from which truths emerge. It cannot verify the love, which, following our discussion of Lacan, relies purely on the two lovers and no third position. Moreover, these two positions themselves are absolutely separate and sexed. The sexed positions, which Badiou labels man and woman, are presented in "What Is Love?" as "strictly nominalist" identities: "there is no question here of an empirical, biological, or social distribution" (Badiou 2000: 266). In other words, Badiou uses these terms as formal positions of relation, rather than making essential claims about sex or gender.[2] This explains why he criticizes surrealism for its mystification of the feminine: it essentializes the sexes, while also rendering these qualities transcendental. And yet, when it comes to the four amorous functions that he uses to identify his nominalist identities, there is perhaps more similarity to the surrealist project than he might like.

The two sexuated positions are distinguished by their adherence to particular functions: a wandering function as opposed to an immobility function, and an imperative function as opposed to a story function. The source of these functions is, Badiou makes clear, the work of Samuel Beckett, which "think[s] the thought of love" (Badiou 2000: 275). Badiou axiomatically defines the "man" position as that which "couples the imperative and immobility" and the "woman" position as that which "couples wandering and storytelling": "man is he (or she) who does nothing [. . .] because he holds that what he has valued once can continue to be valued without having to attest it," whereas "woman is she (or he) who makes love travel, and who desires that her speech constantly reiterate and renovate itself" (Badiou 2000: 276). As Jöttkandt observes in a perceptive account of Badiou's thinking of love in relation to change, the functions appear to fix the positions of the sexuated positions internally: even if the "man" position may be a woman, or vice versa, the relation between wandering and storytelling or imperative and immobility are stuck together (Jöttkandt 2018). Their ways of "going" (wandering and immobility) correspond directly to forms of saying (story and imperative), which fixes them to a particular position in the symbolic. But, while Jöttkandt finds an excellent resolution to this problem in Badiou's pedagogy (a desire to teach desire), my own reasons for raising it are somewhat simpler. In both *Nadja* and *Mad Love* the discussions of love *within* the texts—their immobile imperatives—are counterpointed by the sudden arrival or departure of the lover, whose wanderings seem either to confirm the truth of their love or call it into question, while the insistence on the longevity of a single declaration of love by Breton is contrasted with the iterated declarations by Nadja or Jacqueline Lamba. As much as Badiou's philosophy of love might be inflected by surrealism, there is also a reciprocal benefit to reading surrealism via Badiou's philosophy of love.

Surrealism's "Mad Love"

To understand the continuities between Badiou and surrealism on the matter of love, we need to know what love means for surrealism. Badiou takes us some of the way when he observes that Breton's concept of "l'amour fou" or "mad love" describes "the moment when an event breaks through existence," an "event," moreover, "that is beyond any law," wherein only the lovers "possess that difference by which they experience the world" (Badiou 2012: 79). On the face of things, Badiou finds much in common between Breton's project and his own: the problems, as already demonstrated, lie in not following through ("Conversely, they had little interest in that which endured" [Badiou 2012: 79]) and in an understanding of love that is excessively politicized. Whereas for the surrealists, love will be the basis for aesthetic and political revolution, Badiou remarks to Fabien Tarby that "love begins where politics ends": because politics aims to produce a unity between different groups, it "goes [. . .] from diversity to the same, whereas love consists, on the contrary, in constructing a difference that is accepted as a unique path" (2013: 41). But, perhaps a more fruitful point of departure may be found in their mutual concern, though said some seventy years apart, that love in the contemporary situation—adroitly phrased by Mark Steven as "love in the time of Capital"—is under threat (Steven 2018).

In *Mad Love*, his 1937 text about encountering his second wife, Jacqueline Lamba, Breton would rearticulate a conceit that had been central to surrealism since the publication of the First Manifesto in 1924: "It is the whole modern conception of love which should be reexamined such as is commonly but transparently expressed in phrases like 'love at first sight' and 'honeymoon'" (1987: 53). Earlier in the text, he had clarified this process of reexamination, which would be engineered by surrealist means, stemmed from

> a need to reconcile the idea of unique love with its more or less sure denial in the present social framework, the need to prove that a solution, more than sufficient, indeed in excess of the vital problem, can always be expected when one deserts ordinary logical attitudes. (1987: 42)

Breton's "solution," of course, recalls some of the key tenets of surrealist practice, not least the desire to use "the dream" to solve "fundamental questions of life" (1969: 12), articulated in the First Manifesto with the Hegelian quasi-credo: "I believe in the future resolution of these two states, dream and reality, which are seemingly so contradictory, into a kind of absolute reality, a *surreality*" (1969: 14). To achieve this resolution, the surrealists turned to the use of automatic writing and surrealist objects, "by which one proposes to express," Breton writes, "the actual functioning of thought. Dictated by thought in the absence of any control exercised by reason, exempt from any aesthetic or moral concern" (1969: 26). In this respect, love appears to be a topic on which surrealist practice might operate, but hardly something distinguishable from other forms of avant-gardism in the 1920s, which also found in a commitment to open relationships and free love the means to refuse conformity.

From this unprepossessing beginning, Dawn Ades and Michael Richardson argue, "love, sex and the erotic become fundamental preoccupations [for Surrealism] in a sequence of publications [...] through the 1920s and 1930s, which attempt to lay bare the theoretical grounds for their attitudes to love" (2016: 172). When Badiou refers to surrealism, it is clear he is thinking of Breton himself, but it was a much bigger project for the movement, not only in "the profusion of extraordinary erotic texts that appear during 1928 and 1929" (Ades and Richardson 2016: 176) but in its efforts to create a pseudo-scientific study of love. Before we turn to the novels that trace Breton's specific love encounters—*Nadja*, *L'amour fou* and *Arcanum 17*—we might recall both the "Recherches sur la sexualité" (1928; 1930–2/Pierre 2011) and the "Enquête sur l'amour" (1929/Pierre 2011) that appeared in the last two issues of *La Révolution Surréaliste*. In this respect, we can find an analogy, if not a congruence, with Badiou's own efforts to develop a "pure logic" for love (2000: 266). For, although the pseudo-scientific methods adopted by the surrealists were precisely psychological, which Badiou identifies as the source of "the relative poverty" in philosophical declarations about love (2000: 266), they also attempted to subtract love from its relation to the more general erotic. As Breton would say in the Sixth Session of the Recherches, "the whole point of this investigation is, in love, to establish what part belongs to sexuality" (Pierre 2011: 134).

The Recherches were a series of twelve conversations held in 1928 and then more intermittently from 1930 to 1932 between Breton and other key members of the surrealist movement. They sought, through frank and intimate conversation, to unearth the "the most basic facts of love" (Pierre 2011: 100). Inspired by the revolution in scientific approaches to sexuality inaugurated by both psychoanalysis and sexology, the conversations were Breton's attempt to gather evidence that would prove, in Dawn Ades's words, "both desire and *jouissance* in the union that marked this supreme experience of life were truly reciprocal" (Ades 2011: 266). This concern is well illustrated in the opening question of the first discussion, which interrogated the female orgasm. Of course, the investigations were a failure in every scientific sense: even at the time, Pierre Naville and Louis Aragon observed that the decision to exclude women undermined any claim to scientific credibility, while the casual misogyny and homophobia in the discussions make them difficult to read. Nevertheless, they provide an important point of comparison with Badiou, precisely because they attempt to subtract the physical dimensions of love from their relationship with desire and commitment. And while sex and sexual performance drive many of the conversations, Breton repeatedly returns them to his concern with "what it means to love a woman" (Pierre 2011: 54).

But they are also important because of their relationship to the Enquête sur l'amour. The first two Recherches appeared in the eleventh issue of *La Révolution Surréaliste*. This position was usurped by the Enquête in the twelfth, which replaced discussions of orgasms with a survey that asked the following four questions:

I. What kind of hope do you place in love?
II. How do you envisage the passage from the *idea of* love to the *fact of* loving? [...]
III. Would you [...] deprive yourself for a certain time the presence of the person you love [...]?
IV. Do you believe in the victory of love's glory over the sordidness of life [...]? (Pierre 2011: 158)

These questions and their answers were accompanied by a brief preface that acknowledged the "sudden renunciation" of "patient systematic investigation" (the Recherches) because of "a manifest fact" that "on a particular day and with a particular face, became mysteriously incarnate" (Pierre 2011: 225). But, while this does appear to withdraw into mysticism, Ades makes a compelling argument for seeing the Recherches and the Enquête in dialectical relation with each other. Following Walter Benjamin's perceptive account of surrealism's profane illumination as a dialectical relationship between materialist investigation and mystery, Ades argues that the mysterious hopes of the Enquête are grounded precisely in the material fascinations that guide the Recherches (Ades 2011: 270-1). So, in Benjamin's terms, surrealism's "dialectical optic [...] perceives the everyday as impenetrable, the impenetrable as everyday" (Benjamin 1978: 55). The Recherches and the Enquête combine the everyday matters of sexual practice with the impenetrable mysteries of love's "total attachment to another human being," which, in a telling anticipation of Badiou's terms, Breton would articulate as the "imperative recognition of truth—*our* truth 'in body and soul', the body and soul of this human being" (Pierre 2011: 225).³

While Benjamin's observations were aimed at surrealism's relationship to spiritualism, Ades is right to identify in it "the need perceived by the surrealists to maintain some form of dialectical materialism in their investigations [of love]" (Ades 2011: 271). This materialism is not simply democratic, in Badiou's somewhat pejorative use of the term. In his preface to *Logics of Worlds*, Badiou distinguishes his materialist dialectic from democratic materialism by asserting the existence of truths as exceptions to the democratic assertion that "there are only bodies and languages" (Badiou 2009: 1). In a Mallarméan turn of phrase, he supplements this assertion: "there are only bodies and languages, except that there are truths" (Badiou 2009: 4). Although the Recherches focus, with embarrassing specificity, on describing the interactions of bodies, Breton's recognition of what he calls "*our* truth" in these material bodies invites further reflection on the project's efforts to subtract love from eroticism and sex and so provide that exceptional truth. For, despite the presentation of the Recherches as a democratic acceptance of a plurality of views, they are determined by Breton's commitment to thinking love, above all through what is produced in an encounter between two lovers. When, in the First Session, he asks whether love must "necessarily be reciprocal," and Pierre Naville, Pierre Unik and Benjamin Péret each in turn demure on this point, Breton responds: "It is necessarily reciprocal" (Pierre 2011: 40). Undoubtedly a marker of Breton's domineering personality, it also marks an insistence on a particular truth that Breton attests to, despite its departure from the Sessions' focus on material relations between bodies.

This last claim is bold, but is, I think, borne out by the biographical details in Breton's life. By this point, he had met Suzanne Muzard (they met in November 1927; the First Session was held in January 1928), who was likely the "particular face" mentioned in the Enquête. He qualifies his claim about the necessity of reciprocity by admitting he had believed the opposite but "had recently changed my opinion" (Pierre 2011: 40), which seems a direct allusion to his encounter with Muzard. It is now something of a commonplace to identify Muzard as the enigmatic "you" Breton addresses himself to in the final section of *Nadja* (Polizzotti 1999: xxv), where his committed avowal of love presents a striking contrast to his equivocations about loving Nadja (Léona Delacourt) in the previous two sections, which were written before his fateful encounter with Muzard. Where Breton's narrator worries that continuing to see Nadja will be "unforgivable [. . .] if I do not love her" and questions "don't I love her" (Breton 1999: 90), this uncertainty is stripped away when he addresses Suzanne:

> All I know is that this substitution of persons stops with you, because nothing can be substituted for you, and because for me it was for all eternity that this succession of terrible or charming enigmas was to come to an end at your feet. (Breton 1999: 158)

If his fascination with Nadja was due, in part, to her enigmatic otherness, Suzanne is not only "not an enigma for me" but has "turned me from enigmas forever" (Breton 1999: 158). We might be skeptical of these claims about "eternity" and "forever." In 1934, Breton would meet Jacqueline Lamba: an encounter he would immortalize in *Mad Love*. Soon after their final separation in 1943, he would meet Elisa Bindhoff Enet, with whom he would travel to the Gaspé Peninsula in 1944 and for whom he would write *Arcanum 17* in the same year. In *Mad Love*, we find the idea of substitution repeated, a substitution that, nevertheless, "tends towards an always clearer definition of the physical aspect of the beloved," "the *last* face loved" (1987: 7). In *Arcanum 17*, he expounds on a love that, if it does not last forever, "allows itself a whole lifetime [and] only consents to find its object in one single being" (1994: 38). This repeated sloughing of prior encounters for a final, true love appears to contradict the claims that such loves are forever. Indeed, this is the problem to which Badiou alludes when he criticizes Breton for being only concerned with the encounter and never the maintenance of that encounter point by point. But this seems to mistake Breton's texts for philosophical treatises about love, when a more compelling resolution to this paradox is to think of them as documents of the love encounter itself.

By calling them documents of the love encounter, I mean that they serve as accounts of Breton's changing understanding of the relationship during the writing process. Their failure to avoid Breton's sexism, his inability to transcend his tendency to mythologize his beloved despite every effort to do so; these qualities compromise the works as novels, but they attest to their value as the necessarily one-sided understanding of love since they express the view of love as it is experienced by *one* of its parties. In *Nadja*, he makes clear the profound disconnect between the time before he met Suzanne and the time after: "If I were to reread this story," he confesses in the third section, "I hardly know, to be faithful to my present sense of myself, what I would leave standing. I do not insist on knowing" (1999: 151). At the same time, he believes that the "voice that speaks in them still seems to me to deserve a hearing," because they detail how he "lived badly or well [. . .] in the hopes [that Nadja] left me" (1999: 151). And yet, he continues to vacillate on the book's purpose: after he declares that Suzanne has turned him from enigmas forever, he wonders whether her existence makes it "perhaps not so necessary that this book should exist" (1999: 158). Again, its value lies less in present agreement than "in memory of the conclusion I wanted to give it before knowing you and which your explosion into my life has not rendered vain" (1999: 158). In other words, the contingencies of the encounter are, themselves, the contingencies that mark a break between the second and third sections of *Nadja*, a break that if not detrimental to its surrealist aesthetics, do nevertheless subordinate these aesthetics to the love encounter itself.

Still, the reflections testify to a refusal to understand the encounter as simply instantaneous. Although its effects are felt to be so, the point of tracking these movements, of action and of thought, lies in mapping how the encounter with Nadja played out, and how those experiences jibe against the encounter with Suzanne. Likewise in *Mad Love*, where he wonders, "Who goes with me in this hour in Paris without leading me and whom, moreover, I am not leading?" (1987: 44), his answer to this question must come through the patient resurrection of his encounter with Jacqueline Lamba. Or in *Arcanum 17*, where, writing of Elisa's understandable tendency to "create pure night inside" herself in response to her daughter's death, he announces: "Each time you recall these atrocious events, in my love I have not recourse but to keep watch in secret" (36). In each, we find Breton following the consequences of his relationships, point by point.

Conclusion

This chapter has moved in two quite different directions. On the one hand, it has insisted on a deeper engagement with surrealism in Badiou's writing on love than has hitherto been discussed. On the other hand, it has challenged Badiou's reading of Breton, by suggesting that closer readings of his texts do yield a greater commitment to the duration of the encounter, and not merely its instant. Moreover, they provoke questions as yet undeveloped in Badiou's writing: namely, how to read the serial multiplicity of love encounters presented in *Nadja*, *Mad Love* and *Arcanum 17*. A superficial response might dismiss these encounters as ultimately obscurantist, since Breton's own response is to imagine them as successive, substitutive and teleological. If we set aside Breton's mystical explanation, however, to recall his insistence, in the encounter, that *this love* is forever, then we begin to catch the outlines of the love event in its entirety. Discussing his own amorous histories, Badiou hints at a succession of love encounters in his life. This suggests that not all such truth procedures terminate in abandonment; fidelity to that procedure, as it wanes, might simply be to concede that it happened, that love was there. In this case, Breton's texts become an archive of betrayal, not because he has different lovers, or that they appear serially, but because he testifies to them at the expense of his previous love encounters.

It is here that surrealism's issues with sexual essentialism remain. But there is, in the wider archive, a potential resolution to this problem. For Breton's texts can be supplemented by the biographical details they deliberately skew, where these encounters are moderated by a historical facticity that announces a disjunctive position. By putting Breton's texts together with more straightforwardly biographical accounts of his lovers, we might begin to articulate the world that emerges out of the resulting dialog, a logic less committed to generic functions of wandering, immobility, story and imperative than Badiou might like, but, nonetheless, texts that come closer to being actual documents of love itself.

Still, it is perhaps in modernism that this coincidence finds its true value. Badiou's more recognizable precursors—Lacan, Beckett—provide crucial answers for how love must be thought. But it is the surrealist tradition that offers perhaps the best correlative to why love must be thought: as a modernist reaction to love construed as a contemporary dilemma, which finds its resolution neither in pure hedonism nor mysticism, but in some materialist dialectic enjoining the two.

Notes

1 See, for instance, Jöttkandt (2010b), Burchill (2018); Cooke (2018); Park (2021).
2 In recent years, it has been observed that Badiou has changed his position on this matter (Burchill 2018; Jöttkandt 2018), though these changes haven't emerged in any clear form in *The Immanence of Truths*.
3 As for Badiou's St. Paul, body and soul here are "indiscernible," insofar as they just reflect the transformation of the lover in their entirety (Badiou 2003: 68).

Works Cited

Ades, D. (2011), "Afterword," in J. Pierre (ed.), *Investigating Sex*, London: Verso.
Ades, D. and M. Richardson (2016), "*Amour fou* – Mad love," in K. Fijalkowski and M. Richardson (eds.), *Surrealism: Key Concepts*, 171–181, London: Routledge.
Badiou, A. (2000), "What is Love?" in R. Salecl and S. Žižek (eds.), *Sexuations*, 263–281, Durham: Duke University Press.
Badiou, A. (2003), *Saint Paul: The Foundation of Universalism*, trans. R. Brassier, Stanford: Stanford University Press.
Badiou, A. (2007a), *The Century*, trans. A. Toscano, Cambridge: Polity.

Badiou, A. (2007b), *Sur Duchamp*, transcript F. Duvert. Available online: http://www.entretemps.asso.fr/Badiou/Duchamp.htm (accessed March 21, 2023).

Badiou, A. (2008), *Conditions*, trans. S. Corcoran, London: Continuum.

Badiou, A. (2009), *Logics of Worlds: Being and Event 2*, trans. A. Toscano, London: Continuum.

Badiou, A. (2022), *The Immanence of Truths*, trans. S. Spitzer and K. Reinhard, London: Bloomsbury.

Badiou, A. and D. Rousselle (2019), "Love Must be Reinvented," *Theory & Event* 22:1, 6–17.

Badiou, A. and F. Tarby (2013), *Philosophy and the Event*, trans. L. Burchill, London: Bloomsbury.

Badiou, A. and N. Truong (2012), *In Praise of Love*, trans. P. Bush, London: Serpent's Tail.

Benjamin, W. (1978), "Surrealism: The Last Snapshot of the European Intelligentsia," *New Left Review* 108, 47–56.

Breton, A. (1969), *Manifestoes of Surrealism*, trans. R. Seaver and H. R. Lane, Ann Arbor: University of Michigan Press.

Breton, A. (1987), *Mad Love*, trans. M. A. Caws, Lincoln: University of Nebraska Press.

Breton, A. (1994), *Arcanum 17*, trans. Z. Rogow, Los Angeles: Sun & Moon Press.

Breton, A. (1999), *Nadja*, trans. R. Howard, St Ives plc: Penguin.

Burchill, L. (2018), "Woman\s Adventures with/in the Universal," in A. J. Bartlett and J. Clemens (eds.), *Badiou and His Interlocutors*, 105–126, London: Bloomsbury.

Clemens, J. (2006), "Had We Worlds Enough, and Time, This Absolute, Philosopher," *Cosmos and History* 2:1–2, 277–310.

Cooke, B. (2018), "Everything Must Become Nothing (and Vice Versa): Love and Abstraction in Badiou and Lacan," in A. J. Bartlett and J. Clemens (eds.), *Badiou and His Interlocutors*, 159–176, London: Bloomsbury.

Gibson, A. (2006), *Beckett and Badiou: The Pathos of Intermittency*, Oxford: Oxford University Press.

Jöttkandt, S. (2010a), *First Love: A Phenomenology of the One*, Melbourne: re.press.

Jöttkandt, S. (2010b), "Love," in A. J. Bartlett and J. Clemens (eds.), *Alain Badiou: Key Concepts*, 73–81, Durham: Acumen.

Jöttkandt, S. (2018), "'With a Lever. . .': Beckett, Badiou and the Logics of Sexual Difference," *Philosophy Today* 62:4, 1189–1206.

Park, Y. J. (2021), "A Lacanian Supplementation to Love in *L'Immanence des vérités*," *Humanities and Social Sciences Communications* 8, 185.

Pierre, J. (2011), *Investigating Sex*, trans. M. Imrie, London: Verso.

Polizzotti, M. (1999), "Introduction," in *Nadja*, ix–xxvii, St Ives plc: Penguin.

Steven, M. (2018), "Love in the Time of Capital," *SubStance* 47:3, 147–166.

Part II

Modernisms' Multiple Badious Conditions and Manifestations

7

Twisting Modernism around Mallarmé's White Hair

Badiou versus Rancière

Joseph Shafer

cast skyward by the spume glance down
on islands of the deep mermaids
we'll never see   or hear   yet each

wave rolling brings in brightest
phosphorescence their hair

—Barbara Guest

In an essay Jacques Rancière adapted from a 1999 colloquium paper on Alain Badiou, first published as "Esthétique, inesthétique, anti-esthétique," then revised under "L'inesthétique d'Alain Badiou: les torsions du modernisme," a pithy summation of Badiou's inaesthetics is offered: "In short, Badiou's incontestable modernism is a modernism with a twist" [*un modernisme tordu*] (2004: 96). That deduction is ostensibly audacious. Its provocation, however, does not simply come from considering Badiou's inaesthetics to be another derivation of that "anti-aesthetic" which informed postmodernism. Rancière argues instead that Badiou's inaesthetics actually reemploys the core tenets of modernism. In a seemingly contradictory fashion, then, inaesthetics will be seen as adhering to the criteria by which traditional theories of modernism have defined art and aesthetics. Rancière thus takes a quite untraditional stance in not only identifying the avant-gardism of modernist theory with what is contrary to aesthetic experience but in jointly delimiting the novelty of inaesthetics. The audacity of Rancière's thesis lies, moreover, in rendering the conformity of Badiou's inaesthetics to modernism "incontestable." Incontestability is a striking if not unexpected assertion for a champion of aesthetics like Rancière, for whom any thought may show its paradoxical face. Badiou himself bemoaned this typically teetering form of argumentation in Rancière, inclined as it is to flip any sense of a thing into what Badiou described as "a skillfully constructed paradox, on the general incline of premature conclusions. His [Rancière's] books are neither conclusions nor directives, but *arrest clauses*" (2005c: 111). And yet, that tendency in Rancière to see paradoxical or opposing senses in any thing or work is not why the irrefutable modernism of inaesthetics undergoes what Rancière calls "a twist."

The twist comes after inaesthetics has organized the work of art according to modernist standards and eventually abandons the unruly surface of art in pursuit of a Platonic Idea. For, on the one hand, Rancière outlines how Badiou initially sides with founding theories of modernism. Badiou does this by reestablishing criteria for distinguishing materials of true art from those of non-art. Pure art is anti-mimetic and produces newness, for example, outside the economic circulation, valued representations or purpose of everyday objects and social forms of life. Pure art is thus removed from politics. To elucidate this division, a model for modernism and inaesthetics alike will classify and separate forms of art by medium, to understand how each artform obtains newness through the anti-mimesis of its own ascribed language. Understanding how each artform is organized by one kind of purifying communication, separate from other kinds, is necessary if we are to learn how true art does not appear in any old form of work or thing. On the other hand, Badiou will not apply this schema of prescriptions and categorizations for the purpose of disclosing the essence of a composition as Greenbergian modernism has. Badiou didactically does so in order to retrace the procedure by which an Idea detached from the sensory surface comes to pass through the work. As Rancière attests, that twist is even more symptomatic of inaesthetics than its modernist program, given that the eventful pass of Badiou's infinite Idea must further disregard the sensible composition of dis-orderly appearances.

We might then say that, for Rancière, the theory of modernism is a particularly despised example of a certain partitioning of the sensible. Modernism becomes a framework for classifying what bodies or materials can and cannot appear in a given order. The body of a poem cannot be that of painting or dance. Art too should be autonomous from, and not thereby simultaneously bound to, non-art, the socio-political, ideologically inscribed. That loosely constructed framework of separations then resorts to periodization for its footing. So modernism links art to a period that nevertheless began undoing its proposed rules even before its official start dates. Put with a finer edge, "To counter its lack of follow-through and establish its own beautiful chain of reasoning, modernism has contrived an exemplary fable in which art's homonymy is tied to the contemporaneousness of an era" (Rancière 2009: 68). That unfolding era, which Badiou affirms as modernism, will be "the century" which trailed the poet Stéphane Mallarmé.

Of course we may also recognize that Badiou's imperative to divide the arts has not been his most defended axiom when engaging Rancière. His response is louder in texts like *Metapolitics* when imploring Rancière to partake in organization. Convincing Rancière to rejoin the organization needed for politics, outside the also necessary organization of art, is paramount. "What Rancière calls 'politics' is not of the order of the prescription or the organized project" (Badiou 2005c: 115). Organizing is what transforms party politics, the so-called party. Like Mallarmé's Syntax for Badiou, organization guarantees the exclusionary structure of thought wherefrom a body might appear. Organization is pre-scribed in order for Badiou's philosophy to extricate a truth from separately defined conditions (from poetry/art, politics, love or mathematics). Their disagreements over the need for organization in conditions such as politics or art in general can seem rather abstract, however, in comparison to how an artwork must or must not be organized. The more vividly decisive matter is what exactly is allowed to appear in a single work of art?

Interrogating mere appearance is definitive of both Badiou's philosophy, in structuring his educational science or "logic of appearing," and Rancière's emphasis on the untaught self-sufficiency behind "free appearance." The different conclusions drawn from questioning appearance have no doubt shaped their opposing views on aesthetics. Rancière promotes "the politics of aesthetics," where any body or material whatsoever discounted by an order is also appearing therein. Only then can a subject play as the supplement to an opposition made apparent, as if seen inside and outside, playing as neither inside nor out. The once invisible part of a material body can be seen opposing the visible, like perceiving two opposed classes in one (one ruled and the other ruling without right), or like an object withdrawing from and in service to society. But far too little if anything can substantiate politics proper here for Badiou. He sees Rancière's commitment to a supplemental equality among materials and bodies as unproductive and uninvolved, being without a master. Meanwhile, Badiou's "inaesthetics" separates art from politics to instruct us on how certain designated points, in each of seven artforms, produce an event or new idea. Yet Rancière contests neither politics nor art can exist under such categorization or classification. It is this ongoing debate which makes their readings of two related poems by Mallarmé so illustrative. "A la nue accablante tu" [Hushed to the crushing cloud] and its evolved form, *Un coup de dés jamais n'abolira le hasard* [A throw of dice will never abolish chance], are the stage where this debate is held. The different materials or medium-mixing in Mallarmé's visual poems force Badiou to modernist tactics, of delineating only one language of anti-mimetic points capable of producing a new idea, all while disavowing the other (dis)appearances Rancière admits. More specifically, the point of contention hinges on and is magnified by the extent to which traces of a white page can appear in "A la nue accablante tu" and *Un coup de dés*.

That kernel in their mutual criticism was noted in Badiou's addendum to *Logics of Worlds*. His digression there confirms the "unending dispute" with Rancière is epitomized by a conflict between Rancière's Mallarmé, in *Mallarmé: The Politics of the Siren*, and the Mallarmé of Badiou's cited corpus, "'mon' Mallarmé (de *Théorie du sujet*, de *Conditions*, de *L'Être et l'événement*, du *Petit manuel d'inesthétique* . . .)" (2006: 586). Badiou's list of citations implies a seriousness presumably missing in the one "brief" monograph by Rancière. This despite Badiou not mentioning his books dedicate only passing invocations or chapters to Mallarmé, not a monograph, to exemplify this poet like so many of Rancière's (*Le destin des image*, *Aisthesis*, *La chair des mots*, *Parole muette*, *Malaise dans l'esthétique*, etc.). Ownership, still, is obviously not the wager. Badiou underlines a real difference: "The difference is already patent in the subtitle chosen by Rancière: *The Politics of the Siren*" (2009a: 561). Indeed the siren is a critical figure for the two poems Badiou next quotes: "À la nue accablante tu" and *Un coup de dés*.

The first poem, "À la nue accablante tu," was an octosyllabic sonnet originally printed in the magazine *Pan* in 1895, then inserted as the penultimate poem in Mallarmé's carefully prepared yet posthumously published second-edition of *Poésies* in 1899, released just twenty-three weeks after the poet's death. One reason the sonnet stirred controversy was for its lack of punctuation. All punctuation is absent apart from the parentheses and commas highlighting the word "foam" [*écume*]—"(tu Le sais, écume, mais y baves)"—effectively pronouncing the white space which "slobbers on" nearly everywhere else. Punctuating spaces have also been detected in other poems of *Poésies*, visually or implicitly linking blanks with the collection's recurring white analogies, as "foam" waves on the rim of a chalice during a toast in the opening lines of the lead poem, "Salut": "Nothing, this foam, virgin verse / Only to designate the cup." "À la nue accablante tu" recommences with this white sea-foam tossed upon a wave by an unknown cause. Internal speculations ensue over whether this foam is a white sail from a sunken "mast" [*le mât*] or, in the end, the floating "white hair" of a submerged "siren" or mermaid [*sirène*]—the "so white hair trailing" [*si blanc cheveu qui traîne*].

In *Un coup de dés*, first published in the journal *Cosmopolis* in 1897, the same string of figures is pitched on this "bleached" [*blanchi*] surface among debris of a possible shipwreck: the initial "foam" [*écumes originelles*], "this alternative sail" [*cette voile alternative*] and "siren" [*sirène*]. But in *Un coup de dés*, ranging font sizes, swirling lines and decorative typographical spacing unfold across double-page layouts or folios, producing infinite effects. Consider the small black-and-white column of words and spaces, shadow and light, spiraling down from "The lucid and lordly crest" to "a delicate dark form," informing "its Siren twist" [*torsion de sirène*]. A siren's glimmering tail thus still trails with its "impatient terminal scales" [*impatientes squames ultimes*], though the poem now concludes with a white "feather" hovering above the sea under a star "constellation." When editors at *Cosmopolis* trimmed the poem's spacing for publication, Mallarmé attached a preface with that iconic line: the "blanks . . . assume importance."

The importance of the siren is therefore not what Badiou disputes when saying Rancière's subtitle is misdirected. It is the politics of the siren Badiou cannot see [*vois*], neither in Rancière's reading nor in the lines addressing the siren in either poem: "car je ne vois nulle politique dans le 'si blanc cheveu qui traîne,' pas plus que dans les 'impatientes squames ultimes'" (2006: 586). This rebuke, as terse and narrowly isolated as it is, speaks directly to a central rift. The foam and climactic white hair had been a key thread in Badiou's seminal work, *Theory of the Subject*, in a chapter written in 1976 on "À la nue accablante tu." In 1992, for *Conditions*, Badiou performed another reading of the sonnet's trailing white hair for his chapter on art, and ended its first chapter on philosophy by quoting *Un coup de dés*. Between those projects, the siren and its associated coruscations in *Un coup de dés* were featured in *Being and Event*, where Badiou announced: "The event in question in *A Cast of Dice* is therefore that of the production of an absolute symbol of the event" (2016: 203). An equally blunt statement was published two years prior when reading *Un coup de dés* "as the greatest theoretical text that exists on the conditions for thinking the event" (2015: 10-11). The poem's signature lines are quoted frequently throughout *Logics of Worlds* as well: "One will recognize the style of my teacher Mallarmé: nothing has taken place but the place, except, on high, perhaps, a Constellation" (2009a: 4).

Nevertheless, there was an abrupt reckoning in Badiou's appropriation of Mallarmé over the years, one which modifies his admission of being unable to see any politics in traces of a siren. *Theory of the Subject* had explicitly performed a Maoist interpretation of the foam/white hair by developing a dialectic between the printed words and white page. As we'll see, it was after *Theory of the Subject* that both politics and page fall out of the picture. Poetry thenceforth comprises nothing other than the linguistic power of words when describing an imaginary place. Perhaps this is why Badiou humbly closes his digression in *Logics of Worlds* with an observation Rancière made at the colloquium: "But Rancière demonstrates, in a brilliant talk, that I am torn between two contradictory Mallarmés, that my current Mallarmé disowns the one of twenty years ago" (2009a: 561). If that remark bears any witness to the modernism Rancière was targeting in Badiou's later inaesthetics, the actual effrontery in Rancière's *Mallarmé* may enter the picture.

Not only did Rancière explain in an interview with Robert Boncardo and Christian R. Gelder that his monograph set out to debunk "the representation of Mallarmé as the hero of modernism," and did so by demonstrating how, against modernist dicta, the poems "implied a transformation of poetic language on the basis of nonlinguistic forms borrowed from music, dance, or from ceremonies, as well as on the basis of analogies with the movement of waves, the explosion of fireworks, or the movement of fans" (2017: 53). This reality, of nonlinguistic forms performing within the linguistic, is a harsh reminder for modernist frameworks which, like Badiou's, understand art by separating the mediums and dividing their different forms of communication; though this general reminder is not explicitly thrown at Badiou. Nor is the scale of such criticism revealed when Rancière concurs with interviewers that Badiou's reading of Mallarmé was taken into account. The boldness of Rancière's *Mallarmé* is not even contained in the endnote where he gave Badiou that sole nod via citation, after a statement which closed chapter one: "[the poet] leaves the famished ogre only a trace, a siren's white hair, of the trick that he played on it" (2011: 24). The trace of a painterly white *blanc cheveu*—that appearing white in the poem on the page—is the subject of Rancière's opening chapter, "The foam of the poem: *the white concern*."

Here Rancière favors what Mallarmé termed "the total arabesque" (Mallarmé 2007: 188). In this way, Rancière adds, the sonnet's white hair provided Mallarmé the summary and visual cue for *Un coup de dés*. The foam/white hair is an anomaly bouying along the page, fanning beside the letter. And, in this manner, the page acts as a stage for mixing different materials and genres, e.g. dance, theater, painting, music and poetry. That assemblage is ipso facto against the modernist baseline or schemata of inaesthetics, whereby the militant apprehends a poem once poetry presents only words for description. "The arabesque works to dispel the illusion that the poem is about describing," says Rancière, since a painterly white also leaps or dances on the page to trace the siren, if only as "an ironic trace of its ephemeral and deceptive appearing: a white piece of fairy hair, which we can therefore identify with the white line of the foam" (Rancière 2011: 2–3). That appearing white line on the page is the precise matter or space Badiou's definition and procedural reading of poetry will always already void, while Rancière, in *Aisthesis* as in several works, elaborates how Mallarmé's writings on and reappropriations of the stage dancer Loïe Fuller showcase countless aspects brought by light: those appearances of interlacing skirt folds and moving white fabric. Mallarmé himself compared the dancer's flashing cloth to "sea foam" (2007: 137). Rancière continues, "Mallarmé used to call these forms and elementary relations of forms 'aspects,' which he readily metamorphosized as the folds and unfolding of a fan, swaying hair, or the foam on the crest of a wave. For him all these aspects symbolize the pure act of appearing and disappearing" (2011: 98). The poetic feet of dancing words can appear to disappear only because the foregrounded fabric can as well. As Rancière detailed in *Mallarmé*, once the gold-coating of raised words turns to dust, words can appear cupped with white foam waving in the air as if toasting to the coming community.

The bone Rancière is picking, pace Badiou, will therefore have less to do with whether Badiou's earliest readings of Mallarmé contradict those of his matured philosophy. A trail of white hair tends to suggest a situation was remedied at a formative phase in Badiou's oeuvre. That bone is rather linked to the measures Badiou adopted when bypassing predicaments overtly encountered in *Theory of the Subject*. Mallarmé was not the hero then. The structural dialectic Badiou chained to the signifiers in "A la nue accablante tu"—between words like "foam" and the white page—wound up culminating. In a prudent exegesis of the Maoism Badiou juxtaposes to the sonnet in *Theory of the Subject*, Boncardo reminds us that Mallarmé gets construed as a "radical conservative and idealist, whose poetic operations repress the irruptive force of revolutionary change" (2015: 1). The obstacle Mallarmé's sonnet failed to traverse was its closing relation between the poem's foam trace and paginal white hair.

An earlier warning suspiciously involving Mallarmé can be found in a footnote to Badiou's 1967 essay, "Mark and Lack." It comes after the one-sentence paragraph, "Science is the Outside without blind-spot" (2012: 172). Badiou is affirming the axiomatic power of science (for historical materialism and psychoanalysis) which shall no longer function like the typical "logic of the signifier." The chain of signifiers had, while based on lack, operated from one signifier to another by blindly incorporating an identity, a subject, ideology. No more. Each written line, mark, letter, grapheme or trace must now symbolize ideology and adhere to a structured logic, a "perfect syntax," to maintain a fidelity to lack, to negation, to systematically summon an "undecidable statement." The footnote citing Mallarmé advises readers who would be wise to emulate this science or mathematics, to expose ideology by producing an epistemological break, to stop tarrying in that "delectable" image of writing which merely "sports the ideology of difference."

It is "weak difference" Mallarmé succumbs to in *Theory of the Subject* rather than pushing onwards through "strong difference." Weak difference or "minimal difference" is the difference in the metonymic chain between one word and another word. Badiou reads "A la nue accablante tu" as beginning with the word "foam." The mark *foam* is then replaced by "horn" [*trompe*]—the horn of a shipwreck (but also a horn foreshadowing the siren, since *sirène* is both horn and mermaid). The ship's *horn* next produces the thought of debris from a "mast." At this juncture, there is a jump to another chain. Badiou relinks *foam* to *siren*; then *siren* to her tail or "flank" [*le flanc*]; then *flank* to the poem's final trace of "hair" [*cheveu*]. In sum, Badiou writes, "The ship is evoked only by the abolition, not even of its own massivity but of its mast, supreme jetsam; or by the hypothetical sound of an inaudible horn. The siren is reduced to its youthful head of hair—except that it is only a single white hair" (2009b: 178). Whether it is "a single white hair" or strands of trailing white hair could be beside the grander point of there being two diverging chains. One tracks a mast and the other a siren.

A thinking through these figures—foam, mast, siren—unfolds dialectically through disparate forms of negation. The first negation is the vanishing term *foam*, which is immediately purged or swallowed by the abysmal sea or lack from which the thought of *ship* surfaces. The second form of negation is "annulment." Annulment is radically different from vanishing because the arriving *siren* had not caused the thought *ship* to disappear in the same way as the vanishing terms in the chain *foam-horn-mast* or *foam-siren-flank-hair*. The line of thought about a submerged mermaid completely annuls that of a ship. Annulment is an exceptional break from a chain. Vanishing is more like Leninism, says Badiou, in destroying the apparatus of the old bourgeoisie, while annulment is Maoist, producing "the destruction of the bourgeoisie twice" (2009b: 80). Such chains and negations may be forceful, but what constitutes the subject is the effect of strong difference.

Strong difference is posited from the outset between "foam" and page. *Foam* will have named that place, space or "splace," the abyss or "paper void" where the series of traced figures disappear. The word "foam" is a metaphor for the page's vacant surface. It is the initial trace inscribed upon paper, "the poet's first written trace on the paper void." That relation is of "the void and the atoms, the blank page and the signs." A pending problem, however, rests in this very premise: the described white "foam" is a metaphor for "the white page where everything is inscribed" (2009b: 76). Recognizing "the white page" itself as a visible factor in the reading may anchor the metaphor, but it will also produce an unwanted bind when the "white hair" consequentially winds up resembling the sensibly perceived white page and not exclusively the inscribed trace of "foam" this white was originally imagined as and imagined from.

Badiou's reading of the siren chain-link concludes somewhat hastily with this unraveling knot. A passage steams through the white hair finale before going back over what we learned from the break between the ship and its annulment. The chains which are enframing this white hair seem to have ceased in a split when the white hair of foam manifests as both written trace and paper, a "double-nature": "As for the splitting, it too is manifest, with regard to the foam's double-nature. The foam certainly is a trace, and thus it is captured in the network of mundane differences, as opposed to the unlimited nature of the cloud. But on the other hand, it holds out only thanks to a resemblance to the abyss, of which it indicates the negative power and the underlying effect of abolition" (2009b: 79). What is this "resemblance" [*apparentement*]? Does the word "foam" signify an imaginary whiteness resemblant of an imaginary and thus absent page forever blank, a virgin page sans trace? If so, that never inscribed page would not be the white page where everything is inscribed, the poem's underlying surface, the place under the signifiers, that place under which the poem's ship and siren went. Conversely, the "white hair" does trail on the poem's white page. Badiou's "hair of foam" resurges in upholding a resemblance, kinship, relationship, representation or alliance with the white page in writing. Therefore, would this white hair, lingering as it does with the foam that slobbers on, resemble a white tress woven into the trace, a co-written line of virgin verse, the flash of a less repressed paginal body? Or does the double-nature of foam, as linguistic trace and painterly white page, not more dangerously invite what Badiou accedes to here as a mermaidesque "leap in the superficial heterogeneity of the visible"?

If an appearing color factors in this traced line of thought—in hindsight, in the imaginary, or in lightning flashes—would not such a nonlinguistic indication, paper-laden image or whiteness become a trace too? The split elicits an almost undecidable route. Except there cannot be a visual resemblance, alliance, imitation or representation between atomic traces and their paper void if their "strong difference" is to build rather than collapse. It is thus to Badiou's dismay that Mallarmé and his sonnet apparently conclude with such split hairs while a militant would press on: "Mallarmé stops. Mao does not stop." Badiou proceeds by rewriting the poem with his own invented stanza pasted onto the end of the sonnet to reinvoke the mast and prolong "the plunging ride." And he laments, "Oh, but Mallarmé would much rather not show this subject that the structural will of his dialectic stumbles up against! If only all this could be kept within the homogeneity of the poetic operations" (2009b: 88).

Mathematical and poetic operations are what Mallarmé suddenly masters in Badiou's subsequent publications. What is no longer part of any operation is the "textual splacement" Badiou posited and dismissed regarding "A la nue accablante tu" and *Un coup de dés* in *Theory of the Subject*, where splacement more or less facilitated a dialectical arrangement waylaid and prematurely interrupted by text vis-à-vis the white page. Going forward, both of these interlinked poems, especially *Un coup de dés*, proffer a formalization comparable to mathematics. Mathematics is a science that marches on by thinking itself letter-by-letter. But whereas mathematics cannot think the event it induces and confronts, a Mallarmé poem does think the undecidability of an event: the chance of a shipwreck, or else. "For me," Badiou discovered, "Mallarmé represents the person who launched a poetic challenge to mathematics by assuming that the rigour of poetic language could equal the rigour of mathematics, but moreover also assumed the power of Chance, something mathematics cannot do" (Boncardo and Gelder 2017: 85). In achieving this singular status, as thinker of the event, Mallarmé ushers in another century for Badiou. The century being a new Idea of art.

In his chapter on art in *Philosophy and the Event*, the contemporaneousness Badiou speaks of as if always in scare quotes is a rupture still hailing from the modernist canon: "What we're the contemporaries of is a petering out . . . of the constellation of events that reoriented things at the beginning of the twentieth century," events like Picasso and Braque from 1912 to 1913, Bauhaus architecture and

Schoenberg's twelve-tone debut (2013: 71). Although Badiou stipulates "modernity is the infinite desire of new forms," true art produces newness not through formalism but the abstraction of a new universality or Idea, "a new infinite content" (2004). The splitting difference of a white square on a white canvas in Malevich's *White on White* broaches a new idea for Badiou in "Fifteen Theses on Contemporary Art," as it does again in *The Century* and "Manifesto of Affirmationism," where Malevich, Picasso and Schoenberg are grouped with Mondrian, Kandinsky, Pirandello, Brecht, Faulkner, Mandelstam, Woolf, Beckett, Wallace Stevens and so on. Yet all Badiou honors as the "avant-gardes" and "the century" is repeatedly traced back to the eventual breakthrough of Mallarmé's poetry: "The twentieth century kicks off in an exceptional fashion [with] 1898, Mallarmé dies, shortly after having published the manifesto of modern writing, *Un coup de dés*" (2007: 20–1).

By privileging works like *White on White*, as turning points in the wake of *Un coup de dés*, Badiou can stress the basic qualifications for a modern composition. One is anti-mimesis. He would write, "The modern poem is the opposite of a mimesis" (2005a: 21). An anti-mimetic operation has been examined by Robert Lehman through Badiou's notion of "purging" the sensible. "Purging" was a term used in *Handbook of Inaesthetics* to explain how Beckett and Mallarmé exercise language. An oozing of words, or Mallarmé's "never direct allusive words," is to write nothing or the nothing that is the unnamable power of language itself (2005a: 103). What is being described is an act of inscribing that erases its description. Lehman conveys this process of purgation by comparing Badiou's "eradication of resemblance" in *Conditions* with statements made by Denis and Greenberg about modern painting:

> The treatment of avant-garde art's vocation as essentially purgative—"the eradication of resemblance, representation...."—echoes, in more combative terms, the familiar caveat directed to aspiring painters in the late nineteenth century by the Symbolist Maurice Denis: "We should remember that a picture—before being a war horse, a nude woman, or telling some other story—is essentially a flat surface covered with colors arranged in a particular pattern"; as well as Clement Greenberg's characterization of the history of avant-garde painting as "a progressive surrender to the resistance of its medium; which resistance consists chiefly in the flat picture plane's denial of efforts to 'hole through it for realistic perspective space.'" This process, Badiou observes, reaches its apogee with Kasmir [sic] Malevich's *White on White*, "the epitome of purification." (2010: 55)

Quoting Denis and Greenberg, to support the flattening resistance of a white canvas in *White on White*, does inform and aptly contextualize the process of anti-mimesis in purgation. But it also raises a conflation renounced by inaesthetics between Mallarméan purgation and painting; that is, between Badiou's logic for the medium of *Un coup de dés* and that of *White on White*. Other critics do certainly read *Un coup de dés* as a visually arranged pattern of words which has its significations interrupted by the white paginal plane, contributing to anti-mimesis. Badiou does not. His concept of avant-garde writing purging its own written language in a void stands opposed to the parallel logic of modernist painting attending to its white canvas. Regardless, there is a shared operation.

Badiou says the "subtractive protocol" in *White on White*, as "constituted through the erasure of every content, every upsurge," "is very close to the one that Mallarmé makes within poetry" (2007: 56). It is very close because neither work lets Badiou wander among its dis-appearances, between their materials and representations, between the sensible and idea. Each work is rather viewed or read as erasing a designated string of representations and resemblances on its surface, to systematically (re)produce and clear the ground for the eternal Idea to pass—for the truth of this breaking event. The rupturing difference in *White on White* is not between a white square and the square white canvas it resembles. One white square's shape and color cannot resemble the shape and color of another in the painting. Neither will the foam/white hair any longer resemble a white page in "A la nue accablante tu." Instead, anti-mimesis must purify each artwork's finite medium-specific points: color and shape for painting; words for poetry. Purgation purges the very representation, de-scription or naming being placed on a canvas in painting or in a voided space in poetry. Purgation maps the steps of a Dantean, purgatorial ascension from the hell of ideological representations toward the eternal. The work of philosophy is then subtracting the infinite within this protocol. The infinite for *White on White* would be the Idea, or the thought of the thought *square*, subtracted from a purified white. Thus the event is the gap in knowledge production that occurs between the flattening purification of the color white and the passing Idea of a square shape. Purifying and erasing the sensible for the Idea to pass in poetry occurs differently.

In "A la nue accablante tu," a break will be retraced between the purged word "foam" (as if it were the last word) and a pure Idea of the abyss invoked. Similarly, in *Un coup de dés*, a gap results between a single white "feather" upon a sea and the heavenly Constellation of an Idea. As Badiou wrote in *Conditions*, "Philosophy wants to and must be established in this subtractive point where language, divested of the prestige, or mimetic incitement, of images, of fiction and of narrative, is consigned to thought" (2008: 43). So too will he define "the modern poem" via Mallarmé accordingly in "What is a Poem?": "The modern poem is the opposite of a mimesis. In its operation, it exhibits an Idea of which both the object and objectivity represent nothing but pale copies. This means that philosophy cannot grasp the couple that is the poem and the matheme through the simple opposition between the delectable image and the pure idea" (2005a: 21). Yet what is this "delectable image," charged as it is with setting up such a break? Of what can the image or sensible consist, if it is to reproduce and not derail the schema by which the Idea must eventually come to pass?

The modern poem "is the sensible," Badiou assures us, a sensible "that presents itself within the poem" (2005a: 21). Or, as adumbrated in "Fifteen Theses on Contemporary Art," "an artistic truth is a happening of the Idea in the sensible itself" (2004). And while Badiou will state in *Philosophy and the Event* that art is "what is seen, what is heard," in "the order of appearing," he restricts these senses in the subsequent paragraph with the proviso, "A poem is rendered in a particular language" (2013: 67). In "What is a Poem?" for instance, poetry seems to be neither seen nor heard. "The poem remains enslaved to the image, to the immediate singularity of experience," yet it is only comprised of linguistic signs, words, and a "linguistic power" to purge that language (2005a: 18).

This thinning scope for each medium enables any sensible to comply with one type of grammar for a "configuration." A configuration is a set of points that allows a "configuration to think itself": "*a configuration thinks itself in the works that compose it*" (2005a: 18). A configuration amasses, in other words, not in the sensible per se but through the intraphilosophical effects of the sensible. "The configuration thinks itself through the test posed by an inquiry that, at one and the same time, reconstructs it locally, sketches its 'to come', and retroactively reflects its temporal arc" (2005a: 14). In order for a configuration of the sensible to unfold a logic, it cannot involve any effect produced by another language.

Multimedia would therefore threaten thinking the sensible. In Badiou's fourth thesis on contemporary art, multimedia is said to be an old form of falsely making newness. Integrating one medium with another, albeit pictures or music with poetry, is to fancy a totalization of all forms; a dream of absolute totalization equated with globalization. Dismissing mixed-media helps to explicate, in theses five and eight, how newness or "new forms" can be traced through the development of a specific medium, as *White on White* introduced. It's a position eerily resonant with Greenberg's position against collage, after collage supposedly peaked from 1910 to 1914 in Picasso and Braque, as against what he called "medium-scrambling" in a 1971 lecture (Greenberg 2000: 131–3). Greenberg casts scrambling or "content-mixing" as a trendy, academic maneuver pretending to be new, "risky" and "far-out." Tactics like making two-dimensions appear three, or "poetry that makes a pictorial pattern on the page" has the least chance of producing newness. For Greenberg had likewise declared that brushstrokes attending to a flat canvas could purify a work mainly because those materials belong to modernist painting alone. The task was "to eliminate from the effects of each art any and every effect that might conceivably be borrowed from or by the medium of any other art. Thus would each art be rendered 'pure', and its 'purity' find the guarantee of its standards of quality as well as of its independence" (Greenberg 1993: 86). Modernism must then downplay not only the painterly visibility of writing, as script, concrete object or hieroglyph, but repress the material page or sensory coloration. With that modernist paradigm in mind, the sensible becomes efficaciously organized *a priori* for inaesthetics, for the purpose of tracing one form of knowledge in the production of the new.

Rancière would not need to chronicle the theatricalities of Mallarmé's pages, Apollonaire's caligrammes, the letterism of Braque's collages etcetera to note the theoretical untenableness of modernism and inaesthetics in light of the age's "reality of mixtures" [*la réalité des mélanges*] (Rancière 2002: 482). Such hardline modernisms as Badiou's and Greenberg's shy from readings like Paul Valéry's when first seeing *Un coup de dés* as "the figure of a thought for the first time placed in our space," where "expectation, doubt, concentration were visible things," with "silences" taking shape "there, on the very paper," a "scintillation" of "stars" constellating, given that his friend "tried, I thought, at last to raise a page to the power of the starry sky" (Rancière 2011: 56). Rancière too will quote Valéry's observations here in *The Politics of the Siren*, then rearticulate, in *Aesthetics and Its Discontents*, the adverse principles of Greenbergian modernism to qualify his argument against Badiou:

> Literary modernity thus comes to consist in the exploitation of the pure powers of language, freed from the obligation of communication; pictorial modernity, the conquest, by a type of painting set free from naked women and combat horses, of the powers intrinsic to its bi-dimensional surface and the materiality of coloured pigment; and musical modernity, in a twelve-note language that bears no analogy to expressive language. A "specific of art" is thereby defined which each art allegedly realizes by its own specific means, means that are fully distinct from those of its neighboring art. By the same token, it is claimed, this also substantiates the global distinction between art and non-art. (2009: 69)

This standard model of modernism is heuristic for Rancière. His own aim and approach in clarifying it, however, is not to prove Badiou's inaesthetics simply conforms to that wider consensus. It is to locate four indicative ways Badiou embraces its criteria when springing from them. The first concerns a more widespread misunderstanding of mimesis. Mimesis, Rancière interjects, "was not the obligation of resemblance—with which schoolchildren and a good number of their teachers stubbornly identify it." Mimesis was foremost a principle that divides up modes of appearance (imitation from appearance), to understand what objects can be used to educate truth and which cannot, to classify different human activities and kinds of objects for comparison. When materials are therefore typified and categorized in order to separate artforms, for the sake of classifying artists or artforms from others and non-art, it is not anti-mimesis unless radically conceived.

Second, he sees potential in Badiou's theory of cinema. For while Badiou takes cinema as "the seventh art," he deems it an "impure art" that assimilates other mediums, just as its productions straddle the threshold to non-art. "No painting will ever become music," wrote Badiou, "no dance will ever turn into poem. All direct attempts of this sort are in vain. Nevertheless, cinema is effectively the organization of these impossible movements" (2005a: 82). What Badiou terms an "impure movement"—"falsest of them all"—could be contrived to reaffirm aesthetics, Rancière contends, except Badiou isolates cinema to again teach the points through which an idea comes to pass. Cinema becomes "the breached frontier where an idea will have passed, an idea whose visitation the cinema, and it alone, allows" (2005a: 82). But cinema is not alone for Rancière. Its multiple aspects can be found in other mediums as in the market, although multimedia is not a nightmare of totalization, subsuming all. Art is not totalizing. It is a separate world, Rancière reiterates, since anything can belong to it.

Third, it is Badiou's modernist taxonomy for teaching how the Platonic Idea comes to pass that makes inaesthetics an anti-Platonic "modernism with a twist." Art, unconducive to Plato's education on the Idea, is now conducive. That anti-Platonic twist can be spun once the Idea need not stick to the planes of modernism, or need not remain immersed in a surface's representative points for that modernist procedure which produces the Idea. In modernism, the purification of art basks instead in "the essence—pure or opaque—of language," in the separate anti-mimetic language as each medium. With inaesthetics, that purified language serves that Idea which will pass through the medium (Rancière 2009: 70). Thus inaesthetics can now use art to educate because the passing Idea will not get tangled or lost in the sensible. If the sensible can be reduced to a single type of configured points, and that configuration is executing an anti-mimesis which purges itself from the work, then a road is paved and cleared again, through the disorderly state of the sensible, for the Idea to pass unobstructed. As Rancière writes, Badiou "wants eternity to pass in the ever renewed separation which shines the Idea forth in the fading of the sensible, to affirm the absolutely discrete and always similar character of the advent of the Idea, by not allowing its cipher to disappear in the muteness of stone, the hieroglyph of the text, the décor of life or the rhythm of the collection. He wants this less for the purpose of reserving a specific domain for poetry or art than of preserving the educative value of the Idea" (Rancière 2009: 73).

A primary example of these twists resides in the contrast Badiou makes between non-art and art for the production of the new Idea. This often arbitrary division is displayed routinely and foundationally when Badiou conceives some of Mallarmé's poetic texts as plain discourse about art, to better qualify the different arts Mallarmé refers to, and to read Mallarmé's other texts as strictly poetry and not discourse. Mallarmé's prose pieces are therefore used as an outside instrument for defining the poem as against dance, theater, music. Rancière noted this "recurrent opposition" in Badiou. For Badiou reads the artful nature of essays like those collected in *Divagations* as philosophical discourses about the disjoined arts to teach and rehearse the passing Idea in each art separately. It could not matter, Rancière replied, that *Crise de vers* is not a text on poetry but "a piece of Mallarméan poetry" (Rancière 2009: 74). Badiou has to treat Mallarmé's prose pieces as non-poetry and non-art across *Handbook of Inaesthetics* to organize the arts and classify them. Keeping Mallarmé's prose from poetry, and his poetry from the other arts (arts addressed, mimicked and implicated in his prose and poetry) is a praxis Badiou enforces on behalf of the Idea. And it is a practice which finds Mallarmé playing an exceptionally uncanny role in *Handbook of Inaesthetics*.

Mallarmé's instructions or declarations on visually arranging materials, blanks or a white "*blanc*" in space cannot transfer to the page, or else poems would resemble and overlap with Badiou's perception of Cubism, where a "reconstruction of the visible is wrought through geometrical forms and arrangements in space" (2013: 71). Nor could readings of *Un coup de dés* be redirected by the deluxe edition Mallarmé began devising with his collaborator and Symbolist artist Odilon Redon, who would resketch the page-space as a reflection of cloudy white faces glancing at a bubbly constellation. Mallarmé's 1876 collaboration with Manet for the publication of "L'après-midi d'un faune" could not mix genres either. In Badiou's essay on "L'après-midi d'un faune," he agrees the poem was written as theater, but theater, he writes, "is an assemblage of extremely disparate components, both material and ideal, whose sole existence lies in the performance" (2005a: 72). Badiou may continuously describe Mallarmé's poetry as theatrical, but the body of the poem cannot perform. Mallarmé's poetry is more like dance, says Badiou, since dance is distinct from the "décor of theatre." Both in dance and Mallarmé's poetry, there are only male and female bodies. But in dance, Badiou adds, bodies do not signify their relation to the stage or voided air. The floating bodies of dancers disappear in becoming air themselves. Mallarmé's poems, on the other hand, could never perform as if waving fabric. Poetry's words do not become air but signify a virginal void.

The poem's singular function is to linguistically signify and narrativize an absence. Or, stated differently, the absence can be a place in the poem in so far as a linguistic system of signs forms an uninterrupted narrative describing it. The necessity for narrative therefore takes precedent over the sensible. Philosophy must be free to reconstruct a logical narrative of the void even if it means overlooking the perceptible word-order and punctuation. Narrative is what permits Badiou to read "L'après-midi d'un faune" and poetry in general as "prose." And, in this respect, Mallarmé's poetry is true prose. Unlike the poetic prose Badiou thinks as discourse, the poem's prose is double-edged. A poem must tell a "story" about a place while that place being named must remain in doubt. "That is the very essence of the Mallarméan notion of mystery: A trace that does not amount to proof, a sign whose referent is not imposed upon us . . . The sign is the sign of the undecidable itself under the fixity of the name" (2005a: 130). The image a Mallarmé poem conjures is therefore not the written page or the writing but the imaginary place being systematically described, through vanishing, (annulling) canceling, a foreclosure and undecidability.

Badiou often recalls how Mallarmé supplied us with a rule capable of extracting the poem's embedded prose narrative: the guarantee of syntax. Syntax gives structure to the narrative. But because the existing syntax in Mallarmé's lines is poetic, Badiou's philosophy is duty bound to preemptively choose, rearrange and reinsert choice words and punctuation to prescribe a proper syntax. Jean-Jacques Lecercle has struggled to justify this interpretive practice in Badiou, which begins by "glossing" and "translating the poetry into prose" for "syntactical reordering" (2010: 101). A syntactical reordering of a poem into a prose configuration is most blatantly warranted when reading and quoting from *Un coup de dés*. It's not just that the written page needs to be elided from discussions in *Being and Event*. Any indication of spacing, enjambment or given word-order are removed when quoting at length. The nonchalant manner of quoting such reinvented prose passages is evident in essays like "A Poetic Dialectic: Labîd ben Rabi'a and Mallarmé." Typographical spacing, enjambment and fragmented syntax in *Un coup de dés*—all of which generate different word associations—are manufactured into prosaic quotations with added punctuation, parentheses and commas, ensuring syntactical effects (2005a: 55). What matters is the naming and description of a real void, through a logical narrative untethered from a sensible already limited to words in a vacuum. The instantaneous result is an absent place represented as an oceanic abyss likened to the truly absent Bayda desert symbolized in Labîd ben Rabi'a's *Le Désert et son code*.

Nowhere is this procedure better documented than in Badiou's discussion of "A la nue accablante tu" in chapter five of *Conditions*, under "Mallarmé's Method: Subtraction and Isolation." The chapter begins by quoting Mallarmé's demand for logic in *Music and Letters*, a "melodic encipherment, of the combinations of motifs that compose a logic" (2008: 49). And that call for a pre-scribed logic does seem contained within a single discourse, with Mallarmé's following paragraph in *Music and Letters* qualifying "Letters" as a "mental quest, carried out as discourse" (2007: 188). The essay, Badiou alludes, is a discourse of letters about a logic that ought to be ascribed elsewhere in art (although music should require a separate logic). Then again, the sentence invoking "melodic encipherment" is the one after Mallarmé claims "the total arabesque" ties music and letters together. Such is the "means of Mystery": "Let us forget the old distinctions between Music and Letters, which only divide them, voluntarily, for their subsequent fusion: the one evocative of prestige situated at the highest point of hearing, or almost abstract vision, being well versed, which, spaciously, grants the printed page an equal range" (2007: 188–9). The letters of discourse and poetry seem to be combining, along with music and letters, hearing and seeing, prestige and spaciousness. But if we hear all that is unsaid and said in Badiou's introduction, discourse is divided from art, music from letters, writing and page from signified motifs, in order to discern the logic.

This chapter's progression is meant to represent how Badiou traces his thinking of the event in art; yet it traces more than that in returning to a poem thought problematic before his philosophy of the event. While the method may have changed, various traces of the former reading are present. For example, the two-paragraph storyline Badiou submits as his prose "translation" of "A la nue accablante tu" is taken verbatim from *Theory of the Subject*. Badiou also includes his old bullet points: notes for accurately interpreting the poem's "grammatical construction" and the only guidelines to allow "all the material to be integrated," including a comma he insists we imagine printed after the word "fury" (2008: 52). What is new about this version is a method guaranteed by two minor yet decisive omissions.

The first is any acknowledgment of paper, page or the white page. This omission pronounces *the white concern* in Rancière's introduction on mixed material appearances in *The Politics of the Siren*; since, again, any appearance of white within Badiou's logical configuration would be out-of-place, premature, catapulting his procedure into a collagic detour of spiraling points, tails or strands. Or it would reveal that what is ordered outside and invisible is also visibly inside against. So, true poetry must be comprised solely of linguistic signs writ under a purifying anti-mimesis from which the infinite Idea can be ultimately subtracted. Thus the poem's words or tropes of white cannot resemble or present the muslin, foamy or canvas-like white aspects. That fundamental difference is displaced here between the word "foam" and what it names, "the void of place." Place being the "merging sea and sky," the great "abyss," "being *qua* being." Removing the white page from the equation is not a simple act of substitution either, as if its place were kept under another name, "the empty depths of the marine abyss." Excluding the white page from the premise and picture means a truth-procedure—carried through a prescribed configuration of select words—cannot be spontaneously interrupted. Nor can the splitting of "foam" entail any impatient leaps in the superficial heterogeneity of the visible. That phrasing too has been eliminated. All that remains is the vanishing word or "foam" trace. Now the event can transpire within this "undecidable foam": between the placed name "foam" and its naming of the abyss abolishing it. That scission in "foam" itself is only suspended by the choice of its cause—ship or siren—which is the undecidability of the event.

Works Cited

Badiou, A. (1986), "Est-il exact que toute pensée émet un coup de dés?" *Les conférence du Perroquet* 5 (janvier).
Badiou, A. (2004), "Fifteen Theses on Contemporary Art," *Lacan Ink* 22.
Badiou, A. (2005a), *Handbook of Inaesthetics*, trans. A. Toscano, Stanford: Stanford University Press.
Badiou, A. (2005b), "Manifesto of Affirmationism," trans. B. P. Fulks, *Lacan Ink* 24/25.
Badiou, A. (2005c), *Metapolitics*, trans. J. Barker, New York: Verso.
Badiou, A. (2006), *Logiques des mondes*, Editions du Seuil.
Badiou, A. (2007), *The Century*, trans. A. Toscano, Cambridge: Polity.
Badiou, A. (2008), *Conditions*, trans. S. Corcoran, New York: Continuum.
Badiou, A. (2009a), *Logics of Worlds*, trans. A. Toscano, New York: Continuum.
Badiou, A. (2009b), *Theory of the Subject*, trans. B. Bosteels, New York: Continuum.
Badiou, A. (2012), "Mark and Lack," in *Concept and Form, vol. 1*, trans. Z. L. Fraser and R. Brassier, New York: Verso.
Badiou, A. (2013), *Philosophy and the Event*, trans. L. Burchill, Cambridge: Polity.
Badiou, A. (2015), "Is it Exact That All Thought Emits A Throw of Dice?" trans. R. Boncardo and C. R. Gelder, *Hyperion* IX:3 (Winter).
Badiou, A. (2016), *Being and Event*, trans. O. Fentham, London: Bloomsbury.
Boncardo, R. (2015), "Mallarmé in Alain Badiou's Theory of the Subject," *Hyperion* IX:3 (Winter), 1.
Boncardo, R. and C. Gelder (2017), *Mallarmé: Rancière, Milner, Badiou*, London: Rowman & Littlefield.
Greenberg, C. (1993), "Modernist Painting," in *The Collected Essays and Criticism, Volume 4: Modernism with a Vengeance, 1957–1969*, ed. J. O'Brian, Chicago: The University of Chicago Press.
Greenberg, C. (2000), *Homemade Esthetics: Observations on Art and Taste*, Oxford: Oxford University Press.
Lecercle, J. (2010), *Badiou and Delueze Read Literature*, Edinburgh: Edinburgh University Press.
Lehman, R. (2010), "Between the Science of the Sensible and the Philosophy of Art," *Angelaki* 15:2, 171–185.
Mallarmé, S. (2007), *Divagations*, trans. B. Johnson, Cambridge, MA: Harvard University Press.
Mallarmé, S. (1994), *Collected Poems*, trans. Henry Weinfield, Berkeley: University of California Press.
Rancière, J. (2002), "Esthétique, inaesthétique, anti-aesthétique," in *Alain Badiou, penser le multiple*, 477–96, Paris: L'Harmattan.
Rancière, J. (2004), *Malaise dans l'esthétique*, Paris: Galilée.
Rancière, J. (2009), *Aesthetics and Its Discontents*, trans. S. Corcoran, Cambridge: Polity Press.
Rancière, J. (2011), *Mallarmé: The Politics of the Siren*, trans. S. Corcoran, New York: Continuum.
Rancière, J. (2013), *Aisthesis*, trans. Z. Paul, New York: Verso.

8

Reflections on Cinema and Philosophy

Alex Ling

First published in 2018, Alain Badiou's "Cinema and Philosophy" is doubtless one of the most lucid and accessible accounts of his own understanding of cinema and what it means for philosophy in general. Originally delivered as a keynote address at the University of New South Wales, Australia, the lecture itself constituted something of a culmination of his philosophical comprehension of film, an intellectual engagement that stretches back at least as far as 1957 with the publication of his remarkable (and remarkably prescient) article on "Cinematic Culture."[1] The address moreover served as an occasion to respond to a number of potential issues concerning the somewhat uncertain and even conflicted position that cinema appears to hold in his own philosophical system, complications which arise in particular from its apparent status as an "inessential art."[2] With this in mind, the purpose of this chapter is to provide some general considerations on the meaning of cinema and its relationship to both art and philosophy—a relationship which is itself closely tied to a historically modernist ethos—as well as offer some critical reflections on Badiou's responses. In doing so we see how cinema not only sheds crucial light on the other arts but also reveals Badiou's own approach to art as one that simultaneously reflects and repudiates certain core tenets of aesthetic modernism.

Composed and delivered in English, and exhibiting his typically methodical approach, "Cinema and Philosophy" revolves around a series of six fundamental and interrelated questions which might be summarized as follows: (1) What is cinema? (2) What is the relationship of cinema to philosophy? (3) Is cinema an art? (4) What is cinema's relationship to the other arts? (5) Is the relationship between cinema and philosophy singular? (6) How close is this relationship? At the risk of oversimplification, we will say straightaway that Badiou offers the following answers: (1) Cinema is a complex multi-dimensional structure such that it lies in excess of all definition. (2) Cinema is a crucial condition of philosophy since it says something new concerning images and the real. (3) Cinema is an impure art in the sense that it is intrinsically contaminated with (but not corrupted by) non-art. (4) Cinema is a porous art in so far as it is necessarily complicated with (but not compromised by) the other arts. (5) The relationship of cinema to philosophy is exceptional in that it presents a "democratic dialectics" (6) There is a dissymmetrical symmetry between cinema and philosophy, in that they both, each in their own way, orient us toward the good life.

As is so often the case, however, these answers are themselves less revealing than their complicated workings out. Indeed, our thesis here is that while Badiou's propositions are on the whole correct, certain of their premises remain problematic and in need of further clarification. For the sake of simplicity, as well as for other reasons that will become clear as we move forward, we will regroup these questions under two broad categories: "what does cinema mean?" (encompassing questions 1, 3 and 4); and "what does cinema mean to philosophy?" (incorporating questions 2, 5 and 6). Limitations of space mean that we need to restrict our focus here to the first set of questions, leaving a more detailed consideration of the second group for another time.

What Does Cinema Mean?

From the moment of its premature birth in the late nineteenth century, philosophers, theorists, journalists and critics alike have been trying to come to terms with what cinema actually *is*, or to define the very nature of cinema. More specifically, they have asked what it is about film that is truly unique and original: What is it that "singularizes" cinema and sets it apart from the other arts? This fact alone is enough to lead us to our first critical point, which is that, when considered in isolation, the question "what is cinema?" actually makes precious little sense, much in the way that an adequate definition or ontology of "art" in general (divorced from the question of particular form or quality) is neither forthcoming nor especially beneficial. Rather, any enquiry into what we mean by "cinema," if it is to be of any real use, must be coupled with an examination of what cinema actually *means*, that is, what it signifies or expresses. Or again, in asking what cinema means, it is crucial that we consider this in both its "passive" (or definitional) and its "active" (or operational) senses: not only "what is cinema?", but equally important, "what can it do?"; what is it that cinema and cinema alone makes possible? This twofold question has generally been posed in four different ways, such that we can isolate four principal or elementary approaches to "thinking cinema."

Broadly speaking, the first approach recognizes cinema as the supreme art of images, whose greatness lies in its ability to stage the complex interplay between what *is* and what *appears*. Cinema is then understood as an ontological art: as not only the first art (*pace* photography) to credibly represent the world in all its infinitely complicated glory, but moreover the art that most successfully envisions the relations between being and appearing. Philosophically speaking, this approach actually predates cinema by some millennia, going at least as far back as Plato's *Republic* and his famous proto-cinematic allegory of the cave.[3] In our own age, however—which is of course the age of cinema—it is André Bazin who is most synonymous with this approach.

A second approach concerns cinema's relation to time and tells us that a film's great power lies foremost in the manner by which it "transforms time into perception" (Badiou 2013a: 236), or the way it allows us to, in effect, "see" time itself. Its most famous philosophical exponent is unquestionably none other than Gilles Deleuze, whose two great books on cinema continue to exert an extraordinary influence on the philosophy of film. Indeed, the temporal approach arguably remains to this day the most common philosophical entry point into the question of cinema.

A third approach concerns cinema's relation to the other arts. Broadly speaking, cinema is here either praised for finally presenting the profound synthesis of the other arts, or else it is condemned as little more than the superfluous "plus-one" of the arts, an art which thrives parasitically off its more sophisticated sisters while offering nothing back in return. The key historical philosophical touchstone here is of course no less than G. W. F. Hegel (who, as Badiou himself notes, died over half-a-century before the birth of cinema),[4] while its first great champion—at least in its positive formulation—was the pioneering film theorist and critic Ricciotto Canudo.[5]

Reciprocally, the fourth and final approach concerns cinema's relation to non-art. The idea here is that cinema's uniqueness—and equally its power—is paradoxically to be found in its inexorable artistic impurity: in its being the least "refined" of the arts, or in the simple fact that even the undisputed triumphs of cinema necessarily remain hopelessly complicated with non-art. While many theorists have laid claim to variations on this argument (both negative and positive), its most forceful contemporary adherent is arguably none other than Badiou himself.

So, in sum, we can ask what cinema is—and, crucially, what it does—by examining it as an ontological art, as a temporal art, as an art which is inextricably tied (for better or worse) to the other arts, or as an art that is itself complicated (again: for better or worse) with non-art. Moreover, we can easily associate these distinct approaches with proper names like Bazin, Deleuze, Canudo and Badiou.

An Indefinable Experience

If we are to truly come to terms with what cinema *means*, however, it is critical that we not restrict ourselves to any single one of these approaches and instead engage with all four at the same time (in a manner analogous to how philosophy treats its conditions). This is in fact one of the principal reasons as to why we have opted here to rearrange and conflate three of the key questions Badiou raises in "Cinema and Philosophy"—namely: (1) what cinema is; (3) whether it constitutes an art; and (4) what its relation is to the established arts—under the single heading "what does cinema mean?" For as we have already indicated, in order to provide a clear answer to the question of what cinema *means*, it is essential that we have an understanding of what it *does* (or can do), and this necessarily involves taking into account the relation it has to the other arts, and reciprocally, to non-art. Indeed, it cannot escape comment that Badiou's own self-confessedly unsatisfactory answer to this first fundamental question—namely: that cinema constitutes a complex multi-dimensional structure which exceeds definition, such that "We cannot really know what cinema is" (Badiou 2018a: 19)—results at least in part from his ironically limiting his initial considerations to only the first two of the classical approaches to thinking cinema, that is as constituting an ontological and a temporal art, while treating the remaining two (regarding art and non-art respectively) as wholly distinct questions.[6]

As our thesis is that the problems posed by question (1) cannot be adequately addressed without reference to questions (3) and (4), it is worth taking a moment to consider Badiou's response to this initial question in some detail. In asking what cinema is, Badiou first notes that it is clearly not enough to simply say that a film consists of images, since this would obviously fail to differentiate it from other arts such as drawing, painting and photography. Nor does it suffice to understand cinema as being uniquely composed of images-in-movement, since this neglects the constructive level of editing: the combination of different "movement images" into distinct sequences; the deliberate juxtapositions and careful orchestrations of montage. In addition to this, we of course need to recognize the crucial dimension of sound (incorporating diegetic phenomena like dialog and environmental or "natural" noise, as well as additive elements such as music, narration, sound effects, etc.), together with various key contextual traits inherited from other established artistic fields such as literature (narrative structure), theater (acting and mise-en-scène), dance (the choreography of movement) and so on. Note also how the belated addition of synchronized sound—which only first appeared almost three decades after cinema's birth—further complicates matters in that it draws attention to the "latent infinity in cinema" (Badiou 2018a: 19), or to its evolutionary, assimilative nature: to the fact that cinema has historically existed in a state of constant transformation and increasing complexification following the introduction of new dimensions like sound, color, 3D technology, streaming services and so on.

To this end, Badiou understands cinema as not only expressing the totality of relationships between shots, sequences, editing, sounds and so on, thus as "a complexity of practically all dimensions of perception" (2018a: 18), but furthermore as being historically incomplete: the development of cinema—the successive constitution of its particular infinity—remains an ongoing process, such that we are incapable of registering its ultimate form; even today "we are inside cinema without knowing exactly its conceptual signification" (19). Being irreducible to any single one of its elements, cinema might be at best classified in vague terms as a multiform composition: a complex multi-dimensional structure-in-becoming that eludes determination. As Badiou admits, "it's impossible—this is my proposition—to give a clear definition of cinema"; ultimately "we have an experience of cinema, but not really the definition" (2018a: 18).

Yet this of course raises a further complication, in that without being able to say what cinema really is, at a basic, constitutive level, this makes it very difficult to be able to say what it *does*. Or in other words, cinema's lack of conceptual definition means that we do not have any real operational or "artistic" definition either, such that we cannot identify any clear criteria with which to distinguish an ordinary film from a true work of art. And yet, paradoxically, it is this very point of indistinction that Badiou isolates as "the first exceptional point concerning cinema" (2018a: 18). Indeed, this indefiniteness is in his eyes what foremost distinguishes or "singularizes" cinema, since none of its sister arts exhibit such indeterminacy. To the contrary, each and every one of the other arts can, according to Badiou, be given very precise artistic definitions. Poetry, for example, figures "the maximal intensity of language," by which the poem seeks "to extract from language something new" (Badiou 2018a: 21). Or in other words, in poetry, language is forced to say something previously unsayable, something that could not until then have been formulated in the existing language. Similarly, the objective of painting is to make visible what would otherwise remain in-visible, such that a real painting marks "the production of an image of something that has no image" (21), an image of what is strictly speaking un-imaginable. Theater likewise aims to present "the relationship of humanity to itself in the distance between the spectacle and the audience," such that the performance would "present to humanity a figure of humanity" (21). Similar definitions can be provided for all the other arts—sculpture, music, dance, architecture, drawing, literature and so on—and Badiou has devoted countless pages to their detailed study.[7] Out of all the established arts, cinema alone eludes artistic definition.

The Task(s) of Art

At this point we are obviously required to say a few words about Badiou's conception of art itself. For not only is it clear that he characterizes—and by doing so, *legitimizes*— each of the other arts according to what he recognizes as their peculiar mission or objective; moreover, this operation invariably involves the presentation of something that is both constitutive of its "essential" nature, and at the same time, radically new. This is plain to see in the examples cited earlier (where poetry figures "the maximal intensity of language," etc.), just as we find it in his definition of, say, contemporary drawing as "the material visibility of pure invisibility" (Badiou 2006: 45), where the elementary material of drawing is visible lines and marks on a (for all intents and purposes) blank surface, while transfiguring the in-visible into the visible amounts to a form of creation.

Placing the question of cinema (which at first glance appears to be formally excluded from such a characterization) momentarily to one side, it is of course precisely this prescriptive approach to the arts that more than anything seems to position Badiou on the side of a historical modernist discourse. After all, the words, concepts and ideas he employs when speaking of art—"The stake of poetry is to attain the pure; the poetic machine is subtractive only with a view to a purification" (Badiou 2008: 59); "Artistic activity can only be discerned in a film as a *process of purification of its own immanent non-artistic character*" (Badiou 2013a: 139)—clearly evoke the writings of the great ideologists of twentieth-century modernism. Here we cannot help but think of Clement Greenberg—who, as Fredric Jameson asserts, "more than any other can be credited as having inventing the ideology of modernism full-blown and out of whole cloth" (2012: 169)—and in particular his enormously influential work on "Modernist Painting," where he observes how "the essence of Modernism lies [. . .] in the use of the characteristic methods of a discipline to criticize the discipline itself, not in order to subvert it but in order to entrench it more firmly in the area of its competence" (Greenberg 2003a: 774). It is worth quoting Greenberg at length here:

> What had to be exhibited [in modernist art] and made explicit was that which was unique and irreducible not only in art in general, but also that which was unique and irreducible in each particular art. Each art had to determine, through the operations peculiar to itself, the effects peculiar and exclusive to itself. By doing this each art would, to be sure, narrow its area of competence, but at the same time it would make its possession of this area all the more secure. It quickly emerged that the unique and proper area of competence of each art coincided with all that was unique in the nature of the medium. The task of self-criticism became to eliminate from the specific effects of each art any and every effect that might conceivably be borrowed from or by the medium of any other art. Thus would each art be rendered "pure," and in its "purity" find the guarantee of its standards of quality as well as of its independence. (2003a: 774–5)

While it is hard not to recognize in this decidedly "purificatory" account Badiou's own espousal of "a subtractive protocol of thought" (2007: 56) at work in art, we would be wrong to conflate Greenberg's "purification" with Badiou's "subtraction." Indeed, Badiou has gone to considerable lengths to distinguish between the aggressive logic of purification, which embraces destruction as the necessary precursor to all creation, and the more subtle logic of subtraction, which instead "attempts to *measure* the ineluctable negativity" (2007: 54) and in doing so carve out a space for thought. Moreover, while both logics exhibit what he identifies as a profound "passion for the real"—a passion which, we should add, "is always a passion for the new" (2007: 56)—they differ markedly in the way this passion is expressed. On the one hand, we find "a passion for the real that is obsessed with identity: to grasp real identity, to unmask its copies, to discredit fakes"; yet there also exists "a differential and differentiating passion devoted to the construction of a minimal difference" (2007: 56). While the former (purificatory) approach effectively equates destruction with creation—something we can see especially clearly in the case of the artistic avant-gardes[8]—making it "a process doomed to incompletion, a figure of the bad infinite" (2007: 56), the latter (subtractive) approach realizes itself instead as "the invention of an outline," proceeding "not by grasping a pre-existing totality" (57) but rather by staging "a minimal, albeit absolute, difference" (56).

So whereas Greenberg's modernism effectively reduces everything to the medium itself and accordingly champions purification as a means of "restor[ing] the identity of an art" (Greenberg 2003b: 566), Badiou's subtractive approach is contrarily concerned first and foremost with isolating the constitutive gap or "minimal difference" between semblance and the real, and in particular, with affirming the way by which such art can "invent content at the very place of the minimal difference, where there is almost nothing" (Badiou 2007: 57).[9]

Minimal Differences

We might then say that Badiou reconceives the great modernist project in terms of a subtractive passion for the real, the aim of which is not to grasp (maximal) identity, but rather to produce (minimal) difference. Accordingly, far from promoting an "autonomizing" framework whereby each of the arts would be rigorously separated and exclusively committed to exploring its own medium[10]—what Alberto Toscano derisorily refers to as "the belaboured narrative of aesthetic modernism" (2007: viii), and what Badiou recognizes as a non-dialectical process of *destruction*—Badiou instead holds that the subtractive task of art is "to exhibit as a real point, not the destruction of reality, but minimal difference" (2007: 65), the "invention of an outline" that constitutes a space for thinking something new. Or again: if art's goal is the purification of its own content, this is "not in order to annihilate it at its surface, but to subtract it from its apparent unity so as to detect within it the minuscule difference, the vanishing term that constitutes it" (2007: 65).

Moreover, while it is clear that each art is for Badiou entirely differentiated from the other arts, possessing its own particular form, together with its own unique possibilities, modes of expression and so on, it is crucial to bear in mind how an artistic truth is for Badiou always the truth of a particular artistic situation, and a "situation" is for him an exceedingly plastic term in that it can mean any grouping whatsoever. Indeed, there is no special reason to understand an artistic situation as being necessarily medium-specific or limited to a single art (or, for that matter, limited to art *per se*): obviously there are countless examples of mixed artistic situations, even within the modernist tradition. Hence Badiou can celebrate as being emblematic of the subtractive orientation of thought artists as disparate as Kazimir Malevich, whose seminal 1918 painting *White on White* presents us with the minimal difference between the bare minimum effect of structure—the fragile white square *qua* "zero of form" (Malevich 2003: 173)—and that which is radically unstructured (the white void in which the square exists), and Marcel Duchamp, whose infamous "readymades"— and in particular his 1917 work *Fountain*—contrarily expose the fact that the very material of art is first and foremost non-artistic (or that all art is, in effect, ready-made), thereby giving the lie to the very idea of medium-specificity and the notion of artistic purity or "identity" (see Ling 2018: 132–3). Indeed, for all their differences, it is clear that Malevich and Duchamp each proceed subtractively by understanding the real not in terms of identity but instead treating it as a minimal *gap*, the barely apparent "difference between place and taking place" (Badiou 2007: 56)—and as Badiou avers, "it is in this 'barely', in this immanent exception, that all the affect lies" (2007: 65).

The seemingly conflicting approaches of Malevich and Duchamp moreover illustrate something essential and often overlooked about the concept of subtraction itself, which is that it needs to be understood not only as a process of "drawing back," but also one of "drawing forth." Certainly Malevich's *White on White* embodies the subtractive protocol as a systematic process of "drawing back" (through the painting's evacuation of form, color, space and so on), such that we can indeed conceive of the work in quasi-Greenbergian terms as a movement toward artistic "purity" or identity with the medium, with the crucial exception that this identification not only remains necessarily incomplete (i.e., "minimally different") but moreover signals "the first step of pure creation in art" (Malevich 2003: 181). At the very same time, however, Duchamp's ready-mades illustrate the fundamentally extractive (or better yet, *elicitive*) side of this same procedure, namely, its being equally a process that *draws forth* (hence "sub-traction": "to draw from beneath"), in that far from isolating a "pure remainder" by emptying out all surrounding content, the ready-made as "work of art" contrarily establishes impurity as the well from which all purity is drawn. As before, however, it is crucial to note that this does not amount to an identity or an equivalence, but rather foregrounds what Duchamp would himself call an "infrathin separative difference" (1983: unpaginated), being the minimal difference separating art from its subjacent non-artistic material.

Conflicts and Complications

Having carefully distinguished Badiou's subtractive approach to art from the (Greenbergian) modernist program of self-referential purification or "autonomization," we now find ourselves in a position where we can finally make sense of cinema's complicated relation to both art and non-art. Furthermore, the logic of indiscernibility introduced by Duchamp's work in particular casts cinema's lack of a conceptual definition, which had initially appeared as an obstacle to artistic "legitimacy," in an entirely different light, such that we can now recognize its inherent indeterminacy or "inessentialness" as actually constituting a positive and even constructive feature. Indeed, it is with Duchamp firmly in mind that, after having declared its impossibility, Badiou does in fact go on to propose a possible artistic definition of cinema as the "production of the visibility of the conflict between art and non-art in the contemporary world" (2018a: 22).

This is a striking definition, not simply because it confirms our own insistence that any answer to the question of what cinema *means* must take into account its peculiar relation to both art and non-art, but moreover because its determining feature— namely: cinema's conflicted nature—is according to Badiou one of the major stumbling blocks in the way of a definition in the first place![11] We might even say that the question of cinema remains indistinct precisely because of its artistic definition, that is, as a result of the fact that every film is to some degree complicated with both art—or rather, with the other arts—and non-art.

Let us take a moment to unpack all of this. First, cinema is complicated with art in the sense that it "imaginarily propose[s] a totalization of the arts," even if it "does not 'grasp' this totalization in an authentic artistic singularity" (Badiou 2018b: 576; see also 2020a: 115). This in itself of course presents an immediate obstacle to cinema's definition, since "cinema is always a definition that is also the definition of the other arts as a part of cinema itself" (Badiou 2018a: 24). We have seen something of this complication already, whereby cinema is architecture by virtue of montage, painting through the careful composition of the frame, music not only on account of the obligatory soundtrack but moreover due to its status as an art of time, and so on.

Yet while cinema would clearly fall foul here of Greenberg's autonomizing account, Badiou contrarily sees film's artistic permeability as one of its positive features: "All the arts flow through cinema" such that it recapitulates "and magnifies them, according them a distinctive emotional power. There's a power of revelation of the arts, a power of subjugation of the arts in cinema that truly makes it the seventh art" (Badiou 2013a: 7).[12] But of course the corollary of this is that cinema only exists *as* an art by virtue of its sister arts. Thus we return, once again, to cinema's "inessential" nature, or to its figuring as an empty site of appropriation: while cinema may well be the "seventh art" in that it constitutes a recapitulation and even a "democratization" of its more aristocratic predecessors (as in Canudo's formulation), it is equally so to the extent that, in the absence of their support, it remains little more than an artless folly.

But cinema is also—arguably even more so—contaminated by non-art. Certainly Badiou sees cinema as "an art that takes art's possible impurity to its extreme" (Badiou and Tarby 2013: 83). After all, its indisputable industrial nature not only enjoins it to seek out the lowest common denominator by pandering to its receptive (paying) public but also ensures the effective impossibility of realizing a singular artistic vision. For unlike Duchamp's carefully curated ready-mades (which isolate a single non-artistic industrial object and "elevate" this to the rank of art), the problem here is foremost one of scale, in so far as a film "works with an infinity of parameters that are, as such, impossible to control" (Badiou and Tarby 2013: 83). Indeed, cinema's inherent complexity, or its very *magnitude*—understood both in terms of what it encompasses (the sheer scale of the frame and what it contains) and the nature of its composition (the infinite expanse afforded by editing and montage, as well as the duration of the work as a whole)—ensures that "no film, strictly speaking, is controlled by artistic thinking from beginning to end" (Badiou 2013a: 139); that even its undisputed masterpieces will nonetheless contain at least some degree of non-artistic content. Here we are thinking less of the careless inclusion of inferior material (such as superfluous scenes, poor acting, hackneyed dialog, etc.), than of the vast amounts of everyday detritus which are inadvertently captured by the "rather indiscriminate and undiscriminating" (Malevich 2002: 63) camera lens.

Malevich himself responded to this artistic indiscrimination by likening cinema to "a new trash can" (2002: 64), arguing in 1928 that "film now lags behind all arts because its artistic form is obscured by garbage and kissing" (65). Yet cinema's status as an absolutely impure art in no way means that the other arts are by contrast necessarily "pure." We have already seen how Duchamp's ready-mades revealed impurity as a fundamental law of art, in that art always involves the formalization of what was previously formless, the becoming-art of what had formerly been considered non-art (or what, according to the artistic situation in question, had heretofore inexisted). This is after all what allowed us to isolate the properly creative side of the subtractive procedure as a process that formalizes or "brings into form" what was previously formless, or that "purifies" what was impure. It is in fact precisely this movement that Badiou holds cinema as "democratizing," namely, "the process whereby art uproots itself from non-art by turning that movement into a border, by turning impurity into the thing itself" (2013a: 239).[13] Moreover, it is for this reason he can claim that "with only slight exaggeration cinema could be compared to the treatment of waste" (226). Needless to say, we need to recognize this for the (non-Malevichian) affirmation it really is: as one of Badiou's "masters" Jacques Lacan intoned, "a great civilization is first and foremost a civilization that has a waste-disposal system" (2008: 65).

The Art of the Fight

All of this leads us back to Badiou's proposed definition of cinema as "the art of the fight between art and non-art" (2018a: 22). For him, this means that, far from being a peaceful art of quiet contemplation, cinema is contrarily a site of intense struggle, an unrelenting conflict between refinement and vulgarity and, more fundamentally, between "true" and "false images" (22). That this conflict concerns the spectator (who must actively engage with, rather than be passively absorbed by, the on-screen events) as much as the images themselves cannot help but return us finally to the standard point of departure for any philosophical consideration of cinema, namely, Plato's famous cave. But as Badiou is at pains to point out, as an illusion that explicitly announces itself *as* an illusion, cinema is in reality something altogether removed from the classical cave: if Plato's allegory "is an image of semblance that presents itself to everyone imprisoned in the cave as the indisputable image of what can exist" (Badiou 2020b: 190), then a film presents its spectators with the image of this image precisely *as* a subject for dispute. Indeed, if real cinema foments the "war against bad images" and the struggle to affirm what might constitute a "true image" (Badiou 2018a: 22), it is, if anything, closer to the situation outside of the cave looking in, or to the position of the philosopher themselves.

What is essential to bear in mind here, of course, is that a "true image" is not the real itself, but rather a unique relation to the real. On this point Badiou is crystal clear: a "true image" is an image that constitutes "a new thinking of the real" (2018a: 23), hence its crucial interest to philosophy. And yet, as he points out elsewhere, "the difficulty is that the relation between the real and images [. . .] is dramatically contradictory," for the simple reason that the real is, technically speaking, un-imaginable: "as soon as it is captured by the image [. . .] the real is crucified, abolished" (Badiou 2020c: 7), such that in order to successfully approach it "we must disimage, disimagine" (7).[14] Accordingly, a "true image"—one that "says something new concerning the real" (Badiou 2018a: 20)—can only take the form of a contradiction, a dispute or conflict, whereby we can clearly discern "a fight, a visible fight, in the image itself" (23).

This critical conflict, however, should be understood in two different senses, namely, as both "dramatic contradiction," and as "minimal difference." So cinema is finally Duchampian, in that it is an art which draws on its vulgar non-artistic resources to present, in ways that are by turn spectacular and almost imperceptible, a contradictorily "true image": an image which, far from being self-identical, is visibly at war with itself. But there is also a contrasting Malevichian undercurrent, whereby in attempting to realize its own singular artistic being—to, in effect, *define itself*—cinema engages in a series of "incompletable purification operations" (Badiou 2013a: 140), purging itself not only of its immanent non-artistry, but of its (other) artistic content as well. While both approaches certainly carry with them the risk of going too far—of embracing non-art to such an extent that it would suppress its own artistry; of evacuating extraneous content even to the point of sacrificing the image itself[15]—cinema overcomes this primarily by remaining faithful to its properly subtractive nature, that is, by always embracing conflict and difference over compliance and identity. Or again: by countering Duchamp with Malevich, and Malevich with Duchamp.

Neither succumbing to its inherent vulgarity nor negating itself through total refinement, ultimately cinema means something only in so far as it ensures that these differentially subtractive poles remain in constant, unremitting tension. The most conflicted of all arts, cinema *is* cinema to the extent that it remains engaged in a "fight against itself" (Badiou 2018a: 23), a battle which is equally between Duchamp and Malevich (or rather their artistic gestures), and whose triumph is marked by the absence of any clear victor.

Notes

1. Badiou's article on "La Culture Cinématographique," first published in the journal *Vin Nouveau* in 1957, introduces many of the themes and ideas that would come to define his philosophical comprehension of film—most notably its complicated relation to both art and non-art—long before he had developed his own philosophical system let alone his peculiar "inaesthetic" approach to art. An English translation appears in the 2013 edited collection *Cinema*.
2. See Ling (2018).
3. In a separate lecture delivered around the same time as "Cinema and Philosophy," Badiou half-seriously declares that "Plato created cinema in the allegory of the cave" (2018c: 34), and in his "hypertranslation" of Plato's *Republic* goes so far as to recast the famous cave *as* "an enormous movie theatre" (2012: 212).
4. After meticulously detailing the historical evolution of art through its various stages (symbolic, classical and romantic) and its specific forms (architecture, sculpture, painting, music and poetry), Hegel famously concludes that modern comedy not only represents the final form of art, but that "on this peak comedy leads at the same time to the dissolution of art altogether" (Hegel 1975: 1236). In his most recent work *L'Immanence des vérités*, Badiou turns to cinema to examine why Hegel excludes the possibility of a further "dialectical twist [. . .] which would be the abolition of this abolition in a new form"—namely, cinema—which "would be at one and the same time architecture, sculpture, painting, and dramatic poetry, drawing the history of art to a close through [. . .] a redemptive totalization" (2018b: 572–3) (see also Badiou 2020a: 111–12).
5. Less well known that Bazan and Deleuze, Ricciotto Canudo (writing in 1911) recognized cinema as "Art's powerful coadjutor," and held that film would continue to develop and refine itself to the point that we would "recognize cinema as the synthesis of all the arts and of the profound impulse underlying them" (1988: 293).
6. Here again we can observe the prescience of Badiou's 1957 work on "Cinematic Culture," in which he notes how in attempting to isolate what it is about cinema that is truly unique (or in trying to *define* it as such), "all we come face to face with is an

7   absence. This is because an art form's uniqueness is inseparable from its existence, and 'what is unique about cinema' is nothing but all of its different manifestations" (2013a: 30).

7   A short list of the most relevant English-language works here would include books devoted to the arts such as *Handbook of Inaesthetics*, *In Praise of Theatre*, *The Age of the Poets*, *Rhapsody for the Theatre*, *Five Lessons on Wagner*, *On Beckett*, as well as his key works *Theory of the Subject*, *Being and Event* and *Logics of Worlds*. On top of this, one should of course also consult his own artistic works, such as *Ahmed the Philosopher* and *The Incident at Antioch*.

8   As art critic and philosopher Boris Groys observes, "Avant-garde art equated destruction and creation and assumed that, with the rejection of all conventions and the destruction of the tradition, the reality that had been concealed by these conventions, norms, and things would appear by itself" (2014: 147).

9   It is worth noting that Greenberg would go on to qualify his words on purification in art, explaining that "I don't believe there is such a thing as purity in art, or pure art. That was a useful illusion for the avant-garde, for many years, but I don't believe there is such a thing. Now, when I wrote of art in 'Towards a Newer Laocoon' [. . .] I was reporting an illusion without realizing it was an illusion" (de Duve and Greenberg 2010: 146).

10 Jacques Rancière most forcefully pursues this line of thought with regard to Badiou, arguing that his "inaesthetics" "names the way in which art's Platonic heteronomy comes to be adjusted to the modernist dogmas of art's autonomy and play its part in that anti-aesthetic resentment which is the eventual result of the modernist guarantee" (2004: 231).

11 As Badiou observes, "It is clear that cinema has a relationship to practically all the other arts. It's a form of its impurity, precisely: the impossibility to define cinema as such" (2018a: 23). Note that while Badiou's own "definition" specifically refers to the art/non-art distinction at issue in cinema, the fact that cinema's artistic status is for him entirely tied up with the other arts necessarily implicates them in this definition.

12 While never explicitly condemnatory, it is interesting to note how Badiou has since demurred from his earlier somewhat disparaging contention that cinema "does not add itself to the other six while remaining on the same level as them" (Badiou 2005b: 79), such that whenever an Idea visits us cinematically "it is *always* in a subtractive (or defective) relation to one or several among the other arts" (86).

13 Badiou even conceives of this in Platonic terms, observing that "if cinema is [. . .] the chance visitation of the Idea, it is in the sense in which the old Parmenides, in Plato, requires the young Socrates to accept, together with the Good, the Just, the True, and the Beautiful, some equally abstract if less respectable ideas: the ideas of Hair, or of Mud" (1998: 90).

14 Badiou already points to this inevitable contradiction in an earlier piece (from 1983) addressing "a cinema of the encounter [. . .] with the question of the real, as such, in an opening made solely by its representation," noting that there always remains "something that cannot be represented, a real that slips away through the point of obscurity of its capture" (2013a: 58–9).

15 Unsurprisingly, Malevich himself argued that if cinema was to truly "[free] itself from ideological content and [begin] to build its form," it was essential to understand "that art can exist without the image, without everyday life, and without the idea's visage. Only then will cinema contemplate its own culture 'as such'" (2002: 43).

Works Cited

Badiou, A. (1957), "La Culture Cinématographique," *Vin Nouveau* 5, 3–22.
Badiou, A. (1998), "Le Plus-de-Voir," *Artpress*, hors série, 86–90.
Badiou, A. (2003), *On Beckett*, ed. and trans. A. Toscano and N. Power, Manchester: Clinamen.
Badiou, A. (2005a), *Being and Event*, trans. O. Feltham, London: Continuum.
Badiou, A. (2005b), *Handbook of Inaesthetics*, trans. A. Toscano, Stanford: Stanford University Press.
Badiou, A. (2006), "Drawing," *Lacanian Ink* 28, 42–9.
Badiou, A. (2007), *The Century*, trans. A. Toscano, Cambridge: Polity.
Badiou, A. (2008), *Conditions*, trans. S. Corcoran, London: Continuum.
Badiou, A. (2009a), *Logics of Worlds: Being and Event, 2*, trans. A. Toscano, London: Continuum.
Badiou, A. (2009b), *Theory of the Subject*, trans. B. Bosteels, London: Continuum.
Badiou, A. (2010), *Five Lessons on Wagner*, trans. S. Spitzer, New York: Verso.
Badiou, A. (2011), *Wittgenstein's Antiphilosophy*, trans. B. Bosteels, London: Verso.
Badiou, A. (2012), *Plato's Republic: A Dialogue in 16 Chapters*, trans. S. Spitzer and K. Reinhard, New York: Columbia University Press.
Badiou, A. (2013a), *Cinema*, ed. An. de Baecque, trans. S. Spitzer, Cambridge: Polity.
Badiou, A. (2013b), *Rhapsody for the Theatre*, ed. and trans. B. Bosteels, London: Verso.
Badiou, A. (2013c), *The Incident at Antioch: A Tragedy in Three Acts*, trans. S. Spitzer, New York: Columbia University Press.
Badiou, A. (2014a), *Ahmed the Philosopher: 34 Short Plays for Children & Everyone Else*, trans. J. Litvak, New York: Columbia University Press.
Badiou, A. (2014b), *The Age of the Poets, and Other Writings on Twentieth Century Poetry and Prose*, ed. and trans. B. Bosteels, London: Verso.
Badiou, A. (2018a), "Cinema and Philosophy," in A. J. Bartlett and J. Clemens (eds.), *Badiou and His Interlocuters: Lectures, Interviews and Responses*, 17–30, London: Bloomsbury.
Badiou, A. (2018b), *L'Immanence des vérités: L'être et l'événement, 3*, Paris: Fayard.
Badiou, A. (2018c), "The Common Preoccupation of Art and Philosophy," in A. J. Bartlett and J. Clemens (eds.), *Badiou and His Interlocuters: Lectures, Interviews and Responses*, 31–8, London: Bloomsbury.
Badiou, A. (2020a), "Hegel, the Arts, and Cinema," *Journal of Continental Philosophy*, trans. A. Ling 1:1, 97–116. https://doi.org/10.5840/jcp2020421.
Badiou, A. (2020b), "In Search of the Lost Real," *Journal of Continental Philosophy*, trans. A. Ling 1:2, 187–200. https://doi.org/10.5840/jcp20211288.
Badiou, A. (2020c), *The Pornographic Age*, trans. A. J. Bartlett and J. Clemens, London: Bloomsbury.
Badiou, A. and F. Tarby (2013), *Philosophy and the Event*, trans. L. Burchill, Cambridge: Polity Press.
Badiou, A. and N. Truong (2015), *In Praise of Theatre*, trans. A. Bielski, Cambridge: Polity.
Canudo, R. (1988), "Reflections on the Seventh Art," in R. Abel (ed.), *French Film Theory and Criticism: A History/Anthology 1907–1939, Volume I: 1907–1929*, 291–304, Princeton: Princeton University Press.
de Duve, T. and C. Greenberg (2010), "A Public Debate with Clement Greenberg," in B. Holmes (ed.), *Clement Greenberg Between the Lines*, 121–158, Chicago: University of Chicago Press.

Duchamp, M. (1983), *Notes*, ed. P. Matisse, Boston: G. K. Hall.
Greenberg, C. (2003a), "Modernist Painting," in C. Harrison and P. Wood (eds.), *Art in Theory 1900–2000: An Anthology of Changing Ideas*, 773–779, Oxford: Blackwell.
Greenberg, C. (2003b), "Towards a Newer Laocoon," in C. Harrison and P. Wood (eds.), *Art in Theory 1900–2000: An Anthology of Changing Ideas*, 562–568, Oxford: Blackwell.
Groys, B. (2014), *On the New*, trans. G. M. Goshgarian, London: Verso.
Hegel, G. W. F. (1975), *Aesthetics: Lectures on Fine Art. Volume II*, trans. T. M. Knox, Oxford: Oxford University Press.
Jameson, F. (2012), *A Singular Modernity: Essay on the Ontology of the Present*, London: Verso.
Lacan, J. (2008), *My Teaching*, trans. D. Macey, London: Verso.
Ling, A. (2018), "An Inessential Art?: Positioning Cinema in Alain Badiou's Philosophy," in A. J. Bartlett and J. Clemens (eds.), *Badiou and His Interlocuters: Lectures, Interviews and Responses*, 127–139, London: Bloomsbury.
Malevich, K. (2002), *The White Rectangle: Writings on Film*, ed. O. Bulgakowa, trans. E. Batuman, L. Golburt and A. Muza, San Francisco: Potemkin Press.
Malevich, K. (2003), "From Cubism and Futurism to Suprematism: The New Realism in Painting," in C. Harrison and P. Wood (eds.), *Art in Theory 1900–2000: An Anthology of Changing Ideas*, 173–183, Oxford: Blackwell.
Rancière, J. (2004), "Aesthetics, Inaesthetics, Anti-Aesthetics," in P. Hallward (ed.), *Think Again: Alain Badiou and the Future of Philosophy*, 218–231, London: Continuum.
Toscano, A. (2007), "Translating the Century," in A. Badiou, *The Century*, trans. A. Toscano, vi–xii, Cambridge: Polity.

9

Modern Love Theory

James, Badiou and "The Story in It"

Sigi Jöttkandt

With a modest nod toward Plato's *Symposium*, Henry James's short story, "The Story in It," is staged as a charming philosophical debate about love between three friends. Published in 1902, it concerns a young woman, Maud Blessingbourne, who at the time of the story's opening is a guest of Mrs. Dyott. This latter lady, we learn, is conducting an affair with a certain Colonel Voyt—with whom it turns out that Maud, a young widow and voracious reader of French novels, is also secretly in love. On the stormy afternoon against which James's unassuming drama plays itself out, Colonel Voyt comes over to tea and the members of the little love triangle enter into a vigorous debate about international literary amours. Comparing the contemporary French novel with those of British and American "manufacture," Voyt confidently avows the superiority of "the eternal French thing":

> They do what they feel, and they feel more things than we. They strike so many more notes, and with so different a hand. When it comes to any account of a relation say between a man and a woman—I mean an intimate or a curious or a suggestive one—where are we compared to them? (James 1999: n.p.)

As one listens to Voyt's assessment of the passionate French, it is difficult not to be reminded of Alain Badiou. Badiou, whose numerous works include the aptly-named *The Adventure of French Philosophy*, regards love, together with science, art and politics, as one of philosophy's conditions, and he does so in a fashion that at least one literary critic has found perplexing. Terry Eagleton comments that "Badiou speaks of love as though it is a self-evident experience, which may be true for Parisians but not for the rest of us."[1]

Taking up Voyt's opposition between the ostensibly demure English and the adventurous and passionate French, in what follows I explore a complication that Henry James poses to Badiou's theory of love's Two. With its emphasis on rupture, on the utterly transformative power of the event which embodies a "pure beginning" of a "new time," Badiou's philosophy has been already been remarked as inherently modern (Begam 2021: 121), and yet in the dialog confabulated between Badiou and James later, Badiou's French theory finds itself strangely unsettled by a young English woman who, like her author, remains unmoved by dramatic philosophical flourishes. What might James, usually considered only an incipient modernist figure in the literary canon, offer to Badiou?[2] If James's own special place in the French philosopher's heart is openly worn in the form of his cinematic pen-name, "James Strether"[3] it is perhaps as an unconscious acknowledgment that there is still more to be said on the topic of naming and names, and of the void and the *u* in Badiou's otherwise formidable theory of love.

If we turn back to James's story, we see that his character, Maud, certainly seems to share Eagleton's hesitation about the Parisian passions. Maud, unconvinced by Colonel Voyt's panegyric, claims she is tired of "the poverty of the life" that her French novels depict, the eternally repetitive fictions which "give us only again and again, for ever and ever, the same couple." Despite their reputation for salaciousness, the modern French novels come across to her as colorless and unexciting: "I trust your book has been interesting?," enquires Mrs. Dyott. "Well enough; a little mild" is Maud's reply. But "a louder throb of the tempest had blurred the sound of the words. 'A little wild?' 'Dear no—timid and tame; unless I've quite lost my sense'" (James 1999: n.p.).

What Maud wishes to read—and, as we eventually learn, even more wants to write— is a story about an *un*adventurous woman, a woman who remains irreproachable while nevertheless still being "involved." A story of being "in" a relation, and therefore retaining the character of a Jamesian "situation," is what is required but the woman, Maud stipulates, should also be "decent." She explains, "I don't see why the romance— since you give it that name—should be all, as the French inveterately make it, for the women who are bad."

What interest could there be in the story of a "decent" woman? Clearly nothing, at least as far as Colonel Voyt is concerned, who assures her that her search can end only in disappointment:

"I never look," Maud remarked, "for anything but an interest."

"Naturally. But your interest," Voyt replied, "is in something different from life." (James 1999: n.p.)

For Voyt, as for his paramour Mrs. Dyott, the "interest" in a story can only be found in "pictures of passion." Yet Maud wagers simultaneously on the "good" and the "interesting," a bet she ultimately wins—wins metafictionally, that is, in the shape of James's tale itself, for as readers will have quickly understood, Maud's desired story of a "decent" yet involved woman is nothing other than the very one we are reading.

There is, then, a wider discussion nested within our little trio's mock-Platonic dialog. It concerns the future of the novel at the end of the nineteenth century, and it was a question that James was intimately involved with in the decade prior to the story's publication. Indeed, the key debates aired during this "era of discussion" (Besant and James 1885: 52) have distinct echoes in the argument between Maud, Mrs. Dyott and

Colonel Voyt. The original "hint" for the tale was provided by a comment by James's protégé, Paul Bourget, who on being queried why his heroines always must lead such scandalous lives replied that "ladies who respected themselves took particular care never to *have* adventures; not the least little adventure that would be worth (worth any self-respecting novelist's) speaking of" (James 1962: 286). Markedly, it is this same emphasis on "adventure" we hear Colonel Voyt and Mrs. Dyott mutually propounding:

> "Behind these words we use—the adventure, the novel, the drama, the romance, the situation, in short, as we most comprehensively say—behind them all stands the same sharp fact which they all in their different ways represent."
>
> "Precisely!" Mrs. Dyott was full of approval.
>
> Maud however was full of vagueness. "What great fact?"
>
> "The fact of a relation. The adventure's a relation; the relation's an adventure." (James 1999: n.p.)

With this assurance, Voyt repeats the chief claim aired by the popular novelist and critic, Walter Besant, in a public lecture titled "The Art of Fiction" at the Royal Institution in London on April 25, 1884. It was to this insistence on "adventure" that James famously objected in an essay of the same title, which was published in *Longman's Magazine* later that year.[4] To Besant's assertion that "Fiction without adventure—a drama without a plot—a novel without surprises—the thing is as impossible as life without uncertainty" (Besant and James 1885: 34), James retorts, "Why of adventure more than of green spectacles? [...]. Why without adventure, more than without matrimony, or celibacy, or parturition, or cholera, of hydropathy, or Jansenism?" James explains his reasoning in the following passage:

> This seems to me to bring the novel back to the hapless little role of being an artificial, ingenious thing—bring it down from its large, free character of an immense and exquisite correspondence with life. And what is adventure, when it comes to that, and by what sign is the listening pupil to recognize it? (Besant and James 1885: 22)

Maud, the implicit spokesperson for the Jamesian novelist, is similarly heard to query: "Doesn't it depend a little on what you call adventures?" A much fuller picture of modern "experience" is proposed by the English novelistic sensibility, something far richer than what Colonel Voyt and Mrs. Dyott—along with their French naturalist counterparts, Bourget, Flaubert, Zola, Daudet, despite their insistence on representing *all* of "life"—would seem to allow.

Yet if we read "The Story in It" merely as James's virtuosic recapitulation of an historical literary debate, we would miss the more deeply entrenched philosophical question that is at stake, one that Badiou's philosophy of love enables us to explore. Indeed, by bringing Badiou into this debate about the proper reaches of fictive representation that were circulating at the cusp of the modernist experiment in literature, one sees James extending an intriguing invitation to Badiou's theory of love's Two. Expressed in the simplest way—as James himself does in this tale—the question James poses to Badiou is whether the amorous relation that remains secret, the attachment whose object remains oblivious, or, even more strongly, the "romance" centered expressly around the beloved's "not knowing," is able to constitute the "supplement" of the count-as-One in the "adventure" Badiou names "the Two."

We can make our way into the question by recalling how for Badiou love is universal because of the way it enables the lovers to extricate themselves from the realm of the same and inhabit a world from "the perspective of difference." It is this aspect that gives love its well-known "universal" dimension: Love has "universal implications," Badiou comments in *In Praise of Love*: "it is an individual experience of potential universality, and is thus central to philosophy, as Plato was the first to intuit" (Badiou and Truong 2012: 17). The unique "work of love," its novelty, lies in its creation of a Two (Badiou 2003: n.p.). Love's Two is a singular creation for Badiou because it is not a product of the ordinal "count" that underpins the logic of presentation. Instead, in being counted "immanently," a Two is produced not through the addition of two Ones but by the subtraction of a certain remainder that circulates in the situation. This remainder, which Badiou assigns the letter (u), designates the perpetually missed encounter between the sexes, the eternally "disjunct" positions of masculine and feminine experience.

The u is what ensures the failure of the sexual relation for Badiou. Like the Lacanian object (a), with which it shares a clear affinity, the u announces the strict inevitability by which man and woman will only encounter the other sex from disparate positions; each sex will always inhabit the "other" side of a Möbius strip. Whereas Lacan's formulas of sexuation, the key jumping off point for Badiou's intervention here, express the sexual disjuncture in logical terms, Badiou frames it in terms of epistemology. He writes, "'man's' knowledge is made of judgements ordered around the nothing of the Two" [*rien du Deux*]. "And 'woman's' knowledge orders them around nothing but the Two" [*rien que le Deux*] (Badiou 2008: 194).

And yet it seems that, under the philosophical "condition" of love, something happens to the sexual disjunction. In love the point of the eternally missed encounter, the u, becomes mutually internally excised and the lovers begin to construct the world as a scene of inquiry from a new position: the Two. Badiou explains that this "Two-scene" is "an existential project: to construct a world from a decentred point of view other than that of my mere impulse to survive or re-affirm my own identity" (Badiou and Truong 2012: 25). He goes on in a lyrical vein:

> When I lean on the shoulder of the woman I love, and can see, let's say, the peace of twilight over a mountain landscape, gold-green fields, the shadow of trees, black-nosed sheep motionless behind hedges and the sun about to disappear behind craggy peaks, and know—not from the expression on her face, but from within the world as it is—that the woman I love is seeing the same world, and that this convergence is part of the world and that love constitutes precisely, at that very moment, the paradox of an identical difference, then love exists, and promises

to continue to exist. The fact is she and I are now incorporated into this unique Subject, the Subject of love that views the panorama of the world through the prism of our difference, so this world can be conceived, be born, and not simply represent what fills my own individual gaze. (Badiou and Truong 2012: 25)

Although Badiou is quick to explain that this new "Subject of love" is not the physical couple but rather a work, a process, the "hypothetical operator" of an aleatory enquiry, a lingering question remains. Posed by James's short story, the question is whether Badiou's theory of love is capacious enough to include the specifically Jamesian possibility of a romance *tout-seul*?

Let us now turn to Badiou's discussion of the loving declaration in order to understand this Jamesian complication of the philosopher's theory of love. We discover that the declaration or naming of the amorous event-encounter is the pathway through which the lovers enter into the universality of love, making the transition "from the pure randomness of chance to a state that has universal value" (Badiou and Truong 2012: 20). The declaration of love is thus "central," Badiou contends, because it enables the lovers to proceed beyond the hypnotized fascination with the beloved's face in the event-encounter and to embark upon the construction of a "truth." More particularly, he specifies that the loving declaration "seals the act of the encounter" (Badiou and Truong 2012: 35). And while this declaration of love might occur multiple times—as Badiou says, "it can be protracted, diffuse, confused, entangled, stated and re-stated, and even destined to be re-stated yet again" (2012: 43)—this phenomenon of naming the event is decisive insofar as it is "inscribed in the structure of the event itself" (2012: 40).

With this stipulation, Badiou recalls us to the way his theory of the event is organized around three key moments: the emergence and disappearance of the complete novelty that is, for Badiou, the eruption of the inconsistent multiplicity or "void" into a given situation; the void's naming by those who recognize it as an event; and the subject's subsequent militant fidelity to that name in the truth procedure. Thus from Badiou's perspective, Maud's clandestine love for Colonel Voyt should technically be unable to enter into the universality of love. Unspoken, undeclared, her love remains rigorously unphilosophical: Maud's refusal to name her event-encounter means that her love never shakes off its particular being to become a universal truth. Her love, that is, never exits the interiority of the subject to declare itself to a world—even if this world is only the world of the Two.

In "The Story in It," the shorthand for this Two-scene that comprises love's universality is the theater. In James's tale, the formal distinction between the novel and the drama is prescribed by where one falls in the inside/outside opposition. One has to be "in" a relation, we hear Mrs. Dyott aver, if there is to be any "interest" for the novelist. But the "touching" story of how one gets "out" is always the expanse of the playwright's:

The relation's innocent that the heroine gets out of. The book's innocent that's the story of her getting out. But what the devil—in the name of innocence—was she doing IN?

Mrs. Dyott promptly echoed the question. "You have to be in, you know, to get out. So there you are already with your relation. It's the end of your goodness."

"And the beginning," said Voyt, "of your play!" (James 1999: n.p.)

If, in James, the novelist's task is to treat romance in all of its initial, hesitant, uncertain steps toward "a relation," it remains the work of the dramatist to see that relation through. To put it in Badiou's terms, the theater is capable of combining "pure situation" with the "pure point," bringing "out" what the novelist leaves implicit, namely, the paradox of an "identical difference" that makes perceptible the universal in the particular, and the Idea corporeal in the body.

A certain poetic dimension in Badiou's meta-ontological account of the event has already struck a number of literary critics,[5] but what interests me here is the explicit theatricality that comes to the fore in the loving declaration. Badiou asserts that, like actors on a stage, in love's naming "you are also addressing something that cannot be reduced to this simple material presence, something that is absolutely and simultaneously both beyond and within" (Badiou 2012: 85). "Essentially," he continues, "perhaps the theatre was already a metaphor for what love would become later on, because it was that moment when thought and body are in some way indistinguishable" (2012: 84).

Like Badiou, whose philosophical oeuvre includes a number of plays, James had his own intense love affair with the theater. James described his dreams of dramatizing his novels as the most "cherished of all my projects" (James 1981: 37) but already by May 8, 1898, the date of his first notebook entry on his little literary, "*roman de l'Honnête femme*"—James's affectionate name for what eventually became "The Story in It"—his thespian attempts were at an end. His adaptation of *The American* for the stage had met with only lukewarm reception, running for just two months in 1891 while, by 1895, following the traumatic experience with his play *Guy Domville* where its author was infamously booed on the opening night, James resolved to write only fiction again. An 1895 notebook entry captures this resolve: "I take up my *own* old pen again—the pen of all of my old unforgettable efforts and sacred struggles."[6]

Thus in the battle of the novel versus the drama as it is playfully staged (or perhaps "worked through" in the psychoanalytic sense) in "The Story in It," James seems to side decisively with the novel, with fiction's interiority or inwardness over theater's expressive outwardness, and with the literary, or particular "English" over the philosophical, or universal "French." And yet, even as she loves Colonel Voyt from afar, adoring him without any prospect of return, what becomes evident, too, is that Maud's position should not be understood under the framework of the so-called Jamesian "renunciation." For by having Maud carelessly lump the name of Gabriele D'Annunzio in with the unsatisfying French—"'And are they the only ones you do read?' 'French ones?' Maud considered. 'Oh no. D'Annunzio.' 'And what's that?' Mrs. Dyott asked as she affixed a stamp" (James 1999: n.p.)—James would not have us conclude that the literary path is purely aesthetic. If there is any interest in the English or literary loving "relation" for Maud, it must entail more than the mere "pleasure" deriving from the contemplative attitude.[7] This interest for James, as for Badiou, lies in something they each individually call "life." What could "life" mean here?

It is easy to guess what it means for James's two paramours—a "dramatic" or "wild" adventure such as their own thrilling secret affair in which they live out the kinds of freedoms from convention and morals depicted by the avant-garde French writers, passionately entwined beneath "lemon-coloured" covers (James 1999: n.p.), chromatic warnings to readers of the scandalous contents found inside.[8] But as we know for Maud, this definition of "life" appears nothing but tame—recall her word for the French novelists: "mild." The "life" represented by sexual experience seems devoid of riches: "It's the poverty of the life those people [French novelists] show, and the awful bounders, of both sexes, that they represent" (James 1999: n.p.).

"Life" is a key term for Badiou as well. In *Logics of Worlds*, Badiou maintains that "beyond bodies and languages, there is the real life of some subjects" (Badiou 2019: 412). It is a renewed concept of "life" that Badiou seeks for philosophy, distinct from its quotidian signification as mere, various, "empirical correlations" between bodies and language (412). As a counter to today's all-encompassing catch-phrase, "to have a successful life,"[9] Badiou offers the following definition: "to live is to partake, point by point, in the organization of a new body, which supports the exceptional creation of a truth" (Badiou 2006: n.p.). But whereas Badiou maintains that this creation of a truth must be supported by the outward-facing nomination, in "The Story in It" James offers the prospect of a different, inward or "literary" pathway into love's Two and, together with this, new definitions of "life," "story" and indeed of being "in" or "out" altogether. It is again from the question of the love's naming that this other path advances.

For the un-Badiouean twist James introduces in "The Story in It" is the following: what kind of loving "count" is possible if, in the "pure randomness of chance" (Badiou 2012: 20), the proper name of one of the loving parties already happens to be *Void* (Voyt)? In conjoining what Badiou regards as the proper name of Being[10] with the proper name of a person, as James does in this tale, the loving declaration finds itself descending into a tautology. Instead of engaging the expansive movement of Badiou's loving count, "One [name of the void], Two [fidelity to love's new creation], infinity . . ." (Badiou 2008: 189), Maud would falter, able only to stutter, "One [name of the void], One," [Voyt]. Like a broken record, Maud's loving count would halt at the first step, never attaining the possibility of reaching a Two, let alone infinity.

And this is indeed the fate of Maud's rival, the appositely named Mrs. Dyott who, true to her cognomen can conceive of love only in terms of the dyad; she is unable to think love's Two from any position beyond the idea of the couple, which also requires the position of a third, as Badiou notes: "The couple is what, of love, is visible to a third" (Badiou 2008: 187). Mrs. Dyott's love for Colonel Voyt is operative only to the extent that theirs is a forbidden relation, concealed not just from Maud, but also from a briefly named "Mrs Voyt" and, presumptively since we have not heard otherwise, a "Mr Dyott." The result of a triangulation rather than a true Two, her love can correspond only with what Badiou would call "representation," a "state": "The couple names not love but the state (or the State) of love" (Badiou 2008: 187)—and indeed their love affair's essential status as "representation" is underlined by James in his description of how the lovers meet at Mrs. Dyott's house:

> They met, as it were, twice: the first time while the servant was there and the second as soon as he was not. The difference was great between the two encounters, though we must add in justice to the second that its marks were at first mainly negative. This communion consisted only in their having drawn each other for a minute as close as possible—as possible, that is, with no help but the full clasp of hands. (James 1999: n.p.)

In the form of the couple, love is "covered over," as Badiou would put it[11] by a double inscription: a false, public display of indifference and the silent, private, embrace of desire. By contrast, what Maud (and James) gambles on is the potential for a universality constructed by a different means. Maud seeks the creation of love's Two without the risk of falling into the couple—always the death of love in James—while avoiding the repetitive stasis of the loving count that ensues from the pure "random chance" of her beloved's philosophically inconvenient proper name.

As we saw earlier, the clue to "The Story in It" is James's stylistic device through which the reader is invited to "see" something where there is nothing. Indeed, this is closely in line with James's classic pronouncement in "The Art of Fiction" that literature gives one "the power to guess the unseen from the seen, to trace the implication of things, to judge the whole piece by the pattern, the condition of feeling life in general so completely that you are well on your way to knowing any particular corner of it" (Besant and James 1885: 65). Anticipating Adorno's influential pronouncement on modernism as "a different mode of negation" (Adorno 1984: 31), here James invites our contemplation of a "void" that in-appears as the absence of a "story" at the level of content while, in a kind of topological distortion redolent of early modernist experiments in painting, nonetheless erupting at the level of the short story's *form*.[12]

What is the "numerical schema" (Badiou 2008: 189) of Maud's literary amorous "in-adventure"? In Badiou, love is the product of a subtraction, but in James, it arrives—or *in-advenes*— as a superaddition. Maud's love is a matter of doubling down on the very mark that designates solely the fact of the missed encounter between the sexes. That is to say, she makes the *u* itself the object of her love and by these means she transforms it. For in redoubling the *u*, by iterating it, Maud introduces a slight but exigent difference to the atomic element, which emerges from this repetition trailing an enigmatic mark, μ, as the material trace of Maud's love: μ *(mu)*, the Greek letter for the Möbial function. And, with this, she—and James—construct a new work: a specifically "literary" Two, out of her peculiarly "English" romance. Once we realize that to get "The Story *in* It" (my emphasis) is to get the story *out* of it, we find ourselves flipping Möbially between two modes of perceptual inquiry, an inherently double perspective that bears the hallmarks of Badiou's description of love's Two as a fundamental "double reading" (Badiou 2003: 54).

At the end of the tale, Colonel Voyt and Mrs. Dyott refer affectionately but superciliously to Maud's idea as a "theory":

She said it in a tone that placed the matter in its right light—a light in which they appeared kindly, quite tenderly, to watch Maud wander away into space with her lovely head bent under a theory rather too big for it. (James 1999: n.p.)

What the couple call "theory" is James's name for the fidelity that his literary enterprise formally pays to the missed encounter between the sexes. If to read Badiou together with James is to reveal their mutual emphasis on the impossibility of the sexual relation, it also exposes the different avenues by which they arrive at this impossibility: the former through the operation of subtraction, while the latter through the surprising method of superaddition, a doubling-down on the very object that Badiou would excise from love. And yet it is through her fidelity to this wretched "$(m)u$" that Maud's modern love theory enables James to perform a "creative finitization" of the novel form (Badiou 2022b: 98). Previously "unseen" infinities of a different order are glimpsed.

One might designate Maud's "theory" as the "feminine knowledge" of this new "life" that ensues from the "nothing that is the Two," which is also to say that her epistemology of love would know neither "inside" nor "outside." In a proleptic echo of Derrida's famous claim, in Maud's mad love there is nothing "outside," nothing beyond, nothing *than* the *(rien que)* the *(m)u*, a twisting, throbbing, linguistic "tempest" in which all nominations and declarations, all symbolic distinctions including the little characters designating the sexual difference ("m") and ("w"), are swept up and become "blurred." A "mild" fictional drama turned dizzingly "wild" mathematical discovery, James's diminutive English text, so "busy with letters" (James 1999: n.p.), finds philosophy's "eternal French thing" all a bit "timid and tame."

Notes

1 See Eagleton (2003: 252), cited in De Chavez (2016: 281).
2 Describing James's aesthetic sensibility, Marianne Torgovnik assesses him as a "less radical, less Modern" figure (Torgovnik 1985: 37).
3 In his book, *Cinema*, Badiou explained his use of pseudonymous authorship as a means of protection from police harassment: the pseudonym "Georges Peyrol" (a reference to the hero of Joseph Conrad's *The Rover*) was the author of various political or literary texts, while "James Strether" treated cinema, theater and music. In choosing this name, Badiou reflects on his "admiration" for Henry James, noting that Strether is a reference to the main character in *The Ambassadors*, Lambert Strether. (Badiou 2013: 13).
4 Both essays were eventually published together as *The Art of Fiction*, and appeared in several American editions from 1884 to 1885, and in serial form in the Boston journal, *The Writer*, in 1899. For a more detailed account of the debates, see Spilka (1973).
5 See for example Clemens (2003) and (2015). See also Jöttkandt (2005).
6 Entry of January 23, 1895, *The Notebooks of Henry James*, ed. F. O. Matthiessen and Kenneth B. Murdock (University of Chicago Press, 1981), 179.
7 Recall the title of D'Annunzio's first novel, *Il Piacere* (The Child of Pleasure) (1889).

8 See Doran (2013).
9 See Badiou (2006).
10 See Meditation 4, *Being and Event*, which is titled "The Void: Proper Name of Being."
11 "Broadly speaking, I will call 'covering-over operations' the neutralization of any detection of an infinite potentiality in a situation that the dominant power wants to force to remain under a finite law, a neutralization achieved not by a direct and antagonistic denial of the potentiality but by considerations themselves derived from the finitude resources of the initial situation, which cover over any supposition of infinity and render it unrecognizable" (Badiou 2022b: 198).
12 See Clement Greenberg's characterization of modern painting as a flattening of representational surfaces such that in abstract art "pictorial space has lost its 'inside' and become all 'outside'" (Greenberg 1961: n.p.).

Works Cited

Adorno, T. (1984), *Aesthetic Theory*, trans. C. Lendhardt, eds. G. Adorno and R. Tiedemann, London: Routledge & Kegan Paul.
Badiou, A. (2003), "The Scene of Two," trans. B. P. Fulks, *Lacanian Ink* 21: 42–55.
Badiou, A. (2005), *Being and Event*, trans. O. Feltham, London: Continuum.
Badiou, A. (2006), "Bodies, Languages, Truths." Lecture delivered at the Victoria College of Arts, University of Melbourne, September 9, 2006. Available online: https://www.lacan.com/badbodies.htm.
Badiou, A. (2008), "What is Love?" in *Conditions*, trans. S. Corcoran, London: Continuum.
Badiou, A. (2013), *Cinema*, ed. Antoine de Baecque, trans. S. Spitzer, Cambridge: Polity.
Badiou, A. (2019), *Logics of Worlds: Being and Event II*, trans. A. Toscano, London: Bloomsbury.
Badiou, A. (2022a), *The Adventure of French Philosophy*, trans. B. Bosteels, London: Verso.
Badiou, A. (2022b), *The Immanence of Truths: Being and Event III*, trans. K. Reinhardt and S. Spitzer, London and New York: Bloomsbury.
Badiou, A. and N. Truong (2012), *In Praise of Love*, trans. P. Bush, London: Serpent's Tail, imprint of Profile Books.
Begam, R. (2021), "Modernism after Poststructuralism; Or, Does Badiou Save Us from Drowning?" *Modernism/modernity* 28:1, 117–136.
Besant, W. and H. James (1885), *The Art of Fiction*, Boston: Cupples, Upham and Co.
Clemens, J. (2003), "Letters as the Condition of Conditions for Alain Badiou," *Communication & Cognition* 36:1–2, 73–102.
Clemens, J. (2015), "'Eternity is Coming', Review of Alain Badiou," *The Age of the Poets*, *Sydney Review of Books*, February 19. Available online: https://sydneyreviewofbooks.com/review/age-of-poets-alain-badiou/.
De Chavez, J. (2016), "'No Theme Requires More Pure Logic than Love': On Badiou's Amorous Axiomatics," *Kritike* 10:1, 269–285.
Doran, S. (2013), *The Culture of Yellow: Or, The Visual Politics of Late Modernity*, London: Bloomsbury.
Eagleton, T. (2003), *Figures of Dissent*, London and New York: Verso.

Greenberg, C. (1961), "Abstract, Representational, and So Forth," in *Art and Culture: Critical Essays*, e-book ed., Boston: Beacon Press.

James, H. (1962), *The Art of the Novel: Critical Prefaces by Henry James*, intro. R. P. Blackmur, New York and London: Charles Scribners.

James, H. (1981), *The Notebooks of Henry James*, eds. F. O. Matthiessen and K. B. Murdock, Chicago: University of Chicago Press.

James, H. (1999), *Henry James Collected Stories, vol. 2 (1892–1910)*, ed. J. Bailey, e-book ed., New York: Knopf.

Jöttkandt, S. (2005), *First Love: A Phenomenology of the One*, Melbourne: re.press.

Spilka, M. (1973), "Henry James and Walter Besant: 'The Art of Fiction' Controversy," *Novel: A Forum on Fiction* 6:2, 101–119.

Torgovnick, M. (1985), *The Visual Arts, Pictorialism, and the Novel*, Princeton: Princeton University Press.

10

Derrida's and Badiou's Absolute Modern(ist) Surfaces

James Martell

Où maintenant? Quand maintenant? Qui maintenant?
Where now? Who now? When now?
—Samuel Beckett, *L'Innommable/The Unnamable*.

Wörtflächen (Word Surfaces)

The question is not anymore, or at least not only—pace Levin—"*what* was modernism?" Nor is it—pace Williams—"*when* was modernism." The question is now, for us, in the space opened by Badiou and Derrida: "*where* was, and still is, modernism?" Or more specifically, "*what is the surface of modernism*?" Is it modernism's ground or foundation in the avant-gardes, its sociocultural-historic situation or its spatial or superficial relation to both psychoanalysis and the modern sciences? Or is its surface classicism, neoclassicism, romanticism, a set of traditions or the traditional itself as a period, movement or traits *against which* modernism defines itself? Or is modernism's surface perhaps its "upper" limit, post-modernism or post-modernity, the artistic, literary and philosophical wall that defined it—by surpassing it—chronologically and, purportedly, continues to define it formally and thematically? If modernism's surface is not only its limits (temporal, formal and/or thematic) but also the lines or horizons that define its project, perhaps this surface would appear best to our view not necessarily through its foundation, but through the figure of its zenith and culmination, through the work of the ultimate and perhaps last modernist, who accomplished modernism's procedures and questions in the sense of both fulfilling and ending them: Samuel Beckett. What is more, if—as I will try to show—Badiou is not only a modern but also a modernist philosopher and writer, his constant interest on Beckett betrays not only a personal choice, but also a keen insight into the liminal and "superficial" importance of Beckett's oeuvre as our quintessential modernist surface of both thought and experience, that is to say: writing.

As scholars of modernism and of Beckett know, it is not easy to find a clear declaration of intent or definite aesthetic philosophy in Beckett's oeuvre. Most of the statements that are taken as quintessentially Beckettian come either from texts he wrote on other artists ("nothing to express, nothing with which to express" (1987: 103) from "Three Dialogues with George Duthuit") or from fictional works ("Try again. Fail Again. Fail Better" [1996: 89]) where they are enmeshed in singular, formal and poetic strategies. Nevertheless, there is at least one particular statement that is declared in his own authorial and writerly voice, and that, using surfaces as its guiding metaphors, describes what Beckett considers literature should be doing at the present moment—in order to fulfill its modernist promise, we might add. This statement appears in the infamous letter to Axel Kaun from July 9, 1937. Allow me to quote it at large and to underline all the surfaces and the "superficial" effects or events:

> It is indeed getting more and more difficult, even pointless, for me to write in formal English. And more and more my language appears to me like a veil (*ein Schleier*) which one has to tear apart (*zerreissen*) in order to get to those things (or the nothingness) lying behind it (*hinterliegende Nichts*). Grammar and style! To me they seem to have become as irrelevant as a Biedermeier bathing suit or the imperturbability of a gentleman. A mask [or a larva] (*Eine Larve*). It is to be hoped the time will come, thank God, in some circles it already has, when language is best used where it is most efficiently abused. Since we cannot dismiss it all at once, at least we do not want to leave anything undone that may contribute to its disrepute. To drill one hole after another (*Ein Loch nach dem andern in hir zu bohren*) into it until that which lurks behind (*Dahinterkauernde*), be it something or nothing, starts seeping through (*durchzusickern*)—I cannot imagine a higher goal for today's writer.
>
> Or is literature alone to be left behind on that old, foul road long ago abandoned by music and painting? Is there something paralyzingly sacred contained within the unnature of the word that does not belong to the elements of the other arts? Is there any reason [or ground] (*Grund*) why that terrifyingly arbitrary materiality of the word surface (*Wortfläche*) should not be dissolved (*aufgelöst*), as for example the sound surface (*Tonfläche*) of Beethoven's Seventh Symphony is devoured by huge black pauses, so that for pages on end we cannot perceive it as other than a dizzying path (*Pfad*) of sounds connecting unfathomable chasms (*unergründliche Schlünde*) of silence? (2009: 513–14, 518–19)

As we can read and see, Beckett's description of his own task as a writer of his time is laid out as a series of actions, events and desires ("tear apart," "To drill one hole after another," "dissolved") on a series of surfaces ("a veil," "bathing suit," "word surface," "sound surface," "chasms," "path," etc.) and toward what lies underneath or beyond them ("that which lurks behind"). Surfaces here are not metaphors solely for Beckett's particular modernist project. In this dream, they are, rather, the material and topographic enactment of Beckettian modernism as an emphasis of the principality of place in modernist aesthetics and thought. As I have pointed out before, one can see this principality of place in the fact that the first out of the three questions with which *The Unnamable* begins, "Where now?," is the only one that does not shift places in between its two versions ["*Where now? Who now? When now?*" (2006: 285); "*Où maintenant? Quand maintenant? Qui maintenant?*" (2004: 7; my italics)].[1] Thus, if modernism or the modernist dream exists as a viable project in Beckett's work, it is, as Beckett scholars have remarked since the beginning, a project of inscription, sometimes even of perforation. But what has not been pointed out enough is that, ultimately, it is always the project of an exhaustive exploration of what spaces as surfaces (and the concomitant notions, figures and metaphors emanating from them) can do or offer for art and thought. Inside this universe we are always within, on, above, below and so on a surface, and consequently here, as Lacan hinted in his *Seminar XXI*, *Les non-dupes errent*, we are, indeed, always bidimensional (1973–4a: 3; FR 48).

If Beckett's project, as the last modernist oeuvre and the culmination and epitome of modernism, is a performative reflection on and questioning of place and surfaces as the spaces of literature, art and thought, what happens when such literary modernist surfaces as Beckett's touch or get in contact with a philosophical project—another thinking surface—like Badiou's? What is more—and this will be the focus of this chapter—how does an examination of surfaces and place in Badiou's thought appear when compared to another philosophical project such as Derrida's, sensitive too to the literary and artistic surfaces of modernity and modernism, especially when both philosophical projects have their pivotal points in particular radical surfaces [an ultimate set that is not a set (V), a self-effacing receptacle or surface (khôra, subjectile)] sustaining their founding—and sometimes even necessarily foundering into abysses (*Abgründe*)—structures and inscriptions? While I cannot develop here why and how Beckett's work and its emphasis on surfaces of inscription is one of the most extreme thought-events not only of literature but also of modern thought and experience at large,[2] I will try to show how both Badiou and Derrida shared Beckett's (and potentially other thinkers' and artists' like Lucio Fontana or most povera artists, but also Lacan's, through his use of topology) sensitivity to the radical "superficial" nature of modern and modernist thought. In other words, I will present the Badiouan and the Derridean projects as philosophical attempts to think thought (and all the events happening around but also through it) in its own surfaces but also as a superficial or surface-like dimension itself. Both their oeuvres think thought within the irrevocable and perhaps inescapable two-dimensional—that is, always attached to a surface—condition of all experience and cognition.

Traces, Points, Limits Sur . . . face: *l'inexistant* (the Inexistent)

There is something—call it "space" or "*espacement*," for the moment—that is more than a superficial metaphor in the work of both Derrida and Badiou. It is more than a metaphor because it is, precisely, the "space" upon or on which every metaphor as displacement, transport, μεταφέρω [*metá* ("from one place to another") and φέρω, *phérô* ("to carry or take")] takes place. Ultimately—it is one of my hypotheses—this "space" is the reason or mechanism that made Derrida assert, in "La mythologie blanche," the ubiquitous and undecidable character of metaphor or metaphoricity in philosophy—both *against* and *as* literature. Nevertheless, this is not exactly a space or a place, but rather that-upon-which, against-which, on-which, as well as above-, under- and in-which all places and spaces take place. This "space" is—as I mentioned earlier—what sometimes is best expressed by the French term "*espacement*," but that I prefer to designate (for reasons that, I hope, will be clarified throughout this chapter) with the term "surface." The importance of such a "metaphor" or conceptual and experiential notion of surface as the taking place of spacing or *espacement* is at the core of one of the most significant recent reappraisals of deconstruction, Martin Hägglund's *Radical Atheism* (2008).³ Hägglund introduces us to the logic of his book precisely by linking it with spacing (*espacement*) as the first and main trait of Derridean deconstruction as an ontological event:

> To establish the logic of radical atheism, I proceed from Derrida's notion of spacing (*espacement*). As he points out in his late work *On Touching*, spacing is "the first word of any deconstruction, valid for space as well as time" (181/207). More precisely, spacing is shorthand for the becoming-space of time and the becoming-time of space. Although this coimplication of space and time defines all of Derrida's key terms (such as *trace*, *arche-writing*, and *différance*), it has received little attention in studies of his work. Derrida himself does not undertake a detailed elaboration of how the becoming-space of time and the becoming-time of space should be understood, while maintaining that it is the minimal operation of deconstruction that is at work in everything that happens. (2)

To my mind, one of the reasons why Derrida did not undertake a comprehensive, general explanation of the becoming-space of time and the becoming-time of space as surface-*espacement* events, is to highlight and respect the singularity of each instance. In other words, his explanation of *espacement* was extensive rather than intensive, and carried out through all the series of works where he exposed—with a variety of surface-effect strategies—different surfaces of thought and experience, that is, khôra, the subjectile, archi-writing, grammatology, the (im)possibility of (what is) touch(ed) in the work of Nancy, surfaces of inscription and appearances in works by artists as different as Van Gogh, Gérard Titus-Carmel, Artaud, Colette Deblé and so on. This constant attention to surface-effects in Derrida's work has not gone unnoticed by Badiou. In his most direct confrontation to date with Derridean deconstruction, in *Petit panthéon portatif* (2008a), there is an awareness of this particular Derridean desire for the surface. For Badiou, this is a desire to think, mark and penetrate surfaces in a variety of forms, as well as to lay down (*coucher*), to localize, to embrace (*étreindre*) and especially to ex- and in-scribe surfaces: "This desire, this desire for the non-existent (*l'inexistant*), it is necessary, like for all desire, to lay it down (*le coucher*). To lay it down on the white sheet of paper, for example. [. . .] Such was Derrida's desire: locate, touch, clasp (*étreindre*), even for less than an instant, the non-existent of a place, the flight of the vanishing point. To inscribe its/his ex-scription" (2008b: 140; FR 130).⁴ Since here we want to exhibit the modern and modernist surfaces or surface-effects of both oeuvres, it is especially significant for us that it is at this particular point, "*l'inexistant*" or the point of inexistence, where Badiou expresses his commonality or shared space with Derrida:

> The word différance is, at bottom, the operation whereby Derrida tried to lay down (*coucher*) non-existence (*l'inexistant*). To lay it down in the way you lay down something in writing. He tried to lay down the in-existent in différance as an act of writing, as a slippage (*glissement*). Learning from him, I too will try to lay down in-existence by inflicting upon it the slippage from "e" to "a," which signifies, in its wordly way of in-existing, that its being is no less irreducible for that. We are nothing, let us be all. That is the imperative of in-exist*a*nce. There is no way out of that. I thank Jacques Derrida for having been the vigilant keeper of that imperative. (2008b: 143–4; FR 133)[5]

Two years earlier, in *Logiques des mondes* (2006), Badiou had already identified this point of inexistence as the main trait of Derridean deconstruction. In this description, he had even shown an essential trait of surfaces with regards to the space they "cover": their exceptional character as "out-of-place-within-place." Such exceptionality is ultimately what allows the ex-scription to take place by keeping the minimal distances between the "space" where something is in-scribed, the "deeper" "space" underneath the inscription (i.e., the canvas, wooden board or cave wall "underneath" the subjectile or first coat, the khôra "below" the cosmogonic earth, etc.), and the inscription itself. Even if Badiou describes here the deconstructive movement as a point of flight (*point de fuite*), such a point and its strategies necessarily imply a surface of inscription or puncturing that allows the "marking" and/or "moving," a "space of flight" (*espace de fuite*) where all these new ex- and in-scriptions take place:

> Ever since his first texts, and under the progressively academized (though not by him) name of "deconstruction," his speculative desire is to show that, whatever form of discursive imposition one may be faced with, there exists a point that escapes the rules of this imposition, a *point of flight*. The whole interminable work consists in localizing it, which is also impossible, since it is characterized by being out-of-place-in-the-place. To restrict the space of flight, it is necessary to force the signifiers of discursive imposition, to diagonalize the great metaphysical oppositions (being/beings, spirit/matter, but also democracy/totalitarianism, state of law/barbarism or Jew/Arab . . .) and to invent a language of decentring, or a *dispositif* of acephalic writing. (2009: 545; FR 570)[6]

Now, when Badiou describes the particular movement of thought of the same book, *Logique des mondes*, he also describes a superficial movement whereupon one must identify an elemental trace. What such a trace marks is a "*sous-jacent*"[7] or underneath element, below every object, with zero as its value of existence. This is Badiou's theory of the proper inexistent of an object. It is through the connection between these "underground" or "below surface" inexistent elements that we can investigate what could ultimately arrive to a world, in other words: the new or "modern."

In this Book, the movement of thought culminates in the identification, in every object, of an elementary trace of the contingency of being-there. This is the theory of the proper inexistent of an object: there is an element of the multiple underlying (*sous-jacent*) every object whose value of existence in the world is nil. Its link to the forgoing discussion is that every relation between objects links together the inexistent of the one to the inexistent of the other. Relations, which conserve existence, also conserve inexistence. [...] the point of the inexistent is the measure of what can happen to a world. (2009: 302; FR 318)

Given the potential political and cultural implications of these inexistent elements, Badiou connects them to the temporal and historical (as well as conservative or revolutionary) aspects of such inexistence. This temporal dimension brings up the question not only of the becoming-*time* of space in Derrida's own *espacement* but also of the modern and modernist dimension of such inexist*ance* as différance,[8] and thus as a point of contact between Badiou's and Derrida's philosophical projects. As I am trying to show, if we want to understand their positions vis-à-vis not only modernism and modernity but also in front of modern promises of emancipation and/or revolution, we need to pay close attention to the topologies and topographies inaugurated by their thought. These topologies and topographies imply a particular attention to the concretely "superficial" dimension of ontology and philosophy, or in other words, to thought's and philosophy's essential character as "superficial" or surface-structures and surface-events. Contrary to the common understanding of "superficial" as something easy, frivolous, simple or even naïf, to be contrasted with a purportedly depth of thought, both Badiou and Derrida have shown (together with Lacan, Lyotard, Cixous, Deleuze and Guattari, Irigaray, Blanchot and others; as well as the whole history of art in the nineteenth and twentieth centuries) how modern and modernist thought has its proper place as the thinking of, on, above and below—together with all other prepositions, since every discursive and syntactic spatiality always already implies a topology—surfaces. It is the differences between these topological and topographic, superficial thinking events and structures that underline the particular—and perhaps sometimes irreconcilable—idiosyncrasies of their philosophical projects—while they give us the chance to think about them together. Nevertheless, if some of these differences are indeed irreconcilable or too broad to be breached, it is precisely an attention to their thoughts as surfaces-events that will allow us to see both their commonality as well as the points of inflection and flight toward which they invite us to direct our own thought into the future or *l'avenir*. Thus, what exactly are the surfaces of Badiou's and Derrida's oeuvres?

Badiou's Absolute Surface, V or the Space of Thought/Being

If the question of Derrida's proper surfaces passes by the problem of the exact place of inscription of archi-writing and/or grammatology as a grapho-logy or inscription-logy, in the case of Badiou, surfaces are those upon, on, or in which a set or *ensemble* takes place. Given that Badiou's basis for his ontology is set theory, the representation of this philosophical topology challenges the limits of the figurable or imaginable. In other words, if a surface is a "space" through and in which metaphors effect or suffer their movements, Badiou's superficial "metaphors" take place at and as the limits of representation, that is, at the "place" of inscription of (the) infinite(s). In *L'immanence des vérités* (2018), the third volume of *L'être et l'événement*, this "place" of inscription is named "V," and it is *in it*, as "the class of all sets" (60) that all the possible forms of the being-multiple take place. "Here," in the place of all "heres" and sets (which is, consequently, neither a set, nor a here, nor really a class), *Being and Thought are the same as Place*. In other words, it is V *as* ultimate *ground* (similar to the undecidable *Ur-* and *Ungrund* in Schelling's work) or as khôra or subjectile (in Derrida's) that reveals the sameness of Thought and Being, Logic and Ontology, or what Badiou calls "the latent topology of being" (2009: 410; FR 433). "Class V [. . .] is not a set (*ensemble*). It is not a form of being. It is the place (*lieu*) of being, the place thought/being where the formal being of the possible gathers under the guises (*espèces*) of possible forms of multiple-being, namely, of that which constitutes the form of being in a determined world" (Badiou 2018: 60). This place, as place, is also what Badiou calls "the place of the absolute" (Badiou 2018: 60). But what exactly is the relation between the absolute and the place or surface?[9]

Badiou begins *L'immanence des vérités* with a "speculative strategy" that summarizes what has been his "philosophical strategy" for more than thirty years. This exact strategy amounts to establishing what he calls "*the immanence of truths*" (2018: 13). Here, he explains that establishing such an immanence means "to save the category of truth," and to legitimize certain traits of said truths. The first trait is that "a truth can be: // -Absolute while remaining localized" (13). The following ones are: that it can be eternal, "ontologically determined as generic multiplicity" (13) and A-subjective (universal). This order exposes the necessity of a separation or topological distance (ab-solute) as the first condition for all the other exceptional characters (eternal, generic multiplicity, universal) of truths. From this moment on, the book goes on to establish and describe the different relations and approaches that we can have (through philosophy, politics, mathematics and love) to this absolute (as) space. In the prologue, he explains further that the different infinite sets that the book will examine serve us ultimately as possibilities of approaching "the place V, where truths come into a relation with the absolute" (2018: 54). The purpose of this "coming into relation," or "touching" the absolute, is, for Badiou, "to establish that a contemporary materialism, in order to free itself from the—relativist and, ultimately skeptic—democratic consensus on the false value called 'freedom of expression and opinion,' must produce an alternative to the doxa of finitude" (2018: 35). This alternative appears precisely through what he calls a "texture of crossed infinites" that is linked to "the emancipatory element of truths" (35) and which allows the creation of oeuvres instead of "refuses" (*déchets*). Here, the surface appears not only woven through this "texture of crossed infinites" but also in the tracing or drawing (*tracer*) on the worlds of this "touching of the absolute" (35). Ultimately, this "place of the absolute" is the "absolute ontology" that Badiou extracts from set theory, an affirmation of an ontology that, *as place*, is nothing but a topology, a "universe of reference" (36). Like the Platonic khôra,[10] its absolute character of place, detached (*absolutus*) from anything and anywhere else, is thus its de-termination or separation (*ab-solvere*) from any possible content, what makes Badiou call it both "the Vacuum, the big empty (*vide*)," *and* the place of truths, "*the place of all that which can validate the propositions concerning multiplicities in themselves*" (2008: 40). If thus the absolute is the first essential trait of truths, it is because it is precisely the utter topographical detachment of a separate place that allows truths to be *generic* (de-tached and un-defined) multiplicities, eternal (detached from any particular time, even if they emerge in it) and universal (detached from any subject, even if they come to be with the help of one). In other words, truths and the absolute are names for the complete separation, detachment, un-tying of a surface.[11] Consequently, any liberation or detachment (ab-solving) takes place through the encounter or touching of the absolute via an infinite: "everywhere where a human action frees itself from the order that constrains it, we have, in the figure of an oeuvre, an encounter with the infinite" (2018: 279).

Now, what are the particular modern and modernist forms of these movements and possible relations to the absolute? Badiou describes them too in terms of surfaces, in this case of a surface that covers, like a blanket, the ground of infinites of the absolute. For Badiou, "The modern operation of subjectivation of finitude is called 'covering' (*recouvremment*). It aims to cover, through finite *dispositifs* from the alienated present, all that which could bring a new infinite and sanction modern *oeuvres*, yet independent from capital" (2018: 112). These oeuvres are presented as marked surfaces as well since, while finite, they have the imprint of what Badiou calls an index, which is the proper mark of the absolute, and ultimately what defines them as "oeuvres of truth" or "that which, of a process of truth, exists, in a world, under the form of its fragments" (2018: 681–2).

But if these modern works or oeuvres as "truth processes" are defined by the(ir) mark of the absolute, if they are, so to speak, the surface of inscription (of the trace) of the absolute, and that is their modernist trait, could they identify completely (absolutely) with such a mark and define themselves not only through but also *as* their referent, that is to say, as the absolute itself? In other words, if—according to Badiou—modernity's finitude operation is to cover (*recouvrir*) the surfaces of (the) infinites, and modern or modernist truth-oeuvres are those that pierce such a cover—that is, Beckett's desire to pierce language—what kind of works do we have at the extreme of modernism? What happens when the works define and project themselves through this absolute desire for the absolute? Are these works of an absolute modernism that obliterates the distance between the mark and what marks it, or in Derridean language, between the trace and presence?[12] In chapter 20 of *L'immanence des vérités*, when considering "The hierarchy of infinites" and particularly the possibility of "an internal movement of the absolute" (481), and consequently, of a direct relation to it (through a "non-trivial J elementary dip (*plongement*) of V in V" [481]), Badiou creates a list of examples that include some of the commonly considered most extreme exponents of modernism (Wagner, Proust, Mallarmé), together with other authors, movements, systems and events, that have taken the logics of modernism to its extreme conclusions. At the end of this section, Badiou describes their common trait as "an immense hope," and as a topological dream: the hope to go *from* the most absolute place or surface V *to* the most absolute place, V; in other words, the hope that V does a movement (that it traces, draws or creates a mark, a line, a stroke) on V itself. Here is the passage:

> In my view, the rational temptation to install oneself in the absolute referent to work there on the immanent mobility of possible attributes of the absolute without having to worry anymore about difference; that is to say, the desire to let go of the vertical obligation of the differentiating relation, which assures that, that which sanctions the absolute character (*absoluité*) of a truth while being immanent to the absolute is not identical to it, the desire thus to work horizontally, at the level (*hauteur*) of the absolute itself, this temptation, yes, haunts all truth procedures. Wagner's total work of art, Lacoue-Labarthe's poem fused with prose, the end of History for the revolutionaries of the 19th century, Mallarmé's Book, the ecstatic fusional love of Romanticism, the integral recovery of time in Proust's literary project, utopian communism, Hegel's absolute knowledge, the search in Physics for an unfindable unified theory, theater without theater, presentation without representation, Adorno's informal form, Nietzsche's "splitting in two of world's history," Deleuze's big inorganic life or chaos, Bourbaki's completely formalized mathematics, all of that is nothing but—truth procedure after truth procedure—the desire to not having to deal anymore with the gap, the difference, the separation between the absolute reference and the place of absolutization of singular truths. It is an immense hope: to finally find, beyond interminable and disappointing ascents—disappointing because interminable—an ultimate infinite as testimony of a truth without withdrawal (*retrait*) or lack. The ambition, at the bottom, to be, in V, the one who goes from V to V. Then, the dead God would resuscitate in a solemn rational scenery. (480–1)

Notwithstanding the enormous differences between all these projects and works, Badiou's point is that there is a topological desire proper to modernity and modernism. This is the modern desire of all truth processes (works of art, politics, mathematics and love). It is the temptation of a pure horizontality, a negation of verticality and thus of different layers—a negation of difference itself. A temptation, a desire and ultimately a hope, it is the attempt to conceive or create horizontally—superficially—(on and as) the last and first surface of inscription. However, if this desire or temptation is rational, what exactly is the relation between reason and its form, especially as it embodies the modernist dream "form *is* content, content *is* form"? (Beckett 1984: 27). In other words, what is thought and reason here, and how does it get *properly* inscribed: as mathematics, in mathemes, as poetry or as philosophy? Is there truly any inscription or writing anymore in this ultimate "here"? In this rationally dreamt place, we are at V, the absolute surface before all surfaces, before all inscriptions, where every inscription is an immediate and complete presence, and thus, not an in-scription anymore—without the minimal gap to in-scribe. Here, in this empty surface (V: Vacuum and Truths [*vérités*]), the place of the quintessential modern and modernist rational temptation, there is truly no more surface, no more inscription and, consequently, no more writing or trace. In the absolute horizontality of absolute space without depth, there is no trace, and that means both no more history and no more eternity—no more modernity/modernism.

Derrida's Checkboard

In his book, *Derrida, Badiou and the Formal Imperative*, Christopher Norris gives a fair—albeit at times incomplete—assessment of Derrida's oeuvre:

> What Derrida shows through close-readings of singular tenacity and also—*pace* Searle and other detractors—extreme conceptual precision is the possibility of finding out truths that cannot be expressed (i.e. which elude any overt, articulate and logically consistent presentation) in the text under analysis. Moreover, those truths are by no means confined to some purely linguistic or intra-discursive *register* of sense but must rather be seen as possessing *a highly specific referential dimension* and hence as pointing to genuine complexities or unresolved issues with respect to the given subject-*domain*. Beyond that—as emerges with increasing clarity in his later work—they articulate problems intrinsic to certain kinds of discourse on certain topics, those (such as justice, hospitality, forgiveness, friendship, democracy or cosmopolitanism) which analytic philosophers might recognize as belonging to the class of "essentially contested concepts." (2012: 97)[13]

Thus, in this attempt to approach both Derrida's and Badiou's projects and to show their relevance for a dialog between continental and analytic philosophy, Norris explains the relevance of Derrida's work in terms of Badiou's notion of truths. While so doing, Norris somewhat inadvertently highlights not only the topological and topographic significance of Derrida's oeuvre, but also and especially how Derridean deconstruction is, in itself, a topo-logical and -graphic thinking and writerly project. In other words, the radicality of it (in Hägglund's sense of "radical atheism") lies not only in its questioning and examination of some of the basic and foundational notions of Western philosophy, but also in the critical assessment of both their place and "spacing," of the way they take place, and of their relation to the structure of this placing, inscription, or appearing (i.e., Derrida's early insistence on the importance of "centers" and "circularity" for philosophy). Such a complication between the subjects of the discourse and their spatial, topological and topographic dimension is what Norris describes above as a "highly specific referential dimension" related (connected) to different subject-domains. Thus, when Derrida starts his philosophical project by identifying what he calls the age of the "play of the trace," what he is underlining is not only the undecidable complication of a life (death) that is neither pure presence nor pure absence, but also and especially the flat space or dimension, the surface on which any ontology and epistemology take place, their "bottomless checkboard":

> It is this age that we can call the play of the trace. The play of a trace which no longer belongs to the horizon of Being, but whose play transports [*porte*, like a metaphor, JM] and encloses the meaning of Being: play of the trace, or the *différance*, which has no meaning and is not. Which does not belong. There is no maintaining [*maintenance*, which resonates with *maintenant* or "present," JM], but also no depth to, this bottomless checkboard on which Being is put into play. (1982: 22; FR 25)[14]

As we know, Derrida's engagement with different surfaces of inscription and expression became more and more accentuated and complex throughout his career, from his engagement with artistic surfaces and surface-related phenomena like the subjectile and the parergon, to his reappropriation of the Platonic-cosmogonic surface par excellence, khôra, up to his own conscious effort to highlight the complex layered surface of inscription of his own books in works like *Glas*, *Le calcul des langues*, *La carte postale* and so on. However, since in this chapter we want to continue Norris's project and expose the shared surfaces of Badiou's and Derrida's oeuvres, let us look at their shared space where it might be clearer: at the threshold of Derrida's early engagement with Heidegger.

On January 27, 1968, Derrida read, at a conference of the Société française de philosophie, his text "La différance." As we know, this short text, together with "Structure, Sign and Play in the Discourse of the Human Sciences"—presented at Johns Hopkins University on October 21, 1966—is part of the inaugural event of Derridean deconstruction. What underlines "La différance's" foundational or event-like character is its focus on a singular word, as if it was a presentation of the most important concept of a philosophy—a singularization that the text itself, as well as those around it, denies, since Derrida always carefully insisted on how, if ultimately there was a conceptual strategy of deconstruction, it was always a strategy linked to a chain of concepts, and never focused or dependent on a single, unique one. Nevertheless, the singularity of this conference is clear, especially as it exposes the notion of "*espacement*" as the becoming-time of space and the becoming-space of time, and what Hägglund will describe as the key term, in its implication of space and time, of all Derridean terms.[15] What is more, the conference ends by underlining and thus complicating the relation between the "unique word" and the "always and everywhere," that is to say, the all-space and all-time, where "being" "speaks" in "every" "language." Here are the last words and their significant punctuation marks (, . /): "Such is the question: the alliance of speech and Being in the unique word, in the finally proper name. Such is the question that inscribes itself in the played affirmation of *différance*. It bears (on) each member of this sentence: 'Being / speaks / always and everywhere / through / every / language'" (1982: 27; FR 29).[16]

Now, given this underscoring of the "*espacement*" (the imbrication space/time, "always and everywhere") what exactly is the surface of this last sentence, and of "La différance" at large, the affirmation "on" which bears each member of it: *Being, speaks, always and everywhere, every, language* and especially *through* (*à travers*), since a traversing is always of and on a certain surface? As we know, besides its graphic and semantic condensation of the different senses of differing, disagreeing and deferring, "différance" refers as well to the Heideggerian effacement of the trace of the effacement of the difference between Being and beings—what is, perhaps, the main tenet of Heideggerian philosophy. If Derrida is remarking the trace and tracing (*-ance*) of this effacement, and remarking it "always and everywhere," and if he is doing it while underlining the surface of its and all inscriptions ("every / language": is a language always linguistic or purely semantic? Is not the whole Derridean project to show that it is not?), what exactly is this ubiquitous Derridean surface of effacing and remarking? If it is a surface that includes, comprehends all marks (words, punctuation signs and everything in between), where does the question of all the elements of that closing sentence *take place*? What kind of surface is this one? And given that it comprehends it all, can it be understood also as the space of inscription of a set, or of the set of all sets (V), where both the vacuum and truths (V) could take place? However, if Derrida described this space of inscription as a "checkboard without (back)ground (*fond*)," does this lack of depth preclude the affirmation (corroboration, assessment, assent) of the arrival of an event, and what is more, of a truth? In other words, is Derrida's surface flatter—even more bidimensional—than Badiou's? How do we measure the necessary width of thickness that makes possible an inscription, however superficial, or the width of the limits that define a set, especially if, even when purely mathematical, they are still "marked" by (the) infinite(s), "touched" by the absolute's separation? And finally, since both Badiou and Derrida were defined and defined themselves as philosophers—and especially as philosophers belonging to a certain shared age of metaphysics—we can ask: What is the thickness of the limits (in- and exscribed too on a surface, while they are potentially surfaces as well, just as markable as the Berlin Wall or our own skin) that circumscribe philosophy and metaphysics? How are these limits drawn, even for one set? Or worse, for the set of all sets [V or "every / language"], the set of metaphysics, its complete *text*? Are the limits that define it (and define all sets) completely outside, as walls (already undecidably outside and inside) or are they also inside, marking it, traversing it ("*à travers*") like scarifications or the invisible lines of a tattoo? How do we read this complete text and surface (since every text, just as every image, is a surface), and especially *where*, if we are both *comprised in it* as Badiou thinks it, and *marked by it* and its constant erasure, as Derrida continually remarked it?: "The text of metaphysics is thereby *comprehended* (*compris*). Still legible; and to be read. It is not surrounded but rather traversed by its limit, marked in its interior by **the multiple furrow** of its margin" (1982: 24; FR 24).[17]

"Where Now !"

If my hypothesis is correct, the reason we can understand better both the similarities and the differences of Badiou's and Derrida's projects through a topological or surface-focused consideration of their work is because both of them are not only modern philosophers, but also wrote as modernist writers and thinkers—always in contact with their singular and general surfaces of inscription. If Beckett is the quintessential and last modernist writer and thinker,[18] it is precisely because he exposed modernism as a thought and practice of (the) surface(s). In this way, both Badiou's and Derrida's different yet similarly intense interests in Beckett[19] bespeak their own understanding of the place not only of space but also and particularly of surfaces in the inscription and the practice of thought in modernity—and modernism. Thus, *The Unnamable/ L'Innommable*'s first lesson and dictum, that you can switch around the place of the question of the subject ("Who now?") and of time ("When now?") but not that of space ("Where now?") illuminates both Derrida's philosophy of the trace and Badiou's philosophy of set theory as the thought-events of a modern and modernist ontology whose thinking and being necessarily take place in the same place: the surface.

Notes

1. From now on, whenever there is a French original version of a text, it would be specified with FR after giving the English translation reference.
2. In some way, a lot of Beckettian scholarship in the last few decades has been an exploration of some aspect of this question. See, for example, Boulter (2019), Dennis (2020), and Chattopadhyay (2018).
3. For an even more recent examination of the materialistic "base" (or surfaces) of deconstruction, see Goldgaber (2021). The relation between the "materialistic turn" and Derridean deconstruction is the subject of current and rich reflections. Most recently, the journal *Síntesis. Revista de Filosofía* dedicated its most recent issue, "Matters" (edited by Thomas Clément Mercier), to it: https://sintesis.uai.cl/index.php/intusfilosofia/issue/view/36.
4. Translation modified.
5. Translation modified.
6. Translation modified.
7. In *L'immanence des vérités*, Badiou described further this "underlying ontological scene," linking it with mathematical thought and the foundation of his own ontology: set theory. For our purposes, the question remains: what is the necessity of this topological "metaphor" for the understanding and exposition of ontology, and thus, for the understanding of truths and truth-procedures? "[T]he true ordered maze that is, today, the mathematical thought of the infinite appears as the underlying (*sous-jacente*) ontological scene where are confronted, on the one hand, the injunction to finitude, which tries to train humanity in the direction of new servitudes, and on the other hand, the hazardous creation of truths that tries, as much as possible, to protect their innate weakness by separating them from all relapse into deadly finitude through the thick barricade of still unused and even unknown infinites" (Badiou 2018: 468). All quotes from this volume are my own translation.
8. In *Logique des mondes*, Badiou directly equates différance with inexistance: "In homage to Derrida, I write here 'inexistance,' just as he created, a long time ago, the

word 'différance.' We will say that ∅A = inexistance = différance? Why not?" (2009: 545; FR 571).

9   For different but not unrelated reasons, Derrida's deconstruction project takes the notion of the absolute as a particular point to be interrogated in our philosophical traditions. See *De la grammatologie, L'écriture et la différance, La voix et le phénomène, Politiques de l'amitié* and *Donner la mort*, among other texts.

10 Even though Badiou approaches this absolute place more to the Platonic "Idea of the Good," in the sense that, ultimately, it is not really an idea, I think that the notion of khôra as a cosmogonic place that is not really a place, and where, ultimately, everything would have its "place," is closer to V precisely because of its surface-like performance: "Plato would say that V is the Idea of form (of the multiple) in itself, and thus, the idea of an idea. Let us remark that, 'the Idea of the Good,' which was, for him, precisely the Idea of ideas, was not, for Plato, an idea. A little like V that supports the thought of every possible form of the pure multiple, is not itself such a form" (2018: 60).

11 As we know, the paradox of this absolute surface of inscription in modernism—where you can inscribe all while it remains detached from everything—is connected to Freud's *Wunderblock*.

12 For another exploration of what an "absolute modernism" could be, in this case in the work of Maurice Blanchot, see my "Absolute Modernism and *The Space of Literature*," in Christopher Langlois, *Understanding Blanchot. Understanding Modernism* (Bloomsbury, 2018).

13 My italics.

14 Translation modified.

15 *L'écriture et la différance* itself has as its epigraph: "'Le tout sans nouveauté qu'un espacement de la lecture,' Mallarmé, Preface to *Un coup de dés*" (2005: v).

16 Translation modified.

17 Translation modified. Derrida's italics, my bolds.

18 The question remains of how postmodernist writers surpassed this limit and task, or if they ever did.

19 Badiou wrote a short book on Beckett, *Beckett, L'increvable désir* (Hachette, 1995), and references him constantly in other works. Derrida remarked his deep interest in Beckett precisely by avoiding him, going as far as to explain to Derek Attridge in an interview that his avoidance was not due to a distance, but rather to a too close proximity between him and the Franco-Irish writer. See "That Strange Institution Called Literature," in Derrida, J. (1992), *Acts of Literature*, ed. Derek Attridge (London: Routledge), and my own *Beckett and Derrida* (Cambridge: Cambridge UP, forthcoming).

Works Cited

Badiou, A. (2006), *Logiques des mondes*, Paris: Seuil.
Badiou, A. (2008a), *Petit panthéon portatif*, Paris: La fabrique.
Badiou, A. (2008b), *Pocket Pantheon*, trans. D. Macey, London: Verso.
Badiou, A. (2009), *Logics of Worlds*, trans. A. Toscano, New York: Continuum.
Badiou, A. (2018), *L'immanence des vérités*, Paris: Fayard.

Beckett, S. (1984), "Dante... Bruno. Vico.. Joyce," in *Disjecta*, New York: Grove Press.
Beckett, S. (1987), *Proust & Three Dialogues with Georges Duthuit*, London: John Calder.
Beckett, S. (1996), "Worstward Ho," in *Nohow On*, New York: Grove Press.
Beckett, S. (2004), *L'innommable*, Paris: Editions de minuit.
Beckett, S. (2006), "The Unnamable," in *The Grove Centenary Edition. Novels I*, New York: Grove Press.
Beckett, S. (2009), *The Letters of Samuel Beckett I 1929–1940*, eds. M. D. Fehsenfeld and L. M. Overbeck, New York: Cambridge University Press.
Boulter, J. (2019), *Posthuman Space in Samuel Beckett's Short Prose*, Edinburgh: Edinburgh University Press.
Chattopadhyay, A. (2018), *Beckett, Lacan and the Mathematical Writing of the Real*, London: Bloomsbury.
Dennis, A. (2020), *Beckett and Embodiment*, Edinburgh: Edinburgh University Press.
Derrida, J. (1972), "La difference," in *Marges de la philosophie*, Paris: Les éditions de minuit.
Derrida, J. (1982), "La difference," in *Margins of Philosophy*, trans. A. Bass, Chicago: The Harvester Press.
Derrida, J. (2005), *Writing and Difference*, trans. A. Bass, New York: Routledge.
Goldgaber, D. (2021), *Speculative Grammatology*, Edinburgh: Edinburgh University Press.
Hägglund, M. (2008), *Radical Atheism*, Stanford: Stanford University Press.
Lacan, J. (1973–1974a), *Seminar XXI. Les non-dupes errent*, trans. C. Gallaher, Unpublished Manuscript.
Lacan, J. (1973–1974b), *Séminaire XXI, Les non-dupes errent*, Unpublished Manuscript. Available online: http://www.valas.fr/Jacques-Lacan-Les-non-dupes-errent-1973-1974 ,249.
Norris, C. (2012), *Derrida, Badiou and the Formal Imperative*, London: Continuum.

11

Approaching a Non-Modern Historical Theory

Catholic Theology, Alain Badiou and Antihistory

Michael J. Kelly

> A philosopher is always a critic.
>
> —Alain Badiou[1]

> The Antihistorian is not only a critic but a laborer.
>
> —Michael J. Kelly

"I will term situations in which at least one evental site occurs *historical*," says Alain Badiou in *Being and Event* (Badiou 2005: 177). The "evental site" results from, what this chapter argues is proper to call, the *Antihistorical* shattering of the logic of a historical situation, for example, capitalism in the United States, a personal relationship, a family dynamic, a community norm, a local ecosystem, a political party's status quo. This is the moment that Badiou refers to in his conception of history and historical becoming as the "immediate riot," the brief period after the antihistorical "event" has opened up the path toward historical becoming (Badiou 2012, 2013). The antihistorical eventual truth that elicited the immediate riot is contrary to the logic of the prevailing situation (or, world) and cannot as such be sublimated into it. Once this has occurred, Badiou argues, a subjective choice needs to be made, persons must decide between one of three positions to take toward the new truth: whether to ignore what has happened as a genuine event and fetishize the former situation by reinforcing, or "doubling down," on the old ways; whether to accept the event as having happened but reject the need to let it disrupt the situation; or, whether to, and this is our focus in the chapter, become a partisan of the history shattering event. This is the faithful subject that works to short-circuit the logics of the world and construct an alternative one based around the evental truth.

The appearance of the faithful subject develops specifically after the immediate riot, and does so in two stages. The first is what Badiou labels the "latent riot," the period when an evental truth has found traction in disrupting the established situation and a body of faithful subjects emerges and finds some originary cohesion. The antihistorian, acting as a faithful subject to the antihistorical event, believing it to be one that has affected and will affect further change (in thought, in materiality, in logos, etc.), curates a living narrative (or postnarrative[5]) about the shattering of the systemic (objective) modes of the present via the antihistorical non-object's becoming a historical object. The next and final stage is what Badiou calls the "historical riot," which is when the militant, faithful subject has mobilized a movement in the name of the evental truth and proselytizing drastically expands as the antihistorical moves toward becoming the grounding for a new historical situation.

The "historical riot," historical awakening, is a product, then, of the *historical act* that follows after the event, this period when history is produced from antihistory in the name of the alternative historical situation. As Badiou explains, a historical situation is one in which "at least one of its points [is] on the edge of the void" (Badiou 2005: 177). That excess which calls for negation, and which the function Identity in category theory can expose, as Badiou shows, is the point at which Antihistory, the future post-Evental historical category, appears and Badiou's "rebirth of history" starts again.[2]

This assemblage so far of what history is, does, can and should do expresses what I call the theory of Antihistory, a historical theory whose process begins with the *Antihistorical*.[3] It is, I maintain, crucial for wholly explicating and fulfilling Badiou's historical project. The only way for a Badiouian "event" to have legitimate agency within a theory of history and an actually lived emancipatory awakening, for it to have a real meaning and place within Badiou's theory of subjectivity in the form of historical becoming through the faithful subject, is to recognize its very historicity in a way that does not reduce it to the historical. This is what the theory of Antihistory does, by acknowledging the full dialectic of history (and potentially elevating history to the category of a truth-procedure[4]). In so doing, it completes the project of Badiou's historical vision of emancipatory becoming. This chapter provides a pre-modern case study of how this works to solve Badiou's modernist dilemma. In it, moreover, we get to experience Badiou's philosophical reliance on Catholic theology, including the latter's ontotheological inspiration of the mathematical with universal truths, the Christ Event as an "evental site," and emancipatory agency originating in the unpredictable moment of the appearing of truth united with the religious, philosophical and historical conditions as prerequisite for antihistorical appearing.

The theory of Antihistory is influenced by both Catholic theology and the philosophy of Alain Badiou, especially the latter's theory of subjectivity and its application to his proposed model of revolutionary historical becoming with its historical riot and the rebirth of history.[5] As a theorist, and as an advocate of the re-actualization of the communalist Idea since my teen years on Boston's Youth City Council, I am drawn to the emancipatory potential of Badiou's philosophy. As a "practicing historian," as the philosophers like to call us, I am drawn to the Christ Event and the revolutionary potential of the Truth in early Christian theology, as it was expressed by some of its earliest proponents, Origen and Tertullian, the non-Catholics of Late Antiquity, the writings of the Pelagianists, the *De divitiis* and the *De vita Christiana* and the work of Julian of Eclanum. The *De divitiis*, for instance, following the teaching of the Gospels and the wider New Testament, presents the argument that without the rich there would be no poor, it is wealth that creates poverty. This is effectively what is said in the Letter of James as the Evental Truth of Jesus, and is more faithful to that Truth than to the arguments of Julian's contemporary Augustine of Hippo.[6] But I am also drawn in my historical research to what happens a bit later in the Christian Mediterranean, specifically in the Visigothic Catholicism of Spain c. 589–711, because it is there that the entire cycle of the "rebirth of history" has run its course, returning Catholicism to the moments before the Immaculate Conception. It is here at this point, Visigothic Catholicism, that the once radical, emancipatory Evental Truth of the Christ Event has been turned back to the pre-Evental logics of the ancient world into which Jesus was born and which he announced were dead or had been fulfilled.[7] The nomination "Catholic" in Visigothic Spain served, instead, as the bedrock of a politically impotent fetishization of the Christ Event, radical only in the sense of being expressed as utopian, unrealistic and unachievable.[8] This Catholic history provides a case study both of Badiou's theory of subjectivity and its application as theory of historical becoming. It also illustrates the relationship between Badiou's historical thinking and Catholic theology and why this entanglement is important to fulfilling the emancipatory vision of both.

Visigothic Catholics chose ultimately to deny the Truth of the Christ Event as a viable Truth to be lived out as a new historical situation. This is not to say, though, that it was an easy decision to turn into reactionary subjects. Visigothic Catholics knew their theology well, so well that more than once they corrected theological mistakes by the Papacy. In May 688, for instance, at the 15th Council of Toledo, per Julian, the bishop of that royal city, the Visigothic, Catholic Church officially adopted a Christology different from Rome's while also rebuking the Vatican, calling the Roman theologians thoughtless, ignorant and superficial, and accusing a past pope (Benedict II) of superficial attention to Christology.[9] Knowing the theology so well meant that Visigothic Catholics struggled with their own hypocrisy, in riding that fence between fidelity to the truths of the Christ Event and the desire for earthly commitments, authority and pleasures, with building the institution at the cost of abandoning the principles behind its construction.

As Isidore, the Catholic bishop of Seville, c. 600–36, noted in the 630s, before Jerome produced his edition and translation of the Greek-language version of the Hebrew Bible in the 300s, Origen had produced the fifth and sixth editions (Isidore 2006: 139). And in the early 200s, Origin aptly expressed what would become the historical—in the sense of the process of the historical riot, the emergence of the emancipatory Idea as historical consciousness—struggle of Isidore and his fellow Spanish Catholics, as it was for Origen,

> But let us hear what Christ our Lord admonishes his priests: "He who has not renounced all he possesses," he says, "cannot be my disciple." I tremble when I speak these words. For I myself am my own, I say, my own accuser first of all. I utter my own condemnations. For Christ denies that that man whom he has seen possessing anything and that man who "renounces" not "all which he possesses" is his disciple. And what do we do? How do we, who not only do not renounce these

things which we possess, but also wish to acquire those things which we never had before we came to Christ, either read these words ourselves or explain them to people? For since conscience rebukes us, are we able to hide and not bring forth the words which are written? I do not wish to be guilty of a double crime. I admit, and I admit openly to the people who are listening, that these things are written, although I know that I have not yet fulfilled them. But warned from this, let us, at least, hasten to fulfill them. (Origen 2002: 221–2)

"Whoever finds his life will lose it, and whoever loses his life for my sake will find it," Jesus says in Mt. 10:39. In other words, one must submit fully to the Truth, be a radically faithful subject for the new world, for the new history, to become a reality. One must entirely shed their former existence and its commitments in full fidelity to the Truth of the Event to be an actual Christian (i.e., Catholic).

"Truth remains eternal" said Ildefonsus, the Visigothic Catholic bishop of Toledo, 657–67, in his exposition on the universality of the Christ Event through the Virgin Mary (*De Virginitate Sanctae Mariae*) (Ildefonsus 2007, 2011). In Catholic theology, as in the philosophy of Badiou and the theory of Antihistory, truth emerges without advanced notice from an unpredicted location, as does a miracle for Catholics. Once it does, it interrupts the present and demands a decision on fidelity, on radical subjectivity. Badiou's philosophy mirrors this thinking on truth procedures and history, while moving truth into the material and secular (Badiou 2013). These two acts, Catholic theology's and Badiou's, serve as—in an unintended, trinitarian fashion—foundational components of the theory of Antihistory. If we are to follow this unintentional trinitarian logic a step further, we can say that Badiou plays the role of Christ, the Antihistory figure that arrived unexpectedly to reveal a universal truth and make possible the step beyond the collapsing modern (of History) via the universal Holy Spirit. Badiou's theory of subjectivity unchains Catholic theology's potential in a truly "postmodern" philosophy of history (the same "postmodern" potential it failed to live up to in Visigothic Spain).

In Catholic theology, the Evental Truth arrives as a miracle. Badiou's historical thinking on this is especially close to Visigothic Catholic theology. For the most famous Visigothic Catholic, Isidore of Seville, it is not simply a miracle but rather mysticism[10]—or, that is, conditions in the Badouian sense—that sets the stage for the elicitation of truth, and, Isidore says, this truth appears in the world from "bodies and languages" (Isidore 1998: 64, 2018: 69; Badiou 2009: 1). Isidore's philosophy of history operates on complementary levels that express the conditions, the miracle of the (antihistorical) Event, the manifestation of the latent and historical riots and the historical objects that could lead to a forced nomination. On the one hand, the "historical narrative gains its effect as an explanation by its revelation of the deeper meaning of the events it depicts through characterization in figurative (mystical) language" (White 1975: 63). On the other hand, the significant events in the narrative operate as nodes both for alternative historical paths and to signal the defining characteristic of an individual, place or group. Isidore says that history should preserve fidelity to the Event and this is done by the formation of the faithful subject through the process of historical becoming, or, conversion (Isidore 1998: 64, 2018: 69).

In his *Sententiae* (*Thoughts*) 2.8, Isidore fleshes out the categories of resistance to the present world, his version of what Badiou would say are the stages from "intervallic period"—the period when a historical situation is so firmly constituted that its ideology is in no condition to be shattered (Žižek 2009: 27–85)—through immediate, latent and historical riots, the full circle of a Truth's life in the world, from not being in the world to constituting a world (Kelly 2018). Isidore describes this emancipatory process through Visigothic Catholicism's conception of conversion (Kelly 2021: ch. 3). Before there can ever be a convert, the conditions for revolution must be in place for an Event to occur, as Badiou contends throughout his own work (Badiou 2008b), and as Isidore read, for example, in Lk. 8:14-15:

> As for the seed that fell among the thorns, they are the ones who have heard, but as they go along, they are choked by the anxieties and riches and pleasures of life, and they fail to produce mature fruit. But as for the seed that fell on rich soil, they are the ones who, when they have heard the word, embrace it with a generous and good heart, and bear fruit through perseverance.

For Isidore, the process of conversion, as Badiou's process of radical subjectivity, requires both the presence of the correct conditions—the "rich soil" hangs "on the edge of the void"—and cannot be forced, reliant as it is on grace. But once that Event has occurred and a subjective position is demanded, the primary task of the faithful subject, the true convert, is perseverance, endurance, as explained in the Gospels, for example, in Mt. 10:22 "You will be hated by all because of my name, but whoever endures to the end will be saved." Or, in other words, as Badiou would say, the primary task of an emancipatory historical riot is the subjective choice of fidelity in the face of severe resistance from the hegemony, for even though the conditions had emerged for this truth to appear and be recognized as such, it is only later, in the latent period, when the faithful subject will find a community (of believers) (Isidore 1998: 105–14, 2018: 91–97).

The second or simultaneous responsibility of the new faithful subject, the convert, is to recognize that our individual and collective origins do not matter, they have no meaning in the new world, the new landscape of the emancipatory.[11] It is easy to see in this the Badiouian, the Marxist, the Socialist, the genuinely Christian commitment to the Truth beyond any other identities, including familial ties and the nuclear family. Jesus did not come to confirm the present order but to shatter it. As he says in Mt. 10:34-39, "Do not think I have come to bring peace on the earth. I have come not to bring peace but to bring the sword. [. . .] Whoever loves father and mother more than me is not worthy of me, and whoever loves son or daughter more than me is not worthy of me; and whoever does not take up his cross and follow after me is not worthy of me." The unexpected actualization of God as Jesus into the world of Mediterranean antiquity was a radical Event, an antihistorical, logic-shattering short-circuiting of the situation announcing a Truth in opposition to the prevailing Real and demanding radical subjectivity to that Truth, to the Christ Event, for when it happened "The kings of the earth stood up, and the princes assembled together against the Lord and his Christ" (Acts 4:27).

The next expectation of the convert, the radical faithful subject, is then to forge an alternative situation to the present around the Evental Truth. As Catholics translate Isa. 7:9, "If you will not believe, you shall not continue."[12] And as the ever-yearning-to-be-Socialist Bernie Sanders means when he says that the progressive movement is not about him but about us, Jesus says of the Evental Truth, embodied as the Holy Spirit:

> Whoever is not with me is against me, and whoever does not gather with me scatters. Therefore, I say to you, every sin and blasphemy will be forgiven people, but blasphemy against the Spirit will not be forgiven. And whoever speaks a word against the Son of Man will be forgiven, but whoever speaks against the Holy Spirit will not be forgiven, either in this age or in the age to come. (Mt. 12:30-32)

Finally, as Badiou echoes with his latent-riot category, for Isidore, the final layer of the conversion process involves the convert's reaching out to spread the word, to proselytize, whether in actions or words, as historian or liturgist, with patience and humility to let those who were disenfranchised in this world realize that they can become empowered in the next.[13] As the "revolutionary Christian" and philosopher, although not an avowed Badiouan, Cornel West, professor at the Union Theological Seminary, argues, "There's something that's bigger than us, something that's majestic called Truth. [. . .] The condition of that Truth is to allow suffering to speak" (West 2022).

The components of the evental process for Catholic theology are repeated in Badiou's secular (or, ideological) version of it. When a new truth emerges people can either become faithful subjects to it, deny that it has emerged, or accept it but go "all in" on the established historical situation and its logics, its ideology (practices and beliefs). Firstly though, the conditions or the always-being-ready must exist for the Event, grace, the antihistorical to appear and reject the existing situation, followed by the latent and historical riots that pursue the evental truth, as faith, and are rewarded with a new historical situation. (Badiou's philosophy of history lacks the antihistorical as an entity that is distinct yet inseparable from the Event, integral to a historical riot; Catholicism's grace is closer to the concept.)

The evental process of conversion is told by Catholicism not in the form of ontology or philosophy per se, but as narrative, as allegory and as parable. The rejecting of the existing situation (evil) is exemplified, for example, in the story of Isaiah. In Isa. 58:6-10, God says that what he wants Isaiah to tell his people is to "let the oppressed go free." This immediate riot is the moment of sweetness, followed by the period of effort, when God's truth teaches people to share their bread with the hungry and tells Isaiah that then when these things have happened a new dawn, a new historical situation, the period of rest, will emerge: "If you remove from your midst oppression, false accusation and malicious speech; If you bestow your bread on the hungry and satisfy the afflicted; Then light shall rise for you in the darkness, and the gloom shall become for you like midday" (Isa. 58:9-10). Such conversion or historical riot in full requires not a lax or mild fidelity but full faith as exemplified by *the* faithful subject, Jesus, the complete hypostatic union of emancipatory truth and self. As Paul says to Timothy, "If we are unfaithful, he (Jesus) remains faithful, for he cannot deny himself" (2 Tim. 2:13). Badiou similarly claims for his mathematical ontology via the language of category theory that the function Identity (Id) is that which reveals the elements of a set within a situation. Moreover, as Ex = absolute certain existence and M = absolute identity ⇒ Ex = M because one cannot be more identical to oneself, so Id ([elements of] x, y [the two domains of the function]) ⇒ M. Thus, Id (x, y) ≤ Ex (M), or, effectively, one is equal to oneself, or, that is, one cannot deny oneself. As Jesus the figure is represented in a mathematical equation, so Catholic theology is reconstituted as math. This mathematical process of determining similarities exposes, like Jesus, the elements and sets of a historical narrative, of a (small-h) history, of a logic, and of a historical situation, and, in principle, also what elements can be negated (Badiou 2014).

In terms of similarities and what they can reveal, Judaism provided early Catholicism with a fair amount of its theology and ecclesiastical practices, a point well-known to Visigothic Catholics, like Isidore. In his *On the Origins of the Offices* (*De Origine Officiorum*), Isidore lays out explicitly the Jewish origins of Catholicism, in the celebration of Shabbat, the use of "hallelujah" and other Aramaic and Hebrew terms (e.g., abba for abbot and Mazzaroth ⇒ Vespers, end of the day), prayers (specifically the third, sixth and ninth hours of Daniel ⇒ Trinity of daily prayers), vigils, Matins, the triple blessing of the people, blood sacrifice represented by wine, the songs of David → hymns to God, Greeks → antiphons, accompanying lines, Song of Songs → canticles, psalms, Jewish temples → churches, Moses's choirs of ten → Catholic crown choirs, readings from Scripture in Mass, and the twenty-seven texts of the Catholic Bible (New Testament; seventy-three texts as a whole) from the seventy-two elders of Moses and of the Septuagint.

What is distinctly Christian (Catholic), Isidore claims, is what is the most related to the process of historical becoming, the historical riot of Badiou: the Nicene Symbol (Creed) with the Profession of Faith and the Sign of the Cross, as well as the seven steps of Catholic Mass, as per Peter: (1) admonition (warning); (2) invocation of God; (3) prayer for the dead and the sick; (4) a promise of peace be with you all; (5) sanctifying the Eucharist with Hosanna in the Highest, the Eucharistic sacrifice symbolizing the union of the faithful (water) with the body of the faithful subject to be emulated (the wine and bread), thereby permanently entangling faithful subjects of the Event; (6) the confirmation of that through consumption of the Holy Sacrament (Eucharist) and (7) the closing prayer to the grace, or antihistorian, of the Event, with the Lord's Prayer (Isidore 2008). In this, the revolutionary commitment of the rank and file is reaffirmed each week. And, the anti-Judaism that is continually present in Visigothic Catholicism (*c.* 630–710s) is ultimately grounded in the claim by Catholic theologians that Jews cannot find salvation or become fully human specifically because they lack (the ability to have) a historical consciousness (Kelly 2023a).

In Catholic theology, as noted, antihistory as the start of the historical riot disrupts nature, short-circuits the logics of the world, is a sort of miracle, like grace, that emerges from the void when the conditions are right for it to do so, like in the case of Jesus's birth through Mary. The story of the life of Jesus is a veritable case study for Badiou's *The Rebirth of History: The Prequel*. The conditions of Christ's coming into the world were the situation of late-Second-Temple Judaism in which the cult of Jerusalem struggled to maintain its control, both against outside contenders (such as the Roman Empire) and inside "dissidents" (e.g., the Pharisees, the zealots, sicarii, new messiahs), as well as the legacy of a competing temple in Egypt, in Leontopolis. Roman control of Judaea and Jerusalem fostered anti-imperial resistance, influenced by figures like Hillel and Judas the Galilean. In these conditions, Jesus would declare, "I say to you, something greater than the temple is here" (Mt. 12:6).

In the time-ambiguous narration of Jesus's life, the prevailing conditions allow the Event to shatter that world, and that Event itself is beyond chronology and trinitarian: represented by the birth of Christ, the baptism of Jesus by John the Baptist and the Crucifixion. The immediate riot is certainly the arrival of the child Christ into the world via the Immaculate Conception in Nazareth and the virgin birth in Bethlehem, the house of bread. The latent riot and historical riot are Jesus's ministry and the formation of the Church after the Last Supper (Passover, the exodus from bondage) and the Crucifixion and Resurrection of Christ. The revolutionary Truths of this multiplicitous Event constellation demanded gender equality, vegetarianism and the full renunciation of wealth. In Acts 4:32-35, it is said of the early Christians (those of the latent period) that, echoing God's wishes in Isaiah, "The community of believers was of one heart and mind, and no one claimed that any of his possessions was his own, but they had everything common. [. . .] There was no needy person among them, for those who owned houses would sell them, bring the proceeds of the sale, and they would put them at the feet of the Apostles, and they were distributed to each according to need." In Lk. 18:20-25, Jesus says to the rich man wanting to get into heaven, "There is still one thing left for you to do: sell all that you have and distribute it to the poor, and you will have a treasure in Heaven. [. . .]. How hard it is for those who have wealth to enter the kingdom of God! For it is easier for a camel to pass through the eye of a needle than for a rich person to enter the kingdom of God," that is, the new historical situation.

In his lost work on the "Unusual Properties of the Persons of the Father and the Son and the Holy Spirit," Ildefonsus would have added a crucial component to this Christology.[14] In section 3 of his *Perpetual Virginity of the Holy Mary*, he does just this, citing Isa. 7:14 to prove to his imaginary Jewish opponent—who he refers to as drunk (*crapulatus*) on primeval faithlessness (*primaevae perfidiae*) (Ildefonsus 2007: 166, 2011: 16)—that Mary remained a virgin after she gave birth to Jesus.[15] He says from this that "a miracle is apparent if there comes to be in a human conception (i.e., the virgin birth)—that which human nature doesn't know in this circumstance!" (Ildefonsus 2007: 167, 2011: 16). In a Marian sermon of the *Toledo Homiliary* (*Homiliae Toletanae*), variously ascribed to Ildefonsus, the audience is asked, "Is the virgin St. Mary giving birth contrary to nature?"[16] According to Jews, the sermon contends, yes, "E contra Judaeus: Contra naturum, inquit, parere virgo Maria non potuit."[17] Using the light and the glass metaphor, the sermon contends that the virgin birth is a natural phenomenon: Mary remains a virgin after birth, as glass remains the same after light travels through it.[18] This is a problematic argument though because the light maintains its essence after the event, while Jesus does not, Jesus is transformed, incarnated as human. But this is also what makes the whole argument work, as from the solidly Ildefonsine material, that the Marian birth endows Jesus with humanity—our humanity, which suffers birth and death—by the act of a miracle.[19] If a miracle would occur on some occasion when light went through glass, then it too, like the Eucharist, could be transformed into or endowed with another essence, or will, while maintaining its integrity as one entity.

Jesus's humanity is thus contingent, contingent on a miracle, the Immaculate Conception and the virgin birth: a miracle transforms the essence of God from being one nature into being of two natures. In Catholic theology, human nature itself is a historical contingency in that its essence depends on events that determine it, like the first sin and its introduction of death. As Paul says in Rom. 5:12, "Therefore just as through one person sin entered the world, and through sin, death, and thus death came to all." All that is contingent is historical. History is contingent in Catholic theology, in Badiou's philosophy, and in the theory of Antihistory. Contingency is an absolute of "human nature" and of the historical riot, but it is not a generic absolute: in scientific research, contingency does not exist always, as in quantum entanglement; in Catholic theology, God is not contingent. No miracles are required for God to be. God simply is and you either believe that or you don't. The Truth *is* and the historical riot *is a becoming*. Truths are universal yet material, forever yet created, God and Jesus as Holy Spirit, the communist Idea created by humans (Badiou 2008a), Jesus actualized because of our actions. The infinite has its origins in the finite, the Christ Event from us, showing that finite beings can manifest and partake in the infinite, that the finite and the infinite can be one, Marxism and Badiou proving Catholicism, Meillassoux and mathematics proving Catholicism, saving Catholicism.

Antihistory is an is-was-is, the hypostatic union of being and event in which a *christ* enters also the historical riot, a constellation of the non-contingent, the cause and effect, and the effect and the cause. Radical, subjective fidelity, or faith, is made possible in a historical situation, for example, the current manifestation of humanness, with the arrival of the antihistorical, for example, in the form of the Christ Event constellation. Antihistory is the miracle shattering the present logic and demanding a radical, subjective choice of fidelity or denial. Badiou's evental thinking reminds us of the radical potential of Catholic theology's revolutionary imagination of humanness and history, but it is the distinction of the antihistorical from the historical, the antihistorian from the historian, that fully unites the evental with the theory of subjectivity as historical theory, that fulfills the Badiouian historical project (Kelly 2023a).

In Catholicism, in Badiouianism, in Antihistory, truths are universal yet material, forever yet created, the infinite has its origins in the finite, we as finite beings can partake in the infinite. In political terms, we have the power to create society and "human nature" in any way we want and no truth is ever dead, only unactualized in certain historical situations. The communalist truth was manifested by human conditions thousands of years ago, at least, but it is not currently a living truth. But it could be, and the trinity of non-being, event and being, of Catholic theology, Badiou's philosophy, and Antihistory, could help condition that radical event.

This is true, I think, not only in a theoretical sense. This trinity, operating in our rapidly de-democratizing, demoralizing and hopeless world, allows for the conditioning of wide audiences for radical, emancipatory thinking and historical becoming, the conditions that would shatter the logics of capitalism even as we inch toward the privatization and monetarization of our entire, individual existences. The language of this trinity, in short referred to as Antihistory, is better suited for bringing elements to the edge of the void than are the religious or the philosophical, Catholicism or Marxism via Badiou, alone. The audience for a theology of emancipation vastly transcends the walls of academic philosophy and its for-profit output apparatus. Catholic theology shows that human nature and even nature itself are historical phenomenon and as such are not forever. The first step in the conversion from capitalism is this recognition that the present is not all that there is and can be, is not the result of a universal "human nature" or "nature" that no matter what we try will always return us to some form of capitalism. Badiou's theory of subjectivity shows us how "to believe and to continue" to paraphrase Catholicism's translation of Isaiah. And Antihistory, achieving Badiou's historical call, proves that historical consciousness is a step toward historical awakening, to that point where finally suffering can speak.

History creates objects of investigation, that is, we historians create the past and our objects of study: facts and pasts do not simply exist out there for us to find. Historians create the category "history" and ascribe it contents: past, facts, objects and events. We manifest each of these; we manifest events: we present items as historical events, as objects, as relics, as proof, as truths, as evidence of a real item for our category "history," and within that its subcategories. Further classification categorizes, for instance, our objects, for example, texts, aqueducts, psyches, landscapes, ceramics, tropes, fossilized vegetation, ideas and manuscripts.[20] Further classification likewise categorizes our events, for example, transformative, shattering, confirmative and so on. Each type of object works to prove, first, that the primary object of the category "history," past, is real, but also that the category "history" itself is real. The same is the case with events.

The subsequent movement of historical research should reach beyond proofs of historical reality or meaning to answer questions of its purpose—beyond proving that our category, history, is real and that its contents had meaning at various moments: the next stage is to answer the "so what?" In that way, the historical object and event, such as a specific medieval manuscript or a local flood or an individual act, can sate the historian who sees their job as an archaeologist digging up pre-existing, ready-made facts, can also satiate the neo-Rankean/neo-objectivist, the object-oriented-ontologist and the speculist who, not wanting to be either the naïve objectivist or the uncompromising postmodernist, says there must be absolute truths, like contingency, must be objective facts whose status as such transcends my consciousness, and it can also satisfy the theorist of Antihistory, the believer in the antihistorian, and so the entire Badiouian historical project.[21] The antihistorian sees genuine History as a necessarily radical act that embraces the Badiouian emancipatory Event as the starting point of historical discourse: that is, History begins with the shattering of history, that is, the situation, the imagined "natural" order of things, of time, of space-time, of "human nature" and so on. The traditional, vernacular category "history" is a repository of the once revolutionary, a museum of antihistories. Antihistory as a theory of history offers the chance too, then, for a discourse on philosophy's past that does not turn philosophy, as Badiou has feared, into an object in a museum removed from political potential.[22]

Postscript

The theory of Antihistory in conversation with Catholic theology and the philosophies of Badiou and Quentin Meillassoux assists in the creation of immutable stores of "objective fact"—as such by transparently defined method—for perpetual reinscribing into histories. In Badiou's *Topos, Or Logics of Onto-logy*, a topos is equivalent to a mathematical universe "which presents its own internal logic" (Badiou 2014: 89–94). Topos refers, for example, to the full "mathematical" universe of the Christ Event as it became in Visigothic Catholicism. If a historical situation with its internal logic, for example, Visigothic Catholicism, could be mathematized via category theory, then category theory could help in mathing pasts, cryptographically hashing them (into blockchains), and subsequently "writing" (inscribing) histories. We have a lot of work to do on this, from deciding on consensus mechanisms and determining at what point in the inscribing process to introduce AI, all the way up to imagining how histories on UTXOs force us to rethink our valuations and determinations of being's transactions, being's presence. Badiou's philosophy is a core component of this decentralizing of history and academic output and the ushering in of the New (Web3) Digital Humanities.[23]

Notes

1 Badiou (2010).
2 It is important here to note that Badiou separates nature from history, following Hegel, Marx and others. The theory of Antihistory argues instead, following Catholic theology, the grounding of much of Badiou's philosophical thinking, that nature, including "human nature," is historical and eventual and so can be shattered and reconstituted in an entirely alternative form, the Event can arrive via the excess of nature (Badiou 2005: 173).
3 See Kelly (2022, 2023b and forthcoming).
4 For Badiou, a truth can emerge from one of four truth procedures: art, love, politics and science. For a basic introduction, see Kelly (2014).
5 See Badiou (2005: Part IV, 2012, 2013: Part III).
6 For a recent call for Catholicism, and Christianity more widely, to return to its emancipatory mission, see Hart (2019). For further discussion of the Pelagianists and Augustine, see Brown (2012: chs. 18–23). For Jesus's thoughts on wealth and the requirement to renounce it to follow him, see Mt. 6:24, 10:34-39, Lk. 18:22-28 and Acts 4:32-35.

7   Alain Badiou argues in "On Three Different Concepts of Identity" that the ontological principle of the being of non-being means that the multitude of inexistents are all equal to each other (Badiou 2014). This promises the universality of an Evental Truth until it is forced into a nomination, exactly as we have with the universality of God in relation to the Christ Event and its appearing as Visigothic Catholicism.

8   Recent scholarship (e.g., Whelan 2019) tends to prefer the terms "homoian" and "homoousian" for "Arian" and "Catholic," respectively, but the Visigothic bishops spoke of themselves as Catholics, not homoousians, and of their Church as Catholic not homoousian. See, for instance, Isidore (1998: 55–60, 2018: 64–6, 92).

9   For an accessible edition, see Julian of Toledo's *Apologeticum De tribus capitulis* of 688 at Patrologia Latina 96, cols. 525–36. For the 15th Council of Toledo, see Martínez Díez and Rodríguez (2003: 291–344) or, with Spanish translation, Vives (1963: 449–74). For more criticism of the Papacy from Visigothic bishops, see Braulio of Zaragoza's letter to Pope Honorius in the 630s, listed in Braulio's letter collection as *Ep.*, 21. The letter can be found in modern translation in Claude W. Barlow, trans., *Braulio of Saragossa*, Iberian Fathers 2 (Washington, DC: The Catholic University of America, 1969), 51–6, and, as Ephesians 16, in Ruth Miguel Franco, trans. (Sp.), *Braulio de Zaragoza, "Epístolas"* (Madrid: Ediciones Akal, 2015), 121–4. For more on the letters between the Visigothic Catholic Church and the Papacy, see Ferreiro (2018, 2020).

10 Like the function Id in Badiou's reading of category theory, for Isidore and his Catholic theology mysticism reveals the elements of a set that can be negated. See Badiou (2005: Meditation 7, 2008b: Part III, 2014a).

11 See for this idea also Isidore of Seville, *De Origine Gothorum* (*History of the Goths*). Rodríguez Alonso, 1975; Donini and Ford (1966).

12 "si non credideritis non permanebitis" in the Latin Vulgate. The Hebrew Bible has this as "If you will not believe, you cannot be trusted" ("אם לא תאמינו כי לא תאמנו"). Faith is the essence of trust in both cases, but in Catholicism it is expressed as clearly central to the process of the historical riot.

13 And yet it is important for Isidore—as part of the inner struggles of Catholic theologians vis-à-vis institutionalism—that the Evental Truth should not be forced because once truth is nominated it retreats as a truth. For Badiou's thoughts on this forcing, see Badiou (2008b: 113–44). On Isidore's views of conversion as a gradual process of learning, see again his *Sent.*, 2.8 but also Isidore of Seville 1964: 149–50. In the secondary literature, see Benveniste (2006); Drews (2006: 91–110, et *passim*); Fontaine (1967).

14 *Opusculum de Proprietate Personarum Patris et Filii et Spiritus Sancti* (Patrologia Latina 96, col. 44A): The book is now lost, but we know that it did exist thanks to Julian of Toledo's reference to it in his *De Viris Illustribus* biography of Ildefonsus (see following note). On the relationship between Ildefonsus and Julian, see the latter's *Elogium Ildephonsi* (Patrologia Latina 96, cols. 42–4), a biography of the teacher by the student added to Ildefonsus's *De Viris Illustribus*. For a scholarly discussion of this, see Hillgarth (1958).

15 A real Jewish opponent, as Ildefonsus makes clear in the passage, would have disagreed with Ildefonsus at the very least on simple semantic grounds. The Vulgate Latin version of Isa. 7:14 reads "the virgin shall conceive" ("ecce virgo concipiet"), while the Hebrew Bible says that a young woman is pregnant ("הנה העלמה הרה").

Ildefonsus lambasts his imaginary Jew for reading this as a "young woman" instead of as a "virgin."
16 Patrologia Latina 96, col. 232A: "Et Virgo sancta Maria non potuit contra naturam ex iussu Dei Filium generare?" For a recent discussion of the Toledo Homilary see Chase (2020); Grégoire (1966).
17 Patrologia Latina 96, col. 231D.
18 Patrologia Latina 96, col. 232B: "Solis radius specular penetrat, et soliditatem eius insensibili subtilitate per trajicit; et talis videtur intrinsecus, quailis et extrinsecus [. . .] Specular ergo non rumpit radius solis; integritatem Virginis ingressus aut regressus vitiare poterat Deitatis." On the history of the analogy in Christianity, see Breeze (1988).
19 In *De Virginitate Sanctae Mariae*, Ildefonsus repeats the arguments of the Athanasian Creed, that God/Jesus are in hypostatic union and that Jesus earns his human nature through Mary.
20 As is a category in the category theory that Badiou employs, in which an identity morphism is, we could say, for instance, a chronological narrative bridging source (past) and target (present) (Badiou 2014: 265–8; Marx 1993: 100–8, 704–6, 880–1; Marx 1990: 125–30).
21 The antihistorian proposed here should be not confused with the antiphilosopher in Badiouan discourse (Badiou 2011). For more on my theory of Antihistory and the concept of the antihistorian, see Kelly (2022: 1–15).
22 "The history of philosophy is today more than ever its own court, and the verdict handed down by this court is almost always one of capital punishment [. . .] For my part, I shall propose a violent forgetting of the history of philosophy [. . .] Forget history: this means, above all, making decisions of thought without turning back towards a presupposed historical meaning" (Badiou 2008b: 4–5).
23 I am currently preparing two articles in conversation with each other on, respectively, the concept of "value" in a historical world and on the use-value of blockchain for encoding pasts and inscribing history. I lecture a course and run a lab at Binghamton University in which we attempt to math pasts and develop a history blockchain.

Works Cited

Badiou, A. (2005), *Being and Event*, trans. O. Feltham, New York: Continuum.
Badiou, A. (2008a), "The Communist Hypothesis," *New Left Review* 49, np.
Badiou, A. (2008b), *Conditions*, trans. S. Corcoran, New York: Continuum.
Badiou, A. (2009), *Logics of Worlds: Being and Event II*, trans. A. Toscano, New York: Continuum.
Badiou, A. (2010), Interview, *Hardtalk*. Available online: https://www.youtube.com/watch?v=OpH5GTTIZ3k (accessed June 19, 2022).
Badiou, A. (2011), *Wittgenstein's Antiphilosophy*, trans. B. Bosteels, New York: Verso.
Badiou, A. (2012), *The Rebirth of History: Times and of Uprisings*, trans. G. Elliott, New York: Verso.
Badiou, A. (2013), *Theory of the Subject*, trans. B. Bosteels, New York: Bloomsbury.
Badiou, A. (2014a), "On Three Different Concepts of Identity between Two Multiples or Two Beings," in A. Badiou, *Mathematics of the Transcendental*, trans. A. J. Bartlett and A. Ling, 265–268, New York: Bloomsbury.

Badiou, A. (2014b), "Topos, Or Logics of Onto-logy," in A. Badiou, *Mathematics of the Transcendental*, trans. A. J. Bartlett and A. Ling, 13–161, New York: Bloomsbury.

Benveniste, H.-R. (2006), "On the Language of Conversion, Visigothic Spain Revisited," *Historein* 6, 72–87.

Braulio of Zaragoza (2015), *Letters*. Claude W. Barlow, trans. *Braulio of Saragossa*. Iberian Fathers 2, Washington, DC: The Catholic University of America, 1969. Ruth Miguel Franco, trans. (Sp.), *Braulio de Zaragoza, "Epístolas."* Madrid: Ediciones Akal.

Breeze, A. (1988), "The Blessed Virgin and the Sunbeam through the Glass," *Barcelona English Language and Literature Studies* 1, 53–64.

Brown, P. (2012), *Through the Eye of a Needle: Wealth, the Fall of Rome, and the Making of Christianity in the West, 350–550 ad*, Princeton: Princeton University Press.

Drews, W. (2006), *The Unknown Neighbour: The Jew in the Thought of Isidore of Seville*, Boston and Leiden: Brill.

Ferreiro, A. (2018), "The Bishops of Hispania and Pope Innocent I (401–47)," *Visigothic Symposia* 3, 19–35.

Ferreiro, A. (2020), *"Epistolae Plenae": The Correspondence of the Bishops of Hispania with the Bishops of Rome: Third through Seventh Centuries*. The Medieval and Early Modern Iberian World, Boston and Leiden: Brill.

Fontaine, J. (1967), "Conversion et culture chez les Wisigoths d'Espagne," *Settimane di Studio* 14, 87–147.

Hart, D. B. (2019), "What Lies beyond Capitalism: A Christian Exploration," *Plough* 21, np.

Hillgarth, J. N. (1958), "St. Julian of Toledo in the Middle Ages," *Journal of the Warburg and Courtauld Institutes* 21:1/2, 7–26.

Ildefonsus of Toledo (2007/2011), *De Virginitate Sanctae Mariae*. Valeriano Yarza Urquiola, ed., *Ildefonsus of Toledo, "De Virginitate Sanctae Mariae."* Corpus Christianorum Series Latina 114A. Turnhout: Brepols; Malcolm Drew Donalson, trans., *The Perpetual Virginity of the Holy Mary*, Lewiston: Edwin Mellen Press.

Isidore of Seville (1964), *De Viris Illustribus*. Carmen Codoñer Merino, ed., *El "De Viris Illustribus" de S. Isidoro*, Salamanca: Consejo Superior de Investigaciones Científicas.

Isidore of Seville (1966), *De Origine Gothorum* (*History of the Goths*). Cristobal Rodríguez Alonso, ed. and trans. (Sp.), *Las Historias de los Godos, los Vandalos y los suevos de Isidoro de Sevilla*, León: Centro de Estudios e Investigación "San Isidoro," 1975. Guido Donini and Gordon B. Ford, Jr., trans., *Isidore of Seville's "History of the Kings of the Goths, Vandals, and Sueves."* Boston and Leiden: Brill.

Isidore of Seville (2006), *Etymologies*. Stephen A. Barney, W. J. Lewish, J. A. Beach and O. Berghof, trans., *The "Etymologies" of Isidore of Seville*, Cambridge: Cambridge University Press.

Isidore of Seville (2008), *De Origine Officiorum*. Thomas L. Knoebel, trans., Isidore of Seville, *"De Ecclesiasticis Officiis."* Ancient Christian Writers 61, New York: The Newman Press.

Isidore of Seville (2018), *Sententiae*. Pierre Cazier, ed., *Isidorus Hispalensis "Sententiae."* Corpus Christianorum Series Latina 111, Turnhout: Brepols, 1998. Thomas L. Knoebel, trans., Isidore of Seville, *"Sententiae."* Ancient Christian Writers 73, New York: Newman Press.

Julian of Toledo. *Apologeticum De tribus capitulis*. Patrologia Latina 96, cols. 525–36.

Julian of Toledo. *Elogium Ildephonsi*. Patrologia Latina 96, cols. 42–44.

Julian of Toledo (2010), *Prognosticum futuri saeculi*. Tommaso Stancati, trans., *Julian of Toledo, "Prognosticum futuri saeculi" ("Foreknowledge of the World to Come")*. Ancient Christian Writers 63, New York: Newman Press.
Kelly, M. J. (2014), *Alain Badiou: A Graphic Guide*, London: Icon Books.
Kelly, M. J. (2018), "Introduction: Evental History and the Humanities," in M. J. Kelly and A. Rose (eds.), *Theories of History: History Read Across the Humanities*, 1–15, London: Bloomsbury.
Kelly, M. J. (2021), *Isidore of Seville and the "Liber Iudiciorum": The Struggle for the Past in the Visigothic Kingdom*. The Medieval and Early Modern Iberian World 80, Boston and Leiden: Brill.
Kelly, M. J. (2022), "Truth & Anti-History," in C. Taranu and M. J. Kelly (eds.), *"Vera Lex Historiae": Constructions of Truth in Medieval Historical Narrative*, 1–15, Binghamton: Gracchi Books.
Kelly, M. J. (2023a), "The Logic of Control: Postulating a Visigothic Ontology of Human Being," in D. Castro and F. Ruchesi (eds.), *Leadership, Cohesion and Identity in the Visigothic Kingdom*, 63–101, Amsterdam: Amsterdam University Press.
Kelly, M. J. (2023b), "The Visigothic Idea: Are the Visigoths Still Networking?" in M. J. Kelly and K. Patrick Fazioli, *Social and Intellectual Networking in the Early Middle Ages*, 13–26, Binghamton: Gracchi Books.
Kelly, M. J. (forthcoming), "Medieval Manuscript as Anti-Historical Object?" in A. Dorofeeva and M. J. Kelly (eds.), *The Art of Compilation: Manuscripts and Networks in the Early Medieval Latin West*, Binghamton: Gracchi Books.
Marx, K. (1990), *Capital*, trans. B. Fowkes, New York: Penguin.
Marx, K. (1993), *Grundrisse*, trans. M. Nicolaus, New York: Penguin.
Marx, K. (2002), "Theses on Feuerbach," trans. C. Smith. Available online: https://www.marxists.org/archive/marx/works/1845/theses/ (accessed October 1, 2022).
Meillassoux, Q. (2012), *After Finitude: An Essay on the Necessity of Contingency*, trans. R. Brassier, New York: Bloomsbury.
Milanović, B. (2019), *Capitalism, Alone: The Future of the System that Rules the World*, Cambridge: Belknap Press.
Origen (2002), *Homilies on Genesis*. Ronald E. Heine, trans., *Origen, "Homilies on Genesis and Exodus."* Washington, DC: The Catholic University Press.
Toledo H. and N. Chase (1966), *The "Homiliae Toletanae" and the Theology of Lent and Easter*, Leuvens: Peeters, 2020. Réginald Grégoire, *Les homéliaires du moyen âge. Inventaire et analyse des manuscrits*, Rome: Herder.
Visigothic Church Councils (1963), *La Colección Canónica Hispana*, eds. Gonzalo Martínez Díez and Félix Rodríguez, Madrid: Consejo Superior de Investigaciones Científicas, 2003. J. Vives, trans. (Sp.), *Concilios Visigóticos e Hispano-Romanos*, Barcelona and Madrid: Consejo Superior de Investigaciones Científicas, Instituto Enrique Flórez.
West, C. (2022), "Philosophy in Our Time of Imperial Decay," at The New School for Social Research, March 2022. Available online: https://www.youtube.com/watch?v=k5ydesBadno (accessed July 4, 2022).
Whelan, R. (2019), "Ethnicity, Christianity, and Groups: Homoian Christians in Ostrogothic Italy and Visigothic Spain," in Y. Fox and E. Buchberger (eds.), *Inclusion and Exclusion in Mediterranean Christianities, 400-800*, 167–198, Turnhout: Brepols.
White, H. (1975), "Historicism, History, and the Figurative Imagination," *History and Theory* 14, 48–67.
Žižek, S. (2009), *First as Tragedy, Then as Farce*, New York: Verso.

12

Badiou, Music, Novelty

Adity Singh

Badiou claims that "music was an avant-garde art and still is" (Badiou 2013: 208). When it comes to the "still is" part of this statement, the music in question is specifically a particular Western classical canon, whose only legitimate practitioners in the twenty-first century, for Badiou, are the high modernists who "from Schönberg to Brian Ferneyhough, liquidated tonality and constructed a universe of musical singularities, serial and post-serial" (Badiou 2013: 147).[1]

But is there something about music itself that makes it the avant-garde art *par excellence*? After all, the twentieth century, which Badiou sees as "the century of avant-gardes," has as its "most admirable distillate" the music of Anton Webern, Schönberg's disciple, who wrote some of the earliest "serial" music: aphoristic pieces that were distilled examples of the sort of music that could be written after having broken with the legacy of classical tonality.[2] Yet, while formal innovations form the core of progress in music history, formal *breaks* are not quite so obvious. Music, like the other arts, has often been at the vanguard of its times, while remaining a product of its times. Indeed, innovation in music as often as not has had to do with external factors, whether they be the whims of the patrons or the public, or the strictures of the church, to name a few. A desire to make a formal break with the past purely *for the sake of* making such a break is not so easily discerned.

Thus, what makes the example of atonal music after Schönberg paradigmatic is the "formal break" that it explicitly and *programmatically* declares from the "preceding artistic schema," the very definition of the "avant-garde" for Badiou. Moreover, the key difference between any radical innovations that earlier artists might have made and the one that Badiou credits Schönberg with is that the latter's work does not attempt immediately to please, and is thus avant-garde in another sense that it breaks with "the consensus about what does or does not substantiate a judgement of taste" (Badiou 2007: 132–3). This indifference, even hostility to public taste, makes the music of the avant-garde an excellent illustration of what Badiou calls the "absoluteness" of a work of art, which is characterized by the "profound intellectuality" of its endeavor, rather than any effect it may have on our senses (Badiou 2022: 474).[3]

Thus, while music has "continued to be" an avant-garde art, "the moaning of popular music," for Badiou, cannot be called "music" at all (Badiou 2013: 235), and "the only thing that in the twentieth century [merits] the name of 'music,'" he declares, is the "serial organization of pitches" (Badiou 2009a: 81).[4] Accordingly, when he names, somewhat arbitrarily, and only in passing, the "three types of music" of the twentieth century—"post-romantic," "jazz," "serial and post-serial"—he only credits the last of these with "a continuation through rupture of veritable musical creation" (Badiou 2013: 147).

Yet, in the scattered musings on music in his written texts and, in particular, in an eight-episode radio series with *France Musique*, Badiou shows himself to be a discerning and eclectic listener, at least of the Western classical canon, where he shows a love for Bach, Mozart and Tchaikovsky, as much as for Debussy and Wagner. Indeed, what is surprising is that his canon ends somewhere in the mid-twentieth century— even Stockhausen, Nono and Cage get barely a mention—and so far we have seen nothing touching upon contemporary work in Western classical music, let alone any attempt to discern innovations outside of what may be considered the Western classical canon (Badiou 2009a: 84).[5] What becomes clear is that Badiou's own musical tastes don't precisely match what his philosophy approves of. Although he makes a valiant attempt to get the two to align, especially in his discussion of serialism, this falls short as he admits that the later serialist works are not quite to his taste. In fact, even as he appreciates their "extreme complexity," he still finds Webern's works a bit "dry" and "algebraic" for everyday consumption (Badiou and Esparza 2018c).

An earnest attempt to align the two, his tastes and his philosophy, is his book on Wagner, where Badiou bemoans the declared end of "high art" after (and due to) Wagner and proposes that "a second Wagner" can be "invoked" to make "high art [...] a creative project for the future" (Badiou 2010: 83). Thus, rather than call for a fidelity to the consequences of the break made by Schönberg (or a call to seek another eventual break) Badiou calls for a "resurrection" of Wagner in the present. The question then arises about what future music Badiou expects between the absolute discontinuities of breaks and the discontinuous continuities of resurrection. In other words, what precisely is novelty for Badiou, particularly in the context of music?

If there is a pivotal question that can be placed at the center of Badiou's philosophical enterprise, one that Badiou always returns to, it is the question of novelty. How can anything new emerge in this world? This question animates every stage of Badiou's philosophical enterprise. For example, when it comes to the distinction between being and event, the latter is necessitated by the problem of something *new* occurring when being is structured mathematically. An analogical (though not strictly equivalent) distinction between the world and the existence of something *new* therein is the core of his exploration of phenomenology in *Logics of Worlds*.[6] The question of the subject and truth is, ultimately, the question of novelty itself. How can something new occur in a sustained manner so that something in the old situation/world is definitively changed? And who can be credited as an agent for this change if the event that occurs perchance creates mere possibility and doesn't necessitate anything definitive? Then, the concepts of Idea, eternality, and absoluteness are brought in to ensure that a new truth, "having been created in history" will not, by the mere passage of time, "slip back into nothingness," that is to say, to ensure the stability of a novel construction (Badiou 2009a: 64). Finally, with the concept of resurrection, an act by which a "faithful subject can also reincorporate into the eventual present the fragment of a truth whose bygone present has sunk under the bar of occultation," he can allow for a subject of a particular world to participate in potentially infinite number of worlds and equally, for truths, created in any world, to become available in a transtemporal transworldly manner (Badiou 2009a: 66).

Western classical music is thus paradigmatic for Badiou in another sense. He posits that as a type of music that has a fixed written form that is brought to life in every performance, it exemplifies his distinction between being and existence, between the ontological and the phenomenological and especially between creation and resurrection, where the score from a time past can be brought to life in different worlds and can thus become something new in a world not its own (Badiou and Esparza 2018e). However, here a fine distinction is drawn between the resurrection of a truth and reaction, where the former creates another faithful subject in a new context, the latter tries to "resist the call of the new" and thus creates, oxymoronically, "reactionary novelties" (Badiou 2009a: 54). In music, this is exemplified by what Badiou calls "baroque reaction," a term that dismisses the early music revival movement *in toto* as reactionary. Indeed Badiou, spurns "the plurality of 'musics'—folklore, classicism, pop, exoticism, jazz and baroque reaction in the same festive bag" as reactionary inasmuch as incapable to allowing a new musical subject to be formed in the present.

In fact, even contemporary high modernism doesn't go unscathed and he claims that "today [. . .] the serial subject is equally unpromising" and cannot hope to create sustained truths nor "resuscitate" the dying body of truths "scattered into unorganized bodies and vain ceremonies" (Badiou 2009a: 89). Oddly, what he allows in the name of novelty and resurrection is neoclassicism in music: "Berlioz's return to Gluck; the lessons drawn by Ravel from the clavicembalists of the eighteenth century" (Badiou 2009a: 76). One might be hard-pressed to imagine in what way "the neo-classical nostalgia of the ruins" is less "reactionary"—in Badiou's terms—than the early music revivalists' search for authentic performances of music of the past (Badiou 2009a: 207). The argument, one can assume, is that the attempt to *write* new music inspired by classical examples can count for the resurrection of old truths, but the attempt to merely *perform* old music in contemporary times with an eye to *reviving* something old is, for Badiou, thoroughly reactionary.[7] Yet, when it comes to the future of music as "high art," Badiou invokes the name of Wagner, who he claims is still relevant in the present, which raises the issue of how precisely his "resurrection," so to speak, is to be envisaged (Badiou 2010: 129).

Music, we can note, is not the most privileged example of an artform in Badiou's writings. That place would go to poetry, but it is still accorded a fairly elevated place. Yet, Badiou is somewhat reluctant to write on music, as he himself acknowledges.[8] This reluctance, however, goes to the extent that in his book on art, *Handbook of Inaesthetics*, music is noticeably absent, except as a passing remark, although Badiou identifies "dodecaphonic music" as one of the main "artistic configurations that have marked the century" (Badiou 2005b: 14). The key musical example in Badiou's work, dealing with the second Viennese school and its serialist successors, is tellingly named a scholium, a marginal note, which, while both brilliantly illustrative of Badiou's philosophy and an intriguing application of Badiou's concepts to explain a (canonical) periodization of music history, remains but an example. There are other musical examples in *Logics of Worlds*, including Berlioz and Dukas, but again, the former is mentioned in passing, in reference to Virgil, and the latter's opera *Ariadne and Bluebird* is dealt with entirely at the level of plot. Following "a day-long event devoted to Wagner," organized with his composer friend Francois Nicholas in 2005, we have Badiou's only work entirely devoted to a question of music, *Five Lessons on Wagner* (Badiou 2010: xi–xii). Yet even his reading of Wagner shines through with hesitancy when it comes to writing about music. All descriptions of musical passages are evocative but impressionistic. Badiou is at his philosophical best when writing about the complexity of plots and characters of the operas, when it comes to an analysis of music, he is hesitant and reluctant, perhaps rightly so.

In *The Immanence of Truths*, Badiou includes an analysis of Olivier Messiaen's *Blackbird*, on whose behalf he'd earlier asked for "a concession to sheer personal taste" (Badiou 2009a: 528). Badiou here attempts to engage more carefully with a musical example, attempting to show, as hinted in the marginal notes to *Logics of Worlds*, both how Messiaen's use of birdsong "celebrate[s] in the music itself, the correspondence between music and world" and how "haunted by the modern possibility of the miracle," it allows for "a discreet shift in the relations between existence and inexistence" (Badiou 2009a: 528). There might again be a feeling of aposiopesis in the analysis presented in *The Immanence of Truths*, insofar as it remains an example brought in only to illustrate a concept of Badiou's philosophy (and leaves us feeling that this may be another half-attempt to align his tastes with his philosophy). Messiaen's example returns, more tantalizingly, in the radio series with *France Musique*, as indicating an "other modernity" in twentieth-century music, one that might be equally modern, even if it may not be the "major" and "official" line opened by the Schönberg-event (Badiou and Esparza 2018c) and yet distinct from any Wagnerian resurrection, which, for Badiou, is still "on the horizon" (Badiou 2010: 129).

In this chapter, I will trace the complex interactions between Badiou's understanding of music as an "avant-garde" art, the influence of his musical taste on his philosophy (and vice versa), and his understanding of novelty, in particular, musical novelty, in terms of prophecy and resurrection, ruptures and continuity, tradition and innovation, nostalgia and futurity, structure and temporality, all concepts that he deploys in his major writings on music. The first (and the last) reference will be to Wagner, who, for Badiou, is a figure of the past to be resurrected in the future. Wagner's figure helps clarify the concepts of novelty and innovation and their fraught relation with history and tradition in music. Wagner's towering figure, for Badiou, will be seen to be of the past but also modern, contemporary and prophetic.

Schönberg, who is an heir to Wagner inasmuch as he breaks out from within the fold of Wagnerian modernism, is the second major reference. Schönberg and his heirs constitute, for Badiou, what can be called the "official" musical modernity. Badiou presents their example to illustrate the formation of a novel subjectivity in a world that has become "saturated," thus exemplifying the torsion of the old and the new. Schönberg's example deploys the subjective affects of anxiety, courage, superego (here:

"terror") and justice, that had earlier been set out in *Theory of the Subject*, to illustrate the subjective becoming of the new in terms of ruptures and continuities, openings and points.

Messiaen, the third, "minor," reference, is the more interesting, in that it points toward an "other" modernity for Badiou, one that is supple enough to be able to make something archaic—something referring to the plenitude of nature and cosmos rather than to a discipline of structural ruptures—a figure of the modern. This example complicates the picture of what musical modernity could be. Badiou here brings in the question of the relation of time and space—dynamics and statics—to structural novelty, and poses the question of what it is that makes something a work of art. Here, he sets out the concepts of singularity, universality and absoluteness to discuss how a new form may shift the limits of what is possible.

I will return to Wagner's example, in its "prophetic" dimension, as a conclusion to this analysis. Badiou attributes to Wagner the invention of "an original experience of time," which could provide a possible direction for the reinvention of "high art" (Badiou 2010: 122). This analysis points to a new idea of contemporaneity which is all the more "modern," in that the dialectic of the eternal and the contemporary—of the universal Idea and its singular local appearance—brings out, in all its complexity, what it may be to be modern for Badiou.

Wagner: Past and Future

Wagner, as we noted, is so central a figure in Badiou's music canon that in the only book he wrote on music he takes upon himself the task of "reopening the case of Wagner" so as to mount a defense of Wagner's contemporary relevance in the face of a series of condemnations from Nietzsche to Adorno and Lacoue-Labarthe.[9] Badiou here presents Wagner's figure as "prophetic" for the future of art, in particular, "high art." Indeed, for Badiou, Wagner is a key figure for novelty, for the passage from the old to the new, for the struggle between tradition and innovation, and in particular, he is the figure of resurrection of "high art," one of the central concerns for Badiou.

When it comes to the question of innovation, Wagner's *Meistersinger of Nuremberg* is representative for Badiou, as the very problem of novelty is the central question of the opera. In Badiou's reading, the two male protagonists Hans Sachs and Walther represent the "dialectic of genius and mastery in the realm of art," which at the same time is the dialectic of innovation and tradition (Badiou 2010: 109).

Walther who wishes to become a Mastersinger by composing something "new" says of himself, "new is my heart, new my mind/new to me is everything that I begin." Yet, his novelty is not the one that the guild of Mastersingers was expecting. Their rules are simple: he must, through a composition where he has invented both the poem and the melody, "set a new path" [fügt eine neue Weise]. Technically, then, his "new" melody fits their criteria. But there is one additional criterion that regulates this novelty. In all innovation, he must follow their "rulebook" [Tafel der 'Leges Tabulaturae']. Thus, when he first performs it, he is laughed off stage, as his song is, for the majority, "nonsensical" and "ear-torturing" [Eitel Ohrgeschinder] (Wagner 1868). Clearly, it is difficult to tolerate, at first encounter, what Badiou calls "the sheer anarchy of formal rupture" (Badiou 2010: 108).

He has only one supporter, the cobbler-poet Sachs, who is struck by Walther's song as if by an event: "I feel it and cannot understand it; / I cannot hold on to it, /nor yet forget it; / and if I grasp it wholly, I cannot measure it!" (Wagner 1868). By the invention of this melody, the "rulebook" has become obsolete. In Badiou's terms, Walther's new composition has "displaced, in one point, in a single perception, in a moment, the frontier between the impossible and the possible by the laws of the world," and is thus "prophetic," as by so doing, it has "declared as a formal promise, that finally a new world is possible" (Badiou 2019). Yet, despite being "immeasurable" by the former set of rules, the novelty of the melody is not so absolute that no one could grasp it. Sachs initially exclaimed, "it sounded so old, and yet was so new" (Wagner 1868). Indeed, at the end of the opera, the song gets quasi-universal acceptance, first by the public, and eventually, also by the Mastersingers, who fulfill Sachs's condition to "forget their own tracks and seek the new rules [der eignen Spur vergessen, sucht davon erst die Regeln auf!]." A song that first got "derision and disgrace [Spott und Schmach]" now gets universal applause not for finally fitting in the rules, nor for breaking the rules, but for being "so gracious and familiar, however far off it soars [So hold und traut so fern es schwebt]" (Wagner 1868).

As Badiou points out, the work of art is not only "formal subtraction" but also "historicity." At the end of the opera, when Walther is crowned Mastersinger, he first refuses the title, perhaps considering his work, in Badiou's terms, "a break with the past, radically new creation, irreducible originality" (Badiou 2010: 108). It is Sachs who convinces him to finally accept the title and, in this sense, "proposes a synthesis between innovation and tradition," convincing Walther to "incorporate" his art's "historicity into the new." Walther, as the innovator of new forms, must thus have the "courage" to "[acknowledge] that innovation is innovation on the basis of something that *isn't* new." But in Badiou's view it is Sachs rather than Walther who is "the real master," for he is the one "who is able to sacrifice himself in a timely manner so that the new can be incorporated into the old, so that artistic innovation can be synthesized with tradition" (Badiou 2010: 107–9).

This dialectic of innovation and tradition is reiterated in Badiou's reading of *Parsifal*, which is much more ambiguous on this question. Badiou sees *Parsifal*'s central problem as that of the possibility of a "modern form of ceremony" that could be a "true *creation*" rather than a "restoration" of the old (Badiou 2010: 156). However, the opera only manages to show that eventually "there is no clear distinction between restoration and innovation, or between nostalgia and the creation of something new." This "indeterminacy" or "undecidability" comes from the fact that *Parsifal*'s central theme is that of the fulfilment of a prophecy, where they must await the "pure fool [der reine Tor]," Parsifal, to redeem Amfortas from his cycle of guilt and torture and to install a "new ceremony." However, by virtue of being prophesied, Parsifal's coming is "of the order of necessity or law" rather than of "rupture or discontinuity." In this sense, Wagner fails to answer the question of novelty that he posed in *Parsifal*, and thus "the decision between nostalgia and the creation of something new had to remain suspended" (Badiou 2010: 155–7).

Yet there is a prophetic dimension to *Parsifal* itself, as a work of art, in that it "invites us" to "intrude into future celebrations." While the character Parsifal's prophesied arrival as the redeemer of the redeemer could be seen as a return to order and law, according to Badiou, it is instead a sort of "infinite reopening" toward the future. Similarly, even when "nostalgia" seems to weigh down the innovativeness of the work, there is an element of futurity that is always present, that stops the novelty from being reduced to "mere restoration" (Badiou 2010: 141, 159).

Badiou's use of "prophecy" is worth dwelling on here. Rather than create a fixed idea of the future as fated—reducing the future to a mere reiteration and extrapolation of the present—a prophecy opens the future to polyvalence and uncertainty. Brünhilde, at the end of the *Götterdämmerung*, is a "prophetess" of precisely such uncertainty. At the point where the end of the old world of the gods is assured but the new world of humanity has not yet taken shape, she "indicates an uncertain future," which comes in the form of an "interrogation": "what will humanity make of itself?" (Badiou and Esparza 2018f).

In a recent lecture on contemporary art, Badiou puts forth that works of art have a localized "prophetic function" in that they can locally represent "a future that will be a grace given to this place of the world and to the world itself." This grace consists in that the work "opens a way and gives new means to wait without despairing," so that "it is at this place of grace that we would wish to install ourselves to wait for a future that is adequate to this place [. . .] we can await a new world without losing hope" as we can "await the coming of the becoming possible of the impossible." It is also in this prophetic function that art comes close to politics. It affirms, by making it possible to wait with hope, that "the future of humanity is not yet fully formed—that in this limited and sometimes provocative form there is a promise of a tolerable future" (Badiou 2019).

Future I: The Vanished Schönberg-Event

In Badiou's historical periodization, serialism is a specific "deployment" of experiments in atonality inherited from the world of late nineteenth-century Wagnerian and post-Wagnerian music, which came to its *floruit* in the early twentieth century with the prescription of dodecaphonic music by Schönberg and his successors and came to a (sort of) conclusion in the mid to late twentieth century with the dispersal of its experiments into the various forms of "contemporary" classical music. Badiou sees this sequence as animated by an event, the "Schönberg-event" that "breaks the history of music in two," so that there is music *before* an imperative of dodecaphony was introduced and music *after* (Badiou 2009a: 80).

A "work of truth," Badiou claims, "only exists in the movement [. . . of its] construction" (Badiou 2022: 457). Thus it is no wonder that in *Logics of Worlds*, the choice of example for explaining the production of truths from a vanishing event is a "musical variant," the epitome of movement, which for Badiou can provide a "distilled [. . .] version" of his theory of the subject (Badiou 2009a: 79). This example, to wit, the "becoming of serial music," does not take the form of an analysis of a particular musical work, but an episode of recent music history. Badiou specifies that the episode is complete—has reached "its finition" in that one cannot draw any more consequences—"'interesting' deployments, significant mutations, local completions"—from the initial event (Badiou 2009a: 81).

This example presents a veritable *distillate* of Badiou's understanding of how something new may arise in a situation. The world of late nineteenth-century Western classical music has reached a point of "structural totalisation," where the "classical style" from which it developed has undergone "extensive distortion" and "emotional saturation."[10] At a point of such complete totalization, any search for novelty from within the paradigm—the old "classical" sequence—is condemned to "anxiety" and a "hopeless search for effect," as any points that offer the possibility of a decisive break cause an anxious "retreat" into "continuity." In such a world, then, what was required—and supplied by the "Schönberg-event"—was a "systematic exploration" of a "counter-effect" (Badiou 2009a: 85–6). It is by thus "affirming the possibility of a sonic world no longer ruled by the tonal system" that this event "breaks the history of music in two" (Badiou 2009a: 80).

Schönberg himself, notably, is both of the old world and the new. He shares the overwrought tonal world—breaking at its seams—inherited from Wagner, Mahler, Strauss, Bruckner, Korngold, to name those Badiou mentions (Badiou 2009a: 79–80). Indeed Schönberg himself sees his development of the twelve-tone system as "also the emancipation of Wagner's, Strauss's, Mussorgsky's, Debussy's, Mahler's, Puccini's, and Reger's more remote dissonances" (Schoenberg 1984: 217).[11] This "emancipation," he clarifies, "refers to its comprehensibility" in that, while these dissonances do not have a "lesser degree of beauty," they are not yet understood in the paradigm of the preceding schema of consonances and tonal centers. He thus saw it as his task—and that of his "pupils" Webern and Berg—to explore the new forms that would emerge from this "emancipation of dissonances," which would lead to the development of a "new procedure in musical construction," where having broken from the tonal hierarchies of the diatonic paradigm, the twelve tones (the same ones as in the preceding schema) are now "related only with one another" (Schoenberg 1984: 216–18).

Badiou picks up on this and argues that while the Schönberg-event might have "disappeared" in twenty years, its "trace" remained in the form of an "abstract formula" that took a prescriptive form for all music to come after it. Thus, the event, through the imperative of its trace, could animate the musical works that embodied the subject of the event. The subject, notably, is not the artist, nor the work, but rather "the history of a new form as it is incorporated in works," and thus manages to have an "active orientation" or a "dynamics" that can effect an "eventual rearrangement" of the preceding world by drawing the consequences of the vanished event (Badiou 2009a: 79). Thus, the history of the twelve-tone form as explored by Schönberg's first followers, Berg and Webern, and culminating in the works of Boulez, Nono and Stockhausen constitutes the subject of change that allows for a new paradigm to emerge in the world.[12]

The subject, as Badiou notes, is "a sequence involving continuities and discontinuities, openings and points," where there is a constant struggle with the inertia of the old world—a desire to be in continuation of tradition—and a reckoning with decisive points of change, where confronted with "closures imposed by the old world," there have to be new "obligatory opening[s] of the possible" (Badiou 2009a: 82). In Badiou's account, Berg is an example of the former anxious tendency in that his desire to find continuity with the old by creating operatic works that could become repertory classics relegates him to a "reactive" tendency.[13] Webern, who for Badiou is all "courage" is on the other hand the one "who opens up the future" and "in the name of whom [. . .] the new sonic world will be generalised and consolidated" (Badiou 2009a: 84). Thus Badiou, as in *Theory of the Subject*, can form a neat picture of left and right deviations from Schönberg in his two pupils, Berg's to the right, which would "deny the possibility of the new inherent in the old" and Webern's to the left, "denying, so to speak, the old inherent in the new" (Badiou 2009b: 12).

Webern's music, which Badiou elsewhere calls "the century's most admirable distillate," is one that ends up "without descendants" (Badiou 2007: 213). It is finally Berg, with his compromises with the old, while still holding on to the truth of the new, who gets inducted in the canon. Badiou posits that only when confronted with "zones of indiscernibility," where "event and world are superimposed in a confused becoming" that we see the consequences truly emerge as a subject-body. The subject is thus a "compromise" between the "statics" of the subject-body still pulled by the inertia of the old and the "dynamics" of the trace-declaration, the "manifesto," which orients the subject toward the horizon of the new (Badiou 2009a: 79).

Badiou further classifies the various composers by what he calls their "subjective affects," which he insists are all essential in the subject formation. Webern, courage, exults in the "plurality of points"; Berg, Stravinsky and Dutilleux, characterized by anxiety, show a desire for continuity and a fear of decisive points of novelty; and Boulez, initially terror and later justice, first showed a "desire for a Great Point [. . .] a decisive discontinuity," but later came to accept that what novelty requires is a "delicate crossing" between "points and openings." Thus Boulez, along with Nono and Stockhausen (who are barely mentioned), rescues the Schönberg event from obscurity by making sure that it becomes neither an "established result" of reactive academism nor so "esoteric and abstract" that it merely "opens up the future" without calling for "descendants" (Badiou 2009a: 84).[14]

Future II: Messiaen's Modernism in Minor

It is not insignificant that for Badiou "only the serial sequence opened by the Schönberg-event pronounces the truth of the post-Wagnerian musical world" (Badiou 2009a: 85). In a very brief mention of the other possible heirs of Wagner—Stravinsky, Bartok, Messiaen, Debussy, Varèse—Badiou relegates the lot of them to the other side of the "split" in the "subjectivizable body" of musical works, on the side of the "statics" of the world, no matter the brilliant innovations that they can be credited with. Indeed, musical innovation itself is divided into two by this split. On the "dynamic" side of serialism, there is a focus on "pitch" and "structure." Here it is form and its transformation that is key to musical innovation. On the other "static" side, the search is for innovation in terms of "duration" and "timbre," where the concern is rather with "auditory sensation" (Badiou 2009a: 79–82).

In fact, when it comes to the question of musical modernity, Badiou calls the modernity of the Schönberg–Berg–Webern trio the "official modernity," leaving open the question of the unofficial modernities that may make the question of novelty in twentieth-century music much more complex. In passing, Debussy is credited with novelty in the domain of orchestration in that he gives a "contemporary autonomy" to timbre, making it more than merely "decorative".[15] Scriabin is credited with attempting a new "art of time" in music where he tries to "spatialize" something that has traditionally been temporal and thus finds a "natural vitalism," which is also modern but distinct from the "intellectual structuralism" of Schönberg and his followers (Badiou and Esparza 2018g).

Badiou thus opposes two "great tendencies" in twentieth-century music, algebraic structuralism and cosmological vitalism, where the former is the confident "official" modernity, the "dominant motif" that attempts to give form to something that was hitherto formless, while the latter remains a "tentative" secondary sequence [tâtonnement], a motif "in minor," which attempts to take tonality to its limits, but without making a clear formal break with the preceding schema (Badiou and Esparza 2018g). The two tendencies, Badiou argues, lean toward two solutions to the problem of the "conjunction of space and time," which he asserts is the key problem of twentieth-century music: serialism on the side of time and structure, which though evident in the musical score, may be difficult for the audience to immediately grasp thus making the "consistence" of its sonic universe a problem, and vitalism on the side of space, which creates a rich sonic world for the audience but often turns out to be "athematic" and "disoriented" (Badiou and Esparza 2018g).[16]

The "cosmological tendency," centered around the ideas of "cosmos, nature, and ecstasy," offers an alternative "natural" solution to the problem of space/time rapport by appealing to nature directly to grant it consistency. Messiaen is invoked here as someone who has the "cosmos itself" as his "musical model." The "unity" of his world comes from the unity of nature, which is united under a "spiritual guarantee," and the music that is part of this world is all a "prayer" to the absolute, who guarantees its consistency. This solution may be an "archaism," but it is an "archaism as an instrument of modernity." Messiaen's spiritually charged cosmos, while archaic in that it appeals to the beauty of a world past, has found "a new form, musically invented" that makes the old lost rapport world/God find "new expression" in the present. It does not merely refer nostalgically to a past world but innovates in the new and installs itself in the present, in a world that is Messiaen's "own" (Badiou and Esparza 2018g).

This invention of a "new form" is key to understanding Messiaen's modernity. In *The Immanence of Truths*, Messiaen's *Blackbird* is Badiou's chosen example to illustrate the "power of form" that makes it possible to discern what makes something a "work" of art, which is distinguished not only by its "singularity" and "universality" but also its "absoluteness." It is this last that separates a work of art from other objects of the world that may be beautiful and universally pleasing but are not works *per se* and *a fortiori*, not works of art.

A brief comment on the three terms would help grasp Badiou's point. The singularity of the work is what ties it to a particular world and even a particular moment: "it is constructed with finite materials from a determinate world and is ascribed to a determinate subject" (Badiou 2022: 448). It is singular also in its "immediate effect" in that it can cause "an intense 'artistic' emotion" to arise in those that perceive it (Badiou 2022: 473–4). A work is universal in that it can potentially appeal to *all*: it is not determined by the laws of the world in which it finds itself and can thus partake in "eternity" insofar as it can "come back to life in a world other than the one in which it was created" (Badiou 2022: 448). Finally, the absoluteness of a work has to do with the "concept of form": it is that which, beyond the mere "materiality" of sensory perception, through the conception of its "form," makes an object a work of "profound intellectuality," that is, a "work of art" (Badiou 2022: 474).

What "absolutizes" a work of art is that it becomes "endowed with a new concept of form," something that shifts the boundary between the impossible and possible, between "form and formlessness" as established by the "previous canons" (Badiou 2022: 474–5). Messiaen's example is illustrative of this. Badiou sees his work as not merely exalting nature made sacred but as being in "secret rivalry" with it. His *Blackbird* is neither a mere imitation of the bird's song, nor a "submissive prayer" to the vast glory of God reflected in nature, rather it goes "beyond" these "by means of highly sophisticated and unexpected formal innovations" that attest to a very *human* labor and indicate the "musician's pride" in their technical brilliance. The flute, which is somehow expected to imitate the blackbird, does not *imitate* it but rather *represents* it through human "virtuosity." All that remains of the blackbird's actual song is a "familiar schematism." The being of the musician's bird is rather in the "score" and its existence in the world is brought forth "each time in the performance," where every repeated performance illustrates the "possible becoming of the impossible" (Badiou 2022: 481–2).

Messiaen's *Blackbird*, by illustrating the "absolute idea of what it means to imitate the blackbird" shows, perhaps inadvertently, how human art is "superior." After all, the blackbird can have no concept of imitating and representing other sounds, it can only continue to be what nature decrees, while the musician, through the "desire to imitate it, and, in failing to imitate it" can "produce the music-Idea of the blackbird," something that grants the work thus produced singularity, universality, and absoluteness despite its finitude and makes it capable of presenting "what humanity always and everywhere, is capable of" (Badiou 2022: 487).

At this point, it may serve us to return to Wagner's example as prophetic, particularly as heralding the appearance of the new as an experience of time.

Future III: Wagner's Contemporary Modernity

Badiou credits Wagner with the invention of "three distinct types of time that were signature conceptions of his," through which he creates and presents "an original experience of time" (Badiou 2010: 122). The first of these, which Badiou names "the time of disparate worlds" is, according to him, exemplified in the orchestral interlude between the first and second scenes of the first act of *Parsifal*, where Gurnemanz leads Parsifal from the woods into the castle. The dialog between the two first signals this metamorphosis:

PARSIFAL:
I barely walk,
yet it seems I am already so far.
GURNEMANZ:
You see, my son,
time here becomes space. (Wagner 1882)

The following orchestral interlude, named tellingly *Verwandlungsmusik* (Metamorphosis Music) signals a scenic change, with intercalating themes that end in a decisive and clear "pealing of bells." This short interlude for Badiou presents "a host of transitions from one world to another," which allows for the creation of a "very powerful feeling of an experience of time," where, in Gurnemanz's words, it is time itself that transformed—into space, signaling a complete disappearance—from immediate sight at least—of the old space. There is something dream-like in this "time of wandering," which call to mind cinematic sequences to come (Badiou 2010: 123–124). This experience can be contrasted with the second type of time that Badiou discerns in Wagner's work, the "time of the period of uncertainty," which is a time of waiting in which the new hasn't yet come about, where "the creation of something possible is still in abeyance, when it is on the agenda but has not yet been put into effect." A third type of time, which Badiou names "the time of tragic paradox" confronts the immediate surface of the present with its vast past by opening a "gap" behind the facts of the present "so as to disclose behind it a much more extensive temporality in conflict with it" (Badiou 2010: 125–6).[17]

These three experiences of time—of sudden transition, of uncertainty and confusion, and of abyssal fate—inspire Badiou to see Wagner's music as something prophetic. Of the two acknowledged twentieth-century successors of Wagner—the structuralist-algebraic and the natural-cosmological—it is the latter perhaps that shows evidence of the three Wagnerian temporalities:

i. Time has become space, there was no lifting of curtains, they hardly seemed to have walked, but they somehow found themselves elsewhere, the scene has changed.
ii. The future is still in abeyance and the past hasn't been reckoned with. No clearcut has been made and there is an "effect of dispersion." As Badiou puts it, "something has occurred that is no longer practical but [. . .] what is to come is still in the offing."
iii. The power of the past is overwhelming and extensive. All present is still determined by an "underlying layer" of classical tonality as by a guiding hand of fate (Badiou 2010: 122–6).

It is no wonder then that Badiou's own idea of the place of music as an art falls into a Wagnerian paradox. The "prophesized" future, if Wagnerian, is not and cannot be a break from the past. In fact, the old has immeasurable power over anything new that can arrive. If the high-art to come is to be defined through a set of Wagnerian "rules"—as Badiou proposes—then a lot of what might be innovative in music might not find a place in the canon—and perhaps it might not really care to.[18]

What then can we make of Badiou's statement that "music was an avant-garde art and still is"? (Badiou 2013: 208). In fact, we may even ask, what the "time" of the modern could be. The modern is on the one hand a transition, precipitous, from what was not yet modern, and is thus punctual and interruptive. Yet, what was not yet modern continues to exist in the same present as the modern and have another trajectory into the future, thus being both an alternative modernity and a reactive insistence of what remains stuck behind the times. Moreover, the present can be split open to reveal an abyss of the past. Two layers of time are revealed in this opening: time present, which is quick, melodic, clear and time past, which is slow, vast, immeasurable, like an "unsuspected inner ocean suddenly revealed to us in a gap" (Badiou 2010: 127). For Badiou, then, the modern is both interruptive and continuous, evanescent and eternal, a continuous becoming of the past and a disappearing shard of the present, weighed down by the impossible demands of the past and rich with radically new possibilities in the future. Music as an eternally and ever newly "avant-garde art" exemplifies this dialectic.

Eventually, what is it to be modern for Badiou? It is to find oneself holding on to a point between the creation and resurrection of a truth, which as an Idea *in the present* forms a constellation with an Idea *of the past*.[19] Thus, the resurrection of Wagner would require a dual temporality, or rather a double sense of contemporaneity. On the one hand, there must be the fragile, local appearance of an event that makes Wagner something of the present, something evanescently contemporary, but as a Wagner-Idea, the truth is already eternally available across worlds, so eternally contemporary. The present that "welcomes, point by point, the new truth," is thus poised upon truths that are "created for eternity" and available in the form of an "invariance existing across worlds" (Badiou 2009a: 53, 70, 9). No matter which particular world—particular spatial or temporal circumstances—a truth is born in, it is henceforth eternally available, that is, available across worlds, to find new sequences in new worlds, where it can be created anew around an evental trace.

However, potentially infinite worlds do not entail actually infinite worlds. Which truths become active in a particular world depend entirely on *local* circumstances, in this all truths are profoundly *singular*. An event may appear and disappear, but for a subject of a new truth to be born in that particular world, in those particular circumstances, a transtemporal Idea must provide *local* shelter. Only thus "shielded [...] by the Idea" can individuals become subjects that participate in the eternity of truths (Badiou 2009a: 514).

Thus, contemporary art, which Badiou defines as "a sort of creative exception at the very heart [...] of modernity," only allows for a *local* subtraction from the laws of the world, where it posits a new "formalization" in defiance of these laws. It is in this manner that it *locally* shifts the "frontier between the impossible and the possible." This local struggle, however, is linked to eternity through the "prophetic" function of art, which allows us to wait, with the hope that "the future of humanity is not yet fully formed." Music exemplifies this activity and this "grace" par excellence, but whether Wagner, or any others of Badiou's canon can hold this prophetic role for some music of the future remains to be seen (Badiou 2019).

Notes

1 Badiou doesn't always clearly distinguish the terms "atonal," "dodecaphonic" and "serial" in his writing, using one in the place of the other without emphasizing any historical or musical differences between the uses and applications of these terms, though elsewhere he shows himself clearly aware of the differences cf. (Badiou and Esparza 2018c).
2 Alex Ross, in his excellent account of the times and the music, gives the epithet "aphoristic" to Webern himself. Cf. *The Rest is Noise*, "from the operatic Berg to the aphoristic Anton Webern" (Ross 2007: 38).
3 c.f. Milton Babbitt's (in)famous article "Who Cares If You Listen?" (High Fidelity), a case in point (Babbitt 1958).
4 At another point, Badiou claims, somewhat patronizingly, that popular music used for entertainment ("divertissement") should not be "despised," because one of its functions, as dance music, is to help in the art of seduction (Badiou and Esparza 2018a).
5 Others, however, have attempted to extend Badiou's canon by applying his method. One excellent example is Michael Pisaro's "Eleven Theses on the State of New Music," where he posits the possibility of John Cage's music as an event (or event site) and posits that there "were two (or perhaps three) musical truth procedures in 20th century (Western) music: first, Schoenberg and his circle though Boulez, Nono, Xenakis, Lachenmann and so on; breaking off into Cage, his circle, and those who continue to pursue the experimental direction (time will tell if *this* will have been a real event); and secondly, the music which grows out of the deterritorialization of the Western harmonic system by African-Americans: Jazz (from Armstrong to Miles Davis, Ornette Coleman and Coltrane), Blues (Charley Patton, Robert Johnson, Muddy Waters), Rock'n'Roll (from Presley, to Sam Cooke and Aretha Franklin to the Sex Pistols and the Clash), and so on—wherever this music attacks the *status quo* (a kind of music that, in the capitalist world of 'popular' music, is increasingly hard to find)" (Pisaro 2006).
6 While "ontology demonstrates that the event is not," for Badiou, it is necessitated by the fact that "there is some newness in being" (Badiou 2005a: 190, 209).
7 cf. (Badiou and Esparza 2018d) where he clarifies his position a bit further regarding this problem of baroque reaction. He considers baroque revivalists to be somewhat "primitivist" and obsessed by a "cult of origin." Badiou bemoans the "dogmatic of ancient instruments," that is, the search for an "authentic" sound, so as to hear the music as it would have been played in the time in which it was first written. He points out that the musical score, the "work," lives while the author may die, and can

thus undergo "metamorphoses" and be "resuscitated" in other times, can "traverse the centuries" and be interpreted in ways "not foreseen by the author." While one can agree with Badiou's sentiment, to dismiss the whole of early music movement as a "cult of origin" is a bit of a straw man argument here.

8   In the first episode of his radio series with France Musique, Badiou admits that despite the importance of music in his thought, and notwithstanding his experience as an amateur flautist, he hasn't had a "serious and intellectual engagement" with music, especially when it comes to musical commentary, which would require some technical expertise (Badiou and Esparza 2018a).

9   He names the "case of Wagner" a series of defences and condemnations from "Baudelaire to Lacoue-Labarthe, François Regnault, Slavoj Žižek and myself, by way of Mallarmé, Nietzsche, Thomas Mann, Adorno and Heidegger" (Badiou 2010: 71).

10 Badiou posits that "the Classical Style" as set forth by Charles Rosen in *The Classical Style* presents an example of the "Haydn-event," with Mozart and Beethoven as immediate successors, who are mirrored by Berg and Schönberg as successors of the "Schönberg-event" cf. (Rosen 1972) (Badiou 2005b: 13). It is not very clear how far we can draw the analogy as, although he mentions the "Haydn-event" in several places, Badiou doesn't elaborate any further on this. Something to note is that he sees the post-Wagnerians as inheritors of the *classical style*, which has become distorted, so presumably there is no Wagner-event, despite an episode titled "L'évènement Wagner" (Badiou and Esparza 2018b) in his series with *France Musique* (Badiou 2009a: 84–5).

11 In fact, he insists that "composition with twelve tones [. . .] is not the end of an old period, but the beginning of a new one" (Schoenberg 1984: 120).

12 Or alternatively, it is still somewhat active in the works of composers like Brian Ferneyhough, whom Badiou mentions in passing, but is presumably "unpromising" (Badiou 2013: 147) (Badiou 2009a: 89).

13 Yet, Badiou later declares that of the three, it is Berg that is his favorite. To be fair, it looks like he has changed his mind about Berg at this stage. He classifies Schönberg as "the nostalgic founder," too attached to the old world, Webern as "the radical experimenter," too pure and strict in his fidelity, and Berg as "the one who seeks to seduce from the interior of the novelty itself [Le fondateur nostalgique, l'expérimentateur radicale, et celui qui cherche à séduire de l'intérieur de la nouveauté elle-même]." Berg is praised for being able to "do everything," for his facility with diverse forms, old and new, so that his "mission" is to "deal with novelty in the new world on a grand scale." Thus, of Berg, Badiou says, "he is the one who wants to seduce: he seduced me; I can certify his effectiveness" (Badiou and Esparza 2018c).

14 Sarah Hickmott comments that being centered around such "filial" relations, Badiou's narrative is entirely teleological, and not only reaffirms "an entirely conventional narrative of European music history" but can also neither understand "non-filial relations such as the ways in which Webern influenced Schoenberg" nor "offer us any way of understanding works within a composer's oeuvre that break the teleological narrative (such as Schoenberg's late return to elements of tonality and even neo-classicism)." As she rightly comments, such a "conventional narrative" necessarily "ignores the contribution of women composers" even those whose works may be "incorporable into the serial body" and "refuses the possibility that influences from other domains (especially when it comes to technology and what Badiou would term 'entertainment' music)" (Hickmott 2020: 140–1).

15 In fact, Badiou calls Debussy the "French Schönberg," whose legacy, however, was innovation in "musical timbre and tone, not formal construction," and thus he did not "experiment [. . .] in the direction of the construction of a new." The bigger issue is that even if there was a Debussy-event, the consequences, according to Badiou, were not properly drawn. On the one hand, Debussy's innovations could be seen as merely an effort to render "flexible [. . .] existing languages," on the other hand, he "did not immediately have deserving successors" who could draw new consequences from his "radical lesson." Badiou names Milhaud, Poulenc and Jollivet as worth considering, but as ultimately "a bit reactive, a bit conservative," whose contribution was to show that "conservation itself can continue to be inventive, by distortions, by adjustments [aménagements]" (Badiou and Esparza 2018c). In other words, they are to Debussy, what Mahler and Strauss were to Wagner.

16 This maps on well with the argument presented by Simon-Shaw Miller who speaks of two "streams" of modernism in music: "formal modernism" and "contextual modernism," where "one sees it as a paradigm of abstract formal techniques, the other regards it as a powerful multi-sensory or multidimensional model." Like Badiou, he contends that "formal modernism becomes the dominant model for the first half of the twentieth century. Contextual modernism begins to re-emerge in the second half of the twentieth century and eventually becomes equated with postmodernism" (Shaw-Miller 2016: 604–5). In fact, Badiou recently notes that the "contemporary sequence" of modernist music, comprises not only "serialism" but also "spectral music" which considers "timbre" rather than "structure" as its domain of innovation, and a lot of what goes under the name of "experimental music," which might be more diverse than what could be shown as a simple consequence of the Schönberg-event (Badiou 2019).

17 To illustrate the "time of uncertainty" Badiou takes another orchestral piece—this time a Prelude—from the beginning of the last act of *Tannhäuser*, where Elisabeth is waiting for Tannhäuser to return from Rome, praying that he may have received absolution, but without any guarantee. Badiou characterizes this as presenting "an experience of time constructed by a unique sort of thematic interweaving," which gives an "effect of dispersion" rather than "organic affirmation." The uncertainty and the waiting, he notes, is different from that in *Tristan*, which he has earlier characterized as a somewhat Beckettian "waiting in vain," as it is rather an "uncertainty about what has happened" and where its consequences might lead. Badiou's example for "the time of tragic paradox" is, somewhat obviously, the *Götterdämmerung*, where there is an unfathomable hand of fate behind the actions of the characters on stage—sometimes revealed explicitly, but present throughout. Musically, Badiou notes, Wagner presents an "explicit theme" that is set "against deep, subterranean layers of the music, usually orchestrated in the low register" (Badiou 2010: 122–6).

18 Cf. (Badiou 2010: 130–3), where Badiou gives "five rules [. . .] perhaps five directions, or five clues—concerning what greatness [. . .] might be," derived from an analysis of subjective possibility in Wagner's operas, where Wagner, according to Badiou, gives us a "topological" lesson concerning "the relationship of the local to the global."

19 Here Badiou follows Baudelaire's dictum that "La modernité, c'est le transitoire, le fugitif, le contingent, la moitié de l'art, dont l'autre moitié est l'éternel et l'immuable"—"Modernity, it is the transient, the fugitive, the contingent, the half of art, the other half of which is the eternal and the immutable" (Baudelaire 1885: 70; my translation).

Works Cited

Babbitt, M. (1958), "Who Cares If You Listen," *High Fidelity* VIII:2, 38–40.
Badiou, A. (2005a), *Being and Event*, trans. O. Feltham, London: Continuum.
Badiou, A. (2005b), *Handbook of Inaesthetics*, trans. A. Toscano, Stanford: Stanford University Press.
Badiou, A. (2007), *The Century*, trans. A. Toscano, Cambridge: Polity.
Badiou, A. (2009a), *Logics of Worlds: Being and Event 2*, trans. A. Toscano, London: Continuum.
Badiou, A. (2009b), *Theory of the Subject*, trans. B. Bosteels, London: Continuum.
Badiou, A. (2010), *Five Lessons on Wagner*, trans. S. Spitzer, London: Verso.
Badiou, A. (2013), *Cinema*, trans. S. Spitzer, Cambridge: Polity.
Badiou, A. (2019), *Du moderne au contemporain - L'art, ou la possibilité de l'impossible*, video, October 22, 2019. Available online: https://www.youtube.com/watch?v=LC9Zp00l60c (accessed May 03, 2022).
Badiou, A. (2022), *The Immanence of Truths: Being and Event III*, trans. K. Reinhard and S. Spitzer, London: Bloomsbury.
Badiou, A. and L. Esparza (2018a), "Le temps des découvertes," *Alain Badiou, philosophe et mélomane*, ep.1, France Musique, July 08, 2018. Available online: https://www.radiofrance.fr/francemusique/podcasts/alain-badiou-philosophe-et-melomane/alain-badiou-philosophe-et-melomane-1-8-le-temps-des-decouvertes-6617248 (accessed September 01, 2022).
Badiou, A. and L. Esparza (2018b), "L'évènement Wagner," *Alain Badiou, philosophe et mélomane*, ep.2, France Musique, July 15, 2018. Available online: https://www.radiofrance.fr/francemusique/podcasts/alain-badiou-philosophe-et-melomane/alain-badiou-philosophe-et-melomane-2-8-l-evenement-wagner-1173742 (accessed September 01, 2022).
Badiou, A. and L. Esparza (2018c), "Les temps modernes," *Alain Badiou, philosophe et mélomane*, ep.4, France Musique, July 29, 2018. Available online: https://www.radiofrance.fr/francemusique/podcasts/alain-badiou-philosophe-et-melomane/alain-badiou-philosophe-et-melomane-4-8-les-temps-modernes-7637136 (accessed September 01, 2022).
Badiou, A. and L. Esparza (2018d), "Jouer!," *Alain Badiou, philosophe et mélomane*, ep.5, France Musique, August 05, 2018. Available online: https://www.radiofrance.fr/francemusique/podcasts/alain-badiou-philosophe-et-melomane/alain-badiou-philosophe-et-melomane-5-8-jouer-7359560 (accessed September 01, 2022).
Badiou, A. and L. Esparza (2018e), "L'opéra, mais sans Wagner," *Alain Badiou, philosophe et mélomane*, ep.6, France Musique, August 12, 2018. Available online: https://www.radiofrance.fr/francemusique/podcasts/alain-badiou-philosophe-et-melomane/alain-badiou-philosophe-et-melomane-6-8-l-opera-mais-sans-wagner-3605163 (accessed September 01, 2022).
Badiou, A. and L. Esparza (2018f), "Retour à Bayreuth," *Alain Badiou, philosophe et mélomane*, ep.7, France Musique, August 19, 2018. Available online: https://www.radiofrance.fr/francemusique/podcasts/alain-badiou-philosophe-et-melomane/alain-badiou-philosophe-et-melomane-7-8-retour-a-bayreuth-5967651 (accessed September 01, 2022).
Badiou, A. and L. Esparza (2018g), "Le bel aujourd'hui," *Alain Badiou, philosophe et mélomane*, ep.8, France Musique, August 26, 2018. Available online: https://www

.radiofrance.fr/francemusique/podcasts/alain-badiou-philosophe-et-melomane/alain-badiou-philosophe-et-melomane-8-8-le-bel-aujourd-hui-7347388 (accessed September 01, 2022).

Baudelaire, C. (1885), "Le Peintre de la vie modern," in C. Lévy (ed.), *Œuvres complètes de Charles Baudelaire tome III: L'Art Romantique*. Available online: https://fr.wikisource.org/wiki/L'Art_romantique (accessed September 27, 2022).

Hickmott, S. (2020), *Music, Philosophy and Gender in Nancy, Lacoue-Labarthe, Badiou*, Edinburgh: Edinburgh University Press.

Pisaro, M. (2006), "Eleven Theses on the State of New Music," Edition *Wandelweise*. Available online: https://www.wandelweiser.de/_michael-pisaro/11theses-12-06.pdf (accessed September 27, 2022).

Rosen, C. (1972), *The Classical Style: Haydn, Mozart, Beethoven*, London: Norton.

Ross, A. (2007), *The Rest Is Noise: Listening to the Twentieth Century*, New York: Picador.

Schoenberg, A. (1984), *Style and Idea: Selected Writings*, ed. Stein L., trans. Black L., Berkeley: University of California Press.

Shaw-Miller, S. (2016), "Modernist Music," in Peter Brooker, Andrzej Gasiorek, Deborah Longworth, and Andrew Thacker (eds.), *The Oxford Handbook of Modernisms*, 599–617, Oxford: Oxford University Press.

Wagner, R. (1868), "Die Meistersinger von Nürnberg (libretto)," trans. D. Murashev. Available online: http://www.murashev.com/opera/Die_Meistersinger_von_Nürnberg_libretto_English_German (accessed September 27, 2022).

Wagner, R. (1882), "Parsifal (Libretto)." Available online: http://www.operafolio.com/libretto.asp?n=Parsifal&translation=UK (accessed September 27, 2022).

13

The Thinking of Representation

Badiou and Modernist Theater

Eloïse Mignon

In *The Century*, Badiou writes: "Now, it can be argued (and this is an important symptom) that the twentieth century is the century of the theatre as art" (2007a: 40). At first glance this claim seems unexceptional. Modernist drama, which spans, for most theater scholars, the plays of Henrik Ibsen from the 1870s to those of Samuel Beckett, Jean Genet and Peter Handke into the 1960s, infinitely expanded the possibilities of the form. Moreover, throughout this period theater became engaged, more than ever before (or arguably since) with ideas: philosophers wrote plays (Jean-Paul Sartre; Albert Camus); practitioners produced critical tracts (Bertolt Brecht; Antonin Artaud) and theater was the object of serious treatises (Walter Benjamin's *Origin of the German Trauerspiel* (1928) and Nietzsche's *The Birth of Tragedy from the Spirit of Music* (1872) among them). However, much of the attention afforded theater by modernist aestheticians was pejorative. Because it requires spectators, and because it assembles diverse media, theater was deemed impure, corrupting of the drive to autonomy of art and individuation of form. Furthermore, theater was denounced for operating in the mode of representation; critiqued as politically problematic and aesthetically naïve. In view of these pressures, contemporary theater scholars have interpreted modernist theater's artistic flourishing as an effect of internalized "antitheatricality." The latter term, popularized by Jonas Barish in 1981, formulates this period's formal experimentation as the telos of a trajectory begun with Plato and traversing Western culture, whereby theater and theatricality are held to be socially and morally degenerate—conditions incompatible with truth, whether artistic or political. From this perspective, modernist theater's becoming-art is legible as a sequence of conscious self-denunciations and self-negations.[1]

Badiou localizes the sequences of modernist theater within one of the twentieth century's most significant intellectual undertakings: the thinking of representation. He writes: "Much of the century's greatness lay in its commitment to thinking the relationship—often obscure at first—between real violence and semblance, between face and mask, between nudity and disguise" (2007a: 48). Modernism's preoccupation with representation at once problematized theater *and* produced thought that proceeded in theatrical terms—a peculiarity that can be grasped with Badiou's dialectical apprehension of how "theater thinks" (2005b: 72). Like Plato (and like many philosophers since Plato) Badiou recognizes theater's place of imminence to power. "Theatre is an affair of the State" Badiou declares numerous times in "Rhapsody for the Theatre"; invariably so: "all theatre has been one of the affairs of the State and remains so to this day!" (2008: 189, 187). Elsewhere, Badiou reiterates and refines this claim: from its (Greek) inception theater has been wielded as a "function of the State": rich Athenian citizens were made to fund the City Dionysia; Shakespeare, Molière and Racine were all men of the court; Napoleon was concerned to issue decrees on La Comédie Française from his occupation of Moscow (2007a: 22, 2013: 82–3). As Badiou describes in *Éloge du théâtre* the bond between theater and the State is "objective, organic": "À la fin des fins, le théâtre est une institution, proche à certains égards de L'éducation nationale" (2013: 83). And yet, despite its uneasy proximity to power, Badiou has consistently maintained theater to be "an artistic truth procedure," subjectively capable of producing exceptional thought (2013: 67). On this seeming irreconcilability turns the value of Badiou's project in engaging with the contradictions and capacities of this artform and the philosophical discourses it has generated. Surpassing what can be formulated with simple negation, for Badiou, modernist theater's becoming-art affirmed this form's capacity to *think* representation—indeed, to *represent representation*: to expose both the incompleteness and very real effects of the ideological figures that operate on everyday life.

The Discourse

As Badiou describes in *Handbook of Inaesthetics*, "the veritable slogan of modern art commands that you subtract yourself from the despicable and decadent grip of the theatrical" (2005b: 69). Badiou associates the diffusion of this "antitheatrical aesthetics" with Nietzsche, whose rupture with Wagner took place around 1876. Theater scholar Martin Puchner also names Nietzsche among three theorists—the others are Walter Benjamin and Michael Fried—who "explicitly define the values of modernism through an attack on the theatre" (2002a: 2). According to Puchner, Benjamin's treatment of the respective value of actors for theater and film in *The Work of Art in the Age of Mechanical Reproduction* (1935) becomes an "anti-theatrical tract in which the living actor [i.e., the theater actor] becomes the obstacle for a truly modernist art" (2002a: 4). Fried's polemic is the plainest. In *Art and Objecthood* he writes: "Theatre is now the negation of art"; "Theatre and theatricality are at war today, not simply with modernist painting ... but with art as such—and, to the extent that the different arts can be described as modernist, with modernist sensibility as such" (1998: 153, 163). That Fried's primary concern is with plastic arts has raised suspicion that modernist aesthetics sought theater's exclusion from art's entire remit. In effect, Toril Moi credits Fried with initiating theater omission (even Ibsen's!) from the "usual narratives of modernism" which, she writes, "start with Baudelaire, Manet, and Flaubert—that is to say, with poetry, painting, and the novel" (2006: 27). What is interesting, however, is that Fried goes on to note that an anti-theatrical sensibility had been at work *within* theater for several decades already: "This is perhaps nowhere more evident than within theatre itself, where the need to defeat what I have been calling theatre has chiefly made itself felt as the need to establish a drastically different relation to its audience. (The relevant texts are, of course, Brecht and Artaud.)" (1998: 163).

The apparent contradiction in Fried's invective—his pitting of "art" against "theater" while calling up as exemplary the twin pillars of theatrical modernism—tells us something important. Indeed, it expresses a conviction that numerous thinkers of the theater have held, too: that there exists a Theater and a *theater*; a theater of art and a theater of not-art; or, in an antagonism Badiou presents in "Rhapsody for the Theatre": there is "Genuine Theatre," Theater (with a capital T) and "*theatre*" (in lowercase italics between inverted commas); the former associated with the disruptions of the event and the generic production of truths; and the latter with repetition, Catholic pageantry and the naturalization of interested hierarchies. Badiou writes:

> Here is what I would propose: bad theatre, "*theatre*," is a descendant of the Mass, with its established and substantial roles, its natural differences, its repetitions, its falsified event. It is where one gets a taste of, where one gobbles up, the virgin, the aging hysteric, the tragic actor with the loud voice, the virtuoso of lamentations, the shivering beloved, the poetic young man, just as one eats, in the guise of the host, God. . . . Genuine Theatre turns every representation, every actor's gesture, into a generic vacillation so as to put differences to the test without any supporting base. (1998: 220)

Badiou's Theater/"*theater*" opposition formalizes a desire—especially pronounced by practitioners of modernist theater—to see *two* theaters at odds with one another.[2] The collection of texts in which Artaud presents his project for a Theater of Cruelty is called *The Theatre and Its Double* (1938). Here Artaud describes the existing theater, "which consists of having people sit on a certain number of straight-backed or overstuffed chairs placed in a row and tell each other stories" as the anathema, or "*perversion*" of what this artform is truly capable of (in Derrida 2008:10). With a similar method of censure and prescription Brecht formulated his epic theater against the longstanding influence of the principles presented in Aristotle's *Poetics*, and, more locally, as an antidote to Wagner's *Gesamtkunstwerk*. Further back, Rousseau enthused, in his *Lettre à d'Alembert*, about the social benefits of public theater festivals—of the community coming together "under the sun"—while critiquing the moral consequences of Parisian drama's submission to the protocols of classicism.[3] Nietzsche's initial admiration of Wagner—grounded in the hope that his operas might revive the ideal of Greek choric transcendence—turned to disgust when the composer was sponsored by Prince Ludwig II and institutionalized at Bayreuth (Puchner 2002b: 528–9). Nietzsche's about-face on the topic of theater is expressed in the distance between *The Birth of Tragedy* and *The Case of Wagner* (1888), where he writes of his ex-friend "we are antipodes" (1911: 56). As Badiou notes, in line with the invariant desire for one type of theater to eclipse another, Nietzsche's late critique of Wagnerian "histrionics" went alongside a celebration of music deploying "the metaphor of dance" (2005b: 69). In each of these examples a projected "new" theater is presented as an overturning of, or curative for, an existing type of theater—a theater complicit with the status quo, the prevailing morality, the state of aesthetics, the representations of bourgeois ideology and the institutions of State: a theater complicit with power.

Theater's modal and objective proximity to the institution and operation of power has been known since Plato, who first articulated the function of mimesis in indoctrinating citizens into the State's prevailing "image of reality" (Havelock 1982: 251). Across the Socratic dialogs, mimesis is figured as a vector of transference: spectators at theatrical performances are compelled to identify and empathize with the imitations of actors (who, like the Sophists, imitate but pretend not to), facilitating the transmission of mores and thus inducing successive generations into the Athenian *ethos*.[4] As is well known, Plato's projection for a new city oriented by truth—the political hypothesis advanced in the *Republic*—therefore excludes theater for its role in molding subjects fit to an untrue, unjust State.[5] As Jacques Rancière has shown, Plato's polemic, consciously or not, underpins many modernist projects for theatrical reform, including those of Brecht and Artaud (2021: 6-8). Indeed, as Derrida explains, Artaud theorized imitation, or representation, to be at the crux of theater's complicity with power: "Artaud wants to have done with the *imitative* concept of art . . . This representation, whose structure is imprinted not only on the art, but on the entire culture of the West (its religions, philosophies, politics), therefore designates more than just a particular type of theatrical construction" (2008: 8). The existing representational theater was for Artaud a site where Western hegemony is reinforced and reproduced; so integrally that, as Derrida goes on to point out, Artaud secretly "desired the impossibility of the theatre, wanted to erase the stage" (2008: 17). Later, Artaud-inspired Gilles Deleuze, in his essay "One Manifesto Less," articulated how theater reinforces power by its very taking place:

> the elements of power in the theatre are those which assure at once the coherence of the subject dealt with and the coherence of the representation on stage. It is at the same time the power of that which is represented and the power of theatre itself. In this sense the traditional actor has an ancient complicity with princes and kings—the theatre, with power: thus Napoleon and Talma. (1993: 207)[6]

All theater unavoidably performs officialdom, as Deleuze goes on to say: "the theatre is an institution, the theatre—even the avant-garde, even the popular—is 'official'" (1993: 218).

Whether it was possible to negate theater's complicity with power by abolishing representation or by severing its institutional bonds was a question driving twentieth-century practitioners. As Puchner shows, two countervailing positions defined the situation of modernist drama. While an "anti-theatrical" faction problematized theater's imitative mode, there also existed a "pro-theatrical avant-garde"—among them futurists, Dadaists and surrealists—who placed a high value on theatricality-as-such while repudiating the institution of theater itself (2002a: 6-8).[7] The latter desire, for pure theatricality without institution, is expressed by F. T. Marinetti's call for "'teatralità senza teatro' (theatricality without theatre)"; coupled with his declaration: "everything of any value is theatrical" (in Puchner 2002a: 7). The inverse desire, for "theatre without theatricality," is exemplified by Peter Handke's *Offending the Audience* (1966), a *Sprechstücke* (speak-piece) in which four people appear on stage and refuse all conventions of performance: "We don't imitate. We don't represent any other persons and any other events, even if they statistically exist" (1997: 25). Handke's speakers go on to accuse the spectators in the auditorium of being the performers; calling attention to the compatibility of theatrical representation with the everyday representations of bourgeois ideology: "You represent something. [. . .] You are a society that represents an order. [. . .] You were born actors. Play-acting was in your blood, you butchers, you buggers, you bullshitters, you bullies, you rabbits, you fuck-offs, you farts" (1997: 16, 30). Crucially, what was at stake in both the anti-theater and anti-theatrical positions was a desire for *scission*. In Puchner's terms, both sought "an irreversible dissociation of the value of theatricality from the realities of the actual theatre" (2002a: 7). In Badiouian terms, what modernists and avant-gardists sought was the division of what was known as "theater" from One into Two.

The Form

This desire to split theater in Two in order that a *true* Theater might subtract itself from the prevailing impurity of "*theater*" is consistent with a description of politics that Badiou puts forward in *L'Immanence des vérités*. Politics takes place when a critical antagonism immanent to the word "politics" reveals itself: when "politics," used to encompass the set of processes that constitute the maintenance and management of State power, is shown to be irreconcilable with "politics," when it names a conviction that the current order must be overturned. When it takes place, Badiou writes, "*politics presents itself as a non-consensual discussion on politics itself*" (2018: 640; original emphasis). Analogously, in Barish's terms, theater-as-art emerges only when theater antagonizes theater: "When the theatre grows self-satisfied, when it ceases to question itself, when it believes too uncritically in its own pomps, it begins to suffer from a kind of fatty degeneration" (1981: 450). Accordingly, the various "anti-theatrical" negations of modernist theater—theatricality without institution (Marinetti); theater without theatricality (Handke); affect without text (Artaud); alienation without identification (Brecht); negation toward minimal difference (Beckett); "pure appearance" flickering on "pure nothingness" (as Sartre describes the theater of Genet)—become legible as various attempts to affirm (true) Theater against its degenerate State-like double, "*theater*" (Sartre 1954: 31). Like true politics, theater must work to sustain itself as subject-of-art against theater-as-function-of-the-State.

Interestingly, Badiou complicates the received understanding of theater's institutional status as a mark of its degeneracy. While the history of Western theater is unquestionably the history of an institution *of* power (*pouvoir*), there is something about theater's proper infinite potency (*puissance*) that escapes what the State can know of it. Indeed, this *known unknown* has conceivably constituted the cause for the State's historical vigilance when it comes to theater. In Badiou's words, the State's "permanent interest" in theater owes to the fact that people gather there "to listen to remarks and discussions which are perhaps uncontrolled" (2013: 82). That theater draws a crowd makes it an efficient tool for disseminating controlled communication but means that it equally poses a threat—theater provides an opportunity, as a 1537 letter from the Duke of Suffolk to Henry VIII's regent Thomas Cromwell warns, for the "idell people" to assemble (in Ingram 1992: 77). Theater's institutional status, then, is an effect of the State's concern to append theater to itself in order to surveil it. That theater remains in many places a publicly funded institution today distinguishes it from more "private" artforms like cinema, which, as Badiou remarks, doesn't truly require a crowd (or even a spectator) to take place, but unwinds—on a phone screen as in a film house—"implacably" (2013: 92). Theater's public bearing is implicated in its essence. Strung between the State and the crowd, theater carries the responsibility of an institution:

> everything that the theatre pronounces is official in an obscure sense. It is something for which we can hold the authorities accountable. Cinema is capitalist and private. Nobody is responsible for it, other than a producer and his employees. Whatever is said in theatre, even in a schoolyard illuminated by two small lamps, is said with *majesty*. (Badiou 2008: 203)

So, if the State—from Athens onwards—recognized theater's power and, by appending it to itself as an institution, sought to instrumentalize and delimit its capacities; modernist theater, which recognized theater's infinite power, sought multiple ways to negate its proximity to the State. That the set known as "theater" expanded as a result of these multiple negations is taken up by Badiou as indicative of a formal singularity that he claims Plato to have known, too, in formulating his philosophy as dialog: theater is "the greatest machine ever invented for absorbing contradictions: no contradiction brought to the theatre frightens it" (2013: 37–38).[8] Yet in this way, too, theater resembles Badiou's conception of the State: an operation of tireless inclusion.

I should emphasize here that Badiou is allergic to the formulation "political theatre." Indeed, his work helps to clarify the relation between—rather than collapse—these two distinct procedures. To Nicolas Truong, Badiou says: "I have said it again and again: politics—but in reality especially the problem of State power, from which politics will one day have to liberate itself—is an essential material of the theatre" (2013: 81). This remark offers a fresh view of the formal oddities that put theater out of joint with modernist aesthetics: its incapacity to disentangle itself from representation; its taint of pedagogy and social concern; its dependency on bodies, spectators and time.[9] Theater is an assemblage of disparate materials. In the instance of performance these materials inhabit "a signifying space"—depending on their arrangement appearance and use they animate, as Una Chaudhuri describes it, "that tension between symbolism and literalism that is the hallmark of theatrical art" (1994: 28). When Handke's speakers say: "we don't represent anything and are no others than we are. We don't even play ourselves. We are speaking. Nothing is invented here. Nothing is imitated. Nothing is fact. Nothing is left to your imagination," that tension is being targeted, even if it remains impossible to wholly eradicate (1997: 25). While other modernist arts liberated themselves from the constraints to which they had traditionally referred—the system of classical tonality in music, the pictorial "copy of nature" in painting (the going-beyond of which, in a recent pamphlet, Badiou names as the "point" of twentieth-century artistic truth)—theater struggled, despite diverse attempts, to entirely abstract itself from referring to an image of "reality" outside the site of performance (2022: 12). Indeed, theater's "essential material"—gods, princes, families and other structural units of power—proved stubbornly hard to eradicate, as an anecdote Badiou relates in "Rhapsody" reveals: Mao's attempt to replace the "squires and damsels" of the Beijing opera with "workers, peasants and soldiers" never took off. "Mao wasn't even dead yet when it failed: squires and damsels were back on the stage . . . Theatre is more solidly statelike than the State itself" (2008: 202).

If State power constitutes theater's "essential material," modernist theater's anti-theatricality may have been partly compelled by the theatricalization of twentieth-century politics. In *The Century*, Badiou cites Benjamin's formulation: "The (fascist) aestheticization of politics must be opposed by the (revolutionary) politicisation of art" (2007a: 41). Elsewhere, Badiou has pointed out that, despite what he identifies as their "formal analogy" and parallel positions at the threshold of the State and the crowd, (true) theater's trajectory is not concurrent to that of (true) politics—quite the contrary (2008: 200). "The height of theatre in France, between Richelieu and Louis XIV, is coextensive with the construction of absolutism, which eliminated practically all free politics. Inversely, the French Revolution gave almost nothing to theatre" (2013: 81). Theater became art in a century forced to reckon with the disorienting excesses of representation. Just as the State "reveals itself" when there is a genuine political event, as Badiou writes in *Metapolitics*, the scope of theater's capacities come into focus when the State seeks to delimit theater's place according to its own protocols of reality and fiction (2005c: 145). Indeed, if the twentieth century produced National Socialism as an example of the State seizing the means of theater for the purposes of absolutizing its own distortions—a regime Philippe Lacoue-Labarthe and Jean-Luc Nancy characterize, beyond Benjamin, as "a fusion of politics and art, *the production of the political as work of art*"—it should be remembered that this regime was also concerned with confining theater itself to "the repetition of the tragedy and the tragic festival" (1990: 303). In response to finitizing instrumentalization of this kind, theater is induced to show its essential difference with the State, which Badiou formulates simply—while the State "*does not think*," "theatre thinks" (2005c: 88, 2005b: 72).

At this point it is important to insist on the exceptionality of Badiou's thought, which can account for structural invariances across the history of theater *and* for what is singular to the subjective sequences of modernism. By displacing ontology onto the materialist thought of modern mathematics; by rethinking philosophical categories with the forms of pure multiplicity presented by the axioms of ZFC, Badiou rationalizes the relation between the two terms whose association with theater have attracted metaphysical suspicion: "representation" and "the State." For Badiou, the State is an operation of finitizing constraints that codify and partition a situation's existents while discursively advancing a claim to its own total and infinite representation. Theater's place in a politico-historical situation is one of immanence to this representational meta-structuring, and, by redoubling the State's mode—representation—theater is apt to reveal the falsity of the State's claim to infinite unity. In other words, all material situations, being situations of being, are thinkable according to the parameters of ontology: excess and the void (Badiou 2005a: 104–11). Theater takes place on the threshold of declaring their ineluctable relation. One of the critical ways in which Badiou distinguishes Theater from *"theater"* is by the former's decision to declare the State that assigns its existence: "'*theatre*' is of the State, though it has nothing to say about this. It perpetuates and organizes the easygoing and grumpy subjectivity that is needed for the State. For its part, Theatre always *says* something about the State, and finally about the state (of the situation)"(2008: 200). *Saying something* about the State/state amounts to representing the set of constraints that limit what is possible for that situation, whether moral, aesthetic, or explicitly political.[10] Among artforms, theater is uniquely compelled to this:

> caught in the habit of the State, is theatre not the only art to establish a certain *visibility* of the State? The only art to show the State? What does the theatre talk about if not the state of the State, the state of society, the state of the revolution, the state of consciousness relative to the State, to society, to the revolution, to politics? (2008: 206)

"Rhapsody for the Theatre" culminates in a declaration: "theatre indeed, represents: it *represents the representation*, not the presentation. The State, not the emergence of its place" (2008: 206). In French, *une représentation* translates as "a performance": an instance of theatrical taking-place. When theater happens, then, it engages a dialectic of system and singularity, of State and art, of being and event. It is axiomatic for Badiou that "A theatrical representation will never abolish chance . . . each and every time, the performance is evental, that is, singular" (2005b: 74, 72). An instance of true theater shows the structuring of structure; disrupts and de-naturalizes received notions and hierarchies to illuminate infinite possibilities. Faced with these, "The spectator must decide whether to expose himself to this void, whether to share in the infinite procedure. He is summoned, not to experience pleasure (which arrives perhaps 'on top of everything,' as Aristotle says) but to *think*" (Badiou 2008: 220).

The Subject

In *The Century*, Badiou names the subject of the twentieth century's symptomatic art: the theater director and the mise-en-scène. He writes:

> It is the twentieth century that invented the notion of the *mise en scène*. It transformed the thinking of representation into an art in its own right. . . . The theatre director is something like a thinker of representation as such, who carries out a very complex investigation into the relationships between text, acting, space and public. (2007a: 40)

Mise-en-scène intervenes in the structural dialectic of *representation* and *une représentation*: it is a procedure that seeks to make and re-make meaning from a peculiar arrangement of theatrical materials, while giving the never-abolished chance a chance.[11] There are infinite possibilities afforded by the set of components whose coming-together defines the theater event: bodies, languages, spectators, lights, costumes, places, props, music. Decision by decision, a director builds a world from these materials. The tension between the desire to construct a coherent meta-structure and the resolve to ultimately *incomplete* this montage is characteristic of modernist mise-en-scène: allowing for revelation of "the gap" between the representation and what it fails to wholly incorporate induces the instance of theater to dismantle "the intimate and necessary links joining the real to semblance" and call into question the "reality" that it represents (Badiou 2007a: 48).

A consciousness of how performance elements are structured beyond the text is traceable across many oeuvres of modernist theater. Rabindranath Tagore created a new dance form for his dance-drama cycle *Rabindra Nritya Natya*; Konstantin Stanislavski and Vsevolod Myerhold advanced new acting techniques; Peter Brook intervened in Shakespeare; Ibsen gave long descriptions of stage setting at the top of each act; Beckett's texts included detailed instructions for staging, objects and gestures. An orientation to mise-en-scène also characterizes the innovations of Brecht and Artaud, the two practitioners who Fried places on the art side of his art/theater antagonism. Like Plato, Brecht saw in the inclination of spectators to empathize with characters the key to theater's role in abetting the unthinking replication of ideology. As a means to interrupt this tendency Brecht proposed an acting style derived from his experience of watching the Chinese actor Mei Lanfang: once European actors learnt to *show that they were showing*, European spectators would stop identifying with characters—the *Verfremdung* (alienation) effect would force them from passivity into conscious critique.[12] No less than Brecht, Artaud sought to eliminate the passivity Plato diagnosed in spectating mimesis. His Theater of Cruelty intended to liberate theater from the constraints of representing texts and unleash endless compositional possibilities that would constitute "The triumph of pure *mise en scène*" (in Derrida 2008: 9). It is worth remarking, after Susan Sontag, that while Artaud used words like "passionate" and "violent" to describe the intended effect of his productions, he placed a high value on controlling their arrangement: "The aggressiveness that Artaud proposes is controlled and intricately orchestrated, for he assumes that sensory violence can be a form of embodied intelligence" (2001: 40–41). Both Brecht and Artaud sought to alter the static European stage-spectator relationship and restore theater to its "cognitive function" (Sontag 2001: 41). That their methods are generally seen as opposing—Artaud sought to *eradicate* the distance typically produced by the stage-spectator relationship, while Brecht sought to *emphasize* it—accounts for their frequent positioning at the respective limits of twentieth-century anti-theatricalism. To this effect, Rancière writes: "Modern attempts to reform theatre have constantly oscillated between these two poles of [Brechtian] distanced investigation and [Artaudian] vital participation, when not combining their principles and their effects" (2021: 7).

Twentieth-century dramatists and practitioners explored the infinite means by which the overall structure of a piece of theater could work to illuminate the operations of structure itself. Accordingly, extra-theatrical discourses took note of theater's capacity to organize and re-organize inquiries into prevailing representational set-ups. Among Lacan's remarks about *Hamlet* in *Seminar VI* (1958), he says: "The manner in which a work of art touches us, and directly affects us in the deepest way . . . lies in the terms of its composition, of its arrangement" (2013: 323). Lacan's interest in *Hamlet* owes not to the so-called psychopathology of the character Hamlet (which had attracted enough attention) but to the aggregate assemblage of discourses that constitute *Hamlet* the play-text. Within "the depths of the play's weave," Lacan claimed, "an entire mechanism" is at work, within which can be placed "the problem of the articulation of desire" (2013: 324). Badiou himself recently used Genet's *The Balcony* (1956) to cut through the "pornographic" discombobulations of contemporary life and declare its emblems of power. Badiou's use of a play-text in order to "produce a real analysis of the images of the present age" substantiates a remark he makes elsewhere: "For denouncing the confusion between the imaginary and the real theatre is the most effective of means, even though it gets blamed for perpetuating it" (2020: 2, 2013: 43). While the foregoing examples show Lacan and Badiou using texts and not performances for their respective psychoanalytic and philosophical inquiries, it is precisely the notion of mise-en-scène as it was invented in the twentieth century that affirmed that a text written for theater can be endlessly returned to; indeed that by its very form—which, after Lacan, Badiou places in the order of the "not-all"—a theater text holds infinite potential to be resurrected, in each world inciting spectators to *rethink* rather than *reproduce* the prevailing image of reality (2008: 212).[13]

From its inception theater has shown a capacity to elucidate the means by which the dominant orientation of thought discerns and classifies truth and semblance. This is the thesis advanced by Jean-Pierre Vernant and Pierre Vidal-Naquet, who observe that Greek tragedy flourished at a time when the evolving laws of the *polis* were challenging the prelegal values upheld by myth. Tragedy was born, they write, "when the myth starts to be considered from the point of view of a citizen. But it is not only the world of myth that loses its consistency and dissolves in this focus. By the same token the world of the city is called into question and its fundamental values are challenged in the ensuing debate" (1988: 33). When theater came into being it exposed and unsettled not only the mechanisms of myth, whose traces in the *polis* constituted its ostensible material, but the mechanisms behind the operation of representation that, determining its protocols to be beyond myth, opened a space for theater to take place.

The Condition

For Badiou, genuine Theater is rare, but it happens. Though what prevails is its double—its "orthodoxy," "theater,"—there are events in which "Theatre detaches itself as a rather implausible lightning bolt" (Badiou 2008: 187). When theater splits itself in Two, philosophy's role is to seize upon this subjective rarity and index its existence. More precisely, philosophy's role is to think, in an infinite register, the absolute singularity of the thought that theater presents in its own terms: the thought that it thinks from its singular place in the politico-historical situation. Modernist theater and the mise-en-scène—theater's becoming-art—is symptomatic of an epoch compelled to think the real effects of representation, both political and artistic. With Badiou we can see that the sequences of modernist theater, though interpretable in line with the anti-theatrical tendencies of modernist aesthetics, were induced to this thought by the problem of theater's conjunction with the discursive figure of State power. In this sense, *anti-theatrical* can only take us so far: modernist theater, as many have acknowledged, *affirmed* the infinite capacities of theater; and it did so by bringing its own corruptions and contradictions into form. Badiou writes: "In the twentieth century, theater is more than just putting on plays. For better or worse, its stakes seem to have changed: it is now a question of collective historical elucidation" (2007a: 41–2). These stakes animate Badiou's own plays, in particular the *Ahmed Tetralogie*, for which he re-populated a classical comedic structure with the figures and discourses of late twentieth-century France. These four plays' protagonist, Ahmed—a generically-named worker from the housing projects—takes on the role once animated by the figure of the slave in Roman comedy or the valet in Molière: him who, through linguistic and gestural play, dismantles the authority of the social structure that wilfully misrecognizes him. Badiou's theatrical praxis (he played Socrates at Avignon!) alongside his numerous turns to Aeschylus, Brecht, Genet and other playwrights in his philosophical writing is evidence of the direct relationship that he has maintained with this condition, and not only with the history of its discourse. This is important: critical interventions that seek to define Theater against "*theater*"— that is, to discern a Theater that *thinks* the statist power to which it is bound—can only prevent collapse into a statist discourse itself *if a regard is maintained for the generic specificity of the theatrical form*. Badiou's philosophy, founded in the ontological decision that "the one is not," "induces the decided specificity" of theater's place, as A. J. Bartlett and Justin Clemens recently put it (2020: 62). It is critical in today's postmodern situation that Badiou's thought sustains theater against aporetic theories of generalized performance; discourses whose compatibility with the prevailing ideology of democratic materialism have blunted our capacity to see this artform as it has been declared by its proper subjective sequences across time: as "a device for the construction of truths" (2007a: 42).

Notes

1 Alan Ackerman and Martin Puchner summarize the influential thesis of Barish's book, *The Anti-Theatrical Prejudice* (1981): "Twenty years ago, Jonas Barish identified a disposition within Western culture that he termed the anti-theatrical prejudice. He cites instances, from the Greeks to the present, of a bias against the expressive, the imitative, the deceptive, the spectacular and the subject that arouses, or even acknowledges, an audience" (2006: 2). In the book's final chapter

Barish argues that modernist playwrights have internalized this bias: dramatists from Ibsen to Peter Handke "build into their very plays a critique of the theatre" (1981: 450).

2. In the more recent terms of *Immanence des vérités*, Badiou's "Theater" corresponds to an *oeuvre*, a finite multiple engaged in a dialectical relation with the infinite; while "theater" corresponds to a *déchet*, a passive multiple that holds itself to the law of the current situation (2018: 511).

3. As Maria Gullstam explains: "To [Rousseau's] mind the people with power—the *philosophes* and the nobility—were spreading their version of the truth about virtue, wisdom and beauty through the theatre, under the false premise that their enlightenment was the one and only truth to be adopted by all" (2020: 3).

4. Lacoue-Labarthe, in *Typography* (1989), discusses Plato's "problematic of mimetism," as a problem of *plasticity* afflicting both performer and spectator (1989: 125). Onstage, the actor—whom Socrates describes as "capable by his cunning of assuming every kind of shape and imitating all things"—authorizes the groundless principal of imitation itself (Plato 1969: 3.398a). This plasticity is then transferred to the spectator, who is conceived of as similarly malleable. Understood in this double sense, mimesis licenses the "plastic" citizen as Pericles envisaged him, moldable to whatever the Empire requires. For Plato, then, in Lacoue-Labarthe's words, mimesis "is not, as is repeated endlessly, principally a problematic of the lie, but instead a problematic of the *subject*" (1989: 125). More precisely, mimesis is a problem for its function in forming citizens primed to replicate the status quo.

5. That theater will be barred from the *Republic* speaks to Plato's desire to completely overturn Athens as it stands. Across the corpus, Athens is presented as a State whose relationship to reality is mediated by opinion and false knowledge; a "theatocracy," as Puchner has it, enabled by both poet and sophist (2010: 28). As Havelock explains, "*doxa*" is used in the dialogs to label the general compatibility of theater with the prevailing Athenian orientation of thought: *doxa* names "not only the poet's image of reality but [the] general image of reality which constituted the content of the Greek mind before Plato" (1982: 251). Indeed, Havelock continues, poets were once considered stores of knowledge, and given responsibility for transmitting "the general vision" to younger Hellenes (1982: 251).

6. In a manner continuous with Badiou's Theater/"*theater*" opposition, Deleuze goes on to celebrate the work of Carmelo Bene, a director who amputates "the stable components of power" from his staging: from *Richard III* Bene excises the court; from *Romeo and Juliet* he cuts the families; from S.A.D.E. Bene removes the master's sexual power (1993: 205–207). For Deleuze, the value of Bene's amputations exist in their capacity to unsettle established dramatic structures—namely the submission of conflict to theatrical *agon*—and thereby "place in question the power of theatre or the theatre as power" (1993: 217).

7. Puchner's account of the avant-garde's stance against theater as institution corresponds to the influential claims of Peter Bürger, who writes that for European avant-garde movements "what is negated is not an earlier form of art (a style) but art as an institution that is unassociated with the praxis of men" (1984: 49).

8. Anti-theatricalism was a productive force: as Ackerman and Puchner put it, a "paradoxical way of affirming the capacious powers of the theatre" (2006: 15).

9. Toril Moi offers an excellent breakdown of theater's uneasy relation to modernist aesthetic values: "First of all, theatre is a public art exposed to social and cultural

pressures in the way that poetry is not. Moreover, whatever the bodies onstage do, they remain bodies in space, and as such they can never come across as entirely autonomous of social, cultural and political reality. Because audience and actors have to share a length of time together, and because the actors have to do *something* during that time, it is also difficult for them to avoid the taint of mimeticism and narrative" (2006: 27).

10   For example, in *Henrik Ibsen and the Birth of Modernism* Toril Moi convincingly shows Ibsen's drama—from *Emperor and Galilean* (1873) onwards—to have been engaged with exposing and unsettling the prevailing principles of aesthetic idealism and their implications on nineteenth-century life. Idealism, in Moi's telling, consisted of a set of constraints that operated on intellectual life and aesthetics, but also on bourgeois morality, family life and the social role of women. When Ibsen interrogated the limits and consequences of aesthetic idealism in theatrical terms, modern drama was born. As Moi puts it: "*Ibsen moves away from idealism by representing it*" (2006: 216). In Badiouian terms, Ibsen's theater *represents representation*.

11   As Anne Ubersfeld explains in *Reading Theatre*: "Theatre constructs a space that is not only structured, but in which structures become signifying—a spatialized universe in which chance becomes intelligible" (1999: 102).

12   Brecht first presented his ideas for this style of acting in his 1936 essay "Alienation Effects in Chinese Acting." "This new method of practising art would cause empathy to forfeit its dominant role," he later wrote (2015: 127). Even in his poems, Brecht directed actors:

> before you show the way
> A man betrays someone, or is seized by jealousy
> Or concludes a deal, first look
> At the audience as if you wished to say:
> Now take note, this man is now betraying someone and this is how he does it.
> (1987: 341)

13   Indeed, that a play-text holds something supernumerary; something irreducible to finite protocols, is evidenced by the simple fact that no production of a play is the *ultimate production*—that is, no production exhausts the infinite possibilities for staging a play-text. Badiou returns to this idea in *L'Immanence des vérités* with reference to Aeschylus, whose tragedies continue to provoke new thought after two thousand years: "Que les tragédies d'Eschyle soient encore actives, dans des temps entièrement différents et éloignés de leur création, montre qu'il n'y a pas de protocole fixe, arrêté, de leur évaluation, mais qu'il faut toujours recommencer cette évaluation dans un contexte différent, recommencement que, précisément, leur universalité, donc leur absoluité, rend possible" (2018 : 28). Arguably, theater is apt to condition the dialectical thinking required to enter the immanent relation between finitude and infinity; arguably, it is the modern mise-en-scène that exposed the infinite possibilities for theater to illuminate its situation and affirmed the importance of this form for philosophical enquiry.

Works Cited

Ackerman, A. and M. Puchner (2006), "Introduction: Modernism and Anti-theatricality," in A. Ackerman and M. Puchner (eds.), *Against Theatre*, 1–17, Basingstoke and New York: Palgrave.

Badiou, A. ([1988] 2005a), *Being and Event*, trans. O. Feltham, London and New York: Continuum.
Badiou, A. ([1998] 2005b), *Handbook of Inaesthetics*, trans. A. Toscano, Stanford: Stanford University Press.
Badiou, A. ([1998] 2005c), *Metapolitics*, trans. J. Barker, London: Verso.
Badiou, A. ([2005] 2007a), *The Century*, trans. A. Toscano, Paris: Seuil.
Badiou, A. ([1990] 2008), "Rhapsody for the Theatre: A Short Philosophical Treatise," *Theatre Survey* 49:2, 187–238.
Badiou, A. (2018), *L'Immanence des vérités*, Paris: Fayard.
Badiou, A. ([2013] 2020), *The Pornographic Age*, trans. and eds. A. J. Bartlett and J. Clemens, London: Bloomsbury.
Badiou, A. (2022), *Remarques sur la disorientation du monde*, Paris: Éditions Gallimard.
Badiou, A. and N. Truong (2013), *Éloge du théâtre*, Paris: Flammarion.
Barish, J. (1981), *The Antitheatrical Prejudice*, Berkeley and Los Angeles: University of California Press.
Bartlett, A. J. and J. Clemens (2020), "Minus Something Indefinable," in A. Badiou, *The Pornographic Age*, London: Bloomsbury.
Brecht, B. (1987), "Showing has to be Shown," in J. Willet and R. Manheim (eds.), *Poems 1913-1956*, 341–2, London: Routledge
Brecht, B. (2015), *Brecht on Performance: Messingkauf and Modelbooks*, eds. T. Kuhn, S. Giles and M. Silberman, London: Bloomsbury.
Bürger, P. (1984), "On the Problem of the Autonomy of Art in Bourgeois Society," in *Theory of the Avant-Garde*, trans. M. Shaw, 35–54, Minneapolis: University of Minnesota Press.
Chaudhuri, U. (1994), "'There Must Be a lot of Fish in That Lake': Toward an Ecological Theatre," *Theatre* 25:1, 23–31.
Deleuze, G. ([1971] 1993), "One Manifesto Less," in C. V. Boundas (ed.), *The Deleuze Reader*, New York: Columbia University Press.
Derrida, J. ([1978] 2008), "The Theatre of Cruelty and the Closure of Representation," in M. Puchner (ed.), *Modern Drama IV*, London: Routledge. pp. 157-78
Fried, M. ([1967] 1998), *Art and Objecthood: Essays and Reviews*, Chicago: The University of Chicago Press.
Gullstam, M. (2020), "Rousseau's Idea of Theatre: From Criticism to Practice," Ph.D. diss., Stockholm University.
Handke, P. ([1966] 1997), "Offending the Audience," in *Plays: 1*, London: Methuen Drama.
Havelock, E. A. (1982), *Preface to Plato*, Cambridge, MA: Harvard University Press.
Ingram, W. (1992), *The Business of Playing*, Ithaca: Cornell University Press.
Lacan, J. (2013), *Le séminaire, livre VI: Le désir et son interprétation*, ed. J.-A. Miller, Paris: Éditions de la Martinière.
Lacoue-Labarthe, P. (1989), *Typography*, Stanford: Stanford University Press.
Lacoue-Labarthe, P. and J.-L. Nancy (1990), "The Nazi Myth," trans. B. Holmes, *Critical Inquiry* 16:2, 291–312.
Moi, T. (2006), *Henrik Ibsen and the Birth of Modernism*, Oxford: Oxford University Press.
Nietzsche, F. (1911), *The Case of Wagner, Nietzsche Contra Wagner, Selected Aphorisms*, trans. A. M. Ludovici, Edinburgh: T.N. Foulis.
Plato (1969), *The Republic*. Plato in Twelve Volumes, vols. 5 and 6, trans. P. Shorey, Cambridge, MA: Harvard University Press.

Puchner, M. (2002a), *Stage Fright: Modernism, Anti-Theatricality, and Drama*, Baltimore: Johns Hopkins University Press.

Puchner, M. (2002b), "The Theatre in Modernist Thought," *New Literary History* 33:3, 521–532.

Puchner, M. (2010), *The Drama of Ideas: Platonic Provocations in Theatre and Philosophy*, Oxford: Oxford University Press.

Rancière, J. ([2008] 2021), *The Emancipated Spectator*, London: Verso.

Sartre, J.-P. (1954), "Introduction," in J. Genet, *The Maids and Deathwatch*, trans. B. Frechtman, New York: Grove Press.

Sontag, S. ([1980] 2001), "Approaching Artaud," in S. Sontag, *Under the Sign of Saturn*, New York: Vintage.

Ubersfeld, A. (1999), *Reading Theatre*, Toronto: University of Toronto Press.

Vernant, J.-P. and P. Vidal-Naquet (1988), *Myth and Tragedy in Ancient Greece*, trans. J. Llyod, New York: Zone Books.

Part III

Glossary

14

"The Age of Poets"

Christian R. Gelder

Alain Badiou's category of "the age of poets" looks in the first instance like a conventional form of literary periodization—or so it may seem to a scholar of modernist literature. The age of poets designates a period of poetic production that runs "vaguely," as Badiou qualifies, "between the Paris Commune and the aftermath of World War II, between 1870 and 1960, or between Arthur Rimbaud and Paul Celan, with Friedrich Hölderlin being more of an angelical announcer" (Badiou 2014: 3). Although this chronology shares a number of temporal and aesthetic qualities with literary modernism, Badiou insists that the category "does not pretend to offer a periodisation of the different sequences of poetry" (Badiou 2014: 3). What is more, the age of poets is not defined by a judgment of taste or sensibility. Throughout his lengthy career, Badiou has often loudly expressed a preference for Victorian and modernist poets like Victor Hugo, Gerard Manley Hopkins, T. S. Eliot, Wallace Stevens and, more recently, Emily Dickinson, whom he praises in *The Immanence of Truths* (2018) for having the courage to declare at the height of nineteenth-century bourgeois individualism that "I'm Nobody!" (Badiou 2022: 120).[1] But his own taste notwithstanding, these aforementioned poets do not strictly speaking belong to the age of poets. For Badiou, it was Stéphane Mallarmé, Rimbaud, Fernando Pessoa, Georg Trakl, Osip Mandelstam, Celan and Hölderlin who rose above other poets from this era, distinguishing themselves thanks to several shared thematic operations and strategies of verse making.

Neither an attempt at periodization nor a science of aesthetics, nor even a judgment of taste, the category of the age of poets appears in Badiou's philosophical system after the publication of *Being and Event* (1988) to formalize several propositions about the shifting historical relations between philosophy and poetry; the knots that have, to varying degrees of success, bound and unbound these two discourses.[2] First theorized in *Manifesto for Philosophy* (1989)—a polemical companion volume published shortly after the more technical *Being and Event*—and in a long symposium paper delivered in that same year, the age of poets has a triple function in Badiou's philosophy.[3] It is first employed to diagnose a historical lack in philosophy, which poetry between 1870 and 1960 came to supplement; secondly, the age of poets signifies a set of thematic operations Badiou identifies in post-Romantic poetic thinking, operations that link the disparate poets from this category; and thirdly, Badiou employs the age of poets to offer a new articulation of the relationship between poetry and mathematics in modernity, reframing Plato's classic interruption of the poem with the matheme. Although the category appears only briefly in his work, it is central to understanding Badiou's own rethinking of the relationship between poetry, philosophy and mathematics, offering a crucial historical backdrop to the work Badiou went on to undertake in *Being and Event*, *Logics of Worlds* (2006) and the recent *The Immanence of Truths*. Despite the historical connotations of the term, then, the age of poets does not resemble a literary periodization in any strong or formal sense; it is rather a "philosophical category" that "organises a particular way of conceiving the knot tying the poem to philosophy, which is such that this knot becomes *visible* from the point of view of philosophy itself" (Badiou 2014: 3).

As Phillipe Lacoue-Labarthe notes, while the age of poets makes a claim about nineteenth- and twentieth-century poetry and philosophy, it was also invoked by Badiou as a way of interpreting—and intervening into—his own philosophical milieu.[4] When Badiou wrote *Being and Event* and then *Manifesto for Philosophy* in the late 1980s, French philosophy had distilled its faith in the transformative powers of aesthetic production, concentrating an extraordinary amount of philosophical activity on the question of poetry, painting and cinema. A brief sketch of the work undertaken by Badiou's peers during this period is illustrative. In 1983 and 1985, Gilles Deleuze published his deeply influential two-volume work *Cinema I* and *Cinema II*; at the end of the previous decade, Jean-François Lyotard turned his attention to painting, devoting works to Marcel Duchamp and Jacques Monory; Lacoue-Labarthe and Jean-Luc Nancy published their magnificent *The Literary Absolute* in 1978; and Maurice Blanchot, Jacques Derrida and Michel Foucault had all been publishing on literary writing for the best part of a decade. Indeed, as Badiou himself suggested, mid- to late century French philosophy was defined by a *fetishization* of the literary, handing philosophical thinking entirely over to its aesthetic counterpart.

The age of poets was in part employed by Badiou to historicize this philosophical situation, which he argues was the product of a broader philosophical conviction, with a much longer history, that aesthetic production produced a kind of philosophical thinking of which philosophy itself was incapable. To understand the conceptual conditions that provided the ground for such a fetishization—and indeed to revitalize the project of philosophy itself—Badiou notes that philosophy after Hegel enacted a set of what he calls "sutures." Schematically put, for Badiou, philosophy *must* be systematic: it is the "configuration, within thought, of the fact that its four generic conditions (the poem, the matheme, the political and love) are compossible" (Badiou 1999: 61). But this very classical and Platonic conception of philosophy—which involves reconstituting "the entire initial fourfold structure of [philosophy's] conditions (consisting of politics, love, poetry, and mathematics)"—was suspended in the nineteenth century due to a conceptual preference for one particular condition over another.[5] The concept of suture thereby offers a kind of heuristic through which one can read the various splittings in philosophical discourse that occurred in and after the nineteenth century; historical splittings that still reverberate today in the regional (and arguably parochial) distinction between so-called American analytic philosophy and European Continental philosophy. As Badiou notes, the predominant suture in nineteenth-century philosophy was "positivist or scientistic," a handing over of philosophical invention to scientific discovery (Badiou 1999: 62). But the nineteenth century also witnessed the rise of Marxism, wherein philosophy sutured itself to politics by organizing the entirety of experience on the plane of the political. As Badiou concludes, during the age of poets, philosophy was closest to "the scientific condition, in the different avatars of positivism and the doctrine of progress," "the political condition, in the different avatars of revolutionary political philosophy" and even "a mixture of the two, which is reflected in Marxism as 'scientific socialism'—that is, the superposition of a science of History and a political voluntarism whose philosophical projection has been dialectical materialism" (Badiou 2014: 4).

Suturing philosophy to only one of its conditions means that philosophy is doomed to misrecognize the thought proper to its own era, forcing the owl of Minerva to fly in only one direction. However, positivism and politics were not the only sutures taking place toward the end of the nineteenth century. When Friedrich Nietzsche sought to cure philosophy of the so-called Plato sickness, he did so by reversing Plato's faith in the "transparency of the matheme" and his suspicion of "the metaphorical obscurity of the poem" (Badiou 1999: 19). What began with Nietzsche, culminated in Martin Heidegger's phenomenology and then reverberated out into twentieth-century Continental philosophy, was nothing less than a complete suturing of philosophy to the poem. In the total absence of systematic philosophy—where philosophy in its analytic assignation allocated total and uncompromising power to scientific rationality and liberal parliamentary capitalism, and philosophy in its Continental conjunction handed over the totality of thought to the poem—the age of poets thereby designates the set of poets from Hegel to Nietzsche whose verse was shaped by an intellectual pressure emanating from the lack of systematic philosophical thinking; a historical diagnosis which notes how philosophy knotted itself to poetry by way of pure rejection or dogged affirmation.

The diagnostic power of Badiou's category is thus twofold, referring at once to a "moment proper to the history of philosophy in which the latter is sutured—that is to say, delegated or subject—to a single one of its conditions," as well as to how "certain poets, or rather certain poems, [came] to occupy the place where ordinarily the properly philosophical strategies of thought are declared" (Badiou 2014: 5). The second role Badiou assigns to the age of poets thus concerns these poetic "strategies of thought": the thematic "operations" that poets from Mallarmé to Celan employed to deliver a "metaphysics without metaphysics in the form of short poems rather than long treatises" (Badiou 2022: 170). Indeed, the first of these concerns how these poets reflected on their own capacity to produce a poetic metaphysics—"the intrapoetic putting into work of certain *maxims* of *thought*, nodal points of the poem in which the thinking that it is indicates itself as relation or incision of thought 'in general,'" as Badiou puts it (Badiou 2014: 5–6). When Mallarmé, the "exemplar" of the age of poets, wrote in a highly wrought letter to his fellow symbolist poet Henri Cazalis in 1866, "my Thought has thought itself and arrived at a pure Conception," Badiou highlights the quasi- and meta-philosophical signifiers circulating in that letter.[6]

"Thought has thought itself" and "pure Conception" suggest that a certain strand of poetic thinking after Mallarmé sought to situate its poetic inventions in relation to thought as such, articulating a meta-philosophical position once offered by austere classical metaphysics. Moreover, as Mallarmé came to write his final masterwork *Un coup de dés* in 1897, Badiou notes that this poem ends with the line "Toute pensée émet un Coup de Dés"—the qualifier "toute" ("all") bearing a universality that outweighs "the singularity of the poem," establishing an absolute connection "between thought, chance, and number" (Badiou 2014: 6). Similarly, when Rimbaud offered a rebuke of the Cogito—writing in a letter to Georges Izambard, "It is wrong to say: I think. One ought to say: People think me"—Badiou suggests that Rimbaud "authorises [. . .] the poem as [a] dictation of being," displacing the solipsism of the singular Cartesian subject onto the anonymous thinking of generic humanity (Badiou 2014: 6).

Each of these poetic incisions into the totality of thought requires a "method" of poetic making that "establishes guidelines for thought, proposing singular *operations* for it" (Badiou 2014: 6). There were many methods, many "singular operations," tested by poets during the age of poets, like Mallarmé's infamous "Book"—his project to devise a secular spectacle which would rebind the community in the face of the absence of God—or Pessoa's heteronyms, which express "not merely a name different from the author's but also a separate personality who expresses what the author does not or cannot" (Badiou 2014: 6).[7] But as much as different poets created singular methods of poetic making, the poets from the age of poets are nonetheless bound by a set of common thematic operations—the first being "counter-romanticism." This counter-Romantic thrust "takes the form of a series of prohibitions, which aim to *centre* the poem on a tacit concept rather than on the power of the image" (Badiou 2014: 13). In relation to the age of poets, Romanticism for Badiou stands for the theme of meditation and speculation: the sense, as Justin Clemens puts it, that the subject is the "constitutive foundational agency of thought" and that the poem is the privileged site of that thought's expression.[8] But these poets subtract their poetics from the safeguarding of the dream and all the nostalgia that dreaming connotes. As Mallarmé wrote in "Funerary Toast," a poem published in *Poésies* (1887), "where the true poet's broad and humble gesture must / keep them from dreams, those enemies of his trust."[9] However, Badiou rightly notes that poets only trade in metaphors and images. The images employed by the poets of the age of poets are thus not those of transcendence or nostalgia, dreams of the future or of the past. They are rather "that which is *not* sacred or sacralizable, which turns away from complacency with the dream and the image in order to entrust the poem to the rigorous laws of metaphor" (Badiou 2014: 14). Indeed, in Badiou's own writings on philosophy and Romanticism, he similarly calls for a counter-Romantic philosophical orientation, one which counters the primacy of Romantic subjectivism by revivifying the thinking proper to mathematics.[10]

Badiou identifies another related thematic operation: the poetic "detotalization" of the "Great Whole." For him, the poets of the age of poets think "detotalisation, the separate, irreconcilable multiplicity. They impose on themselves the rule of a principle of inconsistency" (Badiou 2014: 14). This principle can take place at the level of poetic subjectivity (or the lyric I): Pessoa's heteronymical method, for example, speaks to the detotalization of poetic subjectivity. For Pessoa, poetry is not produced by a unified and reflexive self; instead, it is the expression of separate, irreconcilable and inconsistent multiplicities, each one a stranger to the other. Whether through the vanishing constellation of *Un coup de dés* or the semantically empty "ptyx" of "Sonnet en yx," Badiou notes that Mallarmé's verse always gestures toward an object that is missing; an object "subtracted, withdrawn from Presence by its own self-dissolution" (Badiou 1999: 77). Mallarmé's linguistic theory was concerned with naming this subtracted object—affirming what has been negated—which the poet does in part by citing the inherently oppositional nature of the words "jour" and "nuit." According to Mallarmé, although the "sense" or signified content of the former word should in principle refer to the properties of day (in this case brightness or lightness), the "sound" of the word is in fact dark. Similarly, the sense of "nuit" is dark but its sound is light. The internal coherency of language is therefore skewed: words show the chance relations governing sound and sense. As Mallarmé envisaged, however, poetry has the power to supplement language's lack: as Jean-Claude Milner writes, for Mallarmé "[v]erse requires a supplementary component comprised of calculations, symmetries, plays of sonority and, running under it all, a design to create, by means of verse, this single word that language lacks, whose sound corresponds with its sense."[11] Verse can thus bring into being a word that—for a brief moment—overcomes the chance that makes "jour" sound dark and "nuit" sound light. Badiou parses this in terms that echo the reading of Mallarmé he gives in *Being and Event*, where the poet's "total word" provides a poetic name for the interruption of inconsistency, namely, an interruption that lies on the other side of ontology—the event. He writes, "[i]t is a question of a statement of the poem *wagering* that a nomination may come and interrupt signification, and from the point of this interruption for a *localisable* thought to establish itself, without any pretence to totality, but capable of being loyal to its own inauguration" (Badiou 2014: 15).[12]

The poetic detotalization of the whole means that for the poets of the age of poets, ontology is decoupled from scientific "objectivity" (the latter being an epistemic virtue that, as Lorraine Daston and Peter Gaston have pointed out, rose to prominence during this exact same historical milieu).[13] Removing ontology from objective presence, the third operation proper to the age of poets is therefore the dissolution of the category of the object. As Badiou writes, "[w]hat the poets of the age of poets attempt to open is an approach to being, precisely where being cannot buttress itself by way of the 'presentative' category of object. Poetry is then on essentially disobjectifying" (Badiou 1999: 72). For Badiou, this poetic dissolution—the ability of poetry to name that which is not given to presence—also anchors the modernist tradition of poetic impersonality.[14] The poetic representation of objects relies on a correlation between subject and object, a gazing subject able to bear witness to what is presented. But if the category of the object is dissolved, then so too must the poets of the age of poets dissolve the category of the subject, which for Badiou explains the recognizable claims to poetic impersonality that define so much of the work of literary modernism. Indeed, Badiou often invokes Mallarmé's remarks about how the "pure work" of poetry implies "the elocutionary disappearance of the poet" to illustrate this point, though he has more recently read Dickinson's verse in the same fashion ("[w]hat is so remarkable" about Dickinson's assertion that "I'm nobody!," he writes, "is that this Odysseus-like assertion serves only to introduce a question, addressed to some unknown person, and thus addressed to generic humanity: 'Who are you?' The utterly astonishing answer is that the person to whom the question is addressed should be assumed to be Nobody him- or herself, too") (Badiou 2022: 120–121).

These three operations—"counter-Romanticism," "detotalisation" and "deobjectification"—bind the poets from the age of poets. But for Badiou, they serve yet another function. Briefly put, in Badiou's own philosophy, he makes a powerful distinction between knowledge (or what he calls in *Being and Event*, the "encyclopedia") and truth. As Clemens writes, "if knowledge is generated by truth processes, truth is also what makes a hole in (the existing state of) knowledges."[15] Indeed, the encyclopedia exists to mask the hole that lies at the heart of knowledge, precluding the possibility of radical novelty. With respect to the age of poets, Badiou notes that it was Heidegger who grasped that "the opposition of truth and knowledge," as well as "the essential disorientation of our epoch," is at stake in the poetic dissolution of the category of the object: "we must reserve the word 'knowledge' for that which is supported by an object, the object of knowledge," Badiou writes, "The delimitation of knowledge supposes that the real comes to experience in the form of the object. Now—this point is crucial—the poem does not aim, nor suppose, nor describe, any object, or any objectivity" (Badiou 2014: 24). However, we recall that Badiou employs the category of the age of poets to reject the Heideggerian suture of philosophy to the poem, arguing instead that philosophy must think the thought proper to science, art, love *and* politics. In *Being and Event*, this classical vision of philosophy is actualized through a reconsideration of the philosophical distribution between mathematics and poetry: via the mathematics of set theory, the former provides a discourse on ontology, whereas the latter has the capacity to produce a poetic name for the eventual interruption of inconsistency. As Badiou writes, then, "the fundamental criticism of Heidegger can only be the following one: the Age of Poets is completed, it is also necessary to de-suture philosophy from its poetic condition. Which means that it is no longer required today that disobjectification and disorientation be stated in the poetic metaphor" (Badiou 1999: 74).

The third and final role Badiou assigns to the age of poets thus precisely concerns this relationship between the poem and the matheme in modernity. For Badiou, Plato's critique of poetry's second-order mimesis and his faith in the literal transparency of the matheme do not accurately capture how the poets from the age of poets thought this relation—not least because poetry during this period did not trade in representations but rather sought to provide a name for that which is withdrawn from presence. Indeed, modern poetry is in fact "altogether aware of a *sharing of thinking* with mathematics," Badiou notes, "since it has blindly perceived that the matheme too, in its pure, literal offering, in its empty suture to every multiple-presentation, was questioning and dismissing the prevalence of objectivity" (Badiou 1999: 76). Badiou here cites Lautréamont—"the dignified heir to Plato, Spinoza and Kant"—who "considers that mathematics saved him, and it did so at the specific point of the destitution of the subject-object or Man-world couple" and Mallarmé, a poet who searched after a visual attestation of that "unique Number which cannot be another" (Badiou 1999: 75). What the poets of the age of poets recognize in mathematics, Badiou thinks, is a similar dissolution of the category of objectivity: these poets "have, it is true, known better than mathematicians themselves that there was no such thing as a mathematical *object*" (Badiou 1999: 76).

The category of the age of poets is thereby a spur to reconfigure Plato's critique of poetic mimesis. But such a reconfiguration also allows Badiou to double-down on his stirring rejection of Heidegger's poetic suture. While Badiou opens *Being and Event* by remarking that "Heidegger is the last universally recognisable philosopher," Heidegger does not share Badiou's own classical conception of philosophy (Badiou 2006: 1). Rather, for Heidegger, the poem represents nothing less than philosophical salvation from the technological nihilism of mathematics and the sciences: Heidegger positions poets as the "shepherds, the vigils of [the question of Being] which technology renders universally unpronounceable" (Badiou 1999: 50). Although Badiou praises Heidegger for "having been the only one to pick up what was at stake in the poem, namely the destitution of object fetishism, the opposition of truth and knowledge, and lastly, the essential disorientation of our epoch," he also notes that Heidegger "constructs the antinomy of the matheme and the poem in such a way as to make it coincide with the opposition of knowledge and truth" (Badiou 1999: 74). By reviving the question of the truth of mathematical invention in *Being and Event*, then, Badiou closes the ages of poets.

What makes Badiou's category of the age of poets so compelling is its triple function in his philosophical system. The age of poets is employed to diagnose a historical lack in philosophy, to outline the poetic operations proper to this moment in post-Romantic verse thinking, and finally to rethink the relationship between poetry and mathematics— all in the name of recommencing philosophy itself. Badiou identifies the specific set of poetic operations at work in the age of poets only in order to turn these operations upside down—to reconceptualize, thanks to the mathematics apparatus employed in *Being and Event*, counter-Romanticism, detotalization and deobjectification. The importance of the age of poets thus lies precisely and paradoxically in the fact that it has not featured prominently in Badiou's post-*Being and Event* writings. Indeed, by placing philosophy under the political, amorous, artistic *and* scientific conditions, Badiou does something else—he effectuates the end of the age of poets. So how might this relate to modernism as a literary period and aesthetic orientation, given that the age Badiou both identifies and closes is borne out of a specific post- (and counter-) Romantic tradition? While Badiou provides his own account of the philosophical distribution of labor effectuated by poetry and mathematics in *Being and Event*, the method that typifies his way of reading the age of poets consists of turning the categories proper to this age upside down. Although Mallarmé, the exemplar of the age of poets, might make consistent invocations of the category of the infinite—and so resists the modernity of finitude that Badiou so stirringly critiques—that invocation happens at the level of natural language. For Badiou, by contrast, the deductive, univocal and rule-bound nature of mathematical language gives it logical consistency, rendering mathematics capable of *formalizing* the infinite, as well as detotalization, in a way that poetry can only figure. Wagering on the power of formalization over natural language figuration, Badiou aims to shore up what modernism can only ever metaphorize: that is, the general laws of ontology and the spark that makes it new.

Notes

1. I thank Sam Warren-Miell for alerting me to the significance of Badiou's reading of Dickinson, which he expertly sketches in "Lyric, History and Genericity: Virginia Jackson and Alain Badiou on Emily Dickinson" (Unpublished Thesis: University of Cambridge, 2019).
2. For two excellent works dedicated to Badiou's account of poetry and poetics, see Eyers (2016) and Betteridge (2020).
3. The papers delivered at that symposium have been published in the following collection: Badiou (1992).
4. As Lacou-Labarthe writes of the age of poets, "it is quite impressive in its comprehensiveness, in its assurance, and in the abruptness with which it attempts to overturn a tradition that Alain Badiou cannot be accused of ignoring or misunderstanding—and within which, by the way, he places me, along with a few others" Lacoue-Labarthe (2007: 17–18).
5. Lacoue-Labarthe (2007: 17).
6. "ma Pensée s'est pensée et est arrivée à une Conception pure." Mallarmé (1995: 342).
7. Jones (1977: 254), quoted in Frow (2014: 215). For further discussion of Mallarmé's Book, see Meillassoux (2011: 1–11, 106–13).
8. Clemens (2015: 284).
9. "Où le poëte pur a pour geste humble et large / De l'interdire au rêve, ennemi de sa charge." Mallarmé (1998: 55).
10. See in particular Badiou (2004: 22–40).
11. Milner (2014: 94–5).
12. Beyond the reading Badiou gives in Meditation 19 of *Being and Event*, see also Badiou (2016: 16–30).
13. See Daston and Galison (2007).
14. For more on this tradition, see Maud Ellmann's classic *The Poetics of Impersonality* (1988).
15. Justin Clemens, "Absolute," in *The Badiou Dictionary*, 5.

Works Cited

Badiou, A. and Jacques Rancière. (1992), *La Politique des poètes: pourquoi des poètes en temps de détresse*, ed. J. Rancière, Paris: Albin Michel.

Badiou, A. (1999), *Manifesto for Philosophy*, trans. N. Madarasz, New York: SUNY Press.

Badiou, A. (2004), "Philosophy and Mathematics: Infinity and the End of Romanticism," in A. Badiou, *Theoretical Writings*, eds. and trans. Ray Brassier and Alberto Toscano, 22–40, London: Continuum.

Badiou, A. (2006), *Being and Event*, trans. O. Feltham, London: Bloomsbury.
Badiou, A. (2014), *The Age of Poets*, trans. B. Bosteels, London: Verso.
Badiou, A. (2016), "Is it Exact that All Thought Emits a Throw of Dice?," trans. Robert Boncardo and Christian R. Gelder, *S: Journal of the Circle for Lacanian Ideology Critique* 9, 16–30.
Badiou, A. (2022), *Immanence of Truths*, trans. K. Reinhardt and S. Spitzer, London: Bloomsbury.
Betteridge, T. (2020), *Badiou, Poem and Subject*, London: Bloomsbury.
Corcoran, S. (2015), *The Badiou Dictionary*, Edinburgh: Edinburgh University Press.
Daston, L. and G. Peter (2007), *Objectivity*, New York: Zone Books.
Ellmann, M. (1988), *The Poetics of Impersonality: T. S. Eliot and Ezra Pound*, Boston: Harvard University Press.
Eyers, T. (2016), "Alain Badiou, Wallace Stevens and the Paradoxical Productivity of Poetic Form," *Textual Practice* 30:5, 835–855.
Frow, J. (2014), *Character and Person*, Oxford: Oxford University Press.
Jones, M. S. (1977), "Pessoa's Poetic Coterie: Three Heteronyms and an Orthonym," *Luso-Brazilian Review* 14:2, 254–262.
Lacoue-Labarthe, P. (2007), *Heidegger and the Politics of Poetry*, trans. J. Fort, Urbana: University of Illinois Press.
Mallarmé, S. (1995), *Correspondance: Lettres sur la poésie*, ed. B. Marchal, Paris: Gallimard.
Mallarmé, S. (1998), *Œuvres complètes I, Édition présentée, établie et annotée par Bertrand Marchal*, Paris: Gallimard.
Meillassoux, Q. (2011), *The Number and the Siren: A Decipherment of Mallarmé's Coup de dés*, trans. R. Mackey, Falmouth: Urbanomic.
Milner, J.-C. (2014), "Mallarmé Perchance," trans. L. Yamaguchi, *Hyperion* IX:3, 87–110.

15

Maoism

Robert Boncardo

One of the most controversial aspects of Alain Badiou's politics is his peculiar fidelity to the thought and practice of Maoism.[1] In this chapter, I frame Badiou's Maoism as the site of a productive tension between competing modernist and postmodernist tendencies in politics. By "modernist politics" I mean, very schematically, a politics grounded in an historical teleology with universalizing pretensions, such as that evinced by the Marxist-Leninist tradition, which adhered to Badiou for a long time. By "postmodernist politics," by contrast, I mean a conception of the political field as made up of multiple interest or identity groups jostling for greater power or recognition, albeit without any common political denominator. My argument will be that Badiou's Maoism, while initially subordinated to the modernist tradition of Marxism-Leninism, played a key role in helping him overcome that tradition's historical teleology while avoiding a lapse into postmodernist particularism. To make my case, I will focus on the experience of the small Maoist group that Badiou helped lead between 1970 and 1985, the Union des Communistes de France (marxiste-léniniste), or the UCF(ml).[2] As I will show, Badiou's group pushed the Marxist-Leninist tradition to its limits through the use of the Maoist tactic of the mass line. When, at the end of the group's life, they abandoned this tradition, their erstwhile Maoism gave them the means to remain faithful to the universalizing drive of Marxism-Leninism, now shorn of any historical teleology. Yet this also meant abandoning any explicit reference to Maoism as well. Badiou's subsequent group, the Organisation Politique (OP), was thus able to steer a middle course between the twin dangers of regressive modernism and conservative postmodernism.

The place to begin our discussion of Badiou's political trajectory is, unsurprisingly, May '68. While references to '68 are compulsory in discussions of Badiou's politics, what is often poorly understood about his experience of this month's events is that they led him to convert, not to a wholly novel political doctrine—one congruent, for instance, with his later categories of event and truth procedure—but rather to the well-established doctrine of Marxism-Leninism.[3] In contrast to many of his contemporaries, who saw May '68 as invalidating Marx and Lenin's ideas, in an almost rearguard action Badiou took up the rudiments of their thought with extraordinary zeal (Badiou et al. 1970: 4, 12–13, 15, 19–20, 28–9, 45–8). Badiou sharply criticized those who saw the emergence of new social actors, from women to white-collar workers, ecologists to college students, as portending a more diverse—and for this reason potentially more liberating—political field (Badiou et al. 1970: 8–21, 2010: 84–6). Against this nascent postmodernist tendency, Badiou argued, following Marx and Lenin, that industrial workers remained the sole revolutionary class, and that the unique strategic aim of serious revolutionaries was to build a worker-led party that could coordinate the final assault on the bourgeois state before implementing a dictatorship of the proletariat (Badiou et al. 1970: 45–8).

At this formative moment in his political trajectory, Badiou thus adopted an almost dogmatic Marxist-Leninist line, which he articulated using this tradition's three core concepts of class, party and state. Significantly, however, he also introduced a dose of novelty into his version of Marxism-Leninism by adhering to Maoism as well. To be brief, at the time Maoism named a set of innovative organizational techniques that Badiou believed would better serve the cause of building a new communist party than the well-known Leninist ones. These new tactics were encapsulated in the Maoist notion of the mass line (Badiou 2010: 88–9; Michel 2020: 109–14). Where Leninism had favored trained militants rallying the working class and its allies to a line set in advance by a revolutionary party, the practice of the mass line emphasized the perspectives and capacities of those immediately subject to a situation of exploitation and oppression. In the months following May '68, Badiou attempted to steer the party he then belonged to, the social democratic Parti Socialiste Unifié (PSU), in this more Maoist direction by proposing that it build its membership base in the working class and give more power within the party to industrial workers and to those who had led them in the wildcat strikes of May '68 (Badiou et al. 1970: 26). After this proposal was rejected at the PSU's ninth congress, held in Dijon in March 1969, Badiou left the party and joined with Sylvain Lazarus, Natacha Michel, Catherine Quiminal and Cécile Winter to found a new organization that would better express his Maoist principles (Michel 2020: 91–9; Fallet 2021: 24–45). The organization's full name, Group for the Foundation of the Union of Communists of France (Marxist-Leninist), gives us an indication of just how closely the comrades sought to adhere to the practice of the mass line. Rather than proclaim themselves leaders of a new party, the comrades saw themselves as activists who would take the "question of the party" into social movements and "put it back into the hands of the masses," as they wrote in their founding pamphlet *Proletarian Revolution in France*, published in March 1970 (UCFML 1970: 2).

In the Group's second major work, titled *First Year of Existence*, published in 1972, the new comrades analyzed their earliest attempts at applying the tactic of the mass line to situations as diverse as factories, housing estates, educational institutions and slums (UCFML 1972). What is most striking about *First Year of Existence* is that while the Group encountered significant difficulties in pursuing their aim of building a new party, they remained resolutely optimistic (UCFML 1972: 6–7). They believed that the spontaneous inventions of the masses in these struggles were consistent with the Group's overall strategy, even if these inventions were couched in different terms to the standard Marxist-Leninist language and represented only small-scale versions of the larger structures that a communist party would eventually have to build (UCFML 1972: 46–9, 50–61, 62–7). Here Badiou and his comrades' Maoism was manifest in their conviction that the masses' self-education, as slow and uncertain as this process might be, was the key to their eventual success (UCFML 1972: 25). A top down approach would instead only reproduce the alienating structures in place in established communist parties, not least France's own Parti Communiste Français. In other words, the Maoist tactic of the mass line allowed the UCF(ml)'s leaders to maintain their belief in the politically modernist historical teleology posited by traditional Marxism-Leninism, in spite of the vicissitudes of the masses' self-education and the overall unfavourable circumstances they faced. Indeed, it arguably gave them an alibi to take more time to achieve this aim.

At this stage, then, Badiou and his comrades' Maoism was a novel means for reaching a familiar end. While the Group saw much of value in May's radically democratic, or indeed postmodernist, spirit and while they affirmed the right of political actors to organize around their own issues in sites far removed from the traditional loci of class struggle, they saw even more value in the eventual subordination of these movements to the goal of building a new French communist party that could overthrow the French state. This same very traditional vision was equally evident in the way the Group came to structure their organization as a whole (*Le Marxiste-Léniniste*, No. 10, 1976: 1–4). From the mid-1970s onwards, Badiou and his comrades divided their Group's activities into two organizational forms. On the one side were the Communist Cells ("noyaux communistes"), which brought together factory workers who were committed to the Group's line and who studied key Marxist, Leninist and Maoist texts while also engaging in militant work in their respective workplaces. On the other side were the People's Anti-Capitalist Committees ("comités populaires anti-capitalistes"), which united people from sites of struggle outside of the factory, in particular housing estates, and focused on more immediate issues such as the cost of living. The Group were explicit about the logic of this two-part structure: in the new communist party that would be created, the role of the apparently more militant workers in the Cells would be to lead those who belonged to the Committees (*Le Marxiste-Léniniste* No. 10, 1976: 3). The Group saw workers as possessing, thanks to the discipline and structural significance of factory labor, a ready-made revolutionary capacity. By contrast, they imagined the Committees' members as much less politically reliable, even if the organizational experiments they engaged in were useful for giving form and content to the Group's overall program, and helped prevent the broader masses of people from feeling alienated from the Group's activities (*Le Marxiste-Léniniste* No. 5, 1974: 1–3). In short, just as the tradition of Marxism-Leninism stipulated, Badiou's Group held that a particular class had a unique capacity to lead the majority of the population in a party whose aim was to capture the state and eventually emancipate humanity as a whole. While their Maoism might well have inspired them to be open to the new, their overarching project was thus firmly set within traditional—and arguably politically modernist—parameters.

That being said, this two-part structure fails to capture all of the elements of the Group's complex configuration. For beyond the Cells and Committees, the Group also set up or supported other organizations whose members had no common social identity, even if they shared an interest in a particular issue such as the politics of art, public health, or migrants' rights (Fallet 2021: 177–95, 231–40, 243–6, 296–305). None of these sectoral organizations neatly fit into the dual structure that the Group had initially established. Even more significantly, the Group's leaders explicitly affirmed the relative autonomy of these organizations, along with that of individual Cells and Committees, from the UCF(ml) as the central coordinating pole of the Group's activities. For Badiou and his fellow leaders, this was all a matter of faithfully following the Maoist tactic of the mass line. It was not possible, they claimed, to know in advance where and in what form the most significant political battles would take place. It was therefore essential that these various organizations, situated as they were throughout the social field and grouping together an heterogeneous multiplicity of social actors, be allowed to pursue their own ends by their own means, and for the UCF(ml) to learn from their experiences and adapts its line accordingly (*Le Marxiste-Léniniste* No. 5, 1974: 2–3; *Le Marxiste-Léniniste* No. 15, 1977: 4; Badiou 2009a: 286, 2011: 10). This approach would teach both the Group's leaders and the masses how to build a new communist party in such a way as to prevent this party from becoming as oppressive—because separated from the masses' actions—as the capitalist state it was destined to overthrow (*Le Marxiste-Léniniste*, No. 1, 1974: 1).

But what if some or indeed all of these organizations chose not to pursue the Group's ultimate end? How much autonomy could the Group's leaders give them, and for how long? One way of interpreting the Group's structure is as a precarious synthesis between the modernism of Marxism-Leninism and the postmodernism of the radically plural post-May political field. On the one hand, following the Maoist notion of the mass line, the Group encouraged a diverse array of organizations to grow and develop in their own singular directions. On the other hand, they wagered that these organizations would eventually cohere into the form of a new party. But what would a party that brought together such distinct political movements look like? Could it even be a party as this term was understood in the Marxist-Leninist tradition? If one took away the modernist teleology underlying the Group's aim of building a new party, what was one left with if not a postmodernist assemblage of irreducibly distinct political actors?

Badiou and his comrades were unable to give a convincing answer to these questions. As the 1970s progressed, the Group discovered that the French working class was internally divided in a radical way, and that it just as often pursued conformist ends as engage in revolutionary actions (*Le Marxiste-Léniniste* Nos. 27–8, 1978: 10). They also witnessed the depressing transformation of migrant workers, in whom they had invested their most fervent hopes, into a conservative political force (*La Cause Marxiste* No. 1, 1982: 5). Alongside these developments, the amount of activity in the Group's worker Cells decreased, while the number of people who participated in the sectoral organizations increased dramatically. This was particularly evident in the so-called "Anti-Expulsion Vigilance Groups" ("permanences anti-expulsion"), or PAEs, which grew exponentially after the waves of state and popular violence unleashed against migrant workers and their families following the 1978 legislative elections. All of this occurred in the context of the Giscard government implementing a range of neoliberal measures, from expanding the proportion of casual and part-time jobs to cutting welfare. In sum, by the end of the 1970s, Badiou and his comrades had found that reality had invalidated, if not inverted, their vision of the political field.

It was not long before the effects of these developments were felt within the Group itself. In 1982, a small faction led by Catherine Quiminal argued that the large number of people involved in the PAEs relative to the almost inactive Cells showed that the Group's focus on the working class was mistaken (*Le Marxiste-Léniniste*, No. 53, 1982: 10–15, 21–6). Quiminal's faction also claimed that people were no longer inspired by the call to build a new party and that a new conception of organization was therefore needed, one that also decoupled communist politics from the strategic aim of state capture (*Le Marxiste-Léniniste*, No. 53, 1982: 6–7). In response, true to their modernist leanings, Badiou's faction drew on traditional Marxist-Leninist ideas to assert that without a party led by the working class, communism remained an idle dream as it could only be reached via the tactical scansion of the dictatorship of the proletariat (*La Cause Marxiste* No. 3, 1983: 12). Thus, more than a decade after May '68, and after a multitude of often radically novel political experiences, for Badiou there was still only one possible formula for humanity's emancipation.

Everything changed in 1985. The UCF(ml) continued for two years following this fractious debate, issuing a new newspaper to mark the second major stage in the Group's existence, titled *La Cause Marxiste*. Yet the power of the arguments made by Quiminal's faction was clearly not lost on Badiou and the other remaining leaders, for in early 1985 they announced the creation of a new political group, the Organisation Politique, which broke decisively with the UCF(ml)'s line and adopted a position strikingly similar to the one that Quiminal's faction had outlined. In two texts published around this time, *Can Politics Be Thought?* from 1985 and *The Factory as Evental Site* from 1986, Badiou presented the fundamental concepts of the OP's new conception of communist politics (Badiou 2006, 2018a). Instead of class as the crucible of revolutionary politics, Badiou developed the concept of evental site, which, while explicitly mapped in Badiou's piece onto the factory, could also be applied to other situations of struggle (Badiou 2018a: 172–3). And instead of the party as the sole organizational form appropriate to communist politics, with the state as its strategic aim, Badiou envisaged a mode of organization whose means and ends were the localized verification of the axiom of equality, without any guarantee—or need for a guarantee—as to where this process would lead (Badiou 2005: 108–10, 2018a: 99–108, 2018b: 263–7).

All of a sudden, Badiou had abandoned the modernist teleology of Marxism-Leninism. What he and the OP had replaced it with, however, was not the postmodernist conception of dispersed political groupings without any shared ends. Instead, despite relinquishing the drive to unity represented by the party, Badiou affirmed that multiple political processes could achieve the singular objective of verifying people's equality, even if this happened in a unique way in each individual case.

While Badiou might have abandoned the ABCs of Marxism-Leninism, we can still clearly see the legacy of the Maoist mass line in this new political vision. However, where the mass line had once been a means to the politically modernist end of global emancipation, Badiou had now recast it as an end in itself in the form of the localized verification of equality. Yet this also meant that it was no longer a properly Maoist tactic—and Badiou himself no longer a Maoist—since the mass line, particularly during the Cultural Revolution era, had been conceived as a means for reforming the party-state. Without the party-state, its meaning was entirely transformed.

1985 was thus the first year of Badiou's post-Maoist—and, in a very specific sense, postmodernist—political trajectory. Or, to borrow a term from Badiou's later work, whose origins we can now perhaps better understand: 1985 was, politically speaking, Badiou's *first year of inexistence* (Badiou 2009b: 321–4).

Notes

1. For a very small selection of scholarship on Badiou's Maoism, see Boncardo and Cooke (2017: 68–84), Bosteels (2011), Fallet (2021), and Michel (2020).
2. Throughout this chapter I will refer to the UCF(ml) either by this abbreviation or by the term "Group" with a capital letter, for reasons that will become clear further on.
3. Badiou's own later writings are partly to blame for this misunderstanding. See all of Badiou's references, which are far too numerous to cite here, to May '68 as an "event."

Works Cited

Badiou, A. (2005), *Being and Event*, trans. O. Feltham, London: Continuum.
Badiou, A. (2006), "The Factory As Evental Site: Why Should the Worker be a Reference in Our Vision of Politics?," trans. A. Toscano, *Prelom: Journal for Images and Politics* 8, 171–176.
Badiou, A. (2009a), *Theory of the Subject*, trans. B. Bosteels, London: Continuum.
Badiou, A. (2009b), *Logics of Worlds: Being and Event, 2*, trans. A. Toscano, London: Continuum.
Badiou, A. (2010), *The Communist Hypothesis*, London: Verso.
Badiou, A. (2011), *Entretiens 1, 1981–1996*, Paris: Nous.
Badiou, A. (2018a), *Can Politics Be Thought?*, trans. B. Bosteels, Durham and London: Duke University Press.
Badiou, A. (2018b), *Le Séminaire. L'essence de la politique, 1991–1992*, Paris: Fayard.
Badiou, A., H. Jancovici, D. Menetrey and E. Terray (1970), *Contribution au problème de la construction d'un parti marxiste-léniniste de type nouveau*, Paris: François Maspero.
Boncardo, R. and B. Cooke (2017), "1967: The Shanghai Commune, French Maoism & the Case of Alain Badiou," *Australian and New Zealand Journal of European Studies* 9:3, 68–84.
Bosteels, B. (2011), *Badiou and Politics*, Durham and London: Duke University Press.
Fallet, J. (2021), *Les maos de l'UCF: une histoire politique 1970–1984*, Paris: L'Harmattan.
La Cause Marxiste, 3 editions, 1983–1984.
Le Marxiste-Léniniste, 52 editions, 1974–1982.
Michel, N. (2020), *Le roman de la politique*, Paris: La fabrique.
UCFML (1970), *La révolution prolétarienne en France et comment construire le Parti de l'époque de la pensée de Mao Tsé-toung*, Paris: François Maspero.
UCFML (1972), *Première année d'existence d'une organisation maoïste*, Paris: François Maspero.

16

Grace

Baylee Brits

One of the fundamental ambitions of Badiou's work is to construct a philosophical system immune to onto-theology. By positing mathematics as the sole science of ontology and demarcating the concept of truth to philosophy, Badiou manages to reject onto-theology while also making allowance for what he calls "polemical" arguments or "wagers" that respond to "undecidable" situations. Despite onto-theology being a major antagonist, Badiou has not written extensively about religion, though he comments on it in several of his major works, including *Conditions*. Religion is, of course, not a condition from which truths can emerge, unlike art, science, love or politics. Badiou's definition of religion reflects its exclusion from truth: "I propose to call 'religion' everything that presupposes that there is a continuity between truths and the circulation of meaning" (2008a: 24). For Badiou, God counts as a proxy for meaning. In the words of Jon Roffe and Justin Clemens, in their important article "Philosophy as Anti-Religion in the Work of Alain Badiou," this link implies "revealed presence" (2008: 349–51). This conviction closely echoes Lacan's definition of religion, particularly his concern that psychoanalysis might come to resemble a religion in the sense of a "church" rather than a belief system.[1] For this reason, Badiou's work on St Paul, in *St Paul and the Foundations of Universalism*, is often not considered a work on religion. In fact, Badiou writes that he is expressly interested in St Paul only insofar as this figure's life and teachings constitute a refutation of religion as an institution. Nonetheless, this book is perhaps the most fulsome elaboration of why Badiou does not consider religion to be a truth procedure, and a fascinating account of how key religious concepts—like the apostle, Grace and faith—relate to Badiou's philosophical system. As such, Badiou's work on Paul is helpful as a contextualization and, at times, interrogation of his own system.

This chapter will give an account of these concepts, primarily the idea of Grace, and show how these ideas offer a view into Badiou's system as part of a broader achievement of modernity. In particular, Badiou's work with religious concepts allows us to consider his rejection of onto-theology not as a contribution to the death of God, so famously proclaimed by Nietzsche and others, but to Ludwig Feuerbach's idea that "the task of the modern era was the realization and humanization of God—the transformation ... of theology into anthropology" (2019: 355). In other words, to gloss

Feuerbach, this is a transformation of theological questions, methods and assumptions into anthropological ones—a study of the condition of humanity in the world. The "humanisation of God," the "task of the modern era" for Feuerbach, is not solely an atheistic phenomenon. This "humanisation" is associated with theological modernism and the French *nouvelle théologie* movement, which included theologians like Henri de Lubac, Hans Küng, Karl Rahner and religious scholars like Thomas Sheehan. *Nouvelle Théologie* was a mid-twentieth-century French and German movement that emerged after decades of suppression of modernist work in Catholic theology. Theological modernism—not being a coherent or delimitable movement but rather a broad suite of concerns—includes a preoccupation with modern philosophy, including Kant and Hegel, as well as philosophies of experience that reconfigured the relationship between the faithful and the divine. It also involved a renewed focus in the twentieth century on the heresy of Docetism, the immanence of the kingdom of God and the humanity of the historical Jesus Christ, concerns that were famously condemned by Pope Pius X in his 1907 encyclical "Lamentabili Sane: Syllabus Condemning the Errors of the Modernists." Badiou's focus on the materialism of grace and on the universality of Paul's message links his work with the broader concerns of theological modernism; indeed *St Paul and the Foundations of Universalism* can be thought of as a contribution to a modernist reinterpretation of the epistles in the sense in which Pope Pius would have used the term "modernist."

In addition to situating Badiou's work in terms of a broad theological and scholarly trend toward the reinterpretation of Christ, assessing his interpretation of concepts like Grace allows us to consider the strange place of conceptual analogues in his work. Badiou is clear that Paul's "event" does not give rise to a genuine truth, and that his life and work remain only a "fable" from which we can understand how actual events and truths operate. In other words, Paul is constrained as an allegorical illustration of Badiou's system and Grace, as such, is an allegorical illustration of the "supernumerary" quality of the event. Reading Paul's epistles both as fabulous and as unique for their prioritization of the fable allies Badiou with literary modernists like Kafka and Beckett who resurrected the fable as a means of exploring existential conundrums and the relation between finitude and meaning. In this short entry I will canvas some of the problems that arise from this use of allegory or fabulation.

St Paul, and the Pauline epistles, provide regular source materials for modern philosophy—from Kant to Schopenhauer and Hegel to Heidegger, engagements with Paul are too numerous to detail here. The frequency of engagement with Paul is due to his angular relation to the early church, the simplicity and profundity of his reduction of Christian teaching to the claim "Christ is resurrected!" and the universal and cosmopolitan elements of his teachings which echo modern liberalism. Paul is distinct in the Christian canon for his efforts to include Gentiles in the church and to resist the conservative forces of the early church that sought to retain markers of belonging like circumcision. Paul is significant for—as Badiou puts it—preventing "Christianity from becoming a Jewish sect" by advocating for limitations to the observance of the Mosaic Law at the Jerusalem conference. In this very broad sense, it is easy to see how Paul resonates with a particularly modern and twentieth-century philosophical interest in universality, revolution and the nature of the divine.[2] In *St Paul and the Foundation of Universalism*, Badiou explores the radicalism of Paul at the Jerusalem conference, and considers why Paul's epistles were ultimately "appropriated" by the church, arguing that the early church founders preferred to integrate a moderate Paul into the Christian canon rather than leave his work open to interpretation. In this sense, Badiou, like many other philosophers, renders Paul as distinct from the other apostles and as offering a purer and bolder vision of Jesus's significance than Peter or James.

It is well known that Paul's teachings rested on one profound claim: that Jesus was resurrected. This claim emerges from a vision of Christ experienced by Paul on the road between Jerusalem and Damascus which converted him from Pharisee to Christian. Badiou's interpretation of this is thrilling. Badiou writes that:

> Just as the Resurrection remains totally incalculable and it is from there that one must begin, Paul's faith is that from which he begins as a subject, and nothing leads up to it. The event—"it happened," purely and simply, in the anonymity of a road—is the subjective sign of the event proper that is the Resurrection of Christ. (2003: 17)

Badiou associates the necessity and power of Paul's fidelity to Jesus's resurrection with Grace: "This event is 'grace' (kharis). Thus, it is neither a bequest, nor a tradition, nor a teaching. It is supernumerary to all this and presents itself as pure givenness" (2003: 63). Badiou offers an account of Paul's radical "subtraction" of Jesus's teaching to a single statement of the resurrection, associating this with the simplicity of Grace, and the nature of Grace as an incursion of novelty outside of law and tradition. As such, for Badiou, Paul's teachings and his positions at the Jerusalem conference and in his epistles provide an important opportunity to explore the relation between history and event, status quo and novelty, militancy and institution.

Badiou's characterization of St. Paul as a militant figure, brought into being by an event that gives rise to a universal truth procedure (albeit one that remains a fable), allows him to concretize the many abstractions of his philosophy through the narrative of a well-known figure. Paul enables Badiou to present an account of the decisions made by a militant subject, explore the relationship between that militant and truth, and offer a substantial consideration of the textual complexities involved in interpreting the gospel. In particular, Paul functions as a tale of "rupture," bringing "forth the entirely human connection, whose destiny fascinates me, between the general idea of a rupture, an overturning, and that of a thought-practice that is this rupture's subjective materiality" (2003: 2). Badiou is explicit about his dissociation of Paul from Christianity: "For me, truth be told, Paul is not an apostle or a saint. I care nothing for the Good News he declares, or the cult dedicated to him. But he is a subjective figure of primary importance" (2003: 1). Paul is important because he illustrates two key traits of truth: that it is singular, and that it comes from a "subjective declaration." Badiou writes:

> First, since truth is eventual, or of the order of what occurs, it is singular. It is neither structural, nor axiomatic, nor legal. No available generality can account

for it, nor structure the subject who claims to follow in its wake. Consequently, there cannot be a law of truth. Second, truth being inscribed on the basis of a declaration that is in essence subjective, no preconstituted subset can support it; nothing communitarian or historically established can lend its substance to the process of truth. Truth is diagonal relative to every communitarian subset; it neither claims authority from, nor (this is obviously the most delicate point) constitutes any identity. (2003: 14)

This is a striking interpretation of some of the ideas that Paul is famous for: that the wise have no advantage over the unschooled, that the new truth of Christianity makes core aspects of Judaic law redundant, and that there is no distinction between Jew and Gentile. With the emphasis on Paul as a "subjective figure," we can remember Badiou's statements in *Being and Event* about the creation of the subject: "I call 'subject' the bearer of a fidelity, the one who bears a process of truth. The subject, therefore, in no way pre-exists the process. [. . .] We might say that the process of truth induces a subject" (2001: 43). Paul's work, for Badiou, exemplifies "a subject without identity and a law without support" that can provide "the foundation for the possibility of a universal teaching" (2003: 5). And yet, by virtue of the religious content of this "truth," Paul is also "a major figure of antiphilosophy" (2003: 17). This means that "the enunciative position is obviously part of the statement's protocol" (2003: 17). Paul's status as an "anti-philosopher" rather than a genuine subject to truth comes from the subjective nature of his revelation and conversion and the fact that he preaches and organizes on the basis of this singular experience.

Badiou admits to having never, personally, read Paul religiously, and he uses the word "fable" to indicate his own reaction to the epistles but also to unmoor Paul from either history or religion, claiming that his chief obligation is to a subjective process. For Badiou, the content of Paul's truth is dispensable because it is religious. But his conversion, declaration of truth and apostolic ministry are all of primary importance: he is a militant figure that embodies the bringing into being of novelty and the supernumerary qualities of the event. Badiou writes that "Paul is a poet-thinker of the event, as well as one who practices and states the invariant traits of what can be called the militant figure. He brings forth the entirely human connection, whose destiny fascinates me, between the general idea of a rupture, an overturning, and that of a thought-practice that is this rupture's subjective materiality" (2003: 2). So Paul, here, is a militant but one without a genuine truth: he is significant only in abstraction. Badiou resolves this problem by claiming him as a poet-thinker, one who represents key tenets of Badiou's system without actually realizing them. For Badiou, Paul is illustration, not example. Not wanting to be bogged down in exegesis or history, Badiou renders Paul significant for the "poetry" of his life (2003: 2). This rhetorical sleight of hand is common to allegory, where there is a discrepancy between appearance and meaning. A key issue in Badiou's work on Paul is whether this maneuver is successful: can he show that Paul fulfills all the requirements of the militant, but withhold him from the category of genuine truth, and, as such, withhold religion from the category of "condition"?

Roland Boer has addressed this potential knot in Badiou's work in his chapter "The Fables of Alain Badiou," which explores the important and, at times, unsettling tensions between "the rigorous ontology of mathematics and the structures of narrative, or between fiction and argument, image and formula, poem and matheme, or Anglo-American analytic rationalism and continental lyricism" in Badiou's work (2009: 155). He argues, here, that despite the overt "banishing" of theology from Badiou's system, it remains as a ghostly presence, perpetually arising only in order to be contained. One of Boer's most important points is that the "play" between "fable and truth" in *St Paul* is one key indication that theology may resemble a spectral fifth condition in Badiou's work, even though it explicitly violates his axiom that "the One is Not" (2009: xxi, 156). Boer claims that Badiou hits a problem by claiming that Paul's "event is a fabrication and the truth associated with it is a 'fable'" while simultaneously maintaining that the "fable and truth exhibit the exemplary features of the procedures of truth" (2009: xxi). Boer does not suggest that this actually "destabilizes" Badiou's system, but rather that it implies a closer association between the fable and truth than Badiou would admit.

This leads us to a significant feature of Badiou's consideration of Paul. Paul is not only a fable himself but is marked out by the creation or prioritization of a fable that he enacts by declaring that "Christ is resurrected." Rather than prioritizing Jesus's life or teachings, Badiou notes that Paul makes everything revolve around a *"pointe fableux."* In Badiou's words, "A 'fable' is that part of a narrative that, so far as we are concerned, fails to touch on any Real, unless it be by virtue of that invisible and indirectly accessible residue sticking to every obvious imaginary" (2003: 4) Paul focuses not on the teachings of Jesus or the facts of his life, but on the "fabulous element"—the resurrection—which is unverifiable or, in Badiou's words, "cannot be reduced to any objective aggregate, either by its cause or by its destination" (2003: 5). This failure to "touch on" the Real means that Paul's convictions are not ultimately "evental"; the proclamation of the resurrection does not properly constitute a "rupture." Grace is the quality or process that allows this fabulous element of Jesus's life to become foundational for Paul's teachings. For Badiou, Grace "means that thought cannot wholly account for the brutal starting over on the path of life in the subject, which is to say, for the re-discovered conjunction between thinking and doing" (2003: 84). And it is Grace that allows Badiou to posit that it is "the absence of proof" that is all important for those who recognize Paul's truth (2003: 50). For Badiou, then, this means that the Christ-event is "incalculable" (2003: 50).

Badiou argues that Paul departs from the opposition between the Judaic figure of the prophet and the Greek figure of the philosopher to propose a third figure exempt from the laws of the former two. This third figure is the apostle. In contrast to the prophet and the philosopher, the apostle has a militant fidelity to the event. This is not least due to the apostolic position being universally available because it does not require special knowledge. The apostle declares the event of Christ's resurrection, which associates this figure with Grace rather than the knowledge or wisdom of the priest or the philosopher:

Whence the necessity of constantly linking resurrection to our resurrection, of proceeding from singularity to universality and vice versa: "If the dead do not resurrect, Christ is not resurrected either. And if Christ is not resurrected, your faith is in vain" (1 Cor. 15:12-14). In contrast to the fact, the event is measurable only in accordance with the universal multiplicity whose possibility it prescribes. In this sense it is grace, and not history. (2003: 45)

Badiou uses a section from Corinthians (1.1.17) to reinforce this point. Paul claims that "For Christ did not send me to baptize but to preach the gospel, and not with eloquent wisdom, lest the cross of Christ be emptied of its power. For the preaching of the cross is folly to those who are perishing, but to us who are saved it is the power of God. For it is written, 'I will destroy the wisdom of the wise, and thwart the cleverness of the clever'" (2003: 46). Badiou uses this quote to powerfully illustrate the relation between Grace and the Event with the apostolic figure, who is unique because they declare a truth that is "supernumerary" to the law.

The focus on Grace and the universal qualities of the event situate Badiou in terms of a broader modern tradition of interpreting ethics, truth and revolution as exceeding human finitude. This is explored at length by Peter Dews in "States of Grace: The Excess of the Demand in Badiou's Ethics of Truths." Dews argues that Badiou attempts—as many philosophers of modernity have done—to demarcate an ethics in that which exceeds humanity—that "superhumanity" that we see when an individual becomes a Subject to truth in fidelity to an event—but which is no longer religious. This ethics should occupy the domain of the religious transformed by a philosophy of multiplicity and which bears no trace of the One. Dews finds a direct answer to the questions that Badiou poses in *Ethics* in *St Paul*: not only a secularized Grace but a materialized Grace (2004: 114). Badiou writes that "it is incumbent upon us to found a materialism of grace through the strong, simple idea that every existence can one day be seized by what happens to it and subsequently devote itself to that which is valid for all, or as Paul magnificently puts it, 'become all things to all men'" (2003: 66). For Dews, the fact that the event resembles Grace illustrates that "Badiou's ethical thought can be placed squarely within the tradition that understands the ethical demand as exceeding, almost by definition, our finite human capacities to satisfy it" and, despite their antithetical views, this links Badiou to a philosophical tradition, which retains the super-human but foregoes God that is most clearly exemplified by Kant. Dews claims that the core question of Badiou's ethics, and, by extension Badiou's work on religion, is as follows: "how do we escape from the 'animal's desire to grab its socialized chance' and find our way towards the 'Good as the superhumanity of humanity?'" (2004: 114).

Dews also signals an important problem in Badiou's work that the concept of Grace reveals. He shows this problem by contrast with Kant's ideas about Grace, particularly the fact that Kant recognized that Grace implies a separation between action and demand that can never be closed. This gap is, Dews argued, the essence of Grace, and that's why the concept remains a fundamentally religious one (or, perhaps, a religious or ethical one). Dews argues that, by exporting Grace out of religion and into the truth procedures, Badiou closes the gap between demand and action, essentially overriding the concept. Dews contrasts Badiou's notion of Grace with Schopenhauer's, in order to bring into relief the novelty—and potential problem—with Badiou's idea:

for Schopenhauer, we may experience grace, as the dissolution of an oppressive phenomenal reality, but this is not an experience of engagement or activism. On the contrary, since our practical interests are inevitably expressed in instrumental form, they perpetuate the very world of suffering from which we long to escape. Badiou, by contrast, fuses the transformative experience, the truth-event, and the orientation to practice. And it is precisely this which should give cause for alarm. Indeed, one might wonder whether Badiou's ethics should not be regarded as a form of "fanaticism" in the Kantian sense—the articulation of an "imagined inward experience" of being touched by grace. (2004: 117)

Dews's concerns seem to overlap, here, with those of Boer. While Dews worries about the "fusing" of experience, event and practice, Boer is concerned with the ejection of precisely one of the elements that might prevent this "fusing" in other philosophical systems: the presence of the fable.

Badiou's ambition to consider Paul as an example for his philosophical system, while simultaneously denying any association with religion from the "fable," notably results in a figure that at times resembles the twentieth-century Jesus that was imagined by the so-called "modernists" or "neo-modernists" of theology. The need to "materialize" Grace is not exclusive to the atheistic Badiou, and liberalizing figures in the twentieth-century Catholic church, too, sought to recast Grace and "humanize"—to go back to Feuerbach's quote—the figure of Christ in the way that Badiou attempts to "humanize" Paul.

There is only space, in this short entry, to consider one example. Karl Rahner—one of the most important and philosophically interesting theologians of the twentieth century—was deeply influenced by Heidegger. His work was innovative for its opposition to various Christian dualisms—between the human and the divine, the corporeal and the spiritual. In his *Foundations of Christian Faith* he provides a definition of Grace that—while remaining fundamentally theological (and thereby attached to "the One" and linking truth and meaning)—provides a version of the sort of materialism that Badiou seeks. Rahner writes: "In this sense the world is our mediation to God in his self-communication in grace, and in this sense there is for Christianity no separate and sacral realm where alone God is to be found" (1982: 151). This quote resonates with Badiou's own desire to construct a materialism of Grace. Like Badiou, Rahner's Grace has little to do with divine agency or some incursion from a transcendental realm but is thoroughly located in the material world and, as such, is bestowed upon all. In a review of Rahner's *Foundations of Christian Faith*, Thomas Sheehan glosses his notion of Grace, writing that "grace is not added on to nature, as in Luther's simile of snow falling on a dunghill, so much as nature is already embedded in grace. Thus all persons are 'Christian'—that is, caught up in God's universal saving grace—by the very fact that they exist, regardless of whether they are baptized" (1982: n.p).

These sorts of sentiments are echoed by Sheehan, in his classic 1986 text *The First Coming*. Sheehan's reassessment of early Christianity and the significance of the resurrection argues for a reinterpretation of the kingdom of God whereby "God's act of reigning, and this meant—here lay the revolutionary force of Jesus' message—that God, as God, had identified himself without remainder with his people. The reign of God meant the incarnation of God" (1986: 61). Of course, these theological and scholarly interpretations of Grace and their erasure of the separation between the divine and the human, the transcendent and the material, are far removed in intention and discourse from Badiou's work. But the fact that they echo some of his pronouncements so closely demonstrates the persistent association in the twentieth century between the humanization of Christ or the materialization of Grace and the status or structures of religion. This is then illustrative of the complicating factors facing Badiou's foray into Pauline militancy and concepts associated with Christianity, particularly surrounding the impossibility of the association between the One and truth.

The various criticisms of Badiou's work on religion, particularly around his use of the fable, and his association between grace and the event, illustrate the specificity of Badiou's task and the thorniness of appropriating some religious ideas while rejecting the religion itself. The attempt to relegate Paul to the fable is strangely contradicted when precisely the *pointe fableux* of Paul's teachings is what is essential to a declaration of the event. Similarly, the close connection that Dews observes between event and action—co-implicated and even co-temporal in the creation of a subject—is in danger or erasing the specificity that the concept of Grace offers, the quality of exceeding human finitude. And yet Badiou succeeds in the non-religious but recuperative nature of his task in the sense that he clarifies the radicalism of Paul, which is seen most clearly when Paul is held apart from the Church and the other apostles. Whether he manages to contain Paul in the domain of allegory successfully and whether concepts like Grace can travel into philosophy without religious residue is an open question.

Notes

1 See Mads Peter Karlson's work "Badiou's Critique of Religion" for a discussion of this.
2 Each of these topics is addressed in the exhaustive collection *Paul and the Philosophers*, eds. Ward Blanton and Hent De Vries (2013).

Works Cited

Badiou, A. (2001), *Ethics: An Essay on the Understanding of Evil*, trans. P. Hallward, London and New York: Verso.
Badiou, A. (2003), *St Paul the Foundation of Universalism*, trans. R. Brassier, Stanford: Stanford University Press.
Badiou, A. (2008a), *Conditions*, trans. S. Corcoran, London and New York: Continuum.
Blanton, W. and H. de Vries (2013), *Paul and the Philosophers*, New York: Fordham University Press.
Boer, R. (2009), "The Fables of Alain Badiou," in *Criticism of Religion: On Marx and Theology II*, 155–180, Leiden and Boston: Brill.

Clemens, J. and J. Roffe (2008), "Philosophy as Anti-Religion in the Work of Alain Badiou," *SOPHIA* 47: 345–358.

Dews, P. (2004), "States of Grace: The Excess of the Demand in Badiou's Ethics of Truths," in Peter Hallward (ed.), *Think Again: Alain Badiou and the Future of Philosophy*, London: Bloomsbury.

Feuerbach, L. (2019), "From *Principles of the Philosophy of the Future*. (1843)," in Marina F. Bykova (ed.), *The German Idealism Reader: Ideas, Responses and Legacy*, New York: Bloomsbury Academic Publishing.

Karlsen, M. P. (2018), "On Alain Badiou's 'Critique of Religion,'" *International Journal of Philosophy and Theology* 79 (1–2): 36–59.

Rahner, K. (1982), *Foundations of Christian Faith*, Freiburg: Herder and Herder.

Sheehan, T. (1982), "The Dream of Karl Rahner," *The New York Review of Books*, February. Available online: https://www.nybooks.com/articles/1982/02/04/the-dream-of-karl-rahner/.

Sheehan, T. (1986), *The First Coming: How the Kingdom of God Became Christianity*, New York: Random House.

17

Ontology and Greater Logic

John Cleary

The goal of Alain Badiou's philosophy is to demonstrate, against the dominant ideology of relativism, that there are truths. That is, that there are novelties in the domains of science, art, politics and love that are universal and created in a specific context.

Like a number of other philosophers, Badiou articulates these two aspects of truth by grounding them in the difference between being *qua* being and being in a specific place. Truths are creations that draw out what is in that place but does not initially appear. A philosophy of truths as creations therefore must present a theory of these different modalities of being. However, to do so in an essentially modern way requires that this articulation be fundamentally non-theological. For Badiou a contemporary ontology of truths must, in place of hypothesizing the existence of a god or its conceptual expressions, free truth from the sacred and the *aporias* that led to its disrepute.

To accomplish this, Badiou turns to modern mathematics. In *Being and Event* he presents an ontology based on a metaphysical reading of set theory as a theory of inconsistent multiplicity without unity. In *Logics of Worlds* he argues that Topos theory constitutes a greater logic in which multiplicity appears relationally in a purely objective way. In *Immanence of Truths* he returns to set theory, looking this time at the theory of large cardinals, to show that truths must be absolute in order to be both universal and particular. In this chapter, I give a basic outline of the mathematics that he uses to form his ontology and greater logic, and how this relates to his theory of truth, before touching on some basic questions about mathematics and philosophy.

Set Theory and the Ontology of Truths

Set theory has its origin in the discovery by Georg Cantor in the 1870s that the set of natural numbers $\{0,1,2,3,4...\}$ are smaller than the real numbers, which includes the former set plus fractions and irrational numbers like $\sqrt{2}$. This discovery was in fact the case for a more general theorem: given any set A, the set of all possible combinations of its elements—its set of subsets, $P(A)$—is necessarily going to be bigger than it. If a set has n elements we can easily show that the size of the set of its subsets is 2^n. In the case of natural numbers, we can associate every string or subset of natural numbers with a real number, which meant that the real numbers have the same size as the set of all subsets of natural numbers. When applied to infinite sets, this implies that there are different sizes of infinity sets. But, at this point, mathematicians had no way of comparing the sizes of these infinities.

So, Cantor developed a theory of infinite ordinal and cardinal numbers. The smallest infinite number he called ω, which he thought of as coming after all the natural numbers: $1, 2, 3 \ldots n \ldots \omega, \omega+1, \omega+2 \ldots$ Among these infinite ordinal numbers, there are also cardinal numbers whose elements cannot be put in a one-to-one correspondence with any ordinal that precedes it. These mark the different sizes of infinity and are known as the alephs, $\aleph_0, \aleph_1, \aleph_2 \ldots$ The size of the natural numbers is $\aleph_0$, and so the size of real numbers is but what is the cardinality of $2^{\aleph_0}$? Cantor speculated that it was the same size as the next infinite cardinal, $\aleph_1$, so that $2^{\aleph_0} = \aleph_1$. This is known as the continuum hypothesis.

Not long after being proposed, however, set theory was beset in the late nineteenth and early twentieth centuries with some serious paradoxes, most famously of course was Russell's paradox, which shows that, despite what some thought at the time, not every well-formed predicate has an extension. Consider the set of all sets that are not elements of themselves, if it is a member of itself, then it is not a member of itself and vice versa. To avoid these, mathematicians set out the fundamental propositions or axioms of the theory, and the standard version is known as Zermelo-Fraenkel set theory with the axiom of Choice (ZFC). ZFC has about eight or nine axioms (Jech 2002: 3), but we will only look at four to keep things simple:

1. The axiom of the null set: there exists a set ∅ that has no elements.
2. The axiom of infinity: there exists an infinite ordinal, ω.
3. The power-set axiom. To every set x there corresponds the set of all the possible combinations of its elements $P(x)$.
4. The union axiom. To every set x there corresponds the set of all the elements of the elements of the original set $\bigcup x$.

The axioms of ZFC are taken to present the basic structure of the universe of all possible sets known as V, the cumulative hierarchy. This universe is built up of different levels that are indexed by the ordinal numbers beginning from the empty set. Each level is either formed by the power set of the level below, if it is a successor ordinal (e.g., $V_4 = P(V_3)$), or by taking the union of all the levels below if it is indexed by a limit ordinal (like V_ω). V itself, however, is not a set; it does not strictly speaking exist within the universe of sets (see Figure 17.1).

However, two proofs demonstrated that the continuum hypothesis cannot be proved or disproved within ZFC since the hypothesis and its negation are both consistent with the axioms. The first proof by Kurt Gödel uses constructible sets, that is, sets that are definable by a predicate. For example, if we take the predicate ϕ: "the set of natural numbers greater than 1 and less than 7," then the set $M = \{2, 3, 4, 5, 6\}$ is defined by phi. The constructible universe L is the class of all such sets and the axioms of ZFC are true

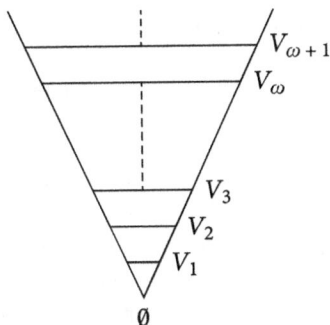

Figure 17.1 The set theoretical universe V.

in it, as is an additional axiom of constructability which says that the universe of sets is the constructible universe ($V = L$). The continuum hypothesis is derivable from the axioms of ZFC plus $V = L$.

The second proof by Paul Cohen uses a technique called forcing over generic extensions. We assume the existence of a set of constructible sets in which the axioms are true. Mathematicians call this a model of the axioms. It is possible to show that there will be subsets of some set, for example of ω, which are not constructible, called generic subsets. They are generic because they have some of the elements of every constructible subset of omega in that model, and so they are not completely describable by any of those predicates. But, since our model is constructible, these generic sets themselves are not elements of the model.

However, we can add them to create a generic extension, and when we do so, certain statements that were undecidable in our model, being neither provable nor disprovable from the axioms, turn out to be decided in the generic extension. For a generic set G, we say that p forces ϕ if $p \in G$ implies that ϕ is true in the generic extension. To set up this relation of forcing one builds a special forcing language in my original model in which a name is given to every element in the generic extension, including the generic set itself. An element p forces a statement ϕ made in the forcing language if and only if the names in the statement ϕ refer to elements in the generic extension that satisfy the statement. Cohen used this general technique to show that we can extend our model with as many generic subsets of ω as we wish such that the number of subsets of ω exceeds $\aleph_1$, thus forcing the continuum hypothesis to be false in the generic extension.

In *Being and Event* Badiou argues that **ZFC** presents an ontology of pure multiplicity in which there is no fundamental unity, either in the form of atoms or a whole. In the set theoretical universe, every set is made up of other sets that are all ultimately generated from the empty set by using the power set and union operations. Once we admit different sizes of infinity, the universe is effectively unlimited in the sense that there is no set of all sets, no whole.

Gödel's and Cohen's proofs form an ontological schema for truths as pure multiples. The being of a situation where a truth emerges is a model of **ZFC**, and Badiou calls the structure of subsets in the model the state of the situation (Badiou 2005: 93). The dominant modality of the relationship between a situation and its state is described ontologically by Gödel's constructivist model (Badiou 2005: 287). Constructivism determines what is possible as what can be constructed via well-defined predicates from already existing things and knowledge. It is consequently a kind of particularism, linking existence always to particular properties. The being of a truth in contrast is a generic set which is universal since any element that is part of the situation can belong to it. However, since truths are processes, the generic set is what this process *would* be, were it completed. The process though is connected to its generic being by the relation of forcing. In *Being and Event*, a truth procedure revolves around certain undecidable statements, and those in the procedure attempt to discover elements within the situation which will force these undecidable statements on the basis of a projection about what the truth as generic set will be (Badiou 2005: 401).

Greater Logic and the Singularity of Truths

If being as such is inconsistent multiplicity, it must nonetheless become consistent, appearing in a unified way and in relations to other beings, otherwise it would be total chaos. Forcing over generic extensions gives an ontology form of truths, but what determines how each procedure appears in a unified and specific way in a given time and place?

In response to these kinds of problems, Badiou proposes in *Logics of Worlds* a greater logic of worlds, object and relations using Grothendieck toposes. A Grothendieck topos is a mathematical universe whose building blocks are categories. A category is a collection of objects and a set of morphisms or arrows between the objects. These arrows satisfy a few axioms, the most important one being that if there is an arrow $f: A \to B$ and an arrow $g: B \to C$ then there will be another arrow $g \circ f: A \to C$, the two paths between A and C being identical, as in the following diagram:

Basic examples of categories are sets and functions, groups and group homeomorphism, and topological spaces and continuous functions.

Arrows between categories are called functors. A functor $F: C \to D$ maps every object A of the category C to an object FA in the category D and every arrow between two objects A and B is mapped to an arrow between FA and FB. We can in turn take functors as objects of a category, and the morphisms between them are known as natural transformations. These are crucial for looking at structural analogies between different branches of mathematics.

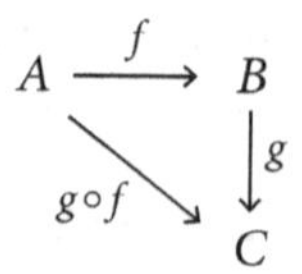

$$A \xrightarrow{f} B \\ \searrow_{g \circ f} \downarrow_{g} \\ C$$

Figure 17.2 Commutative diagram of morphisms.

To analyze the internal structure of objects we need what's called a sub object classifier, which, in *Logics of Worlds*, Badiou calls the transcendental. One way of specifying a subset of a set is via what is called its characteristic function: take a set A, the set $2 = \{0, 1\}$, and all the functions between A and 2. If $A = \{a, b, c\}$, we can think of a subset $B = \{b, c\}$ of A as being characterized through a function χ_B such that $x \in B$ if and only if $\chi_B = 1$. We can similarly determine the elements of A as the characteristic arrows χ_y where $\chi_y = 1$ for one element only of A.

A sub object classifier generalizes this idea: it is an object Ω in a category and the morphisms between any other object A and Ω allow us to determine A's sub objects. In this context, an element of A will correspond to an arrow f between A and Ω where $f(x) = f(x') \rightarrow x = x'$. Badiou calls these atomic functions, because they are the basic units of objects (Badiou 2009: 248). A point to note here is that because the sub object classifier is an ordered set it is also a category, with its elements as objects and the order relation $\alpha \leq \beta$ as its arrows $\alpha \rightarrow \beta$.

If the sub object classifier is a complete Heyting algebra, which means that there is a maximum and minimum element, and every subset is bounded from above and below, it can also be used to determine the internal logic of the category. Take the sub object classifier $\Omega = \{0, 1\}$ and say that the statement "$a \in A$" is true when the characteristic arrow for the element a gives me the value 1 and false otherwise. The ordering properties of the sub object classifier allow us also to give a semantic value of words like "and," "or" as well as "for all . . ." and "there exists . . ." In particular, we can give a value to the statement "there exists a c" such that if c is assigned the maximum value then it exists absolutely in the category, whereas, if it is given the minimum degree then it "inexists" as Badiou says. Consequently, changing the sub object classifier will change the logic of the category: if the classifier is $\{0,1\}$ and $0 \leq 1$ then we get a classical logic where the law of the excluded middle holds (every statement is either true or false). However, a sub object classifier that has a different structure (non-Boolean) will produce a different non-classical logic.

A Grothendieck topos is a category of functors, called sheaves, from a sub object classifier to the category of sets. Given a set A, a functor in this category $F_A : \Omega \rightarrow Set$ associates with each $p \in \Omega$, the subset B of A whose elements are those atomic functions whose value is P. For this functor to give a coherent picture of the structure of A we require first that these atomic functions correspond to the actual elements of A as a set. If f is an atomic function then there must be an $\alpha \in A$ such that the atomic function

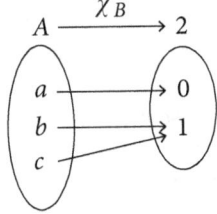

Figure 17.3 The characteristic function of the subset B.

is its characteristic function. Second, the values associated to the various subsets of A must be compatible, meaning that they don't assign different values to the same element. As a result, the order of belonging to the set is synthesized with the structure of the sub object classifier. The arrows of this category are natural transformations between the functors, and they preserve the basic indexation of Ω.

To be a mathematical universe, a category must have, for any object, first, what are called limits. A crucial example of a limit is the product of two objects X and Y, which is equivalent to the set of all pairs of elements of the two objects. A categorical universe must also have the exponential X^Y for any objects X and Y, which gives us the set of all arrows between these two objects. So, in order to be a universe, the category of sets in the topos needs to be big enough to contain all the limits and exponentials, But how big is that?

One standard approach is to assume the existence of a set U as universe for our category of sets such that if $x, y \in U$ then the sets that result from performing the usual set theoretical operation on them (power set, Cartesian product etc.) will also be elements of U (Borceux 2008: 2). Any set with this property is said to be closed vis-à-vis the operations in question. This closure property in our category of our set means that all the constructions that we want in the topos will exist.

Badiou sees in the theory of Grothendieck toposes, a materialist theory of worlds because the relational or virtual structures of arrows that determine appearance are grounded in the constitution of an underlying universe of sets or, to put it another way, the sets are the matter upon which morphisms operate. More specifically, he argues that Topos theory presents two postulates of materialism. The first is the correspondence between elements and atomic functions (Badiou 2009: 250), whereas the second is the dependency of the existence of all relations (limits and exponentials) on the closure properties of the underlying set (Badiou 2009: 317).

The first postulates make possible the synthesis of the underlying set and the transcendental in the structure of the object. The most important consequence of this is that every object has an inexistent element. For any set A there is a function that assigns to all of its element the lowest degree of the transcendental, and this function is atomic. By the postulate of materialism, this is a function of appearing of an $\alpha \in A$, making α the inexistent of the object (Badiou 2009: 341). The second principle implies that all relations are grounded within the world itself (Badiou 2009: 313).

This greater logic allows Badiou to explain the specific or singular nature of a truth procedure in two crucial ways. The first is what is specific to an event. The inexistent has the minimal degree of the appearance, but an event as radical and paradoxical rupture has the effect of making this inexistent appear as completely as possible in the world. This distinguishes an event from other types of changes (Badiou 2009: 376). The second—although we can't present the details of it here—is that the theory of worlds as toposes means he can account for the specific way in which some truth procedures continue, others stall, while others can't manage to start after the event. Mathematically this is dealt with using the theory of points in toposes (Badiou 2009: 403).

Ontology and the Absolute

Conceptually, what this seems to imply is that the duality of sets and relations corresponds to that of absolute and relative, and indeed that does seem to be the position of *Logics of Worlds*. The absolute or maximal appearing of the being of truths would be then the guarantee for their transworldliness, which Badiou argues for at the beginning of that book (Badiou 2009: 9). But under what conditions is the absolute appearing of a set in a world really absolute?

In the *Immanence of Truths* Badiou uses a part of set theory called the theory of large cardinals, which are enormously large counting sets, to approach this question. I don't have space to present all the details here, so I will just give an indication of the general strategy: let us start with the universe of sets V, and rather than operate directly on V, let's take a subclass M of the universe and a map $j : V \to M$, called an elementary embedding. This maps every element of V onto an element of M such that if the statement ϕ is true about α in V, and $j(a) = p, p \in M$, then ϕ will be true of p too. If we can show that there is an elementary embedding that is "non-trivial," meaning that not every element of V is mapped to itself, then we can show that the universe of sets V is not equal to L, that there are lots of non-constructible sets in V, and that the types or forms of infinity in the universe are limitless. It turns out that the existence of such an M and a non-trivial embedding follow from the existence of certain large cardinals called measurable cardinals and a number set theorists call $0^{\#}$, which is not itself a large cardinal, but is closely connected to various types of large cardinals (Jech 2002: 285–92).

There are two important things to note here. First, truths can be absolute creations because they emerge in the difference between the classes M, which Badiou calls attributes of the absolute or the place of absolutization of a truth—suggesting that they are the ontological layer of worlds where truths appear (Badiou 2018: 416). What this implies though is that a truth in a world approximates its absolute being in V (Badiou 2018: 393). Second, as neither $0^{\#}$ nor measurable cardinals can be proved to exist in ZFC, we must introduce axioms into our theory. Thus, it is by axiomatically deciding on the existence of super large forms of infinity that a truth process can touch on its absoluteness (Badiou 2018: 447, 525).

Ontology, Logic and Mathematics

All this raises a series of important questions. The first is, why mathematics? The first answer to this is that mathematics can present an ontology that is not premised on the existence of a fundamental unity. Western metaphysics has traditionally taken unity as its starting point and as such understood the being of something as what gives it unity. This leads, however, to what Heidegger called an onto-theology in which the being of beings is ultimately posed as the highest being that is infinite and transcendent (Badiou 2015: 9). Existence is thus divided between the infinity of a transcendent One and the finitude of the human world. But this is tantamount to the claim that this world cannot truly change, since the forms of finite existence are fixed by this transcendent unity, and what is universal or absolute can only exist in this One. A contemporary example this ontotheological schema is the ideological belief that only one type of society is possible—Capitalism—whose necessity, as the infinite expansion of the market, rules over us as workers and consumers (Badiou 2018: 79). Consequently, understanding being as infinite pure multiplicity must be the starting point for all contemporary ontologies.

But in order to not fall into a form of relativism, this mathematical ontology has to be consistent with a theory of truths as subjective procedures. This consistency is based on mathematics' relationship to what Lacan called the real. For Lacan the real, as the cause of the subject's unconscious desire, is beyond the symbolic and imaginary, and in fact it resists any representation in these registers. It is thus not to be mistaken for the object as the referent of a signifier, which is a product of the symbolic and the imaginary. The real is, as Lacan says, the impossible. However, mathematics provides a model for the theory of the real because mathematical formalization can inscribe its real in discourse through its impasses and paradoxes (Lacan 1999: 93). This inscription can occur because, as a mode of writing, mathematics operates exclusively on letters that are govern by explicit rules, and so it has no external referent (Lacan 1999: 48). What mathematics as a discourse speaks about is consequently entirely internal to it and the impasses that emerge are thus real impasses of it as a discourse.

In *Being and Event* Badiou argues that pure multiplicity is the real of mathematics. The set theoretical universe V is the necessary space within which all forms of sets appear, but whose existence cannot follow from the axioms of **ZFC**. V is nonetheless "sutured" to mathematical discourse by the axiomatic decisions that the sets $\emptyset$ and ω exist, and then built up through operations on these letters (Badiou 2005: 67). The theory's axiomatic formalization is essential to this because a definition of the pure multiple would determine it as an object and hence as a whole, which it is not. An axiomatic system alone can theorize the pure multiple without defining or naming it (Badiou 2005: 29). As the impossible, the real demands that a decision be made about it, which is exactly what an axiom is, not being derivable from any other statements in the theory.

The impasse of **ZFC** is inscribed in it in two ways. First, as the continuum hypothesis, which cannot be proved or disproved from the axioms. Second, as the banned existence of self-belonging sets, which formalize events (Badiou 2004: 98). These two modes of the real are articulated nonetheless through the decision of a subject. It is consistent with the axioms to say that the continuum can be any cardinal larger than ω, so long as it is what is called a successor cardinal (Badiou 2005: 280). How much bigger it is then must be decided, and how the subject decides is bound to their encounter with an event.

The second question is, why does Badiou propose a greater logic? Isn't his ontology sufficient? The first point to make here is that if mathematics is ontology, as Badiou maintains, then he needs to account for category theory since it says something essential about mathematics. In fact, some category theorists would argue it presents an alternative ontology to set theory. Badiou's response to this is that set theoretical ontology presents the form of truths—generic sets—but it doesn't tell us how a generic set emerges in a specific context. This requires a separate investigation, one that is nonetheless mathematical. It is moreover necessarily separate because of the non-completeness of truths and the absence of an absolute whole. If no whole exists, then no necessary connection exists between a given set and the possible relations that it can exist in (Badiou 2009: 36). Consequently, we cannot derive a theory of these relations from a theory of the pure multiple. An important example of this is the theory of the inexistent in a world since such a set may appear as nothing in one world and as something in another.

It would be a mistake, however, to think that mathematics is sufficient for theorizing truth, or for that matter the being of any situation. Mathematics finds its intrinsic limits as a discourse around the event, which it cannot theorize, that being the terrain of poetry (Badiou 2005: 191). Nor can we start with a mathematical theory and derive the structure of a non-mathematical world from it (Hallward 2004: 232). To the extent that we want to know something scientifically about that world, mathematics would indeed have to be involved in this knowledge. But a science must first establish its basic concepts, ideas and problems, and only then can it move back toward mathematics and be synthesized with some fragment of it.

But if that is the case, are truths really generic sets, or worlds toposes? These propositions are certainly not scientific claims, like statements in quantum physics. But a science can't tell us by itself what a scientific truth is, let alone what truth could be for love, art and politics. Philosophy, as a construction of a vision of truth in which its different types can be thought together under a single form must necessarily go beyond scientific knowledge at the same time as being consistent with it. Mathematics presents schemata that delineate an idea of truth that forms an orientation in thinking toward what is universal and absolute. The aim of this idea is not to present an objective structure of the world, but rather to ground new subjective possibilities.

Works Cited

Badiou, A. (2004), *Theoretical Writings*, ed. and trans. R. Brassier and A. Toscano, London: Continuum.
Badiou, A. (2005), *Being and Event*, trans. O. Feltham, London: Continuum.
Badiou, A. (2009), *Logics of Worlds*, trans. A. Toscano, London: Continuum.
Badiou, A. (2015), *Le Séminaire: Heidegger, L'être 3 – Figure du retrait*, Paris: Fayard.
Badiou, A. (2018), *L'immanence des Vérités*, Paris: Fayard.
Borceux, F. (1994), *Handbook of Categorical Algebra*, Cambridge: Cambridge University Press.
Hallward, P. (2004), *Think Again*, London: Continuum.
Jech, T. (2002), *Set Theory*, Berlin: Springer.
Lacan, J. (1999), *On Feminine Sexuality, The Limits of Love and Knowledge, 1972–1973*, trans. B. Fink, New York: Norton.

Contributors

Robert Boncardo has a PhD from the University of Sydney and Aix-Marseille University.. He is the author of *Mallarmé and The Politics of Literature* (2018) and, with Christian R. Gelder, *Mallarmé: Rancière, Milner, Badiou* (2017).

Bruno Bosteels teaches in the Department of Latin American and Iberian Cultures and the Institute for Comparative Literature and Society at Columbia University. His research covers a wide range of topics in literature, culture, and politics in modern Latin America as well as contemporary philosophy and political theory. He is currently preparing two new books, the first a sustained polemical engagement with contemporary post-Heideggerian thought, titled *Philosophies of Defeat: The Jargon of Finitude* (Verso) and the other, its utopian counterpart, The Mexican Commune (Duke University Press), which already has appeared in Spanish as *La comuna mexicana* (Akal, 2021)

Baylee Brits holds a PhD from the University of New South Wales and a research MA from the University of Amsterdam. She is the author of *Literary Infinities* (2017) and the co-editor of *Aesthetics After Finitude* (2016) and *The Covert Plant* (2018).

Arka Chattopadhyay is assistant professor of literary studies and philosophy in the Department of Humanities and Social Sciences at IIT Gandhinagar, India. He has published books including *Deleuze and Beckett, Knots: Post-Lacanian Psychoanalysis, Literature and Film* and *Gerald Murnane: Another World in This One*, and journals such as *Textual Practice, Interventions, Samuel Beckett Today/Aujourd'hui, Psychoanalysis, Culture and Society, Sound Studies* and *The Harold Pinter Review*. He has co-edited the book *Samuel Beckett and the Encounter of Philosophy and Literature* and has guest-edited the *SBT/A* issue on *Samuel Beckett and the Extensions of the Mind*. Arka is the founding editor of the online literary journal *Sanglap* (http://sanglap-journal.in/) and a contributing editor to *Harold Pinter Review*. His first monograph, *Beckett, Lacan and the Mathematical Writing of the Real*, was published by Bloomsbury Academic UK in 2019. He co-edited a volume on Nabarun Bhattacharya for Bloomsbury India in 2020and the volume *Ecological Entanglements* for Orient Blackswan in 2023. Arka has currently finished working on a monograph about Posthumanism, contracted by Orient Blackswan.

Soumyabrata Choudhury is associate professor at the School of Arts and Aesthetics, Jawaharlal Nehru University. He has authored *Theatre, Number, Event: Three Studies on the Relationship between Sovereignty, Power and Truth* (2013) and articles on ancient Greek liturgy, the staging of Ibsen, psychoanalysis, Nietzsche, Schiller and Hegel.

Choudhury is the author of *Ambedkar and Other Immortals: An Untouchable Research Programme* (2018). His latest book is *Now It's Come To Distances: Notes on Coronavirus and Shaheen Bagh, Association and Isolation* (2020).

John Cleary lives in Melbourne, Australia, and is completing a PhD at the University of Melbourne on the philosophy of Albert Lautman.

Justin Clemens is an associate professor in the School of Culture and Communication at the University of Melbourne. He has written extensively on European philosophy and psychoanalysis, and translated many texts of Alain Badiou into English. His recent publications include the translation of and commentary upon *The Pornographic Age* (2020) and *Happiness* (2017), as well as the edited the collection *Badiou and His Interlocutors* (2018), all with A. J. Bartlett.

Sigi Jöttkandt teaches English at the University of New South Wales. She is author of *Acting Beautifully: Henry James and the Ethical Aesthetic* (2005), *First Love: A Phenomenology of the One* (2010) and the forthcoming *The Nabokov Effect*. The co-founding editor of *S: Journal of the Circle for Lacanian Ideology Critique*, she is also co-founder and co-director of Open Humanities Press.

Michael J. Kelly lectures history, critical theory and the philosophy of history at Binghamton University (SUNY) and is a founding co-editor of Gracchi Books. His publications include *Isidore of Seville and the "Liber Iudiciorum": The Struggle for the Past in the Visigothic Kingdom* (2021) and, with Arthur Rose, the co-edited volume *Theories of History: History Read Across the Humanities* (2018). He is currently preparing a monograph on the concept of "human nature" in early medieval law and theology.

Alex Ling is associate professor in communication and media studies at Western Sydney University. He is the author of *Scandalous Times: Contemporary Creativity and the Rise of State-Sanctioned Controversy* (2021), *Badiou Reframed* (2017) and *Badiou and Cinema* (2011) and co-editor and translator, with A. J. Bartlett, of *Mathematics of the Transcendental* (2014).

James Martell is assistant professor of romance languages at Lyon College. He is the co-editor, with Arka Chattopadhyay, of *Samuel Beckett and the Encounter of Philosophy and Literature* (2013); with Eric Larsen has edited *Tattood Bodies: Theorizing Body Inscription across Disciplines and Cultures* (2022); and, with Fernanda Negrete, he has edited the special issue of *Samuel Beckett Today/Aujourd'hui*, "Beckett beyond Words" (2018). He has also published articles on Derrida, Deleuze, Beckett and the cinema of Béla Tarr. His book *Modernism, Self-Creation, and the Maternal: The Mother's Son* appeared in 2019.

Eloïse Mignon is studying for a PhD at the University of Melbourne. She has worked as an actress in Australia and France.

Christian R. Gelder holds a PhD in modern and contemporary literature from the University of Cambridge. He currently works as a research fellow in Macquarie University, Sydney. With Robert Boncardo, he is the editor and translator of *Mallarmé: Rancière, Milner, Badiou* (2017). He has written widely on and translated Alain Badiou.

Jean-Michel Rabaté is professor of English and comparative literature at the University of Pennsylvania, after having taught in Dijon, Paris, Montreal and Princeton. He is one of the managing editors of the *Journal of Modern Literature*. He chairs the Forum for Philosophy and Literature at the MLA. One of the founders of Slought Foundation, and a curator of exhibitions, conferences, lectures and conversations, he has been since 2008 a fellow of the American Academy of Arts and Sciences. He has authored twenty-five books and edited seventeen collections of essays. His recent titles include *Crimes of the Future*, *The Cambridge Introduction to Literature and Psychoanalysis*, *The Pathos of Distance*, *Think, Pig!*, *Les Guerres de Jacques Derrrida*, *Rust*, *Kafka L.O.L.*, as well as four collections of essays, *After Derrida*, *The New Beckett*, *Understanding Derrida, Understanding Modernism* and *Knots*.

Arthur Rose is a postdoctoral research fellow in English at the University of Exeter. He is the author of *Literary Cynics: Borges, Beckett, Coetzee* (2017); *Asbestos—The Last Modernist Object* (2022); and a co-editor of *Theories of History* (2018) and *Reading Breath in Literature* (2019).

Joseph Shafer is lecturer in English at Auburn University, specializing in critical theory, poetry & poetics, aesthetics, and twentieth-century American Literature. He has edited *The Collected Prose of Barbara Guest* and is co-editor of *The Selected Poems of Barbara Guest*. Essays have appeared in edited collections such as *Reading Lacan's Seminar XIII*, *That Tongue Be Time: Norma Cole and a Continuous Making*, and in journals *Textual Practice*, *Oxford Literary Review*, *Arizona Quarterly*, *Journal of American Literature*, *International Yearbook of Hermeneutics* among others. A 2021 interview with Rancière can also be found in *SubStance*. His current monograph introduces the in-differences appearing to arise within typographical space, as within the political and cultural landscapes of post-1945 American poetry.

Adity Singh is currently assistant professor of English and philosophy at the Indian Institute of Science Education and Research, Bhopal, India. She did her MA and PhD in critical theory at the University of Nottingham where she worked on the problem of freedom in Alain Badiou's philosophy. She is currently working on a book provisionally titled *Leaps Out of Circles: On Aleatory Dialectics*, in which she seeks to trace the emergence of a temporal, dialectical and revolutionary subjectivity in the interpretation of dialectical materialism proposed by Althusser and Badiou following Rousseau, Marx and the Epicureans.

Index

Adorno, Theodor 134
Agamben, Giorgio 35
Althusser, Louis 40, 43
Artaud, Antonin 6, 141, 186, 188–9, 194

Badiou, Alain
   "Affirmative Dialectics: from Logic to Anthropology" 28
   Ahmed Tetralogie 196
   Beckett: l'increvable désir 17
   Being and Event 7–8, 43–6, 51–3, 57, 60, 75, 110, 144, 153, 181, 193, 203, 208, 209, 221, 229, 230, 234
   Can Politics Be Thought? 216
   The Century 2, 37, 82, 83, 105, 168, 176, 186, 192, 193
   Cinema 114, 117, 121, 122, 135 n.3
   "Cinema and Philosophy" 113, 115
   Conditions 46–7, 68, 70, 71, 100, 105, 106, 110, 218
   The Factory as Evental Site 216
   Five Lessons on Wagner 169–74
   Handbook of Inaesthetics 18, 19, 30, 33, 67, 105, 109, 170, 187
   The Immanence of Truths 15, 19–24, 51–3, 56, 59, 60, 62, 63, 69, 70, 74, 77, 79, 136 n.11, 144–6, 150 n.7, 171, 177, 178, 190, 198 n.13, 203, 227, 233
   In Praise of Love 81, 84, 130–1
   In Praise of Theatre 124
   Lacan: Anti-Philosophy 3 75–7
   Logics of Worlds 40, 51, 53, 59, 60, 73, 89, 101, 133, 142, 169, 174, 231, 233
   Manifesto for Philosophy 47, 63, 203
   "Mark and Lack" 102
   Metapolitics 77, 98, 192
   Number and Numbers 73–4
   Petit panthéon portatif 141
   Philosophy and the Event 104, 106

   Philosophy for Militants 50
   Plato's Republic 16, 54–5
   The Pornographic Age 3
   The Rational Kernel of the Hegelian Dialectic 42
   The Rebirth of History 159
   "Rhapsody for the Theatre" 187, 188, 193
   St Paul and the Foundations of Universalism 218–21
   Theory of the Subject 43, 45, 78, 100–2, 104, 111, 172
Bazin, André 114
Beckett, Samuel 17–25, 33, 82, 138–40, 146, 150, 151 n.19, 190, 194
Benjamin, Walter 35–6, 186, 187
Berlioz, Hector 82, 84
Besant, Walter 129
Blanchot, Maurice 151 n.12
Brecht, Bertolt 29, 190, 194
Breton, André 82, 83, 86–8, 90, 91

Cantor, Georg 43, 66, 228
Celan, Paul 62, 203
Cohen, Paul 60, 70, 229

Deleuze, Gilles 114, 143, 189
Derrida, Jacques 138–50, 189
Descartes, René 66
Dickinson, Emily 208
Duchamp, Marcel 83, 119–21

Eagleton, Terry 128

Foucault, Michel 35, 41
Freud, Sigmund 38, 151 n.11

Galois, Évariste 59
Genet, Jean 3, 186, 195
Gödel, Kurt 70, 228

Greenberg, Clement   117–18, 136 n.12
Grotowski, Jerzy   26

Habermas, Jürgen   63
Handke, Peter   191
Hegel, G.W.F.   28, 40–8, 115, 204
Heidegger, Martin   57, 205, 209
Hölderlin, Friedrich   7, 8, 54, 56, 57, 203
Hugo, Victor   60
Hyppolite, Jean   40, 43

Isidore of Seville   156, 164 nn.8, 10, 13

James, Henry   127–35
Julian of Toledo   155, 164 nn.9, 14

Kant, Immanuel   66
Kojève, Alexandre   40, 43

Lacan, Jacques   14, 20, 33, 66–79, 84–5, 122, 140, 195, 234
Lacoue-Labarthe, Philippe   57, 58, 192, 204
Lenin, Vladimir   212, 214
Levin, Harry   1

Malevich, Kazimir   105, 106, 119, 121, 124 n.15
Mallarmé, Stephane   13–16, 18, 30–1, 38, 56, 57, 59, 82, 98–111, 205–7

Marx, Karl   28, 29, 40, 76, 212
Messiaen, Olivier   172, 176–8
Milner, Jean-Claude   41, 207

Nancy, Jean-Luc   58, 192, 204
Nietzsche, Friedrich   186, 187, 205, 218

Paul   218–25
Pessoa, Fernando   82
Plato   16, 50, 67, 108, 122, 127, 189, 197 nn.4–5

Rabi'a, Labid ben   31, 32, 110
Rancière, Jacques   57, 58, 61, 97–111, 124 n.10
Rimbaud, Arthur   81, 82, 203

Schönberg, Arnold   171, 174–6, 182 nn.10, 13
Stanislavski, Konstantin   194

Tagore, Rabindranath   194

Valéry, Paul   59

Wagner, Richard   169–74, 178–81, 188

Zedong, Mao and Maoism   15, 212–17
Žižek, Slavoj   157, 182 n.9

Index of Concepts

"Age of Poets"   2, 7, 47, 54–5, 203–10
alienation effect   190, 194, 198
anti-aesthetic   97, 124
anti-capitalism   39, 214
anti-Hegel   42, 47
antihistory   153–4, 156–9, 161–3
anti-mimetic   5, 98–9, 105–6, 108–9, 111
anti-philosophy   68, 75, 77, 221
anti-Platonic   108
antiquity   54, 63, 64, 154, 157
anti-rationalist   74
anti-theatricality   186–90, 192, 194, 196

art   2, 5–6, 20, 25–7, 37, 48, 52, 54, 56, 58–9, 82, 83, 97–9, 104–9, 111, 113–24, 140, 146, 168–71, 173–4, 177–8, 180–1, 186–8, 190–3, 196–8

capitalism   20, 28, 32, 33, 35–9, 56, 62, 69, 76, 78, 145, 162, 181, 191, 205, 215, 234
cinema   5–6, 108, 113–26, 135, 179, 191, 204
conditions   2, 5, 7, 35, 47, 50–2, 61, 63, 69, 75, 79, 81, 99, 101, 115, 127, 130, 156, 157, 186, 204, 205, 209, 218

cosmological tendency 177
covering-over 4, 13, 20–3, 52, 60, 62, 69–70, 78, 79, 136, 145

difference
  identical 130–2
  love/sex 48, 72, 81, 83, 85–6, 130–1, 135
  minimal 42–3, 102–3, 118–20, 122, 190
  negation of 146
  of the one 73
  strong 102–4

eternal return 5, 24, 50–1, 59, 63–4
event 2, 8, 17–19, 27–9, 31, 34, 36, 38, 47, 51, 57–9, 69, 70, 74–9, 85, 87, 99, 100, 104–6, 111, 127, 131–2, 141, 143, 148, 149, 153–63, 169–70, 173–6, 180–1, 188, 192–5, 207, 208, 216, 219–25, 232, 234, 235

fidelity 8, 17, 19, 92, 102, 131, 133, 135, 155–8, 161, 169, 182, 212, 220–3

gesture 4, 15, 26–31, 33–4, 50, 51, 59, 66, 70, 188, 206, 207
grace 7, 19, 31, 32, 157–9, 174, 181, 218–25

history 4–8, 21, 25, 27–9, 33, 37–40, 43, 48, 52–4, 56, 60, 62–4, 66, 69, 77, 78, 105, 123, 143, 146, 153–65, 168, 169, 171, 174–5, 190–2, 196, 204, 205, 221, 223

immanence 33, 45, 51, 53, 59, 144, 193, 219
inaesthetics/aesthetics 2, 5, 6, 17, 18, 30, 33, 61, 82, 91, 97–9, 101, 105, 107–9, 124, 139, 187, 189, 191, 196, 198
infinity 4, 5, 13, 15, 17, 20, 21, 23–5, 43–7, 56, 57, 59–62, 64, 68–75, 77–8, 116, 121, 133, 136, 198, 228, 229, 233

life 2, 24, 32, 35, 62, 87–9, 91, 98, 109, 128, 129, 133, 135, 147, 156, 157, 170, 178, 187, 195, 198, 222

logic 2, 4, 7, 14, 17, 27, 30, 35, 41, 44–7, 51, 57, 59, 70–2, 99, 102, 107, 110–11, 118, 120, 130, 141, 153, 155, 156, 163, 214, 227–35
love 5, 6, 18, 20, 34, 48, 81–93, 127–36

Maoism 15, 42, 102, 212–17
Marxism 161, 162, 205, 212–16
mastery 4, 30–5, 42, 59, 76, 99, 172–3
mathematics 1, 2, 5, 7–8, 16, 20, 38, 42–7, 50, 59, 60, 66–80, 99, 102, 104, 135, 146, 149, 150, 159, 163, 192, 204, 208–10, 218, 222, 227–35
  category theory 7, 78, 154, 159, 163, 232, 234
  Grothendieck topos 230–2
  set theory 5, 7, 43–6, 66, 68–9, 71–4, 78, 144–5, 150, 208, 227–30
  theory of large cardinals 7, 227, 233
May 1968 1, 20, 42, 43, 70, 212–14, 216
militant 7, 50, 51, 101, 104, 131, 154, 213, 214, 220–2
mimesis 5, 16, 30, 54–6, 98, 99, 105–6, 108, 109, 111, 189, 194, 197, 198, 208, 209
modernist studies 1–3
modernity 2–4, 19, 30–3, 35, 62–4, 66, 68–71, 73–4, 78–9, 97–8, 105, 108, 140, 143, 145, 146, 150, 171–2, 177, 178, 180, 183, 204, 208, 209, 218, 223
music 1, 5, 6, 13, 16, 20, 66, 101, 107–11, 115, 120, 168–85, 189, 192
  atonal 168, 174, 181

novelty 3, 6, 38–9, 51, 56, 60, 62, 97, 130, 131, 169–77, 182, 208, 220, 221, 223

ontology 2, 5, 7, 8, 16, 17, 34, 43, 68–9, 74, 75, 77, 79, 114, 143–5, 148, 150, 158–9, 181, 192–3, 207, 208, 218, 222, 227–35
onto-theology 218, 233

poetic operations 15, 58, 102, 104, 203, 205–6, 208, 209
  counter-romanticism 206, 208
  deobjectification 207–8
  detotalisation 206–8

poets   2, 5, 7, 8, 16, 33, 50, 52, 54–6, 64, 67, 197, 203–10
points   72, 76, 83, 99, 106–9, 111, 116, 119, 132, 133, 140–3, 154, 172, 175–6, 180, 205, 222, 225, 232
postmodernism   1, 2, 6, 68, 73, 97, 156, 162, 183, 196, 212–17
presentation/representation   2, 6, 30, 35, 37–8, 45, 48, 70, 84, 89, 98, 101, 104–6, 117, 124, 130–1, 133–4, 136, 144, 146–8, 186–7, 189–96, 207, 208
prophetic function   172–4, 178, 179, 181

resurrection   91, 160, 169–72, 180, 220, 222–3
romantic   20, 47, 48, 58, 63, 69, 71, 123, 206
    post-Romantic   54, 57, 60, 69, 71, 169, 203, 209
romanticism   40, 47, 48, 69, 138, 146, 206, 209

science   30, 42, 44, 48, 66, 69, 75, 78, 82, 99, 102, 104, 138, 205, 209, 218, 235
sexuality   3, 72, 85, 88
singularity   35, 43, 48, 58, 107, 120, 141, 148, 168, 172, 177–8, 191, 193, 196, 206, 222, 230
spacing   100, 110, 141, 147
state, the   6, 15, 33, 38, 77, 78, 133, 187, 189–93, 214, 216
subject, the   2, 6, 8, 13–15, 20, 29, 35, 63, 71–3, 78, 85, 103, 131, 150, 169, 174–6, 189, 193–7, 206, 207, 221, 222, 234
subtraction   17, 18, 26, 28, 29, 31–3, 35, 51, 88, 89, 106, 110, 111, 117–21, 123, 130, 134, 135, 173, 180, 187, 190, 206, 207, 220
surface   5, 6, 98, 100, 103, 104, 106, 108, 117, 119, 136, 138–51, 179
surrealism   5, 14, 82–92

theater   1, 6, 8, 17, 29, 58, 63, 101, 109, 116, 117, 131–2, 146, 186–98
theology   6, 153–63, 218–25
time   5, 23, 36, 48, 53, 57, 62, 72, 90–1, 114–15, 120, 127–8, 141, 143, 145, 146, 148, 150, 160, 162–3, 168–70, 172, 177–80, 183, 191, 198
topology   6, 29, 34, 42, 67, 72, 78, 134, 140, 143–7, 149, 150, 183, 230
truth   2, 6, 7, 16, 18, 19, 25, 31–6, 38, 40, 48, 50–64, 67, 69–70, 73, 77–9, 81, 83, 85–6, 89, 90, 92, 99, 106, 108, 111, 119, 131, 133, 144–7, 149, 150, 153–9, 161–4, 169–70, 174, 176, 180, 181, 186–9, 195–7, 208, 209, 212, 218–25, 228–35
twist   5, 15, 43, 61, 97–8, 100, 108, 109, 123
two, the   6, 18, 45, 81, 82, 84–6, 92, 130, 131, 135, 169, 205

"u"   128, 130, 134–5, 232
undecidability   4, 8, 26–34, 104, 110, 111, 173
universality   48, 55, 77, 105, 130, 131, 134, 156, 164, 171, 177, 178, 206, 219–20, 222–3

"V"   6, 140, 143–7, 149, 151, 228–9, 233, 234
Visigothic Catholicism   155, 157, 159, 163, 164

www.ingramcontent.com/pod-product-compliance
Lightning Source LLC
Chambersburg PA
CBHW052032300426
44117CB00012B/1795